Mind, Brain, and Free Will

Mind, Brain, and Free Will

Richard Swinburne

OXFORD

UNIVERSITY PRESS

OXFORD
UNIVERSITY PRESS

Great Clarendon Street, Oxford, OX2 6DP
United Kingdom

Oxford University Press is a department of the University of Oxford.
It furthers the University's objective of excellence in research, scholarship,
and education by publishing worldwide. Oxford is a registered trade mark of
Oxford University Press in the UK and in certain other countries

British Library Cataloguing in Publication Data

Data available

Library of Congress Cataloging in Publication Data

Data available

ISBN 978–0–19–966256–2 (Hbk.)
ISBN 978–0–19–966257–9 (Pbk.)

Printed in Great Britain by
MPG Books Group, Bodmin and King's Lynn

Contents

Preface

I discussed many of the issues of the present book in a previous book, *The Evolution of the Soul* (1986, revised edition 1997). With a few relatively small exceptions (the nature of the soul, discussed at the end of Chapter 6 of this book, being the main one), my conclusions on those issues remain the same. But many of the arguments by which I support those conclusions are different, and—I believe—deeper and stronger, based on a full discussion of underlying philosophical issues (e.g. the criteria for the identity of events and substances, and the grounds for asserting that a certain state of affairs is metaphysically possible) which underlie differences among philosophers about issues of mind and body. Also, this book includes a far fuller, and to my mind far more satisfactory, discussion than did *The Evolution of the Soul*, of what kind of free will humans possess; and in the process I have been able to take account in the present book of the important results of recent neuroscience about the brain mechanisms which underlie our intentional actions.

I have used some material from the earlier book, as well as material from several articles of mine published in the last few years: 'From Mental/physical Identity to Substance Dualism' in (ed.) P. van Inwagen and D. Zimmerman *Persons, Human and Divine*, Oxford University Press, 2007, pp. 142–65; 'Che cosa mi rende me? Una difesa del dualismo delle sostanze' in (ed.) A.Lavazza, *L'Uomo a Due Dimensioni*, Bruno Mondadori, 2008; 'Could anyone justifiably believe epiphenomenalism?', *Journal of Consciousness Studies*, 18 no 3–4 (2011), 196–216; 'Dualism and the Determination of Action' in (ed.) Richard Swinburne, *Free Will and Modern Science*, British Academy, 2011; and 'How to determine which theory of personal identity is true' in (ed.) G. Gasser and M.Stefan, *Personal Identity—Simple or Complex?*, Cambridge University Press, 2012. Thanks to the editors and/or publishers of these articles for permission to reuse their material. I am most grateful to the two anonymous referees who produced valuable comments on a penultimate draft of this book, as also to those many philosophers with whom I have argued about the issues over numerous years. And my thanks finally to Sarah Barker for typing and retyping earlier versions of the book, and to Peter Momtchiloff for welcoming yet another book of mine and guiding it through the publication process.

Introduction

The focus of this book is the nature of human beings—whether we are merely complicated machines, or souls interacting with bodies; and what follows from this for whether we have free will in a sense which makes us morally responsible for our actions. But I think that we cannot make much progress in these two well explored fields without discussing certain very general preliminary issues of metaphysics and epistemology.

So Chapter 1 is devoted to the general issue of what sorts of things there are, and what are the criteria for one such thing being the same as another such thing. I distinguish three kinds of thing: substances (the constituents of the world such as electrons, planets, and houses), their properties (such as weighing 1000 kg, or being spherical), and events (occurrences at particular times, which consist in substances having or changing their properties). I then consider what are the criteria for two substances, properties, or events being the same substance, property, or event. I must ask those readers who are not professional philosophers to be patient with what might seem the rather abstract hair-splitting arguments of this chapter. For only with clear criteria for the identity of substances, events, and such like can we answer questions about whether mental events are merely brain events (i.e. the same events as brain events), or whether I am the same thing (same substance) as my body. In Chapter 2 I consider what makes a belief that a certain event occurred or that a certain scientific theory is true, or that some proposition is possibly true, a justified (or rational) belief. And again I have to ask those readers who are not professional philosophers to be patient, as the full relevance of my conclusions on these issues will only be apparent later in the book. For it is only when we have a satisfactory account of what makes such beliefs justified, that we will be in a position to assess the justification of a scientific theory that our intentions do or do not cause brain events; or the justification of the claim that (in a certain sense of 'possible') it is possible that I could lose all of my present body and acquire a very different one.

Equipped with important metaphysical and epistemological results, I then come in Chapters 3–7 to examine the relation of our life of thought and feeling to what happens in our brains and so in our bodies. I argue in Chapter 3 that there are two kinds of event in the world—physical events (including brain events) and mental events. Mental events are events to which the subject (the person whose events they are) has privileged access, that is, a way of knowing about them not available to others. Among mental events are pure mental events, ones which do not include any physical event. Among these are beliefs, thoughts, intentions, desires, and sensations, events of which the subject is often conscious and which are then conscious events. I go on in Chapter 4 to argue that not merely do brain events often cause mental events, but mental events (and in particular intentions) often cause brain events, and thereby bodily movements. Many neuroscientists have interpreted the results of recent neuroscientific experiments as showing that our intentions do not cause brain events. I argue that these results do not show that, and that no experimental results of any kind could possibly show that.

In Chapter 5 I argue that this result, that intentions often cause our brain events, needs to be expressed more carefully as the result that persons often cause brain events when they intentionally cause bodily movements. In current philosophical termin-ology, persons are 'agent-causes'. Philosophers and scientists often assume that the causes of events are other events, logically distinct from them; for example, that when the ignition of dynamite causes an explosion, the ignition is a separate event from the explosion, and there is a law of nature (a consequence of the fundamental laws of chemistry) which determines that an event of the first kind is followed by an event of the second kind. I now argue that, whatever might be the case with non-intentional causation (e.g. the ignition of gunpowder causing an explosion, or a brain event causing pain), in intentional causation the cause is the person whose intention it is, a substance and not an event. A person having an intention (in acting) is simply that person intentionally exercising causal power. In Chapter 6 I move on to the issue of the nature of the substance, the human person to whom pure mental events (including intentions) belong. I argue that each human is a pure mental substance, having a soul as their one essential part and a body as a non-essential part; physical properties belong to humans in virtue of belonging to their bodies, and pure mental properties belong to them in virtue of belonging to their souls. Whether or not it is physically or practically possible for the present body of any human to be destroyed and yet for their soul to continue to exist, my claim is that it is compatible with what we essentially are that any human should continue to exist without their present body or any body at all; and so each of us is essentially a pure mental substance. I claim that the arguments in favour of this view, called 'substance dualism', that we are essentially pure mental substances, are—despite its current extreme unpopularity—compelling. Some of the modern hostility to substance dualism arises from the feeling that it leads to the view that having a body and bodily well-being are unimportant. But substance dualism in no way entails that; and I myself certainly hold that having a body is necessary for a worthwhile human existence, and that pleasure arising from bodily causes is a good thing. Substance dualism is a doctrine about what is necessary for our existence, not about what makes for a full and worthwhile life.

Given that human persons cause brain events, the next issue is whether humans are always caused inevitably to cause the brain events they do cause by earlier brain events or mental events; or whether sometimes we cause brain events (and thereby bodily movements) without being caused to do so. I argue in Chapter 7 that although we are always influenced by brain or mental events to form the intentions we do, sometimes (and in particular when we are taking difficult moral decisions) no such events fully determine those intentions. We have a certain freedom to form intentions to act independently of all the influences to which we are subject, which I shall call 'free will'. I then proceed to argue in Chapter 8 that, given that that is our situation, we are often morally responsible for our actions—guilty and deserving blame for doing what we believe wrong, meritorious and deserving praise for doing what we believe to be good actions beyond obligation.

The conclusion I reach is, I think, the view held until very recent years by most philosophers, scientists, and ordinary people in the West. By contrast Buddhism has always denied that humans have souls, claiming that our conscious life consists merely streams of causally connected mental events which do not belong to a continuing substance. Many Muslims, and a much smaller number of Christians, have believed that human actions are totally predetermined by God, and many of these might have allowed that God predetermined our actions through the operation of natural causes (e.g. by causing brain events to cause these actions in conformity to laws of nature). A few early Greek and Roman thinkers and a number of scientists and philosophers since the seventeenth century have claimed that humans are mere physical things operating in accord with physical laws, no more morally responsible for their actions than is a machine morally responsible for its movements. Yet despite these contrary views I suspect that most ordinary people, at least in Western countries, still hold the view implicit in the criminal law that (with exceptions) humans are not fully predetermined to do the actions they do, and are morally responsible for their actions; and also hold the view that humans consist of two parts—a soul and a body, so that even if in fact there is no life after death, there is no incoherence involved in supposing that our souls (the essential part of us) could survive death. In this book I argue that the traditional majority Western view on these issues is the correct view.

1

Ontology

1. What sorts of things there are

This book is concerned with the relation between the lives of intention, thought, and feeling of us human persons, and what goes on in our brains and bodies. Many philosophers and scientists have tried to summarize their views on this topic in brief sentences, such as 'mental events are just brain events' or are identical to them, 'mental events supervene on brain events' or are 'constituted by' or 'realized by' them, 'humans are just complicated physical organisms', 'mental events emerge from brain events', 'mental events cause brain events', 'humans have souls as well as bodies', and so on. But which, if any, of these views is correct depends on what the crucial general philosophical terms mean. What is it for two 'events', or two 'things' of some other kind to be the same, or to 'supervene' on something else, etc? And philosophers and scientists have made claims about what is 'possible' in this area, such as 'it is not possible for a person to exist without a body' or 'necessarily all mental events supervene on physical events'. But whether that is true depends on what is meant by 'possible' and 'necessarily'. In this chapter I seek to develop a clear terminology for discussing what sorts of things there are or could be in the world, which I shall be applying to our particular area from chapter 3 onwards.

Let us understand by 'the (objective) history of the world (or some segment thereof)' everything that has happened, is now happening, and will happen ever or anywhere (or in that segment). I suggest that the whole history of the world can be told with our familiar system of categories: substances, properties, and times. I understand by a substance a particular concrete object: my desk, that person, the photon (particle of light) emitted from this light source which landed on this screen, and so on. Substances may have other substances as parts. My desk has its drawers as parts of it; and it can exist (it is logically possible) independently of all other things of its kind (i.e. all other substances) apart from its parts; and those parts have very many electrons, protons, neutrons, etc. as their parts. Substances exist all-at-once. Whenever they exist, they exist totally. If the desk exists on Tuesday, all of it exists on Tuesday; it's not that some part of it exists on Tuesday, and another part exists on Wednesday. I shall count anything of the kind just described as a substance, whether or not it is of a kind which features in scientific laws or is of importance in our lives.[1]

Substances have properties. A property may be a monadic property of one substance (possessed by that substance by itself quite independently of its relations to other substances), or a relation between two or more substances. Thus being square, or brown, or having zero rest-mass are monadic properties; whereas being-to-the-left-of or being-taller-than are relations. The desk is to the left of the cupboard; John is taller than James. Those are two-term relations; they are relations between two substances. There are also three- or four- or more-term relations. For example, lying-between is a three-term relation; the desk lies between the chair and the cupboard. On our normal understanding of a 'property', which I shall follow, properties (monadic and relational) are universals, that is, they could be possessed by different substances from the ones by which they are possessed (either at the same time, or at different times, or if the world had been different). Many different substances can be brown or have zero rest-mass at the same time. Only one substance can be the tallest man in the world at a given time. But at a different time someone else could be the tallest man in the world; or, if he had grown a bit taller, some other man could have been the tallest man in the world at the original time instead of the man who was then in fact the tallest man. Of the properties which a substance has, some are essential (or necessary) properties of that substance; that is, if the substance did not have these properties it could not exist. 'Occupying space' is an essential property of my desk; my desk could not exist if it did not occupy space. (i.e. it is not logically possible that my desk should exist without occupying space.) By 'it is not logically possible that this should happen', I mean—loosely—it does not make sense to suppose that this might happen. (For a more precise definition, see section 3.) Being negatively charged is an essential property of any electron; if some electron ceased to be negatively charged, it would cease to exist. But some of the properties of a substance are contingent (i.e. non-essential) properties of that substance. Being brown is a contingent property of my desk; if it were painted red instead, the desk would still exist. I count any universal characteristic (in the sense just described) picked out by a predicate as a property, whether or not it features in scientific laws or is of importance in our lives.

Substances have properties or exist for periods of time. My desk existed from 1920 when it was made, and will continue to exist until it is destroyed, maybe in 2020. A period of time (e.g. from 1920 to 2020) is temporally extended, but 'instants' in the

---

[1] My account of substance is—by and large—what the Western tradition since Aristotle has understood by a 'substance', or (more precisely) by what came to be called 'first substance', 'the individual human or the individual horse' (Aristotle, *Categories* 20.11). This is to be distinguished from 'second substance' which is the kind or species (human or horse) to which a first substance belongs; from 'essence', the underlying properties, or 'thisness' (explained later in this chapter) which a first substance or kind of matter has to have in order to be that substance or belong to its kind—for example, the 'thisness' which makes me me, or the underlying chemical structure which makes water or gold what it is; and from the 'prime matter' of which first substances and ordinary kinds of matter are made. See Justin Broackes 'Substance', *Proceedings of the Aristotelian Society* 106 (2005/6), 133–68; J. Hoffman and G.S. Rosenkrantz, *Substance: Its Nature and Essence*, Routledge, 1997, ch. 1.

precise mathematical sense of the term (e.g. the exact moment at which 1920 began) are not temporally extended; they are the boundaries of periods. But when something lasts only a short period of time we often refer to the whole period loosely by a single date within the period, as 'The bomb exploded at exactly 10 a.m. on 30 June 2007', not intending thereby to refer to an instant in the technical sense of the term.

I now follow many philosophers in defining an event as either some substance (or substances, or event or events) having a certain property (more formally, the instantiation of a property in some substance or substances, or event or events) at a certain time, or the coming into existence or the ceasing to exist of some substance at some time. Thus 'the desk being brown at 10 a.m. on 9 June 2008' or 'Birmingham lying between Manchester and London during the twentieth century' are events. In ordinary language only those instantiations of properties which involve change are called events, while the ones which do not involve change are called 'states of affairs'; and so only the desk being made in 1920 or the desk being destroyed in 2020, but not the desk being brown between 1920 and 2020, would count as events. But it is useful to have a word covering all instantiations of properties at times (as well as the comings into existence and ceasing to exist of substances), and I shall use 'event' in this sense.[2] Both substances and events so defined may have relations to other events at a period of time, and so I include these also as events. Thus the event of 'my going to London on Tuesday' has the relation of occurring-earlier-than to 'my opening my mail on Thursday'; and so there is an event of 'my going to London on Tuesday' occurring earlier than 'my opening my mail on Thursday'.

Some philosophers have thought of 'laws of nature', principles determining what has to happen or what probably has to happen, as constituents of the universe, additional to the substances whose behaviour is governed by them. One such modern account, articulated in slightly different ways by Armstrong, Tooley, and Dretske[3], claims that laws are (logically contingent) relations of natural necessitation (or probabilification[4]) between 'universals', that is between properties in my sense. I call this account the 'relations-between-universals' (RBU) account. On this account, for example, Newton's law of gravity, the law that 'all substances attract all other substances with

---

[2] Jaegwon Kim has championed this definition of an event as the instantiation of a property in a substance at a time (though he does not seem to include the coming into existence or ceasing to exist of a substance as an event)—see his 'Events as property exemplifications' in his *Supervenience and Mind*, Cambridge University Press, 1993. But Kim favours a less prolific account of properties than I am advocating; 'it is not part of the account [which he advocates] that the use of different predicates—non-synonymous, logically inequivalent predicates—invariably leads to a multiplicity of properties' (op. cit. p. 43). David Armstrong, *A World of States of Affairs*, Cambridge University Press, 1997, pp. 25–6, also favours a less prolific account.

[3] See Armstrong, op. cit. especially chs 15 and 16; Michael Tooley, 'The Nature of Laws', *Canadian Journal of Philosophy* 7 (1977), 667–98; and F.I. Dretske, 'Laws of Nature', *Philosophy of Science*, 44 (1977), 248–68. Another account of laws of nature which sees them as components of the world additional to substances and their properties, but (unlike the RBU account) regards them as unanalysble components is that of Tim Maudlin. See his 'A modest Proposal Concerning Laws, Counterfactuals, and Explanations' in Tim Maudlin, *The Metaphysics within Physics*, Oxford University Press, 2007.

[4] For the distinction between the different kinds of probability see Additional Note A.

a force proportional to the product of their masses and inversely proportional to the square of their distance apart', is to be analysed as there being a relation of natural necessity joining the universals of 'mass', 'distance', and 'force' of such a kind that when universals of 'mass m' and 'mass m'' are instantiated in two substances at a distance r from each other, there is a force of attraction between them proportional to mm'/r^2. On this view the law is not an event, but a relation between universals which exists whether or not there are any substances and so any events, and so is a different kind of constituent of the universe from those discussed so far. There are however two other kinds of account of laws of nature which analyse them in terms of events. One kind of account, normally ascribed to Hume,[5] is the event 'regularity' account which analyses a 'law of nature' as a regularity in the actual successions of events. Newton's law is to be analysed as the regularity that (for all m, m', and r) all events of two substances of mass m and mass m' being at a distance r from each other always have been, are, and will be followed by an event of there being a force of attraction between them proportional to mm'/r^2. The other kind of account, which was the normal account in ancient and medieval times of the regularities subsequently called 'laws of nature', and has recently been revived by Rom Harre and E.H. Madden and by Brian Ellis,[6] is that they are regularities, not of actual (past, present, and future) successions of events, but regularities in the causal powers and liabilities, which are properties, of actual substances— powers naturally to necessitate (or make naturally probable), that is, to cause effects; and liabilities of natural necessity to exercise those powers under certain circumstances or under all circumstances. I call this account the substances-powers-and-liabilities (SPL) account. The possession and exercise of these powers constitute events in my sense. So Newton's law is the regularity that (for all m, m', and r) every substance of mass m and every substance of mass m' have together the power to attract each other with a force proportional to mm'/r^2, and the liability always to exercise that power when the substances are at a distance r apart. On the SPL account many of the essential properties of fundamental particles are causal powers—having a negative electric charge just consists (at least in part) of having the causal power to attract substances with positive electric charge and to repel substances with negative electric charge. On both the regularity and SPL accounts, the operation of laws of nature consists in the occurrence of events, and if there were no events there would be no laws of nature. I shall be arguing in Chapter 5 that the SPL account is the correct account of laws of nature, but meanwhile I shall assume that 'laws of nature' can be analysed in terms of events in one or other of the ways just outlined.

Each account of laws of nature is connected with an account of causation, which I shall discuss in Chapter 5. But meanwhile I need to make some assumption about the kinds of entities which cause effects. For most philosophers since Hume, causation is

---

[5] For a more detailed exposition of Hume's account, and of subsequent developments to it, see Chapter 5.
[6] R. Harré and E.H. Madden, *Causal Powers*, Basil Blackwell, 1975; Brian Ellis, *Scientific Essentialism*, Cambridge University Press, 2001.

regarded as a relation between two events; it is the ignition of a lump of gunpowder, not—to speak strictly—the lump of gunpowder itself, which causes an explosion. But on the SPL account of laws, it is a substance or several substances together which cause effects; they cause effects normally in virtue of their liabilities to do so under certain conditions—the gunpowder has a liability inevitably to cause an explosion when it is ignited. I shall be justifying this account of causation in Chapter 5. Meanwhile, for the sake of simplicity of exposition and as nothing in my argument before then depends on this account of causation, I shall assume that it is events (e.g. the ignition of gunpowder) and not substances (e.g. the gunpowder) which cause effects. The earlier definition of a substance in terms of its ability to cause may therefore be read as events in a substance having that ability.

I now claim that there is nothing more to the history of the world (in the objective sense of what has happened, is happening, or will happen) than all the events which have occurred, are occurring, or will occur. It is each substance coming into existence at a certain instant, acquiring this monadic contingent property, acquiring this relation to another substance or event (maybe the relation of the substance or an event which is a state of the substance causing the latter), losing that contingent property or relation, and then ceasing to exist at a certain instant. It includes, for example, a particular desk being made, being painted brown, placed 10 ft away from the wall, being moved 15 ft away from the wall, damaging the floor when moved, and then being destroyed. And so on for every substance.

Some have held that there are processes which are not analysable in the above way, for example fluctuations of a quantum field, or interactions of streams of energy. But a quantum field is (in my sense) a substance which has the property of fluctuating in a certain way (and consists of parts which do the same); and a stream of energy is no less a substance for being in motion. Others have held that there are events which are not analysable in terms of substances having properties, for example, flashes and bangs. Yet these events can be analysed as substances having the power to cause most people in a certain place to see or hear certain things and exercising that power at a certain time.

Finally, what about places (regions of space)? In my view talk about places is reducible to talk about substances and their relations to other substances. A place is the place it is in virtue of its spatial relations (of distance or direction) to particular physical objects (substances). The place enclosed by the walls of my garage is the place it is in virtue of being so enclosed. So to say that my garage (i.e. the place enclosed within the walls) is smelly is to say something like that there are substances which have the property of causing most people in the garage (i.e. most people who are situated at relevant distances and directions from its walls) to smell an unpleasant smell; these substances might be the walls of the garage, or the air molecules contained within it. Talk about motion (i.e. change of place) is to be analysed as changing one's distance or direction from certain physical objects which form a frame of reference. Thus 'the car is moving' is elliptical for 'the car is moving relative to the earth'. The earth consists of a system of physical objects (parts of the earth) which maintain constant distances and directions from each other. This account of place and change of place involves a relational view of space. But some have held that there is an absolute space, an invisible framework, such that there would be a difference between our universe being where it is and being a metre to the left of its present location (i.e. relative to absolute space.) But if so, then places would be in my sense substances; they could have properties (e.g. shape) and could enter into causal relations (a certain place or some event which was a state of that place could cause some substance to change in some way). Either way, we do not need 'place' as an additional unanalysable component of our conceptual scheme.

So I conclude (subject to further argument in Chapter 5 about the nature of laws of nature) that we do not need categories additional to those of substance, property, and time in order to tell the whole history of the world.[7]

2. How to tell the history of the world

The history of the world (or of some segment thereof, for example, some spatio-temporal region) is then all the events which have occurred, are occurring, or will occur. The occurrence of some events entails the occurrence of other events. To take a trivial example—there is one event of my walking from A to B from 9.30 to 9.45 a.m., another event of my walking slowly from 9.30 to 9.45 a.m., and a third event of my walking slowly from A to B from 9.30 to 9.45 a.m. But the third event is 'nothing over and above' the first two events. In telling the full history of the world if you list the third event you would not need to list the first two events. To generalize—there are different ways of cutting up the history of the world into events, and there are many different sets of events such that there is no more or less to the history of the world than the occurrence of all the events of that set. There is no more to the history of the world (or some segment thereof) than any subset of events whose occurrence entails the occurrence of all the events; and no less than any least subset which will do this. As I shall illustrate at various places in this book, you can tell the history of the world in many different ways (using different categories of kinds of substances, properties, and times, and so of events), subject to the condition that that system of categories would enable you to list a subset of events which entail all the events.

'Substance' and 'event' are technical terms of philosophy, and I hope that what I have written so far clarifies what a substance or an event is. Yet in order for these terms to have a clear use we need also to clarify what it is for one substance to be the same substance as another one, and for one event to be the same event as another one.

---

[7] Some philosophers have proposed alternative systems of categories which do not include the familiar categories of substance, property, and time in the senses I have been analysing, as reflecting more perspicuously the structure of the world. I relegate to a short additional note (Additional Note B) my reasons for holding that it would make no difference to the force of the main arguments of this book if we adopted either of the two best known alternative systems of categories.

Is the statue of Cleopatra the same substance as the bronze of which it is made, or is Brutus killing Caesar in 44 BC the same event as Brutus stabbing Caesar in 44 BC (when this stabbing caused Caesar's death)? 'Substance' and 'event' being technical terms, it is up to a philosopher to stipulate rules for the identity of 'substances' and 'events'. I am using 'property' in one of its ordinary-language senses in which it means the same as 'characteristic' or 'feature' or 'aspect'; a property of an object is a characteristic of that object. But 'ordinary language' has no precise rules for when two properties are the same. Is red the same property as the property of reflecting light of such-and-such wavelength, or is being triangular (having the shape of a closed rectilinear figure with three interior angles) the same property as being trilateral (having the shape of a closed rectilinear figure with three sides)? Ordinary usage provides no criteria. So again the philosopher who uses the word 'property' must stipulate criteria for when two properties are the same. However, when events are said to happen at a 'time', 'time' is being used in an ordinary language sense, and (as far as discussion of the issues with which I am concerned in this book) it is clear enough what it is for two (periods or instants of) times to be the same (period or instant of) time.

It is important for any science to describe its data as fully as possible, before it proceeds to try to explain them. This book is concerned with the data of the mental and physical life of human beings. In order to set out the events which constitute its data as fully as possible, it must describe them in ways such that if someone knew the 'canonical descriptions' of all the events of a certain subset of all the events, they would know or could deduce from what they knew everything that had happened. This means understanding by the 'canonical description' of an event a description in terms of the substances, properties, and times involved in it by words such that a competent language user would thereby know fully which property, which substance, and which time the event involved. These will be words which always pick out the same property and so on, and tell us fully which property that is; such words I shall call 'informative [rigid] designators'. This requirement that our vocabulary should enable us to tell the whole history of the world constitutes a metacriterion determining when we should deem that two referring expressions pick out the same property, substance, or whatever: They will pick out the same property or whatever iff that property or whatever can be designated by the same informative designator; and so two properties or whatever will be the same iff their informative designators are logically equivalent (that is, each entails the other). ('iff' means 'if and only if'.)

A rigid designator is a word which 'in every possible world, designates the same object',[8] and I shall understand 'the same object' (or 'thing') to mean 'the same substance, property, time, or event'; that is, designates the same object, whatever happens to that object so long as it exists. (By 'in every possible world' is meant 'whatever else might be the case'.) A non-rigid designator is a word which applies to

---

[8] Saul Kripke, *Naming and Necessity*, republished as a book, Blackwell, 1980, p. 48.

something only as long as it has some non-essential property. Proper names are normally used so as to refer to the same person whatever happens to him or her, and whether or not he or others normally use that name to refer to him or her. 'David Cameron' refers to the present British Prime Minister, whether or not he remains Prime Minister and even if he begins to call himself 'John Smith'. Likewise 'brown' always refers to the same colour, even if many brown objects are repainted red. Hence these expressions are rigid designators. By contrast those definite descriptions ('the so-and-so') which designate substances in virtue of properties which are not essential to them are non-rigid designators. 'The Prime Minister', as normally used, is a non-rigid designator; it refers to whoever is Prime Minister at the time in question. If David Cameron ceases to be Prime Minister, 'the Prime Minister' no longer refers to David Cameron, but to his successor. Those definite descriptions which designate (without naming it) a non-essential property possessed by some substance are also non-rigid designators. Thus 'The colour of my desk' is also, as normally used, a non-rigid designator. If my desk is now brown, it refers to the colour brown; but if my desk were to be painted red, then it would refer to the colour red.

But 'normally' is not always. Expressions which pick out an object in virtue of non-essential properties can sometimes be used as rigid designators, and philosophers have a device for bringing out when that is happening; they append to the expression the adjective 'actual'. So, given that my desk is now brown, 'the actual colour of my desk' is used to refer to the colour brown in every possible world. Then if we imagine that my desk (which is in fact brown) is red (and the world is otherwise the same) this involves imagining that British mail boxes have the same colour as my desk, but not the actual colour of my desk. I shall, however, in future (unless I use the adjective 'actual') assume that words are used in the more normal way just described.

Yet not every rigid designator is such that a competent language user knows what is involved in its application to a substance or whatever. There is a class of rigid designators, to which Kripke and Putnam drew our attention in the 1970s, which pick out things (and especially substances and kinds of substances) by certain of their normal superficial properties, but where what makes a substance or a substance of that kind that substance or a substance of that kind is the essence (of which competent language users may be ignorant) underlying those properties, a set of necessary and sufficient conditions for a substance or substance kind to be that substance or substance kind.[9] In ignorance of the latter, we do not fully understand what we are saying about a substance when we say that it is that substance or a substance of that kind.

Thus, to modify an example used by Kripke to illustrate this class of designators, suppose that in days long before people knew the geography of the Himalayas, explorers named a mountain of a certain visual appearance seen from Tibet 'Everest',

---

[9] Kripke op. cit., and H. Putnam, 'The Meaning of "meaning"', republished in his *Mind, Language and Reality, Philosophical Papers, vol. 2*, Cambridge University Press, 1975.

and a mountain of a certain different shape seen from Nepal 'Gaurisanker', and used these names as rigid designators of the mountains. These mountains are in fact the same mountain, but these early explorers—we may suppose—did not know this. Yet, the explorers would have assumed, what made the mountain Everest was not that it had a certain appearance when seen from Tibet, but rather the rocky matter out of which it was made; and similarly for Gaurisanker. But, in ignorance of what that matter was, their having the ability to refer by a rigid designator to these mountains would not rule out their supposing that Everest and Gaurisanker were totally different mountains. Or consider Putnam's example of the word 'water'. Plausibly it was used in the eighteenth century to pick out the transparent drinkable liquid in our rivers and seas; while what made the stuff that stuff was its chemical essence (then unknown). But in ignorance of what made something water, people in the eighteenth century could not be sure whether something which was not transparent or drinkable or in our rivers or seas was water; or whether other rivers and seas could contain transparent and drinkable stuff which was not water. So the explorers who called a mountain 'Everest' or those in the eighteenth century who called a liquid 'water' didn't fully understand what was involved in the application of these terms. Hence I call them 'uninformative designators'. To set out the whole history of the world we need to list the substances, properties, and times involved in events by informative designators.

For a rigid designator of a thing to be an informative designator it must be the case that anyone who knows what the word means (that is, has the linguistic knowledge of how to use it) knows a certain set of conditions necessary and sufficient (in any possible world) for a thing to be that thing (whether or not he can state those conditions in words.) Two informative designators are logically equivalent if and only if they are associated with logically equivalent sets of necessary and sufficient conditions. To 'know' these conditions for the application of a designator—as I shall understand this expression—just is to be able (when favourably positioned, with faculties in working order, and not subject to illusion) to recognize where the informative designator (or, if it is defined in words, the words by which it is defined) applies and where it does not[10] and to be able to make simple inferences to and from its application. (These simple inferences are those captured by what I shall shortly be analysing as the 'mini-entailments' of the application of the designator.) Having the ability to recognize something when favourably positioned with faculties in working order and not subject to illusion,

---

[10] More precisely, if you know this part of the rules for using an informative designator of an object (substance, property, or whatever), then you can apply it (subject to border-line cases) correctly to any object if (1) you are favourably positioned, (2) your faculties are in working order, and (3) you believe that (1) and (2); or if this holds for the words by which the designator is defined. Thus 'red' being an informative designator means that someone who knows what 'red' means can apply it to an object correctly when (1) the light is daylight and they are not too far away from the object, (2) their eyes are in working order, and (3) they believe that (1) and (2). Someone may be subject to illusion if either {(1) and (2)} and not-(3) or {either not-(1) or not-(2)} and (3). By contrast, I shall argue, however favourably positioned you are and however well your faculties are working, you may not be able to identify correctly some liquid not in our rivers and seas as 'water' or some mountain as 'Everest'(when the designator words have their pre-modern senses).

and able to make such inferences, entails knowing what that thing is. In the case of technical terms, it is experts in the relevant field whose knowledge of the relevant necessary and sufficient conditions determines the meaning of a term. Thus it is physical scientists whose knowledge determines the meanings of 'quark' or 'electron'.

Many of the words—for example, 'red', 'square', 'has a length of 1 m'—by which we pick out properties are such that if we know what the words mean we can recognize (subject to the stated restriction) where they do or do not apply, and can make the requisite inferences. Thus we can recognize red objects and distinguish them from differently coloured objects if the light is normal, our eyes our working properly, and we are situated fairly close to them; and we can infer from 'it is red' to 'it is coloured', and from 'it is bright red' to 'it is red'. The satisfaction of the latter requirement means that we know what sort of thing red is—a property, and not a substance; and the satisfaction of the former requirement means that we know which item of that sort it is. Other words by which we pick out properties can be defined by words for which those conditions hold. For example 'has a length of 10^{-15} m' can be defined in terms of the informatively designated property 'has a length of 10 m' and the informatively designated relation of 'being shorter by 1/10th than' (used 15 times). But suppose that instead of using the word 'red' in the normal way, we called an object 'red' if it had whatever actual underlying structure (e.g. reflecting light of a certain wave length) made most of the objectives we now call 'red' look that way, and we did not know what that structure was. That would leave open the possibility that there were red objects which did not look the way red objects look to us. So we would not know fully what we were saying that an object was 'red', and so the word would be an uninformative designator.

While being 'water' (as used in the eighteenth century) is an uninformative designator of a property, being 'H_2O' (as used today) is—I believe—an informative designator of a property. Being 'H_2O' is the property of being composed of molecules, each consisting of two atoms of hydrogen and one atom of oxygen. An atom is an atom of hydrogen iff it has a nucleus consisting of one and only one proton, and (unless ionized) is orbited by one electron. (A rare form of hydrogen has in its nucleus also a neutron.) An atom is an atom of oxygen iff it has a nucleus consisting of eight protons and eight neutrons, and (unless ionized) is orbited by eight electrons. (Rare forms of oxygen have in their nucleus also one or two more neutrons.) (Ionized forms of hydrogen or oxygen may have more or less orbiting electrons.) A proton is a particle of mass 1.67×10^{-27} kilograms, with a positive electric charge of 1.60×10^{-19} coulombs. An electron is a particle of mass 1/1836 that of a proton with a negative electric charge equal to the positive charge of the proton. So both 'electron' and 'proton' are defined in terms of fractions of quantities (kilograms and coulombs), larger values of which are such that physical scientists can determine their value (when favourably positioned, with faculties in working order, and not subject to illusion), and make simple inferences to and from their application. Hence 'H_2O' is an informative designator of a kind of substance. And the same goes for many other (though maybe not all) of the rigid designators of kinds of substances referred to by today's physical scientists. We (or at any rate today's scientists) know what we or they are talking about when talking about 'H_2O'; whereas eighteenth-century speakers did not know fully what they were talking about when they referred to 'water'. Whether or not a word is an informative designator is a matter of the rules for its current use in the language.[11]

3. Logical and metaphysical possibility

The notion of an informative designator will enable us to deal with the issues of 'metaphysical' and 'logical' possibility. These terms have been defined in different ways by different writers. Following many writers, I shall understand 'metaphysical

---

[11] Others have sought to make the distinction between words like 'red' and words like 'water' in somewhat similar ways to mine. Thus David Chalmers distinguishes between the 'primary intension' of words like 'water' (as used in the eighteenth century) which are the superficial features by means of which people pick out a substance such as water, and the 'secondary intension' which is the actual underlying property. It is a priori what is the primary intension, a posteriori what is the secondary intension. Chalmers holds that 'both the primary and secondary intensions can be thought of as candidates for "the meaning" of a concept' (See David Chalmers, *The Conscious Mind*, Oxford University Press, 1996, pp. 57–62). I am, however, assuming (as most writers do) that there are some words (e.g. 'red') which (in their normal use) have only a primary intension (because any underlying property is irrelevant to the applicability of the word) and so are informative designators; and other words (e.g. 'water' as used in the eighteenth century) which (in their normal use) have only a secondary intension and so are uninformative designators. George Bealer makes the same assumption and makes the distinction between what he calls 'semantically stable' and 'semantically unstable' expressions. (George Bealer, 'On the Possibility of Philosophical Knowledge' in *Philosophical Perspectives 10: Metaphysics* (1996), pp. 1–33, see p. 23.) An expression is 'semantically stable iff necessarily in any language group in an epistemic situation qualitatively identical to ours, the expression would mean the same thing. An expression is semantically unstable iff it is possible for it to mean something semantically different in some language group whose epistemic situation is qualitatively identical to ours'. So 'red' is semantically stable, whereas 'water' is semantically unstable because its meaning depends on what is the underlying essence of the stuff picked out by 'water'. But, while Bealer's 'semantically stable' expressions turn out to be the same as my 'informative designators', and his 'semantically unstable' expressions to be the same as my 'uninformative designators', his account of what the distinction amounts to seems to me not quite correct. 'Water' wouldn't have meant something different in the eighteenth century if the underlying essence of the stuff in rivers was something other than H_2O. 'Water' would still have had the 'meaning' (in what I suggest is the natural sense of 'meaning' as 'intension') of 'the actual stuff which has the same chemical essence as the stuff in rivers' and so on; the difference would have been that the reference of 'water' (what the word picked out) would have been different.

necessity' as the strongest kind of necessity there is, and 'metaphysical impossibility' as the strongest kind of impossibility there is, and so 'metaphysical possibility' as the weakest kind of possibility there is. Some event is metaphysically necessary iff it must happen, whatever else is the case; metaphysically impossible iff it could not happen, whatever else is the case; metaphysically possible iff it could happen under some circumstances; metaphysically contingent iff it is metaphysically possible but not metaphysically necessary. But, before these notions can have any content, the expressions 'whatever else is the case' and 'under some circumstances' need to be illustrated by examples and be filled out in a more precise way. An event is metaphysically necessary iff it occurred and would have still have occurred if the world had begun in any different way from the way it did begin (or had always been different in some way from the way it was) and/or had been governed by any different laws of nature (or any other ultimate determining principles) from those which in fact operate. An event is metaphysically impossible iff it did not occur and would not have occurred even under any such circumstances. An event is metaphysically possible iff it would have occurred under some such circumstances. An event may be physically impossible (because ruled out by the laws of nature in our universe), or practically impossible (because even though its occurrence is not ruled out by laws of nature, it is in practice impossible for humans to bring it about) without being metaphysically impossible; physically or practically necessary without being metaphysically necessary; metaphysically possible without being physically or practically possible.

Although I have written of events being metaphysically possible (or whatever), in order to discover whether some event is possible we need (as we shall see) to reflect on what it means to say that that event occurs. And since that reflection involves reflection on the meaning of the sentence which asserts its occurrence, I shall assume that it is best to think of the possibility (or whatever) as belonging primarily to a sentence and secondarily to what the sentence claims, that is, that the event occurs. The possibility (or whatever) belongs primarily to a token sentence (i.e. a particular utterance or inscription of a sentence in a particular context), not necessarily to any sentence of that type (uttered in a different context). This is because, for sentences of some types, the claim that they make about the world varies with the context in which they are uttered—for example, the claim made by 'I am ill' depends on who said it when. But for many sentences (e.g. the sentence 'all humans are mortal'), which claim they make is independent of the context of utterance, and depends only on the rules of the language; and so we can talk about the claim made by the type-sentence, that is, any sentence containing the same words in the same order; and I shall be discussing sentences of this kind except when I specify otherwise. Sentences which make the same claim about the world (whether of the same or different types) are often said to express the same proposition ('content', or 'thought'). Since any sentence which makes the same claim as a given sentence will have the same metaphysical modal status (i.e. if one is metaphysically necessary, so too will be the other one; if one is metaphysically possible, so too will the other be; and so on), we may speak also of propositions being metaphysically necessary (or whatever).

Among metaphysical impossibilities and necessities are ones discoverable a priori, that is, discoverable by mere reflection on the meaning of the sentence—on what is involved in the claim made by the sentence. I'll call these logical impossibilities and necessities. The most obvious example of a metaphysically impossible sentence is a self-contradictory sentence (which I shall in future call simply a 'contradiction'). Such a sentence claims both that something is so and also that it is not so, for example 'he is taller than 6 ft and it is not the case that he is taller than 6 ft'. For such a sentence could only be true if that something was so, and the sentence asserts that it is not so. No sentence could be more obviously or more strongly impossible than such a sentence. Yet any sentence which entails a contradiction is as strongly impossible as a contradiction. Likewise the strongest kind of necessity a sentence can have is that its negation (the sentence which denies the former sentence) is or entails a contradiction. Such necessities and impossibilities are 'logical' ones, in the sense that they are discoverable by mere a priori reflection on the meaning of the sentence.

But what determines the meanings of sentences, in the sense of their truth conditions (under which conditions they are true, and under which conditions they are false), and so which sentences entail other sentences? Sentences of a language mean what its speakers (or—in the case of technical terms—some group of experts, e.g. physicists) mean by them. Each of us learns the meanings of certain sentences by being shown (or having described to us by sentences which already have a meaning in the language) many observable conditions under which the former sentences are regarded as true or as false, and by being told of other sentences to which a speaker is regarded as committed by uttering those sentences, and other sentences which are such that someone who utters them is regarded as committed to the former sentences. Each of us learns the meaning of certain sentence forms (e.g. a subject–predicate sentence, such as 'Harry is old' or 'this table is long') by being shown many observable conditions under which sentences of that form are regarded as true or as false. We learn the sense of a word by being taught the difference to the meanings of sentences of different forms made by that word playing a certain role in those sentences. By being taught the meanings of various sentence forms and the senses of various individual words, we may then come to an understanding of the meaning of a sentence in which those words are arranged in a certain way, even if we have not been shown (or had described to us by sentences already having a meaning) observable conditions under which the former sentence is regarded as true or as false. For example, we learn the meaning of 'there is a cat over there' by being shown observable circumstances under which this sentence is regarded as true, and observable circumstances under which it is regarded as false; and by being told that someone who utters this sentence is regarded as committed to 'there is an animal over there', and someone who utters 'there are two cats over there' is regarded as committed to the original sentence. We learn the meaning of 'there is a dog over there' in a similar way. Thereby we come to know the kind of meaning possessed by sentences of the form 'there is a ϕ over there', and the senses of 'cat' and 'dog'. We need to observe (or have described to us) many different examples of observable conditions under which sentences of different forms and sentences containing certain words in various roles are regarded as true or false, and to be provided with many different examples of the commitments speakers who use such sentences are regarded as having; and this allows us to acquire an understanding of the conditions under which some new sentence of a certain form containing those words in certain roles would be regarded as true or false. We extrapolate, that is, from a stock of supposedly similar paradigm examples of sentences which are regarded as true or false and having certain relations of commitment under certain observable conditions to an understanding of the meanings of sentences in various ways different from those we have used previously. Then, once we understand the commitments of many sentences and words, we can come to understand other sentences and words when they are defined in terms of sentences already understood. Note, however, that the sense of a word which we get from this process may be such as to rule out a few of the supposedly paradigm examples as examples of things to which that word applies. Thus we may derive from many supposedly paradigm examples by which we are taught the meaning of the word 'cat' a sense of 'cat' which rules out one of these examples as being a cat at all; it might turn out to have been a baby tiger instead. I ask the reader to understand future uses of 'paradigm' as short for 'supposedly paradigm'.

Because humans have very similar cognitive mechanisms determining how they learn meanings, and because members of a language group are exposed to very similar paradigm examples (of observable conditions and rules of commitment), members of the same language group normally acquire very similar understandings of the meanings of words and sentences. But because humans do not learn meanings from exactly the same paradigm examples, and do not have exactly the same cognitive mechanisms, we will not all come to understand words and sentences in exactly the same sense as each other. This is one reason why there is always a small range of cases in which it is vague whether some sentence is true or false (or perhaps neither). We may all be taught what a 'table' is by being shown various objects which everyone calls 'tables'. They will all have flat surfaces and be used to put things on. But some of us might also be shown desks and sideboards and told that they too are tables, whereas others might be told that these are not tables even though they have flat surfaces and are used to put things on. These minor differences in the ways that speakers of the same language understand words and so sentences will lead to some minor differences in our beliefs about which sentences commit us to other sentences.

These minor differences get reduced by dictionary compilers and philosophers who 'tidy up' language by laying down rules for correct usage, usually by codifying most people's actual usage. The rules give general descriptions of the observable conditions under which different sentences of the language are true and of the observable conditions under which they are false, and of the kinds of other sentences to which a sentence of a given kind commits the speaker and by which sentences of other kinds a speaker is committed to a sentence of a given kind. The rules include rules about which words are informative or uninformative rigid designators. The rules about the commitments of different kinds of sentences include for example the rules of the syllogism; 'all As are B, and all Bs are C' commits one to 'All As are C'. Given a 'correct' use, a sentence then has a public objective meaning.[12] We may call a rule for what one is objectively committed to by a sentence, a rule of mini-entailment. s_1 mini-entails s_2 iff anyone who asserts s_1 is thereby (in virtue of the rules for the correct use of language) committed to s_2. 'British mail boxes are red' mini-entails 'British mail boxes are coloured'; someone who used the words 'red' and 'coloured' would not be using them in the public objective sense unless they recognized that commitment. s_1 entails s_n iff they can be joined by a chain of mini-entailments, such that s_1 mini-entails some s_2, s_2 mini-entails some s_3, and so on until we reach a sentence which mini-entails s_n.[13]

With such rules we can derive contradictions, and so we have a criterion for sentences being logically impossible or logically necessary. For example the rules for the use of the word 'tall' include the rule that 'taller than' is transitive, that is, 'A is taller than B' and 'B is taller than C' together mini-entail 'A is taller than C'; and the rule that it is asymmetric, that is, 'A is taller than B' mini-entails 'not-(B is taller than A)'. Hence 'John is taller than James, James is taller than George, and George is taller than John' mini-entails 'John is taller than George, and George is taller than John', which mini-entails 'John is taller than George, and not-(John is taller than George)'; and so 'John is taller than James, James is taller than George, and George is taller than John' entails a contradiction and so is logically impossible.

But because it is vague how much agreement by whom is enough to establish a 'correct' use, there are likely to remain some minor disagreements about what entails

---

[12] A sentence is said to be 'analytic' (in one sense of that word) iff it is such that anyone understanding it knows it to be true. Someone understands it iff they know the paradigm examples and inference links which determine its (correct) meaning. If these are such that to deny that sentence mini-entails a contradiction ('mini-entails' a contradiction in the sense defined below, not merely 'entails' one), then they know it to be true. This constitutes an 'epistemological conception of analyticity'. Timothy Williamson rejects any such conception of analyticity on the ground that 'no given...statement is immune from rejection by a linguistically competent speaker.' (*The Philosophy of Philosophy*, Blackwell Publishing, 2007, p. 97.) But (given that 'statement' means 'sentence') all that that shows is that not all speakers, however generally 'linguistically competent', always use a given word or sentence-form in the same sense as all other such speakers. They purport to use these in the correct sense, but they may be mistaken about what that sense is, or there may be no one correct sense.

[13] It will be evident that I am using a concept of mini-entailment and so a concept of entailment much wider than any such concepts used in any particular system of logic. That one sentence entails another is a relation between them which may hold whether or not it has been enshrined in any system of logic. 'This is red' entails 'this is coloured', though—as far as I know—no system of logic captures that entailment. A system of logic merely gives rigorous form to certain kinds of entailment, often ones prominent in ordinary language—as does syllogistic logic. So the axioms of some formal system may in my sense entail a contradiction and so be inconsistent, even if they do not do so by the definitions of 'entailment' and 'inconsistent' provided in that system. Hence, for example, a system which is said to be 'ω-inconsistent' is inconsistent in my sense.

what and whether some word applies to some object, which will mean that some disagreements about which sentences are logically necessary (or whatever) will remain. I will discuss in Chapter 2 the ways in which these minor disagreements can be resolved so as not to cause serious philosophical problems; and go on to consider why occasionally very major disagreements arise about the logical status of sentences, and the extent to which they can be resolved. For the present I will assume that there is an agreed correct usage of language.

I see no reason to suppose that there are any logically impossible sentences other than ones which entail a contradiction (i.e. any sentences which are as strongly impossible as those which entail a contradiction, and whose impossibility is detectable a priori, but which do not themselves entail a contradiction).[14] So I shall assume that any logically impossible sentence entails a contradiction, and any logically necessary sentence is such that its negation entails a contradiction. A logically possible sentence is then one which does not entail a contradiction. A logically contingent sentence is a logically possible sentence which is not logically necessary. Having defined these terms in this chapter, I shall discuss in Chapter 2 the problems involved in showing some sentence to be logically necessary, impossible, or possible.

Kripke and Putnam[15] drew our attention to the fact that there are many sentences which seem not to entail any contradiction and not to be such that their negations entail a contradiction, but which are necessarily true or necessarily false with a necessity as strong as that of logical necessity and whose truth or falsity are discoverable only a posteriori. These sentences were said to be metaphysically, but not logically, necessary or impossible. The examples which Kripke and Putnam gave of metaphysically necessary sentences which were not logically necessary, for example, 'Everest is Gaurisanker' (as used by early explorers) and 'water is H_2O' (as used in the eighteenth century), are all ones which involve at least one uninformative designator of a substance or property (such as 'Everest' or 'water'). Their negations 'Everest is not Gaurisanker' and 'water is not H_2O' might seem to entail no contradiction, and yet are impossible with as strong an impossibility as the logically impossible. But the reason for this is that a competent language user could use these sentences without knowing fully what is being referred to by the referring expressions. When we know fully what we are talking about (e.g. that in talking about 'water', we are talking about 'H_2O'), mere a priori considerations can show whether some sentence is metaphysically necessary or impossible for this kind of reason. Hence there is available a definition of a sentence as metaphysically necessary (impossible or possible) iff it is logically necessary (impossible or possible) when we substitute co-referring informative for uninformative designators, that is, designators which pick

[14] For argument in justification of this claim, see Additional Note C.

[15] See notes 8 and 9. I interpret the claims of Kripke and Putnam about necessity and so on as claims about the necessity of sentences. Kripke makes it clear that his concern is with sentences, and writes that he has no 'official doctrine' of how his account applies to 'propositions'. (op. cit. pp. 20–1.)

out the same substance or property. This definition will capture as metaphysically necessary (impossible or possible) almost all the uncontroversial examples of the 'metaphysically necessary'('impossible' or 'possible') offered by Kripke, Putnam, and others, and I see no reason to believe that any necessities (impossibilities) which cannot be captured by this definition are as strong as metaphysical necessities (impossibilities) of this kind, or that any possibilities which cannot be captured by this definition are as weak as possibilities of this kind.[16]

It follows that the truth or falsity of a metaphysical necessary or impossible sentence depends solely on the conventions of language and on what is in fact picked out by the rigid designators of the language. An explanation of that truth or falsity will consist in explaining how words are used and what is picked out by rigid designators. The truth or falsity of a metaphysically contingent sentence, however, depends not merely on what the sentence claims but on how the world is, independently of how we describe it. If it can be explained why some true metaphysically contingent sentence is true, the explanation will consist not merely in explaining what the sentence claims, but in citing the cause of what the sentence claims to be the case. The explanation of why 'all squares have four sides' is true will consist in explaining what 'square' and other words and the kind of sentence in which they occur (a subject–predicate sentence) mean; but the explanation of why 'the dinosaurs became extinct 60 million years ago' is true consists not merely in explaining what 'dinosaur' and other words and the sentence form mean, but also in citing some extra-linguistic cause which caused dinosaurs to become extinct.

These definitions have the consequence that any identity sentence, in the sense of a sentence claiming that two things (substances, properties, or whatever) picked out by (informative or uninformative) rigid designators are the same thing, is—if true—metaphysically necessary, and—if false—metaphysically impossible. For someone who knows the meaning of an informative designator knows a priori the necessary and sufficient conditions for a thing to be the thing referred to by that designator. Logically equivalent informative designators refer to the same thing, and logically non-equivalent informative designators refer to different things. So if in an identity sentence 'a is b', where 'a' and 'b' are rigid designators, we substitute for either of 'a' or

---

[16] Anyone who makes a claim about what is 'metaphysically' necessary (or whatever) where this is not analysable in this way owes the reader an explanation of why they think that there are sentences as strongly necessary as sentences which are so analysable. It may well be, as Gendler and Hawthorne say, that 'the notion of metaphysical possibility . . . is standardly taken to be primitive', adding in a footnote 'in contemporary discussions at any rate' ((ed.) T. Gendler and J. Hawthorne, *Conceivability and Possibility*, Oxford University Press, 2002, Introduction, p. 4.) For myself, I simply do not understand what is meant by this notion, unless it is analysable as here, or given some other technical definition. It is simply uninformative to say that it is the most basic conception of 'how things might have been' (ibid. pp. 4–5.) For since this 'most basic conception' is supposed to be narrower than logical possibility (as defined by me), it is unclear how the latter is to be narrowed unless in the way I have analysed. In one book I myself unhelpfully used 'metaphysically necessary' to mean (roughly) whatever is the ultimate cause of things or is entailed by the existence of that ultimate cause; and so the 'metaphysically possible' is whatever is compatible with the existence of the actual ultimate cause. See *The Christian God*, Clarendon Press, 1994, pp. 118–19. But this is certainly not the sense which most writers who use the term have in mind, and not the sense in which I am using it in this book.

'b' which are not informative designators, informative designators of things designated, and get a sentence 'c is d' where 'c' is logically equivalent to 'd', the things picked out by 'a' and 'b' must be the same. If some thing is the same thing as another thing (in virtue of both things satisfying the same necessary and sufficient conditions for being that thing), it is necessary in the strongest degree—that is, metaphysically necessary—that those two things are the same. If in the sentence 'Everest is Gaurisanker' we substitute for both names informative designators of the rocky matter referred to, we will—given that these mountains are the same—get a sentence which is logically necessary; and so the identity of the mountains with each other is metaphysically necessary. But if when we substitute informative designators for 'a' and 'b', the resulting sentence is not logically necessary, it must be false. For, non-equivalent informative designators pick out different things. And if one thing is different from another thing (in virtue of satisfying different necessary and sufficient conditions) it is metaphysically impossible for them to be the same thing.

A 'possible world' is a maximal way (a full history) of how things could have happened, be happening, and be going to happen. The logical/metaphysical necessity distinction gave rise to the notion of a metaphysically possible world as one which was different from a merely logically possible world; it had to be *both* logically possible *and* one whose full description involves no metaphysically necessarily false sentences. However, a full description of a world will entail all its events, including the events underlying the visible Everest or water. They will include 'Everest is made of such-and-such matter', 'Gaurisanker is made of such-and-such matter' (the 'such-and-such matter' being the same in both cases), and 'the stuff in our rivers and seas is H_2O'. The full description of the world will then entail the falsity of 'Everest is not Gaurisanker' and 'water is not H_2O'. Since the meanings of 'Everest', 'Gaurisanker', and 'water' are defined by the essence of what they refer to in our world, and since the sentences just cited are incompatible with the substances having that essence, then they cannot (logically cannot) hold either in our world, or in any other one. I thus share Chalmers's view that the distinction between the logically and metaphysically possible 'is not a distinction at the level of worlds, but at most a distinction at the level of statements [in my sense, sentences] . . . The relevant space of worlds is the same in both cases'.[17] That is, any logically possible world is a metaphysically possible world, and conversely. Hence when talking about worlds I do not distinguish between, for example, logically possible/necessary worlds and metaphysically possible/necessary worlds.

This brings me to the notion of supervenience. As originally introduced, it concerned the relation of one kind of property to another kind of property. I shall understand the supervenience of one kind of property on another in Kim's sense of 'strong supervenience', since this is the sense with which we need to be concerned in

---

[17] Chalmers, op. cit., p. 68.

subsequent chapters. Loosely, properties of kind A supervene on properties of kind B, iff which substances have which (if any) A-properties is entailed by which (if any) substances have B-properties. More precisely, a kind of property A supervenes on a kind of property B iff 'Necessarily for any property F of kind A if any substance x has F, there exists a property G of kind B such that x has G, and necessarily any substance y having G has F'.[18] ('Necessarily' in this definition means 'of metaphysical necessity'.) Thus a utilitarian may urge that moral properties supervene on properties measuring human happiness. Let's call the latter properties 'hedonic properties'. If there is such supervenience, then any agent who does an action which has the same hedonic properties (i.e. adds the same amount to or subtracts the same amount from the total of human happiness) as some other such action will be doing an action with the same moral properties as the latter. It must be that either both actions are morally good, or both actions are morally bad. And no action can have a moral property unless it has a hedonic property; an action which neither adds to nor subtracts from the total of human happiness cannot be either morally good or bad, but will be morally indifferent. All of this is what the utilitarian claim of the supervenience of moral properties on hedonic properties amounts to. (I am not endorsing this claim, merely using it to illustrate the notion of supervenience.)

This gives rise to the following definition of supervenience of kinds of events: events consisting in a substance x having a property F of kind A, supervene on events consisting in x having a property G of kind B, iff necessarily for any x which has any property F of kind A, x has some property G of kind B, such that necessarily if x has G, x has F.[19] I read the claims of many philosophers that mental events are 'constituted by' or 'realized in' brain events as meaning the same as the claim that mental events 'supervene on' brain events.

Kim does not discuss supervenience of substances, but I will adopt this natural extension of his definition: A-substances supervene on B-substances iff necessarily for every A-substance x there is a B-substance y, such that necessarily if y exists x exists.

4. Identity criteria for properties and events

There are different ways of cutting up the world into events, because there are different ways of cutting up the world into substances and properties. There are, for example, in the case of properties, innumerable different ways of dividing up animals into kinds. One could group all animals which live in the water as one kind—'water dwellers'; and all animals which fly as another kind 'flyers'. But then in order fully to describe the

---

[18] See Jaegwon Kim, '"Strong" and "Global" Supervenience Revisited' in his *Supervenience and Mind*, Cambridge University Press, 1993, p. 80. In order to conform to my terminology, I have replaced Kim's 'object' by 'substance' and his 'in' by 'of kind'. Kim has made distinctions between various kinds of supervenience, and shown their merits, demerits, and interconnections in various articles collected in this volume.

[19] I put the definition of *Supervenience and Mind*, pp. 98–9 in my own words.

world, we would need to add that many water dwellers breathe through gills, but some (e.g. whales) have lungs; and some flyers feed their young by supplying milk for suckling (e.g. bats), but most do not. Alternatively one can follow the normal zoological classification of animals (dependent on many different overall features of the animals) into fish, birds, and mammals; and then add that most mammals live on land, but some live in the water, and some fly. There is an obvious point in using the normal zoological system of classification: it enables us to tell the history of evolution more concisely—first there were fish, then birds, them mammals. However, either of the two systems of description will enable us to tell the whole history of the world.

But the requirement that we be able to tell the whole history of the world (putting someone in a position to know everything that has happened, is happening, and will happen), by listing a subset of events which entails all the events, does put restrictions on how we can do this, restrictions on the possible identity criteria. The restriction, as we have seen, is that the properties, substances, and times constituent of events must be picked out by informative designators. Since the identity of an informative designator is constituted by the criteria for its application, such designators will pick out the same properties and so on iff they are logically equivalent. So, for example, being red (being the property picked out by the informative designator 'red') and reflecting light of such-and-such wavelength (being the property picked out by the informative designator 'reflecting light of such-and-such wavelength') are not the same property—since having the one does not entail having the other or conversely. If one said that these properties are the same although the designators are not logically equivalent, then knowing that some object had the property picked out by 'reflecting light of a certain wavelength' would not tell you all there was to be known about it; that it is red (i.e. looks a certain way to most people) is a further piece of information about the world. You would need to include this latter piece of information or something which entails it in a full history of the world. But if some object is trilateral, a rectilinear closed figure with three sides (defined as picked out by the informative designator 'trilateral'), that is nothing extra in the world beyond it being triangular, a rectilinear closed figure with three interior angles (defined as picked out by the informative designator 'triangular'). Having the one entails having the other and conversely, so you do not need to mention that some figure is trilateral as well as triangular in order to tell a full history of the world. Since the informative designators of 'trilateral' and 'triangular' are logically equivalent, they pick out the same property.

It is important to distinguish a description of a property P in terms of some property which it possesses, from an (informative or uninformative) rigid designator of P. 'Green' is an informative designator of the property of being green; it applies to it in all possible worlds, and someone who knows what 'green' means knows what an object has to be like to be green. 'Amanda's favourite colour' or 'the colour of spring grass' may function as descriptions of the property green in terms of its properties, possibly (in our world) uniquely identifying descriptions. These words may be used to describe the property of being green by informatively designating a different property—the property of being Amanda's favourite colour or the property of being of the same colour as spring grass—which property the property of being green possesses. 'Green is Amanda's favourite colour' is then a subject-predicate sentence where 'Amanda's favourite colour' informatively designates the property of being Amanda's favourite colour and thereby (in our world) describes the property green. It says that the property 'green' has itself the property of being Amanda's favourite colour. If it were (unusually) being asserted as a statement of identity between two informatively designated properties, it would be false.[20]

It follows from properties being individuated by the informative designators which pick them out that it is a pure a priori matter whether one property is identical with another (depending on whether having the one entails having the other, and conversely). And it is also a pure a priori matter whether one kind of property supervenes on another kind of property; it depends on whether for any property of the former kind its possession by a substance is entailed by the possession by that substance of some property of the latter kind, and it not being logically possible for a substance to have a property of the former kind without having a property of the latter kind.

In recent years, however, many philosophers have commended theories of property identity, which have the consequence that knowing which properties have been instantiated in which substances and when would not necessarily put you in a position to know everything that had happened. These are theories which claim that the only properties are ones whose possession by a substance have effects and so enable us to explain the world better; and so hold that we should regard a property possessed by some substance which doesn't have any effects as really the same as one that does, so long as the latter property is invariably instantiated in the same substance at the same time and place as the former property. Since it is a matter for scientific discovery when two properties are invariably coinstantiated and what effects a substance has and so what enables us to explain the world better, it is then an a posteriori matter (not to be settled by armchair philosophizing) when two properties are the same. Thus Hilary Putnam writes that 'properties can be synthetically identical' (by which he seems to mean that it may be a logically contingent truth that two properties are identical), and that 'the way in which we establish that properties are synthetically identical is by showing that identifying them simplifies our explanatory endeavour in certain familiar ways'.[21] There being an electric discharge of a certain kind in the sky (i.e. the sky being

---

[20] But, as mentioned, any property designator can be turned into an uninformative rigid designator of another property which has the first property, and that that has happened can be made clear by using the adjective 'actual'. 'The (actual) colour of spring grass' can be used to rigidly designate that colour which in the actual world is the colour of spring grass. In that case 'Green is the (actual) colour of spring grass' will be a (true) identity statement. This device of 'rigidification' allows us to turn any uniquely identifying description of something, including a property, into a rigid designator of that thing. But it does not make it into an informative designator of that thing. For someone who knows what the rigidified predicate 'the (actual) colour of spring grass' means need have no ability to identify any colour property (other than that of spring grass) as being that colour property—for they may never have seen spring grass.

[21] Putnam's article 'Putnam, Hilary' in (ed.) S. Guttenplan, *A Companion to the Philosophy of Mind*, Blackwell, 1994, p. 508.

characterized by an electric discharge of a certain kind) is invariably coinstantiated with the occurrence of lightning (i.e. the sky being lit up in a certain way). Yet there being an electric discharge in the sky can explain why we see the sky lit up and such other phenomena as often occur at roughly the same time, such as trees sometimes catching fire; while the sky being lit up explains nothing—Putnam would claim—which is not explained better by the occurrence of the electric discharge. Hence on Putnam's theory the property possessed by the sky of being lit-up is the same property as its property of being characterized by an electric discharge.

This kind of theory of property identity is implicit in the more explicit theories of event identity which have proposed for the purpose for advocating that mental events are the same events as physical events (an issue to be discussed in Chapter 3). Thus U.T. Place, who first advocated the modern version of mental/physical event identity in 1956,[22] claimed that 'a process or event observed in one way is the same process or event observed in (or inferred from) another set of observations . . . if the latter event provides an explanation of the former set of observations';[23] and—he added later—if the two sets of observations refer to the same point in space and time (in other words, if we can attribute the properties to the same substance). Hence the conclusion is again that an electric discharge (property) in the sky (substance) is the same event as lightning in the sky because it explains why we observe what we do when we observe lightning.

The view of property identity implicit in the writing of Putnam and Place has been given rigorous shape by a number of writers who have claimed that all properties simply are powers to produce effects;[24] and so if some description of a property seems to pick out some property that does not produce an effect when instantiated in a substance, what is picked out must really be the same as a property which does produce an effect. If being 'red' does not seem to pick out a property which makes a difference to the world (because what makes the difference is the power to reflect light of a certain wavelength), then, being red must be the same as the difference-making property. Now, I agree and shall argue more fully in Chapter 5, powers to produce effects are among the properties of substances. But on the view just described there are no other properties. However, not all properties could be merely powers to produce effects— given that effects are events in my sense of the instantiations of properties in substances. The assumption that effects are events is shared by philosophers who put forward this view that all properties are nothing but powers to produce effects; and I argued earlier that the history of the world is just a succession of events, and so—as things which happen—effects must be events. Yet if there were no properties other than powers, all properties in that case would be powers to produce powers, and these would be powers

[22] U.T. Place, 'Is Consciousness a Brain Process', *British Journal of Psychology*, 47 (1956), 44–60.

[23] U.T. Place, 'Materialism as a Scientific Hypothesis', *Philosophical Review*, 69 (1960), 101–4.

[24] See, for example, Sydney Shoemaker, 'Causality and Properties', republished in his *Identity, Cause, and Mind*, Cambridge University Press, 1984: 'What makes a property the property it is, what determines its identity, is its potential for contributing to the causal powers of the things that have it.' (p. 212).

to produce other powers, and so on ad infinitum. One power P_1 might differ from another power P_2 in being a power to produce more new powers than P_2, or powers which produce powers, one of which might be produced also by another power P_3; but there would be no difference (or at least no detectable difference) between this whole net of powers and any other isomorphic net of powers.[25] Yet we can recognize the differences between powers in virtue of their having different effects which we can observe as such without being able to observe the effects of those effects, and without assuming that they have any effects. We can recognize independently of their effects, the movements, interactions, and surface features of physical substances (their colour, smoothness, hardness, etc.). If someone claims that all these features are simply the powers of substances to produce different conscious events (e.g. patterns of sensations) in observers, then in that case it is the properties of these latter events (e.g. the sensory properties) which are what they are independently of their effects. In the end there must be more to some properties, and so to the events which involve them, than powers to produce yet further events. These events form the data of science which provide our evidence for scientific theories postulating substances with powers which cause these events. To take an analogy: a government official whose only powers were powers to appoint other officials whose only powers were to appoint yet other officials and so on ad infinitum wouldn't make any difference to the way the country was run. The powers of substances do make observable differences to the universe and its inhabitants.

One could attempt to avoid this conclusion by saying that while the only properties of substances are their powers, we can distinguish between different events (involving different powers) not only by other events which they cause, but by their different 'aspects' or 'modes of presentation'. One could say that when a surface has a certain power, there are not two distinct events of it being red and reflecting light of such-and-such wavelength (which are the same event), but we can pick out that same event by different 'modes of presentation' or 'aspects' (e.g. its visible colour and the reflected wavelength). But that is just to multiply ontological categories unnecessarily. For 'a mode of presentation' or an 'aspect' of an event is just as much a real characteristic of an object as any property. And nothing is left out and much is clarified if we say that visible redness and reflecting light of a certain wavelength are both properties of the surface.

---

[25] Alexander Bird pointed out in response to the claim of myself and others that one could not distinguish between one power and another power if powers were simply powers to produce other powers, that one could make the distinction in terms of the numbers of other powers a given power produces and their causal relations to each other. See his 'The Regress of Pure Powers', *Philosophical Quarterly*, 57 (2007), 513–34; and his *Nature's Metaphysics*, Oxford University Press, 2007, ch. 6. I claim in the text that we need more than that to distinguish between powers. John Hawthorne shows this by pointing out that there can be a world in which two properties have exactly the same effects when instantiated alone, but a different effect when co-instantiated from the effect which either would have separately. The two properties must therefore be different from each other, but one cannot tell by its effects which is which. See his 'Causal Structuralism' republished in his *Metaphysical Essays*, Oxford University Press, 2006, p. 224.

These considerations affect the status of the scientific discoveries such as 'lightning is an electric discharge' analysed by the authors just discussed as identity claims, claims that two properties are the same property. This sentence claims that the property of being characterized by lightning, possessed by the sky, is the same property as the property possessed by the sky of being characterized by an electric discharge of a certain kind. But we must ask more precisely what is it for the sky to be characterized by lightning. Is it for the sky to be lit up in a certain way? In that case, if we are to give a full description of the world and so pick out properties in terms of informative designators, the two properties are certainly not the same; the instantiation of the latter property (an electric discharge) may cause the instantiation of the former property (the sky being lit up), but they are different properties and the one does not supervene on the other. Alternatively, one may answer that for the sky to be characterized by lightning is for it to have that actual property which causes the sky to be lit up in a certain way. In that case the properties are indeed the same, just as (as described already, and see note 20) the property of being green and being the actual colour of spring grass are the same. But then there is another property possessed by the sky which is not the same as lightning—the property of being lit up in a certain way—but whose instantiation is caused by lightening.

As already mentioned, I am understanding by the 'canonical description' of an event one in terms of the informative designators of the substance(s), property, and time involved in the event. The conjunction of those informative designators will constitute an informative designator of the event. We should count any two canonical descriptions as picking out the same event if and only if any possible world which contained an event picked out by the one would contain an event picked out by the other, and conversely. For only then is the occurrence of one event nothing in the history of the world 'over and above' the occurrence of the other event. Events which involve the instantiation of the same properties in the same substances at the same time will therefore be identical. Yet the canonical descriptions of two events may occasionally entail each other without the properties, substances, and times involved all being the same. One case of this is where a substance having some property entails and is entailed by some part of that substance having that property. For example, a table is flat iff that table's top is flat; but the former is not an occurrence in the history of the world additional to the latter, nor is the latter an occurrence additional to the former. Normally, however, it will be apparent that by my criteria events are the same only if the (informatively designated) properties, substances, and times are the same. So the sky being lit up at 3 a.m. is not the same event as the sky having an electrical discharge at 3 a.m.; nor is the table being red (in what is, I think, the normal sense of 'red') today the same event as the table reflecting light of a certain wavelength today.

A rival theory of event-identity to the one which I have just been defending is one advocated by Donald Davidson, that 'events are identical if and only if they have the same causes and effects.'[26] An obvious problem is that it can apply only to events which are caused and which have effects. But even if we suppose that every event has a cause (and I see no reason to suppose that), there is no reason to assume that every event has an effect. Yet even if it is concerned only with events which have causes and effects, there might still seem to be the possibility of obvious counter-examples to Davidson's theory. Cannot there be an event E_1 which has two different effects E_2 and E_3, each of which cause E_4? That can surely happen if neither E_2 nor E_3 are sufficient causes of E_4; each could be a partial cause (i.e. a necessary condition) of the effect, and only together do they fully cause (i.e. are they a sufficient cause of) the effect. So in order for Davidson's principle to be plausible we need to understand by 'each of which causes E_4', 'each of which is a sufficient cause of E_4'. But then E_2 and E_3 could still be distinct events if E_4 is 'over-determined', that is, if either E_2 or E_3 would have caused E_4 without the other. So we need to add a clause 'so long as the effects are not over-determined'—that is, so long as there are not two separate sufficient causes of E_4. Then if E_2 and E_3 are both sufficient causes but not separate sufficient causes, they will indeed be the same sufficient cause of E_4, and so the same event. Davidson's principle, so analysed, is undoubtedly true (of events which are caused and have effects). But the principle provides no criterion for determining whether E_2 and E_3 are or are not separate sufficient causes rather than being the same sufficient cause—that will depend on whether they are or are not the same event. So the theory requires some other criterion of event identity in order to determine whether two events are identical. It is viciously circular; true no doubt (for events which have causes and effects), but quite useless.

5. Identity criteria for substances

To tell the full history of the world, I argued earlier, involves listing all the events of some subset which entails all the events that happen under their canonical descriptions. We saw in the case of properties that that involves picking out the properties involved by informative designators. And we need to informatively designate the substances too—merely giving a description of them, even a rigidified description, won't tell us what was green, or square, or 10 m away from a wall. Properties are timeless things instantiated from time to time in substances. Individual substances, however, belong to a world of change, and continue to exist over periods of time. So we may expect their identity conditions to be more complicated than those of properties. This section seeks to develop categories and results which will be of use in due course in answering questions about whether humans are the same substances as their bodies, and what makes a person at an earlier time the same person as a person at a later time.

---

[26] D. Davidson, 'The Individuation of Events' in his *Actions and Events*, Clarendon Press, 1980, p. 179.

The identity of substances over time is a matter of the extent to which there is
continuity between substances in respect of the properties which they possess, and
perhaps also of something other than properties. For a substance S_2 at a time t_2 to be the
same substance as a substance S_1 at an earlier time t_1, two kinds of criteria have to be
satisfied. First the two substances have to belong to the same minimum essential
kind[27]—I'll just call it 'same kind' in future. We think of particular substances as
belonging to kinds, such that all members of a particular kind share certain essential
properties, which make them a member of that kind. Thus a particular table belongs to
the kind of tables; (whatever their other properties) all tables have to have flat surfaces
which are used for putting things on. If a substance loses the essential properties of its
kind, it ceases to exist. In ordinary talk it is often fairly vague just which properties are
the essential properties of the kind to which a particular substance belongs, but clearly
there are some properties which any substance shares with other substances, such that if
it lost them it would cease to be the same kind of thing and so cease to exist. And, if we
are to give a full description of the world, language would need tightening up so that it
was clear for any substance which the essential properties are of the kind to which it
belongs. Fairly clearly, as I illustrated earlier by a zoological example, there are different
ways of cutting up the world into kinds of substance, any of which would enable us to
give a true and full description of the world. I now use this point to show how it affects
which individual substance is the same as an earlier substance. Suppose I have a car
which I turn into a boat. I can think of cars as essentially cars. In that case one substance
(a car) has ceased to exist and the matter of which it was made has been used to make a
different substance (a boat). Or I can think of cars as essentially motor vehicles, in
which case my car has continued to exist but with different (non-essential) properties
(being a boat instead of a car). All three substances exist (whether we think of them in
the one way or the other way)—the car which is essentially a car, the boat which is
essentially a boat, and the motor vehicle which is essentially a motor vehicle. Yet I can
tell the whole story of the world either by telling the story of the motor vehicle, or by
telling the story of the car and the boat.

The second requirement for a substance at one time to be the same as a substance at
another time is that the two substances should consist of largely the same parts, or parts
obtained by gradual replacement from those of the former substance, the extent to
which this has to hold varying with the genus of the substance. Kinds of substance
belong to different 'genera'. (I am not using this word in its biological sense, but merely

[27] The minimum essential kind to which a substance belongs is the kind consisting of all the essential
properties of a kind which that substance has to have in order to continue to exist. If a is the same substance as
b, there is some f such that a is the same f as b, and such that there is no more determinate kind g such that
necessarily a is the same g as b. Then f is that minimum essential kind. In that case necessarily a is the same h as
b, when h is a less determinate kind than f (such that being f entails being h). If a is the same dog as b, necessarily
it is the same animal as b; but if a is the same animal as b, it does not follow that a is the same dog as b. I thus
endorse David Wiggins's thesis of sortal dependence, (called 'D' in his *Sameness and Substance Renewed*,
Blackwell, 2001, pp. 55–61); and so, for his reasons, I deny the possibility of relative identity—a being the
same f as b, but not the same g as b. On this see *Sameness and Substance Renewed, passim.*

in the sense of a wide class.) Genera differ from each other in respect of the extent of replacement or rearrangement of parts of a substance of a kind belonging to that genus, which is compatible with the existence at any time or over time of the substance. The genera of substances include: simples, organisms, artefacts, geographical features, mereological compounds, and gerrymandered entities. A 'simple' is something which has essentially only one indivisible part; then the existence of that part is necessary and sufficient for the existence at any time of the substance. Some of the fundamental particles such as electrons and quarks seem to consist of only one part and so to be 'simples'. An electron consists of only one part, and that part has to continue to exist for the electron to continue to exist. Organisms are plants or animals, and these belong to kinds (normally 'species' in the biological sense)—they are strawberry plants or oak trees or ants, or whatever. They consist of many parts: cells which can be removed or replaced, and parts of cells which can be removed or replaced. If a certain particular organism, for example, a particular strawberry plant, had never existed, but one with very similar properties had existed instead of it, our criteria are such that we would count it as the same organism iff most of the parts were the same. And we would still count a later organism as the same organism as the original organism even if most of the parts were different, so long as the replacement of parts was gradual; for example, so long as the strawberry plant acquired a few new cells at a time while the organism's other cells continued to exist and to play the same role in sustaining the life and activity of the organism. Just what constitutes 'most' parts or a 'gradual' replacement of parts is of course vague, but there are clear cases of replacements of 'most' parts being the same or not the same, and of replacements which are or are not 'gradual', for us often to be able to say definitely that some substance does or does not continue to exist. If you cut off a branch from an oak tree and graft in a new branch, it is still the same oak tree. But if you cut off all the branches and remove the trunk and roots simultaneously, and replace them by another trunk into which a few old but many new branches and roots are grafted, the old oak tree has ceased to exist and been replaced by another one.

Artefacts are things made by persons (or animals) such as desks and tables, vases and houses. As with organisms, if an artefact had never existed, but one with very similar properties had existed instead of it, our criteria are such that we would count it as the same artefact iff most of the parts were the same. But with artefacts only a small amount of replacement is compatible with the continued existence of the same substance; and if—whether simultaneously or gradually—you replace many parts, the artefact no longer exists. If you replace one of the four legs of a table, the same table still exists. But if you replace the top of the table and also two of its legs, what is left is a different table (having two of the legs of the old table). In the case of artefacts, not merely is it vague what constitutes a 'small' or 'gradual' replacement, but there are two different ways of understanding the replacement requirement, illustrated by the story of the ship of Theseus,[28] the ship had its planks

----

[28] See Thomas Hobbes, *De Corpore*, 2.11.

gradually replaced until none of the original planks was in place; the original planks were then reassembled to form another ship. So we ask: which ship was the same as the original ship—the ship which preserved continuity of organization with the original, or the one composed of all the same planks as the original? And of course our normal criteria for 'same ship' are too vague to enable us to answer this question; but we can make them more precise so that continuity of planks arranged in the same way rather than same planks determines identity, or the other way about. In the former case we can tell the whole story by saying that the ship continued to exist all the time, but that the original planks came to form another ship. In the latter case we can tell the whole story by saying that the ship continued to exist during the replacement of planks, but when the replaced planks were reassembled the continuously existing ship was no longer the original ship—it was the ship formed of the original planks which was the original ship. We can tell the whole story in either way without anything being omitted.

Geographical features are naturally occurring inorganic things like mountains or rivers. In the case of a solid feature such as a mountain it would seem that the component parts have to be and remain largely the same, whereas for a river continued replacement of parts is essential for the identity of the river over time; but in both cases they have to be situated in somewhat the same place (i.e. surrounded by the same other geographical features.) A 'mereological compound' is by definition the same iff all its parts remain the same. A lump of brass, considered as a mereological compound, continues to exist iff every part of it continues to exist. And finally there are 'gerry-mandered entities' consisting of arbitrary conjunctions of two or more substances of the above genera—for example, the entity consisting of the right hand drawer of my desk together with the planet Venus, and which differ from each other according to which of innumerable possible criteria determine their identity, only some of which will ever have been thought of by humans. Some philosophers consider that only substances of kinds of some of these genera are really 'substances';[29] the others are artificial construc-tions. One can of course use the word 'substance' in some restricted sense, which has this consequence. But on the definition of 'substance' I gave at the beginning of this chapter, there are substances of all these genera—particular things which—it is coher-ent to suppose—cause or are caused by other things (or which are such that events involving them cause or are caused). Substances of all these genera exist and have properties. I cannot see any justification for operating with a narrower concept of 'substance'.

A full history of the world, however, will need to mention only substances of certain genera—for example, if it tells us the history of all the fundamental particles (considered as simples), their coming into existence, gaining or losing non-essential

[29] See Peter van Inwagen, *Material Beings*, Cornell University press, 1990, section 13; and Trenton Merricks, *Objects and Persons*, Clarendon Press, 2001.Van Inwagen considers that mereological compounds, artefacts, and gerrymandered objects do not exist, and so of course they cannot be substances.

monadic properties and relations to other particles, that might suffice (if we forget for the present about obvious problems to be discussed subsequently arising from substances having mental properties). There is no more to any substance than its parts (e.g. fundamental particles) and the way those parts are arranged. Sometimes the substances which are parts of larger substances behave differently when they form part of the larger whole (and in particular when they form part of an organism) from the ways in which they behave when they do not form such a part. Then the behaviour of the larger substances can be explained more easily if the behaviour of the parts is analysed in terms of their contribution to the behaviour of the larger substance. We can explain why the plant grows roots in terms of the function of its roots in the economy of the plant—to take in nutriment from the soil. Nevertheless the causal properties of larger substances such as organisms are just the causal properties of their parts, even if the latter have causal properties such that when combined with other parts they behave in ways different from the ways in which they behave separately. The causal properties of a root or leaf just are the causal properties of its cells, even if a cell behaves in different ways when it has a certain location in a plant from the way it would do if were not part of a plant. So another way of telling the whole history of the world, instead of telling merely the history of fundamental particles, might be to include the history of organisms and artefacts, saying when they gained or lost parts or their internal parts were rearranged, and then add only that part of the history of the fundamental particles when they did not form unchanging parts of the organisms or artefacts. There are many different ways of telling the same story.

But what is it for a part to be the 'same part' of a substance as an earlier part? A part of a substance is itself a substance, and so one could define being the same part in terms of what proportion its sub-parts must stay the same for how long. Being the same part may be thought of as a matter of having all the same sub-parts, or some replacement of its sub-parts may be thought of as consistent with being the same part, but in the end either we will reach simples, or—if matter were infinitely divisible, and we wish to operate with a sharp criterion of identity (which we would need to do in order to tell the full history of the world)—we would need arbitrarily to define a level at which any replacement of a sub-sub-part has the consequence that the sub-part is not the same sub-part. So either the level of simples, or this arbitrary level, is the level of what I shall call ultimate parts. Being the same ultimate part will involve, as with any substance, having the essential properties characteristic of the kind– being this electron will involve being an electron; that is, having a certain mass, charge, etc. It will involve also something else for it to be the same token of that kind, that is, for it to be the same electron—a principle of individuation.

What kind of principle we need in order to fully to describe the world depends crucially on what sorts of things substances are. One theory is that substances are simply bundles of co-instantiated properties, properties in the sense of universals, that is, in the sense defined earlier.[30] A substance is just a bundle of properties instantiated together, such as the monadic properties of having a certain shape, colour, hardness, and such-and-such relations to other bundles of instantiated monadic properties. A particular electron is just a bundle of the properties of having a certain mass, charge, and spin, and having such-and-such spatio-temporal relations to various other bundles of monadic properties. The alternative theory is that some substances have thisness.[31] A substance has thisness iff there could exist instead of it (or in addition to it) a different substance which has all the same properties as it, monadic and relational, including its spatio-temporal relations to earlier and later substances having such-and-such monadic properties and relations.

It does look as if two different physical substances[32] could exist at the same time having all the same properties as each other. 'Isn't it logically possible that the universe should have contained nothing but two exactly similar spheres?', asked Max Black.[33] Each could be of the same size, shape, 'made of chemically pure iron', at a distance of two miles from a sphere having all the same monadic properties, and—we may add—situated at a place which has all the same properties as every other place; and each could have had a qualitatively similar history, for example, each could have the past-related property of being spatio-temporally continuous with a sphere having the same monadic properties for infinite past time, and the future-related property of being spatio-temporally continuous with a sphere which ceased to exist at a certain particular moment. A philosophical principle known as the 'principle of the identity of indis-cernibles' claims that there cannot be two things (substances, or any other things) which have all the same properties, monadic and relational.[34] Black's thought experiment powerfully suggests that this principle is not a logically necessary truth.

Qualitatively identical objects having all the same spatio-temporal relations to different qualitatively identical objects could coexist only in a symmetrical universe. But even in a non-symmetrical universe like our universe, where every substance with all the same monadic properties has different spatial relations to other substances (picked out by the conjunction of all their monadic properties), might not the universe

[30] Distinguish this theory from the theory discussed in Additional Note B, that substances are bundles of tropes, that is, particular properties. A trope, for example, a particular redness, is the redness it is independently of which bundle it belongs to. Whereas on the bundle theory being discussed now the redness is the redness it is in virtue of the substance to which it belongs, that is in virtue of the other properties co-instantiated in the bundle.

[31] For a more detailed account of thisness, see my 'Thisness', *Australasian Journal of Philosophy*, 73 (1995), 389–400.

[32] 'Physical substance' will be defined precisely in Chapter 3, but meanwhile the reader should understand such a substance loosely as one all of whose essential properties are publicly observable. Hence a physical substance necessarily occupies space.

[33] M. Black, 'The Identity of Indiscernibles', *Mind*, 61 (1952), 153–64. See p. 156.

[34] This principle is due to Leibniz; for example, 'it is not possible for there to be two individuals entirely alike, or differing in number only' (*The Leibniz-Arnauld Correspondence*, (tr.) H.T. Mason, Manchester University Press, 1967, p. 61.) But while Leibniz sometimes uses it in the form in which it has become established (the claim that any two things which have all the same monadic *and* relational properties are the same thing), he sometimes uses it in the implausible form of the claim that any two things which have all the same monadic properties are the same thing. See my 'Thisness' note 2.

be different if instead of one substance (e.g. a certain electron) there was, always had been, and always would be for the period of time while the first substance existed another substance (a different electron) with exactly the same monadic and relational properties? The difference between two different physical substances having all the same (monadic and relational) properties, if there could be such, would then naturally be described as their being made of different matter from each other. That yields for such substances the 'hylemorphic' theory that the sameness of an ultimate part of such a substance (e.g. being the same quark) requires both having the essential properties of that kind of ultimate part (e.g being a quark) and sameness of underlying matter. Even if some physical substances have thisness, maybe not all physical substances have thisness. Maybe quarks which have a mass do have thisness, but photons (the particles of light) which have no mass (and so may be thought not to be made of matter) do not have thisness. If there are non-physical substances which have thisness, it cannot consist of their being made of certain matter; saying that such a substance has thisness is just a way of saying that there could be (instead of it) a different substance with all the same monadic and relational properties. Identity for non-physical substances which have thisness would be a 'brute' identity, not further definable.

If substances of some kind do not have thisness, then they are the particular substances they are in virtue of the properties of their ultimate parts (additional to the properties of ultimate parts which make them substances of a particular kind of ultimate part). If apples (and so their parts) do not have thisness, an individual apple would be the particular apple it is in virtue of the size, shape, colour, taste, etc. of its ultimate parts and their relations to each other and to other things (e.g. that they are parts of an apple growing on a tree, with certain properties, monadic and relational). The obvious two further properties which we use for individuating ultimate parts of substances, and so for tracing the history of substances, are spatio-temporal continuity and causal continuity (the earlier ultimate part causing the existence of the later one). If substances do not have thisness, it is natural to regard one or other or both of these two properties as essential properties which make an ultimate part (e.g. a quark) the same ultimate part (e.g. the same quark). Then a larger substance—for example, an apple— would be the same substance as an earlier substance of the same kind (e.g. the same apple) iff most of its parts are spatio-temporally continuous with and/or caused to exist by the parts forming the earlier apple, or result from gradual replacement thereof.

So if no substances have thisness, then the history of the world will consist of bundles of co-instantiated monadic properties having further properties, including spatio-temporal and causal relations to earlier bundles, coming into existence and ceasing to exist, and causing the subsequent existence and properties of other bundles. There are many different ways to cut up the world into substances at a time, according to the size of the bundle and which members of the bundle are regarded as essential to the substance which they form. And, according to which members of the bundle are regarded as essential and what constitutes an ultimate part, so there will be different ways of tracing substance continuity over time. There are again alternative ways in which the requirements for being an ultimate part could be spelled out, any of which would allow us to tell the whole story of the world. If we make spatio-temporal continuity necessary for the identity of ultimate parts over time, then we shall have to say that if an electron disappears from one orbit and causes an electron to appear in another orbit without there being spatio-temporal continuity between them, they are different electrons. Yet if we insist only on causal continuity, then they will be the same electron. But we can tell the whole story of the world either way, and both stories will be true; electrons of both sorts will exist. But all we need in order to tell the whole story of the world is informative designators (as well as of properties and times) of substances which pick out substances in virtue of certain kinds of continuities between bundles of properties. If, however, some substances have thisness, a full history of the world could need to describe not merely the continuities of bundles of co-instantiated properties (as well as describing the non-essential properties which the bundles gain or lose), but the continuing existence of the different thisnesses which underlie certain bundles (i.e. of what it is which makes the difference between two bundles of the same properties with qualitatively the same history).

There is nothing more to a substance than its parts and how they are arranged. So although the principle of the identity of indiscernibles is, I have urged, not a logically necessary truth, what is, I urge, a necessary truth is a stronger principle which I will call 'the principle of the identity of composites', that 'there cannot (logically) be two things which have all the same parts having all the same properties, arranged in the same way'. A substance made of the same parts arranged in the same way must be the same substance. For example, if there is a substance composed of certain fundamental particles which each have thisness (e.g. each is made of different matter), with certain properties including relations to each other (and spatio-temporal and causal relations to earlier particles), there could not be instead of it a different substance composed of all the same particles with the same properties and relations to each other. Andre Gallois has called the view that there could be another such substance 'strong haecceitism'. He writes:

Strong haecceitism seems to me incredible. Consider a car on a parking lot. It is not at all incredible to suppose that a qualitative duplicative of the car in question might have existed even if there is no qualitative difference at any place or time as a result. It is incredible to suppose that throughout history all of the atoms that actually exist might have been configured at each time in exactly the way they are actually configured without the car on the parking lot existing.[35]

Given my principle of the identity of composites, what Gallois describes as 'incredible' is necessarily false.

If none of the parts of a substance have thisness, the substance itself cannot have thisness. But if some or all of the parts of a substance have thisness, then clearly a substance made of parts with different thisnesses would be different in this respect. But

[35] Andre Gallois, *Occasions of Identity*, Oxford University Press, 1998, p. 251.

whether that difference would make it a different substance depends on how many parts have to remain the same (or result from gradual replacement) for the substance to remain the same; and that depends on the genus of substance to which the substance belongs. For example, even if electrons and some other fundamental particles have thisness and many cells of a strawberry plant made of such particles are replaced (gradually while the other cells continue to play the same role in the life of the organism), the strawberry plant would still be the same plant.

Nevertheless if parts of physical substances, such as electrons, have thisness (that is, are made of matter), then a full history of the world will have to distinguish between an electron (or other fundamental particle) made of this matter and an electron made of that matter. To do this we need informative designators which designate electrons as the particular electrons they are and tell us fully what it is to be those particular electrons, that is they tell us fully just of which chunks of matter they are made. But we humans could not have access to such ideal designators. This is because we identify substances by their properties, including their properties of spatio-temporal relations to other substances; and so we cannot know what is the difference between a world containing this electron with this history through space and time and a world containing an identical electron with a qualitatively identical history. If physical substances do not have thisness, there is no difference, but if they have thisness there is a difference and we cannot know what it is. In that case we cannot informatively designate physical substances, and in this respect we cannot tell the full history of the world. We may, however, know that two uninformative designators of a substance pick out the same substance at one time—for example, 'the electron seen from this side of the screen' and 'the electron seen from the other side of the screen'—because we can know that whatever the criteria which determine the identity of the two electrons, they are the same for each electron; that is, the informative designators of the two electrons—if we could know them—would be logically equivalent. We might also have good evidence that one electron or other particle is the same particle as a particle at another time; because we could infer that they had the same thisness (that is, was made of the same matter), in virtue of some physical theory about how matter behaves being simpler and so (see Chapter 2 section 5) more probably true than other theories. For it might be that the simplest theory about how matter behaves has the consequence that it always moves along continuous spatio-temporal paths. I shall assume below that—if physical substances have thisness—that theory is true. In that case spatio-temporal continuity is good evidence of the same thisness (that is, being made of the same matter), although it does not constitute it. So given that we can have evidence that the thisness of a certain substance in the actual world is the same as the thisness of a certain physical substance picked out by a different designator at the same time or at different times, we can often rigidly designate that substance by an uninformative designator which will enable us to reidentify it (certainly or probably) in the actual world. Nevertheless we cannot ever know in what the thisness consisted, and so know the difference between a world containing a particular physical substance and one qualitatively identical to it. This is because we could never have (as it were) an 'inside' view of the nature of a physical substance. Later in this book, I shall claim that our access to what I shall call 'mental substances' is different in this respect.

It is a disputed issue in the philosophy of physics whether or not some particles have thisness, an issue which further experimental work may help to solve.[36] Unless and until this issue is resolved, we do not know whether any of the physical substances of our world are composed of particles having thisness, and in this respect we do not know what would constitute a full description of our world, or even—to be more realistic—of any tiny spatio-temporal chunk of it. Although our ignorance of whether physical substances have thisness limits temporarily and perhaps permanently our ability to designate substances informatively, we can still know quite a lot about which ones are identical with which other ones or supervene on them. Thus to take the earlier macroscopic example, as used by early explorers, 'Everest' was an uninformative designator of the actual mountain visible from Tibet. If physical substances do not have thisness, then being Everest consists in being a fused collection of rocky parts having monadic properties (of size, mass, etc.) underlying the shape visible from Tibet at the time it was named, or any collection of similar parts which are spatio-temporally and causally continuous with those parts, surrounded by most of the same geographical features (individuated in a similar way.) That is, a future mountain would still be Everest even if mountaineers had removed some rocks and an earthquake had raised the mountain by adding rocky material to its base, and removed the whole rocky corpus a few metres to the South—all so long as there was spatio-temporal and causal continuity between the old parts and the new parts. But if physical substances do have thisness (i.e. are what they are in virtue of the same matter—something not further analysable), then being Everest consists at least in being a mountain with most of the same rocky matter surrounded by the same features consisting of parts made of certain particular chunks of matter (themselves having a certain thisness); and we cannot know what that matter is so we cannot use an informative designator for that mountain. But although the nature of Everest differs in the two cases, we can know that 'Everest' and 'Gaurisanker' pick out the same mountain at one time, since (as for the electrons discussed above) whatever are the criteria for being the mountain picked out, they are the same for both words. Also, we are likely to be able to pick out the same mountain as 'Everest' on different occasions. For if physical substances do not have thisness, the spatio-temporal and causal continuity of its parts will constitute a later and an earlier

---

[36] See Steven French and Décio Krause, *Identity in Physics*, Oxford University Press, 2006 for a very thorough historical account of the development of views about whether fundamental particles of some kinds differ from each other, not in any properties (in the sense of universals) but in 'thisness', and philosophical analysis of what conclusions about this can be drawn from the present state of quantum theory. Their conclusion is an agnostic one, that 'the formalism' of quantum theory 'can be taken to support two very different metaphysical positions', one in which the particles are regarded as 'non-individuals' in some sense and another in which they are regarded as (philosophically) 'classical individuals', that is as having thisness.

mountain both being Everest; and if they do have thisness, then such spatio-temporal and causal continuity will be strong (although fallible) evidence of it.

Also, merely knowing to which kind a substance belongs often enables us to say that two substances rigidly designated in different ways are not the same—since they do not satisfy some of the necessary conditions for being the same substance of that kind; even though we cannot nearly so often say that two substances are the same. This table may or may not be the same as the one that was here last week, but it is certainly not the planet Venus—for Venus is essentially a planet and the table is not. And we can know that 'that lump of bronze is Cleopatra's Needle' (Cleopatra's Needle being a statue made of bronze) cannot be a true identity sentence since a lump of bronze is a mereological compound, all of whose bits have to be retained if the lump is to continue to exist; whereas a statue is an artefact, some bits of which may be replaced without the statue ceasing to exist. (But there is clearly a sense in which the sentence is true; and the natural way to construe it so that it is true is to define it as claiming that the statue is made at that particular time of that lump of bronze.) Having pointed out the problems involved in individuating physical substances, and acknowledging that the physical substances of some other world might have thisness, since nothing important for the main topics of this book turns on the issue, I shall in future take it for granted that the fundamental particles of our world and so the larger physical substances composed of them do not have thisness—which is, I suspect, the majority view of philosophers of physics. I shall thus assume that physical substances are what they are in virtue of their properties, including the causal and spatio-temporal relations of their parts to those of earlier substances—though, as I pointed out, we can cut up the world into substances in different arbitrary ways and still tell the same world story. An informative designator of a substance will then pick it out in virtue of it having the properties which make it a substance of a certain kind, and the spatio-temporal or other relations of its parts to those of earlier substances which make it the individual substance it is.

For two events to be the same as each other, the events have to happen at the same time. There is an interesting and important philosophical issue about what makes a period of time the time it is. Is it its calendar date, or its relation to the present moment? Suppose today is 31 December 2008. Is my writing this sentence today the same event as my writing it on 31 December 2008? If not, then it would seem that we need to include both events in a full history of the world, told today. And in that case a full history of the world—what has happened, is happening, and will happen—as told on one day, will differ from that history as told on another day, because, for example, only on one day will it be true that 'today is 31 December 2008'. And there is an interesting and important philosophical issue about whether periods of time at places moving relative to each other are ever the same as (i.e. simultaneous with) each other. The Theory of Relativity, as expounded by Einstein, raised the issue of whether each system of physical substances in motion relative to other such systems has its own time scale—so that, to speak strictly, no period in one system is the same period (i.e. is simultaneous with) as any period in another. I shall have a little more to say about the former issue in Chapter 2, when I use it to illustrate a general point. However, since none of the issues which are the primary concern of this book turn on questions about the nature or identity of times, I shall not seek to resolve these issues. But as everything turns on questions about the identity of properties and substances, I have devoted this first chapter to the criteria for such identities.

2

Epistemology

1. Justified belief

Chapter 1 set out a framework (of substances, properties, and events) in terms of which we can tell the history of the world; and an understanding of what it is for some event to be metaphysically possible (impossible, or necessary). In this chapter I analyse certain general features of our criteria for beliefs about what is metaphysically possible, about which kinds of events and substances there are, and about which events cause which other events, being well justified beliefs. While I am not seeking to present a full-scale theory of epistemic justification in a book devoted to a different topic, I do need to make a few very general points. I assure the reader that these points are crucially relevant to my subsequent arguments; for example, about whether a belief that it is metaphysically possible that I could exist without my body, or a belief that conscious events cause brain events, are well justified beliefs.

A person's belief is 'epistemically justified' (and so in some sense 'rational') iff it is (in some sense) probably true; and better justified the more probable it is. But there is a considerable dispute among philosophers about whether a belief being probably true is a matter of it (that is, the content of the belief, the proposition believed) being made probable by the evidence available to the believer—which is the 'internalist' view—or whether it is a matter of the belief being produced in the right way—which is the 'externalist' view—which makes it probably true. (Most externalist theories are reliabilist theories holding that a belief is justified iff it is produced by a reliable process, such as being produced by (what seems to be) visual perception or being taught it at school, when what one learns by apparent visual perception or learns at school is usually true.) I suggest that this dispute, which has seemed in the past to many of its philosophical disputants to concern the true answer to some deep philosophical matter, is no more than a dispute about words. There is not a univocal sense of 'justified'; there are both externalist and internalist senses in which a belief may be 'justified', and more than one sense of each kind.[1] My concern is with the justification of beliefs in the internalist

---

[1] For a short introduction to the different externalist and internalist theories of 'epistemic justification' see Noah Lemos, *An Introduction to the Theory of Knowledge*, Cambridge University Press, 2007, chs 5 and 6. For a much fuller treatment, see my *Epistemic Justification*, Oxford University Press, 2001. For the claim, which is now becoming quite widely accepted, that there are different senses of 'justified', see William P. Alston, *Beyond 'Justification'*, Cornell University Press, 2005.

sense in which a belief is justified iff the belief is rendered (epistemically) probable by the evidence available to the believer and the believer believes it because of that evidence.[2] To spell out this sense requires spelling out what constitutes evidence, and what are the criteria for different kinds of evidence making different kinds of belief probably true. Among our evidence for the truth of some belief may of course be evidence that that belief has been produced by a reliable process, and in the absence of counter-evidence that evidence renders that belief probably true. But if a belief has been produced by a reliable process, but we have no evidence that it has been so produced, that the belief has been so produced cannot make any difference to whether or not we are justified in believing it in an internalist sense.

Epistemic probability is a relation of varying degrees between propositions.[3] For example, '80 per cent of Russians voters voted for Putin to be President, and Ivan is a Russian voter' makes it (80 per cent) probable that 'Ivan voted for Putin'; but '70 per cent of voters in St Petersburg did not vote for Putin, and Ivan is a voter in St Petersburg' makes it (70 per cent) probable that 'Ivan did not vote for Putin'. Usually the only probability relations between propositions are comparative ones (rather than ones with exact numerical values): for example, that a certain proposition makes a certain other proposition very probable, or more probable than not, or more probable than some other proposition. A detective's evidence or a scientist's evidence, which may be written down as a long conjunction of propositions reporting observations, may make some hypothesis about who committed the crime or what are the laws of nature fairly probable or more probable than some other hypothesis or more probable than it would have been without some of that evidence.

A person's evidence consists of the propositions which they believe to be true, but which they do not believe to be true merely because they are made probable by other propositions. In taking any journey we start from the place where we are; and in taking an epistemic journey to a world-view, we begin from those propositions which seem to us to be true but not on the basis of other propositions (always allowing for the possibility that we may come to believe on the basis of other evidence that they are not true after all). These propositions which form our evidence may be called our 'basic propositions'. They will include our beliefs about our mental life ('I have toothache'), beliefs about what we are perceiving ('I see a tree outside the window'), but also our memory beliefs ('I visited Moscow last year'), and our general beliefs about geography, history ('The Battle of Hastings took place in the year 1066'), or science. These latter beliefs are ones which we were no doubt once taught, but which we have by now forgotten by whom we were taught them and when. We think of them as things

---

[2] 'The believer believing it because of the evidence' is usually spelled out as the believer's belief being 'based on the evidence'. For different theories about what constitutes being 'based' see my *Epistemic Justification*, ch. 5, especially pp. 135–9. The present book being concerned with the probability of propositions believed, rather than with the epistemic status of believers, there is no need to investigate the nature of 'basing' further here.

[3] For the distinction between the three basic kinds of probability, see Additional Note A.

which 'everyone knows'. Our basic beliefs differ in strength, in the sense that we are more confident of some than of others; I may believe more strongly that I have toothache than that the Battle of Hastings took place in the year 1066.

In investigating any important topic, we seek to get beliefs as probable as we can get them within a limited time. That involves seeking more basic beliefs relevant to the topic, and in particular reading and listening to what others claim to have seen and established. My arguments in this book will take as evidence both very obvious basic beliefs of a kind which we all have about our mental life and our immediate physical environment, and also scientific results relevant to our topic (which the reader will be justified in believing on the evidence of his or her basic beliefs that they have read my reports of these results, in virtue of the principles of credulity and testimony to be analysed in this chapter, unless the reader has counter-evidence.)

2. The Principle of Credulity

It is, I suggest, a fundamental a priori epistemic principle, which I call the Principle of Credulity, that any basic belief (that is, the content of that basic belief, the proposition believed) is probably true (that is, it is more probable than not that the belief is true) on the believer's evidence that he believes it—in the absence of evidence in the form of other basic beliefs of that believer which makes it probable that he is mistaken. Put in another way, the principle claims that what seems to us to be so probably is so, that our apparent experiences are probably real experiences. This holds paradigmatically for perceptual beliefs, that is, beliefs arising from perception. If it seems (or appears) to me that I am seeing a desk in front of me (that is, I find myself believing that I am seeing a desk), then, in the absence of counter-evidence, probably there is a desk in front of me. Of course in the case of most perceptions I will have sensations (e.g. patterns of colour in my visual field) which I believe to be caused by the object apparently perceived (e.g. the desk). But that I am perceiving that object is not a conscious inference from those sensations; it is a datum which comes with the sensations, providing their interpretation. Likewise, if it seems to me that I have six spots in my visual field, or that I remember going to London yesterday, or that 'all men are mortal and Socrates is a man' entails 'Socrates is mortal', then probably (in the absence of counter-evidence) these things are so. And the more obvious it seems to me that some such thing is so, then (in the absence of counter-evidence) the more probable it is that it is so, and the better justified I am in believing it.

Of course I can normally check out my beliefs by further investigation. In the case of perceptual beliefs, and beliefs about my sensations (e.g. the spots in my visual field) I can look again more carefully. I can check my memory beliefs (that is, my apparent memories) by looking at my diary and asking others what I did: and so on. We seek to have beliefs as probable as we can get them; and that involves looking for more relevant evidence, and (in the case of beliefs which we believe because we believe that they are made probable by our evidence in the form of other beliefs of ours), checking whether the evidence we have does make our beliefs as probable as we think it does. This process of investigation may increase the probability of those beliefs and so make us more justified in believing them, but it may instead lessen that probability and even make it very unlikely that they are true. But what the principle of credulity is concerned with is whether on the evidence merely of having some basic belief (and no counter-evidence), that belief is probably true; and the principle claims that it is.

If we cannot start our epistemic journey from our basic beliefs, we cannot start it at all, and total scepticism would follow. Opponents seek to avoid so strong a conclusion by proposing more restricted forms of the principle of credulity. One possible alternative is to allow that while having a basic belief gives some degree of probability to that belief, it is only (in the absence of counter-evidence) probably true (that is, more probable than not) if it is confirmed by more evidence. That new evidence would take the form of another basic belief (e.g. a belief, resulting from looking a second time at the object which we believed that we had seen before, that the same object was there). If merely having the first belief did not make it probable, the same would surely apply to the second belief. Yet the suggestion is that two or more mutually supporting beliefs together (e.g. two or more successive beliefs with the same content, say beliefs that I am looking at a desk) would suffice to make the original belief overall probable. But the problem with this suggestion is that when we have checked out the original belief and obtained a new belief supporting the original belief, we would be dependent on fallible memory for the belief that we had checked out our original belief two or more times, and, unless that memory belief was probably true merely in virtue of being believed, we would never be in the position of having enough evidence that the original belief was true. And if ordinary memory beliefs are probably true merely in virtue of our having them, so surely are our ordinary perceptual beliefs.

An alternative more restricted form of the principle of credulity would be to claim that to hold a probably true basic belief we require not a number of supporting beliefs, but one very strong convinced belief. On this view only very strong perceptual beliefs and very definite memory beliefs (which might mean beliefs about events within the last few minutes) would be sufficiently probable to be more probable than not (that is, overall probable). But that would have the consequence that we would have very few probably true beliefs. Most of our basic perceptual and memory beliefs arise from one quick glance, or have the form of a rather unspecific memory of what we saw yesterday or were taught at school, and so on. Unless most of our basic beliefs (against which we have no counter-evidence) are probably true merely because we believe them, we would still be virtual sceptics about very ordinary matters. What goes for perceptual and memory beliefs, goes for basic beliefs of all other kinds, such as general beliefs about geography, history, science, and so on, and relatively simple beliefs about arithmetic or beliefs about what entails what. And since surely most of our ordinary basic beliefs are probably true, the restriction that only strong convinced beliefs are probably true is ill justified.

Thirdly it might be suggested that only certain sorts of basic belief are probably true (in the absence of counter-evidence). Alvin Plantinga (without making his point in terms of 'probability') gave the name of 'properly basic belief' to any belief which we are justified in believing without needing further evidence; and he gave the name of 'Classical Foundationalism' to the view that only perceptual beliefs, beliefs about our own conscious states, and 'self-evident' beliefs (such as '2 + 2 = 4') are properly basic.[4] But if we omit memory beliefs and the very general beliefs about history and geography, we will have too slender a basis from which to infer much of what we are justified in believing. And anyway there doesn't seem to be any very good reason for excluding any class of basic beliefs from being probably true except on the basis of evidence that most beliefs of that class turn out to be false. That's why we don't think that anyone should believe basic beliefs arising from palmistry or crystal-ball gazing— experience shows that most such beliefs are false. We all of us have the evidence that experience shows this latter in the form of a generally accepted piece of knowledge, of the same kind as our general beliefs about history and geography.

These considerations lead me to reaffirm the original principle of credulity in its unrestricted form. Either we must be very sceptical, and think that almost all our ordinary beliefs are not probably true, or we must endorse the principle of credulity. But we cannot choose our beliefs at will. Hardly anyone really believes that almost all the normal basic beliefs (about their physical surroundings, their immediate past, the size and age of the Earth, etc.) of most of us are probably false. So in consistency we must endorse the principle of credulity in its unrestricted form. Most of what we seem to experience, we really do experience; what seems to be so probably is so. The rational person is the credulous person, not the sceptic. A person's basic beliefs are probably true merely in virtue of the fact that he has those beliefs—in the absence of counter-evidence. But, if that person has counter-evidence to a basic belief of theirs (which may include evidence that other people have basic beliefs inconsistent with that basic belief) that will diminish its probability, perhaps to the extent of making it improbable. So, assuming the Principle of Credulity, I shall now illustrate its application to various kinds of 'seeming', on which we build our knowledge of the world. I begin by considering how we learn which sentences have which logical modality— that is, are logically impossible, possible, or necessary.

3. Justified beliefs about logical modalities

Among the things which seem to be so, and which we are surely 'justified' (in the above internalist sense) in believing to be so—in the absence of counter-evidence—are apparent 'truths of reason'. I claimed in Chapter 1 that we should regard such truths as truths about the logical status and relations to each other of sentences of some human

---

[4] See Alvin Plantinga, 'Reason and Belief in God' in A. Plantinga and N. Wolterstorff, *Faith and Rationality*, University of Notre Dame Press, 1983, pp. 46–8 and 58–9.

language. A sentence s is logically impossible iff it entails a contradiction. Sometimes it seems so obvious that some sentence entails a contradiction, that we are very well justified in believing this without needing to attempt to deduce the contradiction—unless we learn of some counter-argument to show that we may have made a mistake. 'There are round squares' is obviously logically impossible. But very often it is far from obvious whether some sentence entails a contradiction, especially when that sentence is a mathematical formula or a philosophical claim; and then, in order to be justified in believing the sentence to be logically impossible we need to show that the sentence entails a contradiction by means of an argument having fairly obvious steps. The obvious direct way to show that a sentence s is logically impossible is to deduce a contradiction from it. This is done by finding a chain of mini-entailments from s to a contradiction. An objector may challenge some step in the argument, say the step from p to q, by claiming that q is not something to which anyone is committed when using p in the correct sense. Such disagreement about one step in an argument may have been brought about by the almost inevitable minor disagreements about the mini-entailments of certain words and sentences, to which I drew attention in Chapter 1. But given that the disagreement arises only from this source and not from any deeper source, we may expect it to be overcome or bypassed by finding a route of proof (either to the original conclusion or to its negation) which does not depend on those particular words. Thus the proponent of the claim that s entails a contradiction may get his opponent to recognize some r such that p mini-entails r and r mini-entails q. Or the disagreement may be bypassed if the proponent can find a different sequence of mini-entailments from s to a contradiction which an opponent will recognize. A sentence s is logically necessary iff its negation entails a contradiction; and again sometimes it seems very obvious that the negation of some sentence—for example, the negation of 'all squares have four sides'—entails a contradiction. The direct way to show that some sentence whose status is not obvious is logically necessary is to deduce a contradiction from its negation, in the way just described.

Often too it is very obvious that some sentence does not entail a contradiction, and so is logically possible. A true sentence entails no contradiction, and if it is obvious that some sentence (e.g. 'my desk is brown') is true, then it is obvious that it is logically possible. Often too it is very obvious that some sentence which may be false, entails no contradiction—for example—'my desk is red'. And more generally it is often very obvious that some description of a world very different from our world entails no contradiction—for example, a world in which the law of gravity takes the form that any two bodies of mass m and m' at a distance r from each other attract each other with a force proportional to $mm'/r^{2.01}$ rather than, as is actually the case in our world, a force proportional to mm'/r^2. The postulated world would not be as stable a world as our world, but there is evidently no incoherence in supposing the existence of such a world, and so no contradiction is entailed by the sentence that claims that there is such a world.

When it seems obvious that some sentence is logically possible, we are justified in believing this—in the absence of counter-arguments. But when it does not seem obvious that some sentence is logically possible, it needs to be shown. Since any sentence entails infinitely many other sentences, one cannot show that a sentence does not entail a contradiction by running through all its entailed sentences and showing that there is not a contradiction among them. So the direct way to show that some disputed sentence q is logically possible is to show that it is entailed by some other obviously logically possible sentence p. For if p does not entail a contradiction, then neither does any sentence entailed by p. Often the other sentence p is a conjunction of sentences describing in detail a situation which we recognize as logically possible; it is one such that we can 'make sense' of what it would be like for it to be true. Then by deducing the disputed sentence q from this conjunction we show that the conjunction is one way in which the disputed sentence could be true.

To take an example far away from the issues which are the primary concern of this book, consider how one could show that it is logically possible that there be more than one space. A space is a collection of places at some distance in some direction from each other. There would be two spaces if there were two collections of places, members of each collection being at some distance in some direction from each other but not at any distance in any direction from any member of the other collection. We can show that this is logically possible by describing in detail one way in which it would be like to live in a world where there are two such collections of places, a description which is fairly obviously logically possible and then pointing out that it entails that there are two spaces. C.S. Lewis's Narnia stories depict such a world. In these stories people get from our space to another space, not by travelling for some distance in some direction, but by going into a wardrobe and shutting the door, or by taking a pill and then suddenly finding themselves in a different environment.[5] Though Lewis does not make this point, people could discover that the two environments belong to different spaces by finding that one environment belongs to a closed unbounded space—that is, an environment in which by proceeding in any direction you eventually return to your starting point and so could explore the whole space—and by failing to find the other environment when you explore the whole closed space. (The closed space would be a finite space. But it would not be finite in virtue of being bounded by some surface. Rather it would be the three-dimensional analogue of the surface of a sphere; in whichever direction you travel on the surface of a sphere you eventually return to your starting point.[6]) By reflecting on such thought experiments we can come to see that what might have seemed at first not logically possible—that there could be more than

---

[5] Anthony Quinton describes a Narnia-like situation in order to show the logical possibility of there being more than one space, in his paper 'Spaces and Times', republished in (ed.) R. Le Poidevin and M. MacBeath, *The Philosophy of Time*, Oxford University Press, 1993.

[6] Hans Reichenbach describes a world which observers could naturally describe as being a closed space in his *The Philosophy of Space and Time*, Dover publications, 1958, §12.

one space—is in fact logically possible. I shall be using thought experiments to help to resolve the issue of whether it is logically possible that a person could continue to exist when most of his or her brain has been replaced.

If we understand by some sentence being 'conceivable' that we can apparently make sense of what it would be like for it to be true (i.e. it appears not to entail a contradiction), then if some sentence is conceivable, that makes us justified in believing that it is logically possible. If we understand by a sentence being 'conceivable' that it does makes sense to suppose it to be true (i.e. that it does not entail a contradiction), then 'conceivable' means the same as 'logically possible'; in that case it is apparent conceivability (the fact that we can apparently make sense of what it would be like for it to be true) which justifies us in believing that the sentence is logically possible.

While the direct way to show some sentence to be logically impossible is to deduce a contradiction, and the direct way to show some sentence to be logically necessary is to deduce a contradiction from its negation, and the direct way to show some sentence to be logically possible is to deduce it from some obviously logically possible sentence, there is a less direct way of showing that the requisite entailments exist than by going through the process of deducing them. The direct way relied on the already existing common intuitions of language users about certain words. The less direct way seeks to draw out from language usage new intuitions in the form of common principles underlying the language usage which all users of the language can come to recognize as implicit in their use; and which they can use to draw out new mini-entailments. This less direct way is to use a method which John Rawls called the 'method of reflective equilibrium'.[7] (He used it as a method for assessing the truth of suggested moral principles, but it can clearly be used to assess the truth of any principles about the logical modalities of sentences.) We start with a few examples of obviously logically possible (or whatever) token sentences of some type; and suggest as an explanation of why they are logically possible some general principle about sentences of the type of which the particular tokens are tokens. We would expect there to be such principles, since—as noted in Additional Note C—sentences of a given grammatical form have conditions for their truth or falsity special for that form, and substances belong to kinds and so it is only logically possible for them to have properties which it is logically possible can be possessed by a substance of their kind. So we would expect there to be general principles why all sentences attributing similar properties to similar substances (or denying the existence of certain kinds of substance, or asserting that if some substance has a certain property it will have a certain other property, or whatever) are logically possible (or whatever). We are justified in believing a suggested general principle to the extent to which it is a relatively simple principle and able to explain why many different token sentences of different kinds have the logical status which it seems obvious that they do have, so long as there are no token sentences to which the

---

[7] John Rawls, *A Theory of Justice*, Oxford University Press, 1972, p. 20.

principle denies the logical status which it seems obvious that they do have. Insofar as the principle is justifiably believed, it allows us to resolve the logical status of some token sentence about whose logical status we were doubtful.[8]

Consider the procedure whereby philosophers have tried to construct a general analysis of 'knowledge', that is, of 'S knows that p'. They were aiming at an analysis which is a conceptual truth, and so logically necessary. Philosophers assembled many different examples of circumstances in which a sentence of this form is obviously true and other examples of circumstances in which a sentence of this form is obviously false, and then put forward a simple theory which purported to explain these results. Thus they suggested that if anyone justifiably believes that the First World War ended in 1918, and it did end then, then they know that the War ended then. And so more generally many examples seemed to support the principle that 'S knows that p' iff 'S believes p, S is justified in believing p, and p is true' ('justified' being understood in the internalist sense described earlier). And so many philosophers claimed that all sentences of this form are logically necessary truths, from which it would follow that conclusions could be drawn about sentences whose logical status was dubious. For example, it followed (on the assumption that by the principle of credulity or some other principle, many of us are justified in believing that we are not brains in vats, and that this latter sentence is true), that the sceptical claim 'no-one really knows that they are not a brain in a vat' is not logically necessary.

However, Edmund Gettier produced a kind of counter-example to the suggested principle, subsequently much discussed. Here is one of his examples. Smith and Jones have both applied for a certain job. Smith has strong evidence for the proposition that Jones will get the job, and also for the proposition that Jones has ten coins in his pocket. So plausibly Smith is justified in believing that the man who will get the job has ten coins in his pocket. However, Smith himself gets the job, and—unknown to Smith—Smith himself has ten coins in his pocket. So it would follow from the suggested

---

[8] The two ways of establishing the logical status of sentences discussed in the text are a priori ways. There are also far less direct a posteriori ways of establishing this, if we can find contingent events which make it probable that some sentence is logically possible, necessary, or whatever. One way in which this can happen is when we have authority for such a claim. Thus the fact that some brilliant and hitherto totally honest mathematician claims to have proved that some theorem is a consequence of the axioms of arithmetic makes it probable that the theorem does not entail a contradiction. Another interesting way in which a sentence of a particular kind can be made probable by contingent evidence is the following. It may be that some observed data would be explained very well by some hypothesis, and so be very probable on normal criteria of what is evidence for what, if that hypothesis was coherent—that is, if the sentence expressing it was logically possible. Thus the hypothesis that light is both particulate and wavelike may be shown to be (probably) logically possible, because if it is logically possible it can explain the various phenomena of light—interference, diffraction, reflection, photoelectric effect, Compton effect, etc.; whereas the hypothesis that light is a particle and not a wave, or the hypothesis that light is a wave and not a particle, can only explain some of these phenomena. Without the supposition that light is both particulate and wavelike the occurrence of all of these phenomena would be very improbable; hence their occurrence is evidence for the logical possibility of the hypothesis. This kind of argument, it should be noted, is an argument not from the logical possibility of certain phenomena, but from their actual occurrence. I discuss this type of argument in my *The Coherence of Theism*, revised edition, Oxford University Press, 1993, pp. 48–50.

principle that Smith knows that the man who will get the job has ten coins in his pocket. Yet it would seem obvious that Smith does not know this. It follows that the suggested principle about sentences of the form 'S knows that p' is not a conceptual truth, and so not logically necessary. Hence the suggested principle was rejected, and slightly more complicated accounts of knowledge were proposed instead, which had the desired consequence that Smith did not know that the man who would get the job had ten coins in his pocket. One suggested reason why Smith did not know this, is that he reached his belief by relying on a false proposition ('Jones will get the job'). So a relatively simple new principle was suggested that S knows that p iff S believes p, S is justified in believing p, p is true, and S's justification does not depend on relying on some false proposition (albeit one justifiably believed to be true—e.g. 'Jones will get the job') as his evidence for the true belief. Counter-examples to this new principle were then put forward in the attempt to refute it. In this way philosophers were trying to discover a general principle of the form 'S knows that p iff q' analysing the concept of knowledge which would yield the results that all agreed cases of knowledge were indeed cases of knowledge, and which did not have the consequence that some case which was obviously not a case of knowledge was such a case. Such a principle would enable them to determine whether disputed cases were or were not cases of knowledge.[9] In this way the method of reflective equilibrium can be used to determine the logical status of a sentence, in cases when using the direct method cannot achieve agreement (e.g. because there is not enough initial agreement about which sentences entail other sentences). I shall be showing how this principle can be used to resolve moral disputes in Chapter 7, and go on to use it in Chapter 8 to help to resolve the debate about what makes a person 'morally responsible' for his or her actions.

These ways of showing that some sentence q is logically possible or impossible depend on substantial initial agreement about which relevant sentences mini-entail which other sentences, and—when demonstrating logical possibility—on some substantial initial agreement that some other sentence is logically possible. Such agreement would have been reached by the process described in Chapter 1, of giving language-users similar training by way of similar kinds of examples of observable conditions under which different sentences would be true or would be false, and similar kinds of examples of their mini-entailments. Although more advanced language-users can be given rules (e.g. definitions of words) rather than examples, these rules themselves (and how to apply them) can only be understood by means of examples.

Minor disagreements about what entails what, arising from minor differences in the procedures by which we have learnt meanings can usually be bypassed in the way illustrated earlier so as not to lead to more substantial disagreements; and if they don't,

---

[9] See, for example, Lemos op. cit. ch. 2 for an account of various different analyses of knowledge and the various counter-examples which have been used to try to refute them.

the method of reflective equilibrium may resolve them. But where there is not that substantial degree of agreement about which sentences mini-entail some sentence q and by which sentences it is mini-entailed, or which other relevent sentences are logically possible, clearly the sentence q is ambiguous, either because it contains ambiguous words or because its sentence form is ambiguous. (Where I write about disputes about senses or mini-entailments of 'words', I ask the reader to take for granted that what I say applies also to longer phrases and to the meanings of sentence-forms.) The crucial issue is, then, whether both senses are coherent senses, or whether those who use the word in one of the senses are confused in supposing that they are operating with a coherent concept.

By a 'coherent sense' I understand a sense such that some existential sentences containing that word used in that sense do not entail contradictions. (By an 'existential sentence' I mean one which affirms the existence of something. Thus a predicate term 'splodge' has a coherent sense if 'there are splodges' is logically possible; and 'bodgier' has a coherent sense if 'there are substances which are bodgier than other substances' is logically possible.) If the sense of a word is coherent, then it designates a coherent concept. If each group is prepared to recognize the sense of the word used by the other group as coherent then the language contains two coherent senses of the word, and so two coherent concepts.

One obvious way in which ambiguity arises is when different groups are introduced to the use of a word by different kinds of paradigm examples of observable conditions of its correct application or of sentences mini-entailed by or mini-entailing sentences using it. So long as each group has equal access to the examples on which the usage of the other group is based, the dispute can then be resolved by pointing this out; and then it will normally happen that both groups are prepared to recognize the sense of the word (or longer expression) used by the other group as a coherent sense. This seems to be happening to the dispute in epistemology between internalists and externalists about what makes a belief 'justified'. As I mentioned earlier, internalists hold that a belief is justified iff it is made probable by evidence accessible to the believer. They do so on the grounds that 'S is justified in believing p' mini-entails 'S's belief that p is based on and made probable by evidence accessible to S', and vice-versa. Externalists hold that the justification of a belief depends on the kind of process which produced it; and the normal form of externalism, reliabilism, holds that a belief is justified iff it is produced by a reliable process, that is, a process which normally produces true beliefs. They do so on the grounds that 'S is justified in believing p "mini-entails" S's belief that p is caused by a reliable process', and vice-versa. Each group denied the mini-entailment claimed by the other group. However, many philosophers are now willing to concede that there are different kinds of paradigm examples of the use of 'justified' which lead naturally to different coherent senses of 'justified'; and that the only issue is not which is the correct account, but whether and why justification of each kind is worth having.

There can only be a resolution of this kind to a dispute about whether a sense of a word is coherent in the normal case where members of each group have access to the paradigm examples of the kinds from which the other group have derived their sense of that word. I shall be arguing in Chapter 3 that different people may have been introduced to words denoting sensations (e.g. 'taste of curry' or 'high note') by different paradigm examples because the public events (eating curry or listening to a singer producing a certain noise) may cause different sensations in different people; and that the person whose sensation it is has a privileged access to that sensation which other people do not have. I shall, however, be concerned for the rest of this section with the normal case where people have been introduced to the senses of words (and longer phrases and sentence forms) by publicly accessible examples.

There are, however a few situations where there is massive disagreement about the mini-entailments of words and so ambiguity, even though the disputants have been introduced to the word by exactly the same kinds of paradigm examples of observable conditions of its application. These paradigm examples have led different people to acquire different understandings of the sense of the word, and so to come to hold different views about the mini-entailments of sentences which use the word (without such examples of its mini-entailments constituting paradigm examples of the sense of the word). This is not a normal occurrence because, since humans have similar cognitive mechanisms to each other, they normally derive from the same kind of training in the use of a word the same understanding of its meaning. But when this does happen, the group of those who understand the word in one sense may still come to recognize the sense in which the other group is using the word as coherent, perhaps because it can be defined by other words having a sense shared by both groups.

Sometimes however when two groups use some word (or longer expression) in different senses, at least one group is not prepared to recognize the sense of the word used by the other group as a coherent sense. The only way that I can see to resolve the dispute at this stage is for the two groups to look again at the paradigm examples. The group whose sense is disputed will try to show that the other group has ignored some observable properties of the paradigm examples, properties logically independent of those on which both groups are agreed, and so failed to grasp a possible sense of the word. The other group will try to show that there are no such independent properties which it has ignored.

Two examples of this kind of dispute about whether some sense of a word or expression is a coherent sense are central to the main theme of this book. These are the disputes about the sense of 'causes', and about the sense of 'is the same person as'; both of which I shall need to discuss at length in due course. So I will illustrate how a dispute of this kind goes by a different example, one provided by one of the issues involved in disputes about the nature of time, to which I alluded at the end of Chapter 1.

The history of the world consists of a succession of events. We derive our concept of temporal succession from paradigm examples of events observed to succeed each other (i.e. we observe one event to occur later than another event). On the basis of such awareness of temporal succession, we derive the concepts of 'earlier than', 'at the same time as', and 'later than', governed by various mini-entailments (such as 'a is earlier than *b*, and *b* is earlier than *c*' mini-entails '*a* is earlier than *c*'). Then different cultures create different calendars, different systems of dating the events of which they have learnt. They define one event of great importance to them (the 'original event'), for example, the birth of Christ, picked out by the substance and its properties involved, but not the date of its occurrence, as happening at year 1; and date other events by the number of years they occur before or after the believed time of that event.

The issue then arises whether given all the 'type-events', in the sense of events picked out by the individual substances and properties involved in them, including their relational properties of occurring a certain temporal interval after such-and-such type events and before such-and-such other such type events, but not by the time of their occurrence, could—it is logically possible—have occurred at different times. For example, could the Second World War have begun and ended a year earlier than it did, and the possession of every property by every substance (every type event) in the whole history of the world also have occurred a year earlier than it did? And so, if the world had a beginning, could it have begun a year earlier than it did, while subsequently developing in exactly the same way? Leibniz claimed that this was 'not intelligible'.[10] In his correspondence with Leibniz, Samuel Clarke took the opposite position: everything could have happened a year earlier than it did.[11] Clearly Clarke's understanding of a year being the year it is was different from that of Leibniz, yet both derived their understanding of temporal terms from similar paradigm examples of events which succeed each other.

Leibniz denied that periods of time have any properties other than the properties of which type-events occur at them and properties of occurring before or after other type events, by which they can be picked out. So, for him, a period of time is the period it is in virtue of which type-events happen then, and happen at different temporal intervals before or after that period. He then applied the principle of the identity of indiscernibles to events (in which their time of occurrence was determined solely by properties of the above kind), to claim that any two sequences of events of the same type (involving instantiations of all the same properties in the same substances in the same order) must be the same sequence of token events (because events of the same type, defined as above, would always occur at the same time). Hence he claimed that it would not be 'intelligible' (which he would understand as 'it would entail a contradiction') to suppose that every event might have happened a year earlier.

Clarke did not produce much by way of argument for his rival view. But—even if he were to accept the principle of the identity of indiscernibles—he could have made the point made in the twentieth century by what is known as the 'A-theory of time': that periods of time do have properties additional to the properties of which

---

[10] See (ed.) H.G. Alexander, *The Leibniz-Clarke Correspondence*, Manchester University Press, 1956. Leibniz's fifth paper §55.

[11] Clarke claimed that 'it was no impossibility for God to make the world sooner or later then he did' (op. cit. Clarke's fourth reply §15).

type-events occur at those times and which type-events occur at earlier and later times.[12] Some of the paradigm examples of one event occurring 'earlier than' another event are also paradigm examples of the former event being evidently 'past' when the latter event is evidently present. It is above all from those paradigm examples of one event being earlier than another, that we derive our concepts of 'earlier than' and so its converse 'later than'; and from paradigm examples of one even being present when another event is present that we derive our concept of 'simultaneous with' (that is, happening at the same time as). The presentness of events—that is, that they are happening now—and the pastness of some events which happened very recently are (at the time of observation) observable properties of those events—that is, the memory by which we remember them as 'past' is so clear that our awareness of them as having this property is like observing them. (See later in this chapter on the evidential force of memory.) The paradigm examples of futurity are examples of the property possessed at the time of an event now past by an event now present. The properties of being past, present, and future belong to events only at certain times; whereas if the relations of 'earlier than', 'later than', or 'simultaneous with' relate two events at any time, they relate them at all times. Having distinguished the properties of presentness, pastness, and futurity from the properties of temporal relation (i.e. the properties of 'earlier than', 'simultaneous with', and 'later than' certain type events), we can see that they are, by the criteria for property identity which I advocated in Chapter 1, distinct properties. ('Occurring now' doesn't entail 'occurring in 2012', or conversely.) So we can individuate a year (or other period of time) either by its temporal distance from a year at which some type event occurred, or by its temporal distance from the present year. (If it is now 2012) the supposed date of the birth of Christ can be individuated, not merely as the year at which certain type events having temporal relations to certain other type events happened, but as the year 2012 years earlier than the present year. It follows that there are two possible senses of 'same year'; in one sense an event happens in the same year as another event iff they occur at the same temporal interval after the original event, and in another sense an event happens in the same year as another event iff they both occur at the present moment or at the same temporal interval before or after the present moment. Both senses seem coherent senses. So it is intelligible to suppose— that is, it is logically possible—that every type event might have occurred a 'year' earlier than it did, in the sense of 'year' in which the year is the year it is in virtue of its temporal distance from the present year. At that point the defender of Leibniz (in modern terminology the B-theorist) will try to show that being 'present' does not designate a property of events, or—if it does—can be defined in terms of 'earlier' and 'later'.

I will not take this controversy further. My point here is that one can help someone to see that one sense of a word (e.g. 'same year') derived from the same paradigm examples is a sense which fits those examples and is a coherent sense by trying to draw

---

[12] See, for example, Part 7 of (ed.) Michael J. Loux, *Metaphysics: A Contemporary Introduction*, 2nd ed., Routledge, 2006, for the controversy between the A-Theory of Time, and the B-theory of time.

attention to certain properties of some of those examples (and especially ones involved in one's experience of them) to which his opponent may not have paid adequate attention, and to their logical distinctness from other properties (especially properties of their place in the publicly observable succession of types of events) which both disputants initially recognize. The opponent will respond by trying to show that the former properties are not really properties distinct from the later properties and can be analysed in terms of them. I shall show in due course how (by paying attention to certain properties of at least some paradigm examples of their correct application) we can observe in the same paradigm examples of causation and of personal identity properties distinct from and additional to those involved merely in the patterns of public events, which give rise to concepts of causation and personal identity which are unanalysable, and needed for a full description of the world.

Such are the different ways in which we can obtain justified beliefs about logical possibility, necessity, and impossibility.[13] The logically impossible is metaphysically impossible; and the logically necessary is metaphysically necessary. If all the substances, properties, and so on, in a logically possible sentence are designated by informative designators, then that sentence will also be metaphysically possible. But if the logically possible sentence contains uninformative designators, it needs empirical investigation to acquire a justified belief about what they designate. When we have acquired that, we must substitute the informative designators of the things designated, and then the metaphysical status of the earlier sentence will be the same as the logical status of the resulting sentence.[14]

4. Direct sources of justified beliefs about contingent events

I move on to consider the sources of our justified beliefs about (metaphysically) contingent events, such as my breakfast this morning, or the Battle of Hastings. In order not to continue to use the cumbersome phrase 'justified belief', I shall sometimes simply talk about the sources of our 'knowledge'. As I have noted above, although knowing some proposition is not the same as having a justified belief in that proposition, our only evidence for supposing that we know some proposition is that we have

---

[13] Two modern philosophical movements—Hume's 'concept empiricism' and logical positivism—have tried to enunciate quick general principles by which we can distinguish the logically possible (often called the 'conceivable' or 'coherent', or even 'meaningful') from the logically impossible, or the logically contingent (sometimes called the 'factually meaningful') from the logically necessary or impossible, which—I point out in Additional Note D—have proved totally inadequate for the purpose. We cannot settle issues of the modal status of sentences by evoking such general philosophical principles; they can only be settled by detailed conceptual inquiry on the case-by-case basis described in the text.

[14] For my response to the account different from mine, of the source of disagreement about the logical status of sentences by Timothy Williamson in his *The Philosophy of Philosophy*, see Additional Note E.

a justified belief that it is true. So the sources of knowledge are the same as the sources of justified belief.

We learn about some contingent events (as also some truths about logical modalities just discussed) directly, in the sense that our knowledge of them is not reached by an inference from something else, and does not depend on taking for granted some particular theory of the world. There are three direct sources of knowledge—experience (in a wide sense), memory, and testimony.[15] I shall include as 'experiences', (apparent) perceptions (by means of the senses) of physical events, (apparent) 'experiences' (in a narrower sense) of our thoughts, feelings, sensations, etc., and also (apparent) awarenesses of truths of reason (awareness of 'seeing' some sentence to be logically possible or whatever) which I have been discussing in section 3. (All of such experiences will be included under the category of conscious beliefs and so of 'conscious events', which I shall introduce in Chapter 3.) As I have noted, it is because it seems obvious that 'there are no round squares' is logically necessary, that I have a justified belief that it is so. I do not infer it from anything else, nor does the justification of my belief depend on some general theory of how the world works. I just 'see' it (in a metaphorical sense of 'see'). And that goes, as I argued in section 3, for many other truths of reason.

But it is a similar 'seeming obvious' which provides our justification for believing many claims about perception and 'experience' (in a narrower sense). It is as obvious to me that 'there is a desk in front of me' (I see it), and that I have a headache (I feel it), as that 'anything red is coloured'. The Principle of Credulity applies here too. But as with the truths of reason, so with contingent claims, some are more obvious than others, and less obvious claims become more probable when rendered probable by more obvious claims; and any claims are only justifiably believed in the absence of outweighing counter-evidence. If I seem to see a desk in front of me (but I am not very confident about this), and then I put my hand where the desk seemed to be and the hand seems to pass through an empty space (and I am very confident that it did), then the evidence of the second experience outweighs that of the first; and I am no longer justified in believing that there is a desk there. And the evidence of many experiences outweighs that of a single experience. If I seem to see a desk in front of me and am fairly confident that I do, nevertheless when I look again and look from different angles there is no desk, again I must conclude that the first experience was illusory. But, to repeat the point, unless apparent experience as such has a right to be believed we could never have any beliefs which were (on our evidence) probably true.

The principle of Credulity applies also to memory. It is an epistemic principle derivative from the principle of Credulity, which I call the Principle of Memory, that what we seem to (i.e. apparently) remember having experienced we (epistemically)

---

[15] Part I of Robert Audi's textbook *Epistemology* (Routledge, 1998) entitled 'Sources of Justification, Knowledge, and Truth' has chapters on 'Perception', 'Memory', 'Consciousness', 'Reason', and 'Testimony'. What I have called 'experience' covers what he calls 'perception', 'consciousness', and 'reason'.

probably did experience—barring counter-evidence. I include in 'remember having experienced' both what we remember doing and having happen to us (personal memory) and what we remember that we did or happened to us (factual memory) without remembering doing it or having it happen. In the former case I recall the 'doing' or 'having happened' 'from the inside', how it felt to me as an agent or subject of experience. In the latter case I may simply recall that I did something or that it happened to me, but just as a brute item of knowledge. I may remember how it felt to me going to London yesterday. By contrast I may simply recall as a fact about myself that I went to London when I was five years old without remembering how it felt, and perhaps suspecting that my belief that I went to London then was caused by someone having told me a few years ago that I went then. Personal memory entails factual memory but not vice versa. Among the things of which I have factual memory are that I have been taught various geographical and historical facts, and that I have been taught the meanings of words and sentences in the ways described earlier in this chapter. But all this is compatible with not being able to recall by whom I was taught these things or when and where. Without knowledge arising from memory, our direct knowledge would be confined to our experiences of what is happening now (including present experiences of what we are reading in some written text such as a diary). For all our other knowledge (including knowledge of the meanings of spoken or written words, and knowledge of who wrote those words, and knowledge of what others have told us orally) we depend on what we remember having experienced in the past.

But even with memory, we would have very little knowledge of the world unless we assume that what we read and what other people tell us is—in the absence of counter-evidence—probably true. It is a second fundamental a priori epistemic principle that what people seem to be (i.e. apparently are) telling us that they are experiencing or remember having experienced or remember as facts, they (epistemically) probably do or did experience or probably are facts, again barring counter-evidence. I call this the Principle of Testimony. So many of our beliefs depend on the apparent testimony of others (spoken or written). Almost all we know about science or history or geography depends on what it seems to us that others have told us; and so often they tell us what they do because others have told it to them. If we cannot trust the testimony of others (and that normally involves trusting our memory that someone did tell us so-and-so, even if we cannot remember who that person was), our knowledge of the world would be very limited indeed. In trusting the testimony of others (e.g. that USA has nuclear weapons), we believe that we are trusting their apparent memory (e.g. that other people told them this) and that this was derived ultimately (perhaps via one or more intermediate testifiers) from the apparent experience of others (e.g. to have watched a nuclear weapon being assembled in Colorado). My justification for claiming that this is a fundamental principle on which we must rely is that we do all think and surely think correctly that we are justified in having all the common beliefs that we do—that the earth is spherical, that Russia is a big country, that there were two world wars in the twentieth century, etc.; and we could only have this justification if the principle of testimony is correct.[16] So if someone tells you something, whether about their own experience or some fact they claim to have learnt, that provides prima facie justification for believing what they say. But one's own apparent memory (that one was at the relevant place and time of the event to which they testify and saw that it didn't happen) or the apparent testimony of others that the event didn't happen can outweigh the evidence of the piece of apparent testimony.

Beliefs acquired by apparent experience, memory, and testimony are (epistemically) probably true—in the absence of counter-evidence. Science relies on the applicability of these principles to determine what constitutes evidence. A scientist takes their observations, experiences, and calculations as probably correct, and the probability will be greater if they have looked carefully at the experimental results and checked the calculations. Almost all scientific knowledge relies on apparent memory (e.g. of the results of experiments or calculations only written up the following day). Most scientists rely the majority of the time on the apparent testimony (written and spoken) of observers that they have made certain observations and of theoreticians that they have done certain calculations. And the wider educated public relies entirely on the testimony of scientists with respect both to their calculations and to their observations.

As I have been emphasizing, beliefs acquired by apparent experience, memory, and testimony are, however, open to counter-evidence. Such counter-evidence is often called a 'defeater'. There are two kinds of defeaters—undermining and overriding defeaters. If we have inferred (whether consciously or without thinking about it) the occurrence of some event ϵ from evidence γ, then an undermining defeater is evidence (making it probable) that γ did not occur or is not good evidence for ϵ whereas an overriding defeater is new evidence that ϵ did not occur. If, for example, I seem to hear my telephone ring, and then someone points out to me that the noise is coming from the television set where someone is depicted as hearing a telephone ring, that constitutes an undermining defeater for my apparent experience. It doesn't show that my

---

[16] I have assumed that the Principle of Testimony is a fundamental a priori principle, but all that is necessary for my argument is that it is correct. Some philosophers hold that the principle that what people seem to be telling us that they experienced or remembered they probably did experience or remember is not an a priori principle, but one for which we have good evidence: we have apparent memories that in the past apparent testimony has proved correct. Thus Hume, *An Enquiry Concerning Human Understanding*, section 10, part. 1: 'The reason why we place any credit in witnesses and historians, is not derived from any connection, which we perceive a priori, between testimony and reality, but because we are accustomed to find a conformity between them'. Philosophers have objected that this would not be possible, because it is a necessary condition of understanding a language that one already assumes that speakers normally tell the truth. But even if that objection is not cogent and Hume is right, the authority of testimony would still remain, given that it is supported by apparent memory that people usually tell the truth. But if in fact the evidence of apparent memory were to suggest that apparent testimony is not reliable, then there could not be any justified beliefs which relied on testimony. In that case none of us would have any justified beliefs about geography, history, or science except those which resulted solely from observations and calculations done by ourselves. On the reasonable assumption that we can know more than that, I assume the principle.

telephone was not ringing, but it does show that the noise was not evidence that it was, since the noise had a different cause. Again, if I have come to believe that ϵ happened because some person apparently testified that they saw ϵ, evidence that that person was somewhere else at the relevant time and so could not have seen ϵ undermines the evidence of that individual, and I no longer have reason to believe that ϵ happened. By contrast the apparent testimony of two independent witnesses that they were at the place of the alleged occurrence of ϵ, and that they saw that ϵ did not happen, overrides the evidence of the original witness. But the evidence constituting a defeater of either kind must itself be provided by apparent experience, memory, or testimony. This evidence need not be direct evidence of, for example, testimony that the testifier was not present at the site of the alleged event ϵ, and so couldn't have seen it. It may be fairly indirect evidence, in the sense that it may be evidence supporting a theory which has the consequence that the testifier couldn't have seen the event—for example, evidence supporting a theory that the testifier was blind and so couldn't have seen what they testified to having seen.

5. Indirect sources of justified beliefs about contingent events

The beliefs which we acquire through experience, memory, and testimony, provide grounds for many further beliefs. Deduction provides a very obvious way of extending our knowledge. We can deduce from the content of some of our experiences other items of knowledge; and we saw in section 2 how deduction can add to our knowledge of the truths of reason. But most of our knowledge about events beyond what we have ourselves experienced or remember, or others have testified to, depends on induction (in a wide sense of that term). We infer from the contents of our experiences, our memories, and the testimonies of others to some explanatory theory about how the world works, and thence to events predictable or retrodictable from that theory. Philosophers of science give different accounts of the criteria for evidence making a theory probable, but I suggest that something along the following lines must be approximately correct.[17] An explanatory theory T is rendered (epistemically) probably true (or likely to be true) by evidence insofar as (1) the theory predicts, that is, makes probable, much evidence observed to be true and no evidence observed to be false, (2) the theory 'fits in' with any 'background evidence' (i.e. it meshes with theories outside the field it purports to explain, which are themselves rendered probable by their evidence in virtue of these criteria), (3) the theory is simple, and (4) the theory has

---

[17] For a fuller exposition of this account of the criteria for evidence making a theory probable, see my *Epistemic Justification*, ch. 4. (In ch. 3 of that book I make a distinction between what I call 'logical' probability and what I call 'epistemic' probability; and I call the correct criteria of inductive inference criteria of 'logical' probability. That distinction is not important for the issues discussed in the present book, and what I write in *Epistemic Justification* about 'logical' probability can in general be read as concerned with 'epistemic' probability in the sense with which I am concerned in the present book.)

small scope (i.e. is concerned to explain a small field and makes few and imprecise predictions about it).

The evidence may be direct evidence (of the kinds described in section 4) or be a (deductive or inductive) consequence of another theory itself made probable by direct evidence. By the theory 'predicting' evidence, I understand merely that it makes probable much observed evidence and no evidence observed to be false. (It is, I suggest, irrelevant whether the evidence is discovered before or after the formulation of the theory. Many philosophers of science, however, claim that evidence observed in the course of 'testing' a theory and made probable by it adds much more to the probability of the theory than evidence known before the theory was formulated. For present purposes nothing turns on the issue of this dispute.) The evidence referred to in (1) is evidence which the theory T makes probable without appealing to a 'mesh' with other theories outside the field of T. I contrast this with the 'background evidence' referred to in (2), which is evidence constituting or making probable such other theories. Criterion (2) tells us that if a theory 'meshes' with another theory of a neighbouring field, itself satisfying the other criteria well, that adds to its probability. 'Meshing' is a matter of the two theories together making a simple overall super-theory; and is often a matter of the two theories having the same form. The justification for using criterion (2) thus depends on that of criterion (3). For example, the theory that Mars moves in an ellipse meshes with the theory that other known planets (of our solar system) move in an ellipse. Together they form a simple super-theory—that all planets (of our solar system) move in an ellipse. There may, however, be no relevant background evidence, and then criterion (2) drops out. One case of this is when a hypothesis purports to explain a very large field (as does quantum theory) and so there is little if any evidence about fields beyond it. However, given any finite amount of observed evidence (or background evidence), there will always be an infinite number of theories which render the occurrence of that evidence very probable, but differ in that they make quite different predictions from each other for the future. Hence the vital importance of criterion (3) which allows us to choose between such theories (especially in cases where there is no relevant background evidence).

The simplicity of a scientific theory is a matter of it postulating few kinds of entities (i.e. substances), few properties, few kinds of properties, properties closely related to observation, few laws relating substances to each other, and mathematically simple relations in the laws. Thus a theory which postulates 20 kinds of subatomic particles is more likely to be true than one which postulates 40 kinds—if it satisfies the other criteria (e.g. predicts the observed evidence) equally well. Likewise, a theory which postulates three kinds of colour charge (a property of some subatomic particles) is as such more likely to be true than one which postulates six kinds: as is a theory which postulates three forces of attraction or repulsion between physical objects rather than four. Any theory can be expressed in the form 'a = b', if 'a' and 'b' are given complicated enough definitions; and so—other things being equal—laws in terms of properties which we can readily recognize (e.g. 'mass' which we can measure—for medium-sized objects—on scales) are more likely to be true than ones defined in a very complicated way in terms of the former. The fewer laws the better. And finally, laws which relate values of properties to each other in mathematically simple ways (e.g. '$y = 2x$') are as such to be preferred to ones which relate them in more complicated ways (e.g. '$y = 2x + (x\text{-}1)(x\text{-}2)(x\text{-}3)(x\text{-}4)$'). (These two laws give the same predictions of values of y for values of x, $x = 1, 2, 3,$ or 4.) A number or mathematical function ϕ is simpler than another one Ψ if someone can understand Φ without understanding Ψ, but not vice-versa. Thus addition is simpler than multiplication, multiplication is simpler than powers, scalars are simpler than vectors, vectors simpler than tensors, etc.; not all numbers or mathematical functions can be related in this way to each other, but many can. The scope of a theory is what it purports to tell us about the world. A theory has small scope insofar as it is concerned only with some small field (for example, the behaviour of a certain kind of gas at low temperature, or the movement of one named planet), or makes relatively few or imprecise predictions. Criterion (4) tells us that the more a theory claims (the larger its field and the more precise its predictions), the more likely it is to be false. Simple theories may have large scope, but simplicity carries more weight than scope; scientists consider some theory of enormous scope (e.g. quantum theory which governs the behaviour of all physical objects) quite probable because it satisfies the other criteria, including the criterion of simplicity, well.

Without the crucial a priori criterion of simplicity (affecting criterion (2) indirectly as well as criterion (3) directly) any prediction would be as probable as any other, since for any prediction some theory satisfying criterion (1) as well as any other theory with the same scope would make that prediction. And there will always be an infinite number of such theories.

I take a simple example which illustrates these criteria at work. Newton's theory of gravitation, put forward in 1689, consisted of his three laws of motion and his law of gravitational attraction (that every body attracts every other body in the universe with a force proportional to the product of their masses and inversely proportional to the square of their distance apart). It predicted a vast number of observations of the motions of our moon and of planets and of the moons of other planets, of the behaviour of comets, tides, and pendula. There was in 1689 very little by way of probably true detailed theories about fields outside its field—no theories of chemistry or electro-magnetism, for example—with which it could mesh. Although an infinite number of theories could always be constructed which were such as to predict the observations known in 1689 as well as Newton's did, they would all have been far more complicated than Newton's. For instance, the theories that the force of gravitational attraction between bodies of mass m and m$'$ was proportional to $\dfrac{mm'}{r^{2.00001}}$ or to $\left\{\dfrac{mm'}{r^2} + \dfrac{mm'}{10^6 r^4}\right\}$ (where r is the distance between the massive bodies) would have made the same predictions as Newton's theory, within the limits of accuracy then measurable. And the theory that the force is proportional to mm'/r^2 until the average distance apart of the galaxies from each other exceeds a certain amount (e.g. that to be reached in 2050 CE), after which it is proportional to mm'/r^4 would make exactly the same predictions, then or today as does Newton's theory, within any limit of accuracy. Yet because of its great simplicity and despite its large scope, Newton's theory was surely rightly regarded in 1689 as probably true, and is so regarded today (subject to qualifications imposed by relativity and quantum theories). Newton's theory was so regarded by many in 1689 despite the fact that not merely would more complicated theories make the same predictions; and despite the fact that it predicted no new phenomenon which could then be observed, not already predicted by theories of narrower fields (such as Kepler's theory of planetary motion, or Galileo's law of fall). Newton's great achievement was to construct a simple theory from which the narrower theories of very different fields all followed.

Given an (epistemically) probable explanatory theory, we can then predict future events from the theory and observations of present and past events (about which we may learn later by experience, memory, or testimony); from Newton's theory and the present and past positions of planets, we can infer their future positions. We can also retrodict past and present unobserved events. We can retrodict the occurrence of an unobserved event C on the grounds that, given our theory T, it is probable that such an event was cause of some observed event E. The criteria for it being probable that C caused E are that it follows from (T and C) that E would occur, and from (T and not C) that E would not occur, and more generaly E makes the hypothesis that (T and C) probable on the same criteria as made T probable. Thus learning that the planet Uranus moved along a path which was irregular in comparison with the path which Newtonian theory predicted on the assumption that the only planets were the ones then known, in 1846 Leverrier postulated (as the most probable explanation) the existence of a new planet, Neptune, pulling Uranus out of its regular orbit. And we can extend our knowledge to retrodict more remote events which would in their turn most probably explain the events which, in accord with our probable theory, explain known events. And we can use joint applications of retrodiction and prediction to infer further events—for example, we can retrodict from a crater that there was a large meteor impact in 60m BCE, and then predict that this would have led to much of the surrounding country being covered by a dense dust cloud.

So we have a picture of humans acquiring evidence from apparent experience, memory, and testimony; and inferring thence inductively in various directions. Some of our evidence may be rejected on the basis of stronger (i.e. more probably true) evidence acquired by one of these routes, or on the basis of a theory rendered probable by such evidence. Some evidence likewise may be reinforced by the same process.

6. The causal criterion

A major undermining defeater to a belief resulting from apparent experience, memory, testimony, or inference (deductive or inductive) is evidence to the effect that our apparent experience, memory, or testimony was not caused (directly or indirectly) by the event apparently experienced or whatever. In having beliefs resulting from experience such as the apparent observation of a desk, we assume that the event (of the presence of the desk) experienced caused the belief (with its accompanying sensations), 'caused' in the sense of being a necessary part of a total (i.e. sufficient) cause of the belief.

In perception we seem in contact with the event apparently observed. That event seems to force itself upon us; the presence of the desk seems to force itself upon me, and so I have no option but to believe that it is there. That, we assume, is because there is a causal chain from the desk to the belief—only causes exert 'force'. (This holds, we believe these days, because the desk reflects light rays which land on my eyes and cause the belief.) Hence the generally accepted causal theory of perception. Maybe not any perceptual belief caused by an event constitutes a perception of that event. Maybe the causal route must not be 'deviant'. For example, suppose that I apparently see a tree outside the window. Suppose there is indeed a tree outside my window, but there is a screen in front of the tree, so that light rays from the tree do not reach my eyes. But there is a closed circuit TV camera which takes pictures of the tree and its movements which it transmits onto the screen; and so, indirectly the tree causes me apparently to perceive the tree and so to acquire the belief that it is there. The causal route is then not a normal one but a 'deviant' one; and this leads some writers to claim that I do not then perceive the tree but only the image of the tree. My point is, however, that whether or not we suppose that only certain sorts of causal route from an event apparently perceived to the subject's belief about it constitute perception, some causal route is necessary for perception. Any evidence that such a belief was not caused by a causal chain from an event apparently perceived therefore constitutes an undermining defeater for it—as in my earlier example of the telephone ring.

It is natural to suppose that there is a similar assumption of a causal route involved in our conscious experiences (in a narrow sense). In believing that we are now having certain sensations or conscious occurrent thoughts, we assume that the belief is forced upon us by those events. Some writers have, however, denied that in these cases there is any causal chain, or that we normally assume that there is. They claim that in these cases we have direct access of a non-causal kind to our conscious events.[18] Not much turns on whether the causal account applies to our knowledge of our currently occurring conscious life, and so—for the sake of simplicity of exposition—I shall assume that it does, while drawing attention subsequently to any important consequences of denying it. And likewise it is natural to suppose that some apparent truths of reason which seem obvious to us (including mathematical calculations which we

---

[18] See, for example, David Chalmers, *The Conscious Mind*, Oxford University Press, 1996, ch. 5.

recognize as true straight off) are correct because the beliefs that they are correct are forced upon us by the marks on the paper or the thoughts in our mind symbolizing these apparent truths causing us to have the beliefs that they are correct.

We must also suppose that when we come to believe some proposition because we infer it from a consciously believed premiss by a process of inference where we cannot (or do not) hold all the intermediate stages in our mind at once, that we believe the later stages and the resulting conclusion because we believed the earlier stages. That means that we must believe that each earlier belief caused the next belief; and so any evidence that this is not happening constitutes an undermining defeater for the belief in the conclusion of the inference. But in such a case we must believe, not merely that we are caused to hold each later belief by its preceding belief, but that we are caused to hold each later belief later because of what we see as involved in the earlier belief. If we thought that we were being caused to believe the later proposition by the earlier belief in virtue of some irrational process, we would not really believe it. So the causation of each later belief by its preceding belief must be immediate, not, for example, via a series of non-conscious events. By one event causing another event 'immediately' I mean the first event causing the second event without doing so by causing some third event which in turn causes the second event.

The assumption of the existence of causal chains, although longer ones than for perception (and perhaps for other experiences) and ones involving different kinds of event, does—most writers would agree—seem to undergird our beliefs in the deliverances of apparent memory and testimony. I trust my apparent memory because I assume that it is caused by my earlier belief (which it correctly records) about what I was then apparently experiencing, and that that belief was itself caused by the event which I was apparently experiencing, 'caused' in the sense that the earlier belief and the event apparently experienced were necessary parts of a full or total cause (a sufficient condition). Thus in trusting my apparent memory that I was in London on Monday I assume that it was caused by a belief held on Monday that I was then in London, and that the latter belief was caused by my being in London. Hence the generally accepted causal theory of memory. (Again, maybe the causal route must not be 'deviant'. My point is merely that a causal route is necessary for memory.) Any evidence that the memory was planted in me by a hypnotist or a brain surgeon constitutes an undermining defeater for that apparent memory belief.

In believing someone's apparent testimony to have experienced some event, I assume that they say what they do because they believe that the event happened and have the intention of telling me the truth; that is, their belief and intention causes them to say what they do, 'causes' in the sense of being a necessary part of the total cause. I believe that they believe that the event happened because they apparently remember it, and that that memory belief was caused by a previous belief that they were then experiencing the event, and that the latter belief was caused by the event. So if I get evidence that the words coming out of some person's mouth were not caused by any intention of his (e.g. that the words were caused by a neurophysiologist stimulating that person's neurones to cause his mouth to make the sounds, or simply as in fluent aphasia or Tourette's disease where a neural malfunction causes a stream of words to come out of a sufferer's mouth), that evidence constitutes an undermining defeater to belief in the truth of what that person seemed to be saying. (The intention does of course have to be of a particular kind, an intention to tell the truth; and evidence that the person was intending to deceive me would also undermine his testimony. But my point is simply that evidence that there is no causation at all by the apparent testifier's intention undermines his apparent testimony.) In all of these cases the counter-evidence (in the form of an undermining defeater) must itself come (directly, or indirectly via a theory) from apparent experience, memory, or testimony.[19]

In summary there is an epistemic assumption (EA) behind the justification of scientific theories that:

(1) A justified belief in a scientific theory (which is not itself a consequence of any higher-level theory in which the believer has a justified belief) requires a justified belief that the theory makes true predictions.

(2) A justified belief that a theory makes true predictions is (unless this is a consequence of some higher-level theory in which the believer has a justified belief) provided by and only by the evidence of apparent experience, memory, and testimony that the theory predicts certain events and that these events occurred.

(3) Such justification is undermined by evidence that any apparent experience was not caused by the event apparently experienced, any apparent memory was not caused by an apparent experience of the event apparently remembered, or any apparent testimony was not caused by the testifier's intention to report his or her apparent experience or memory.

And what goes for scientific theories goes, I suggest, for any theory about any metaphysically contingent matters including historical theories about what has happened in the past.

The causal requirement (3) is not an arbitrary one. If we are to hold that our basic beliefs resulting from experience and memory, and our beliefs resulting from testimony (2), are probably true, we must suppose that there is some mechanism which normally guarantees the coincidence between each belief that some event occurred and the occurrence of that event. The most direct mechanism would be for there to be a direct causal chain from each event believed to occur to the belief that it occurred. The shorter the chain, the less that can go wrong with it. So if we are to have knowledge as reliable as we can get about past events in our own experience and that of others, we

---

[19] Audi (op. cit) defends the causal nature of perception, memory, consciousness, and (in effect) testimony. Thus (p. 28) 'perception is a kind of causal relation', (p. 56) 'causal connections to the past are essential to genuine remembering', (p. 81) 'the process by which introspection leads to introspective beliefs . . . is . . . causal', and (p. 137) 'with testimonally grounded knowledge, as with memorial knowledge, there must be a certain kind of unbroken chain from the belief constituting that knowledge to a source of the knowledge in some other mode'.

need a direct causal chain. The only other possible mechanism which would sustain the coincidence would be an indirect mechanism, in the form of there being a common cause of each belief that an event occurred and the occurrence of that event. Maybe sometimes there are such common causes. Suppose some military parade has been very well rehearsed, so that the actual parade on the day looks exactly like the rehearsal. Suppose that a TV station is unable to get a crew to film the actual parade, but having a film of the rehearsal and knowing that the actual parade will look just like that, shows the film of the rehearsal purporting to be a film of the actual parade. The rehearsal is then a common cause both of the detailed events of the actual parade, and of the film shown on TV and so of the resulting beliefs of the TV audience about the detailed events on the parade ground. But there are two independent causal chains in this story—one between the rehearsal and the actual parade, and one between the rehearsal and the beliefs caused by watching the film of the rehearsal. And so a lot more can go wrong; if either chain behaves imperfectly the audience will acquire false beliefs. If we are to have basic beliefs as reliable as possible, they must result from direct causal chains; and if we are to suppose that we have got such beliefs, we need to believe that they do result from direct chains. Hence in order to regard basic beliefs as probable as we do, we must believe that they do result from direct chains. If we come to believe that some basic belief doesn't result from a direct causal chain, we would have no reason to believe it to be true unless we believed that it resulted from a common cause mechanism. But since the supposition of a common cause mechanism is a complicated supposition, and since we have plenty of basic beliefs which we can believe in the absence of defeaters to result from direct causal chains, it would seem ill justified to suppose that there is a common cause at work unless we have evidence, in the form of basic beliefs which are apparently directly caused, that there is such a common cause. We would need evidence provided by more reliable basic beliefs that a cause of a certain kind was regularly followed both by a belief that some event occurred and via an independent chain-by the occurance of that event, if we are to have a justified belief which we believe to have been produced by a common cause mechanism.

The fundamental criterion (FC) behind EA is that justified belief that some event occurred requires the assumption that that event is accessible (in a privileged way) to the believer, or causes an event thus accessible—unless this is justifiably believed to be the consequence of some theory which predicts other events justifiably believed to occur on grounds independent of that theory. By an event being 'accessible in a privileged way' I mean that the event is an event, such as a belief (e.g. about what the believer is perceiving), which the believer has a way of knowing about (by experiencing it) not available to others. (That we have privileged access to our beliefs is something for which I shall argue in Chapter 3.) Then justified belief that a theory makes true predictions requires (unless justified by a higher-level theory for which this holds) the assumption that both a scientist's awareness of the calculations that the theory predicts certain events and the events predicted are accessible to or cause effects accessible to the believer. FC, I suggest, is a criterion central to our judgements about the credibility of any scientific, historical, or whatever theory about the contingent world.

To have a justified belief in a scientific or historical theory of any complexity, where the argument involves many steps from reports of experiments or observations of (to most of us) unknown observers, each of us needs to rely on others, not merely for their reports of observations but for their calculations therefrom. Even the most able physicists can make mistakes in their long calculations, ignore important variables, or make ill-justified assumptions about which terms in an equation can be ignored in order to have an approximately true equation. They need to have the calculations checked by others. Although some physicists might have a moderately well justified belief in a theory, even if they don't have their calculations checked by others, it will not be a very well justified belief. And the non-experts in a field are crucially dependent on experts, in order to have a justified belief in some scientific theory, including, for example, even such an easily comprehensible theory as the theory of Evolution by natural selection. For most of us a scientific theory needs to be publicly established if we are to be justified in believing it to be true.

3

Property and Event Dualism

1. Definitions

In Chapter 1 I clarified the nature of properties, substances, and events, and their different identity conditions; and in Chapter 2 I considered both how we may discover the metaphysical necessities relating substances, properties, and events, and how we may learn which events have occurred. I now come to apply these results to the main topics of this book. I begin by arguing in this chapter that there are two kinds of events, physical and mental, and that a full history of the world must list (or entail the occurrence of) events of both kinds.

There are different ways of making the mental/physical distinction, but I propose to make it in terms of the privileged accessible/public.[1] I believe that making the distinction in this way highlights the traditional worry about how the mental can be connected with the physical; but some other ways of making the distinction may do so as well, and similar results to mine are likely to follow from these other ways. So I define a mental property as one to whose instantiation in it a substance necessarily has privileged access on all occasions of its instantiation, and a physical property as one to

---

[1] There are in the literature other ways of understanding the mental/physical contrast, the most common of which are (what I shall call) the propositional/non-propositional and the non-physical science/physical science distinctions. I expound these distinctions in terms of properties; similar distinctions follow for events and substances. The propositional/non-propositional distinction is the distinction usually called intentional/non-intentional. On this way of understanding the contrast a mental property is one which involves an attitude towards some (apparently) conceivable event under a certain way of thinking about it—it is fearing, thinking, believing so-and-so, when the subject does not necessarily fear, think, believe the same thing under a different way of thinking about it. On that account, 'John believing that David Cameron is friendly' involves the instantiation of a mental property in John, because its occurrence is consistent with John not 'believing that the Prime Minister is friendly'—because although David Cameron is the Prime Minister, John may not believe that. A physical property is then any property whose instantiation does not involve such an attitude. On the non-physical-science/physical-science way of understanding the contrast, a physical property is one whose instantiation can be explained by an extended physics, and a mental property is one which cannot be so explained. The propositional/non-propositional way of understanding the contrast has the unfortunate consequence that pains and sensations of patterns of colour are not mental events (they are what they are independently of the subject's attitude towards them); yet these are the most obvious trouble-makers for 'mind-brain' identity, and must count as mental if we are to deal in any way with the traditional mind-body problem. The non-physical-science/physical science way of making the contrast is hopelessly vague, for it is totally unclear what would constitute an extended physics, that is, a science incorporating present-day physics but much else as well, as still being a 'physics'. Hence my preference for my way of defining 'mental' and 'physical' properties, events, and substances in terms of privileged access.

whose instantiation in it a substance necessarily has no privileged access on any occasion of its instantiation. Someone has privileged access to whether a property P is instantiated in him in the sense that whatever ways others have of finding this out, it is logically possible that he can use, but he has a further way (by experiencing it) which it is not logically possible that others can use. A pure mental property may then be defined as one whose instantiation in a substance does not entail the instantiation of any metaphysically contingent physical property in that substance. Any mental property which is not a pure mental property I will call an impure mental property. Such a property must derive its mental nature from there being an aspect or element of it which consists of a pure mental property; and the subject's privileged access to the instantiation of the mental property then consists in her privileged access to the instantiation of the pure mental property.

In the above paragraph and always in future when I mention a property or event, I ask the reader to assume (unless I state otherwise) that I am mentioning the property or event picked out by the informative designator used in mentioning it—for example, when I mention the property of 'having a toothache', I am thereby mentioning the property picked out by the informative designator 'having a toothache'; I am picking out the property which is present 'on the surface' in all cases of having a toothache, and not some property to be discovered by science which underlies and causes the surface property. So to say that instantiation of one property entails that of another is to say that a sentence affirming the instantiation of the former property picked out by its informative designator entails a sentence affirming the instantiation of the latter property picked out by its informative designator. Two properties are different iff their informative designators are not logically equivalent.

Clearly there are physical properties (as 'physical' is defined by me) such as 'being square' and 'having a positive electric charge' which are often instantiated. And clearly also there are mental properties (as 'mental' is defined by me) which are often instantiated. They include properties of perception picked out by such informative designators as 'seeing a desk'; and 'hearing a telephone ring'. When these predicates are being used informatively, as they normally are, they are such that, given that we know what the words (e.g. 'see' and 'desk') mean, we can recognize when they apply to ourselves (e.g. when I am seeing a desk) and when they do not—unless our faculties (e.g. my eyes) are not working properly, or we are not favourably positioned (e.g. I am a long way away), or we are subject to some illusion (e.g. someone has arranged mirrors in a clever way so that I am tricked into supposing that I am seeing a desk). If we could be as favourably positioned with respect to the mental properties of others as they are (with faculties in working order, and not subject to illusion), we could recognize just as easily as they can which mental properties they are having. How it is that we do know what such predicates mean when they are applied to others, and so what we would experience if we were as favourably positioned as they are, is an issue which I will discuss later in this chapter. And of course the other condition for the predicates to be informative designators is also satisfied: we can make simple inferences from the application of these predicates (i.e. we know their mini-entailments). We can infer from 'I am seeing a desk' that 'I am seeing an item of furniture' or 'I am not blind'. So we know what is involved in seeing a desk or hearing a telephone ring.

These properties are mental because whoever has them is necessarily in a better position to find out whether he or she has them than is anyone else. Although others can be fairly confident about whether I am seeing a desk or hearing a telephone ring, clearly I can be even more confident. I can know better than you or anyone else whether I can see the desk which is in front of me, or hear the telephone ring. Whatever ways anyone else has of finding these things out I can use. They can find these things out (fairly well) by studying my behaviour and also perhaps (when neuroscience has made further progress) by studying my brain events. But I too can study my behaviour—by watching a film of it: and I too can study my brain events by looking at the instruments which record the patterns of my neural discharges. But I have a further way of finding these things out—by my conscious awareness that I seem to see the desk or hear the telephone ring.

The properties just discussed are not, however, pure mental properties; for their instantiation entails that of a physical property; I can only see a desk or hear a telephone ring if I have the physical properties of being causally affected by a desk or telephone. But since there is more to seeing a desk or hearing a telephone than being causally affected by a desk or a telephone, seeing a desk or hearing a telephone must include pure mental properties such as those informatively designated by 'apparently seeing (seeming to see) a desk' and 'apparently hearing a telephone And there are pure mental properties because they entail nothing physical. I can apparently see a desk when there is no desk there, and seem to hear the telephone ring when it is not ringing. There are other pure mental properties which are not components of any obvious impure mental property—for example, the properties informatively designated by 'having a headache' or 'having ten spots in my visual field' or 'hearing a tune in one's mind'. It is, I suggest, obvious that such properties are pure mental properties, since it is obviously logically possible that someone can have a headache or spots in their visual field without this being entailed by any brain or other physical event. But clearly it could be shown to be logically possible by telling an even more obviously logically possible story of two similarly situated cloned persons with qualitatively identical brain states, one of whom had a headache and the other did not, from which it would follow that having a headache did not entail anything (metaphysically contingent) about a person. Clearly there are innumerable such mental properties, as I shall illustrate further in the course of this chapter.

Since the informative designators of any physical properties are not logically equivalent to those of any mental properties (since there are different criteria for applying the designators), no mental property is identical to a physical property. The criteria for being in pain are not the same as the criteria for having some brain property (e.g. 'having one's c-fibres fire'), or behaving in a certain way in response to a bodily stimulus (e.g. crying out when a needle is stuck into you). The criteria for being in pain are how the subject feels, and the criteria for brain and behavioural events are what anyone could perceive.[2] And the same applies to any other pure or impure mental property. Nor do mental properties as such supervene on physical ones. Mental properties would supervene on physical properties iff necessarily for any mental property F, if any substance x has F, there is a physical property G such that x has G, and necessarily any substance y having G has F. But given that x having a pure mental property does not entail x having a (contingent) physical property, no pure mental property will supervene on a physical property; and if pure mental properties do not supervene on physical properties, neither will any properties which include them, that is, impure mental properties. So there is no reason to suppose that any particular mental property supervenes on any physical property at all.

My definitions have the consequence that there are some properties which are neither mental nor physical—let us call them 'neutral properties'. These are properties which are such that some substances have privileged access to whether they are instantiated in it; but other substances do not. These properties include formal properties (e.g. 'being a substance') and disjunctive properties (e.g. 'being in pain or weighing ten stone'). Both I (when I am in pain) and a filing cabinet (which weighs 10 stone) have the property of 'being in pain or weighing 10 stone'. Given that I have privileged access to whether the property of 'being in pain' is instantiated in me and that no-one has privileged access to whether the property of 'weighing 10 stone' is instantiated in me, it follows that I have privileged access to whether the property of 'being in pain or weighing ten stone' is instantiated in me. But a filing cabinet does not have privileged access to whether the property of 'being in pain or weighing 10 stone' is instantiated in it, because, not having a capacity for consciousness, it does not have privileged access to anything at all.

It is now natural to define a mental event along the same lines as one to which the substance involved has privileged access, and a physical event as one to which the substance involved does not have privileged access, and a pure mental event as a mental event which does not entail a metaphysically contingent physical event as that substance. While the instantiation of a mental property will always constitute a mental event, and the instantiation of a physical property will always constitute a physical event, the instantiation of a neutral property may constitute either a mental or a physical event, dependent on the substance involved. With these definitions it follows that no mental event is identical to or supervenes on any physical event. For no pure mental event is identical to or entails any (contingent) physical event involving the same substance, and so cannot supervene on any physical event, and so

---

[2] I compare my argument for the non-identity of mental and physical events with Kripke's somewhat similar argument in Additional Note F.

the same will apply to any impure mental event which includes the pure mental event.

By argument of the same pattern as that just used, we can conclude that it is logically possible that physical properties of the kind, the instantiation of which normally causes the instantiation of pure mental properties of a certain kind might fail to do so in a certain person. And if it is logically possible that this might happen for physical properties of a certain kind, there seems no reason why it should not be logically possible that in a certain person physical properties of all kinds might fail to cause the instantiation of the pure mental properties which they cause in other persons; that is, it is logically possible that there be zombies. Given that the properties being referred to in the sentences of this paragraph, are ones referred to by informative designators, what is logically possible is also metaphysically possible. It is metaphysically possible that there are zombies.[3]

However, on our normal assumption, which I shall argue in section 4 of this chapter to be a justified one, that most human-looking beings are not zombies, it follows that the mental properties which I have been discussing are instantiated innumerably often, and so that a full history of the world must include innumerable (pure) mental events and—distinct from them—innumerable physical events.

Many readers may find this argument for the claim that no mental events supervene on physical events rather quick, in view of the contentious nature of this philosophical issue. But the work of the argument is done first by my definitions of 'mental' and 'physical' events, secondly by my criteria for event identity, and thirdly by the argument of Chapter 1 about the relation between logical possibility and metaphysical possibility. Clearly any philosopher is entitled to define technical terms as they wish; and when I define the terms in my way, it then becomes very clear that (whatever we call them) there are two kinds of properties, and that properties of both kinds are often instantiated. Some of the contentiousness of this issue arises when 'physical' and 'mental' are defined in different ways from mine. Again any philosopher is entitled to lay down their own criteria for event identity; and I have given an argument why we need mine in order fully to describe the world. And for justification of the argument of Chapter 1, I must refer the reader back to that chapter. I now proceed in the sections 2 and 3 of this chapter to fill out my conclusion that mental events do not supervene on physical events, by analysing the different kinds of pure mental events, and by showing that my definition of the 'mental' includes many of the kinds of events which, sometimes in virtue of rival definitions, most other writers also term 'mental' events. Having drawn attention to the existence of impure mental events, my main concern in future will be with pure mental events, and so—unless I state otherwise—my

---

[3] In the article referred to in Chapter 1 note 11 Bealer affirms that it would not be counter-intuitive to say that our doppelgangers are not 'conscious' since (in his terminology) '"conscious", "sensation", "pleasure", "pain"' seem 'semantically stable'.

subsequent discussions of 'mental events' are to be understood as concerned only with pure mental events.

2. Sensory events

Pure mental events are of kinds which differ from each other in two respects, whether they are 'propositional' or 'non-propositional', and whether they are conscious events or continuing mental states.[4] A propositional event involves an attitude to an (apparently) conceivable event under a particular way of thinking about it: a desire or purpose to bring it about, or an (occurrent) thought or belief that it has occurred or will occur. Since that way of thinking about the event could be put into words by a sentence describing the event (not necessarily by its canonical description), it is an attitude to the proposition which is expressed by that sentence. It is for that reason that I call these events 'propositional'. (What I call a 'propositional' event is more normally called an 'intentional' event. But I am avoiding this term, because it leads to a confusion between 'intentional events' and 'intentions' which are only one kind of 'intentional' event.) A conscious event is one of which necessarily the person whose event it is is aware or conscious while it occurs. A continuing mental state is an event which may occur while the person whose it is is not aware of it, but to which they have privileged access because that person has a way of becoming aware of it (by experiencing it) necessarily unavailable to others. Using these distinctions, I shall now proceed to describe the different kinds of pure mental events, and I shall delineate five different kinds of mental events which I will call 'sensations', 'beliefs', 'thoughts', 'intentions', and 'desires'. I shall describe what I mean by these terms, which is in general what is meant by them in ordinary English. But in order to include only those events to which their subjects have privileged access, my definitions will not always coincide with ordinary English usage. Hence if someone claims that we have 'beliefs' or whatever, to which the subject does not have privileged access, I shall simply agree that such 'beliefs' are not mental events in my sense. My interest in 'mental events' is an interest in mental events in my sense, including—I shall claim—most events normally called 'beliefs', 'desires', or whatever.

The only conscious non-propositional mental events are ones naturally called 'sensations' which are conscious events. They are sensory events which involve the instantiation of sensory properties (often called qualia). Sensory events include the experiencing of patterns of colour (when the subject has no belief that they correspond to anything in the outside world) such as having an after-image, lines in the visual field symptomatic of migraine, and images had by the drink or drug addict; the hearing of noises 'in the mind', smelling a smell of roses, or tasting a taste of honey (where the subject may or may not believe that there are roses or honey present), memory images

---

[4] Much of what I have to say here about the kinds of pure mental events summarizes what I have written in my *The Evolution of the Soul*, Oxford University Press, revised edition, 1997. Part I.

(when memory comes to one via images), and the intentionally imaged diagrams or patterns of the imagination. It seems fairly evident that (veridical) perception normally involves two elements on the pure mental side—acquisition (or reinforcement) of beliefs, and having sensations of patterns of colour (or noise, touch, smell, or taste) caused by the event believed to have been perceived. My seeing a rose involves having a pattern of colour in my visual field and acquiring a belief that there is a rose in front of me (or having a previous belief that there is a rose there strengthened) caused by a rose. Hearing someone talk involves hearing noises caused by that person talking, and acquiring a belief that they are talking. And so on.

Other examples of sensations are bodily feelings, such as pains, itches, tickles, and feelings of heat or cold *minus* any desire which accompanies them. Experiences of certain kinds are so regularly accompanied by the desire that the experience cease, that we tend to make it part of the concept of an experience of one of these kinds that the subject desire not to have it. In one sense of 'pain', a pain would not be a pain unless it was unpleasant, that is, the subject desired not to have it. But in these cases one can distinguish between the sensation and the desire. One can see the distinction in the case of pain by noting that a normal pain is a more acute feeling of a kind which would not be unpleasant in a very mild degree. The mildest of pricks or aches is not unpleasant. Note also that when those suffering acute pain are subjected to the brain operation of prefrontal leucotomy, they sometimes report that although the 'pain' is still there, it is no longer unpleasant.[5] While most sensations are involuntary—they just happen— some sensations (and in particular imagined images) are voluntary in the sense that we bring them about intentionally.

It should be evident that none of the sensations such as I have described entail the occurrence of anything physical in their subject, and so sensations are pure mental events. Sensations are as such conscious events, in the sense that—not merely does the subject have privileged access to their occurrence, but he or she is necessarily to some extent aware of them while they are occurring. A 'mental image' of which I was totally unaware while I was having it is no mental image. But sensations are what they are independently of how the subject thinks about them, and so there may be aspects of a sensation of which the subject is unaware, or even—through not paying adequate attention—has false beliefs. Thus I may have an eidetic image (i.e. an image containing all the details) of a page of a book, yet not be aware of the words on the tenth line, and so have no belief about what those words are. Or, to take a much discussed example, I may have an image of a striped tiger without having noticed how many stripes it has. Or, to use a previous example, I may have a pattern of dots in my visual field, and as a result of

---

[5] On this issue see R.M. Hare, 'Pain and Evil' republished in (ed.) J. Feinberg, *Moral Concepts*, Oxford University Press, 1969. And for full-length development of the distinction between the sensation of pain and any other elements involved in what we normally call 'pain'; the fact that some sensations other than pains are unpleasant; and the fact that although many sensations are pleasurable (i.e. we desire to have them), there is no sensation of pleasure corresponding to the sensation of pain, see R. Trigg, *Pain and Emotion*, Oxford University Press, 1970.

a very quick examination of the field, come to believe that there are ten dots, when really there are only nine dots.

One reaction to these examples is to deny that there is any more content to a sensation than the subject is currently aware of. On this view, the image of the tiger, the number of whose stripes I have not noticed, is simply a blurred image, like a blurred photograph which gives a stripy impression without depicting a definite number of stripes. There may indeed be such images. But some images are not like that; they have features of which the subject is unaware. My reason for saying this is that, if asked, a subject can often report features of their images of which the subject was previously unaware, for example, the exact number of stripes possessed by the image of the tiger, without the image appearing in any way to change. And a subject can also correct their initial beliefs—for example, about the number of dots in their visual field. But a part or aspect of a sensation wouldn't be such a part or aspect unless the subject had privileged access to it, and could become aware of it by more thorough introspection.[6]

While the only conscious non-propositional events are sensations, I suggest that the disposition to have sensations is also a non-propositional event, but a continuing mental state. Having such a disposition is a mental event because its subject has privileged access to whether they have this disposition by sometimes experiencing sensations. There may be animals which have a disposition to have sensations and no other mental events.

3. Propositional events

Propositional events involve an attitude to an (apparently) conceivable event under a particular way of thinking about it, which—if put into words—would be a description of it. The event (the 'content' of the belief or whatever) may be described either in a way which entails or presupposes something about the public world or in a way which does not entail or presuppose any such thing. Someone could have a belief that Oxford is a beautiful city, only if Oxford (a public object) exists (for one cannot have a belief about a thing if that thing does not exist); but someone could believe that there is a beautiful city called 'Oxford', even if Oxford does not exist. The former belief is called a 'wide-content' belief, and the latter is a 'narrow-content' belief. Every wide-content belief entails a narrow-content belief, which consists of the former minus any

---

[6] It is of course well established that people are influenced in their behaviour by inputs to their sense organs which do not give rise to sensations of which they are aware. When words are flashed on a screen very quickly subjects deny that they have seen them, but their guesses about which words were flashed are far better than chance; and when those words are the names of advertised products, this 'subliminal advertising' influences people to buy the products. (See, for example, Phil Merikle 'Preconscious Processing' in (ed.) M. Vellmans and S. Schneider, *The Blackwell Companion to Consciousness*, Blackwell Publishing, 2009.) But there seem to me no grounds for postulating that this causal process consists in the input causing an 'unconscious sensation' which in turn via brain events causes the subsequent behaviour, rather than for supposing that the input causes only brain events which in turn cause the subsequent behaviour; and so no grounds for a wider understanding of 'sensation' than that outlined.

presuppositions about the public world; for example, a belief about a public object that it has some property entails a belief that there is a public object which has that property. In my terminology a wide-content belief is a mental event but not a pure mental event (since its occurrence entails the existence of a public object), whereas a narrow-content belief is a pure mental event. But we can give a full description of the world without listing any wide-content beliefs. If there is a public world with the features presupposed in the wide-content belief, then the occurrence of the wide-content belief is entailed by the occurrence of the narrow-content belief and the occurrence of those features; and if there is not a public world with those features, then there is no wide-content belief. Since a full description of the world need include only narrow-content beliefs, and since my main concern is with pure mental events, I shall in future treat all beliefs as narrow-content beliefs. And what goes for beliefs goes for the other propositional events; I shall treat all desires as narrow-content desires, and so on.

There are, I suggest, two kinds of conscious propositional events: thoughts and intentions (intentions in what the agent is doing, that is, their purposes), and two main kinds of propositional events which are continuing mental states: beliefs and desires. Intentions for the future are also continuing mental states, and so too are dispositions to have thoughts or intentions, though of course these latter are definable in terms of conscious events. I will analyse these different kinds in turn.

I begin with beliefs. A person's beliefs are the way the world seems to that person. At any time we all have many beliefs of which we are not conscious at that time. I believe the First World War ended in 1918, that I lived in Essex when I was young, that $5 + 7 = 12$, and so on—while I am not conscious of these beliefs, and am thinking about quite other matters. But the beliefs are (pure) mental events because I have privileged access to them; I can ask myself what I believe about some issue—for example, when the First World War ended, and if I don't find myself saying to myself '1918', then I don't have the belief that that war ended in 1918. Often, when one first acquires some belief, one is conscious of acquiring it; the acquisition of it is then a conscious event. I described various ways in which we acquire beliefs in Chapter 2. We acquire them by apparent experience (in my wide sense), apparent memory, or apparent testimony. Apparent experience includes apparent perception. As already noted, this normally involves having sensations and acquiring beliefs (or having previous beliefs strengthened). Apparent memory, it if is real memory, is—as normally understood—simply the bringing into consciousness of previously held beliefs (though I shall be suggesting in Chapter 4 the possibility of a wider understanding of memory). Apparent testimony often leads us to believe what we are told. The extension of our belief system by means of deductive and inductive inference involves apparent experience of the consequences of already held beliefs. One's beliefs need not be expressed to oneself in words, and indeed one may not have words of the right kind adequately to express some belief.

I include under 'beliefs' also 'inclinations to belief', but for the sake of simplicity of exposition I shall not mention these subsequently to this paragraph. I mean by an inclination to believe some proposition, a belief that there is quite a chance (in numerical terms, a significant probability less than 1/2) that the proposition is true. I shall assume that a belief that some proposition has an (epistemic) probability on the believer's evidence greater than 1/2 (i.e. is more probably true than not) is logically equivalent to a belief in that proposition (i.e. that the proposition is true).[7] (Someone's evidence may be simply it seeming to that person thus, but it may be some other believed proposition.) To believe that it is more probable than not that you will come to see me tomorrow is to believe that you will come to see me tomorrow; and conversely. Beliefs may be of different degrees of strength. The strength of a belief is a matter of the believer's degree of conviction that it is true. If I believe that you will come tomorrow, I may believe it to be virtually certain that you will come tomorrow (i.e. that it has an epistemic probability close to 1) or that it is only barely more probable than not that you will come (i.e. that its probability is marginally greater than 1/2).

Because beliefs may exist while the believer is not conscious of them, they are continuing mental states. Our paradigm understanding of what beliefs are is, however, provided by conscious beliefs, that is, beliefs of which one is conscious. That then gives us the concept of a belief which may exist whether or not one is not conscious of it. A person having a belief that so-and-so is that person having the disposition (or liability) to become conscious that it seems to him or her that so-and-so when whether so-and-so is true is relevant to what they are thinking about, and to be guided by the assumption that so-and-so in the way that person forms their intentions. Thus to have a belief that a certain road leads to town is for the subject to be in a state where that belief would occur to them when it is relevant to that person's thought about how they or someone else could get to town; and to have the intention of walking along that road when they have the intention of getting to town.[8] Beliefs are dispositions to cause conscious beliefs (which are sometimes called 'occurrent beliefs') and behaviour. The disposition itself may be caused by a brain event, but by my criteria of event identity it is not the same event as the brain event, since the subject has privileged access to whether or not they have the disposition, but not to whether the subject has any particular brain event.

I cannot be in error that I have some belief when I reflect on whether or not I have the belief, because my beliefs (in my sense of 'belief') just are the way things seem to me. While a subject who has a belief necessarily can become aware that they have that belief, it may occasionally happen that the subject refuses to reflect on whether they have that belief and thus become aware of it; and even if they are aware of it, the subject may refuse to admit to him or herself that they have that belief. But the belief is still a mental event if the subject can come to know about it, as well as by public means,

---

[7] For justification of this assumption, see my *Epistemic Justification*, pp. 34–8.

[8] This brief summary of the relation of belief to a person's behaviour is over-simplified in not taking account of the fact that the influence of a belief depends on its strength and on the strength of that person's various intentions. For a more adequate account see *Epistemic Justification*, ch 2.

also by introspection better than can anyone else by merely public means. I still have privileged access to my beliefs even if others (including psychiatrists) know better than I do what my beliefs are, because (contingently) I could acquire all the information they have which allows them to infer what my beliefs are, and also (maybe with a psychiatrist's help) access them in a way (introspection) that (necessarily) the psychiatrist cannot use. Yet, to repeat, if there are any 'beliefs' to which we have no introspective access at all, then they are not mental events in my sense. There is an important difference between actions guided by repressed beliefs which need a psychiatrist to help the subject to become aware of them, and bodily movements which occur solely as a result of physiological processes or actions which exhibit patterns of goal-seeking of which the subject has not the slightest (conscious or repressed) knowledge. Beliefs are not merely mental events, but pure mental events; as I shall be arguing shortly, someone's beliefs as such entail no consequences about what they will do unless combined with intentions.

Beliefs are by their very nature involuntary. Believing is something that happens to someone, not something that one does. I believe that today is Monday, that I am now in Oxford, that Aquinas died in CE1274, and so on. I cannot suddenly at a given time decide to believe that today is Tuesday, that I am now in Italy, or that Aquinas lived in the eighteenth century. (I emphasize 'at a given time'. I can of course take steps to investigate whether my belief is true, and that may—or may not—lead to a change of belief. Also, I can try to brainwash myself, so as to come to hold later a certain belief specified in advance; but I will only succeed if I get myself to be caused to hold the belief at the later time by some cause, e.g. some brain event, which I am not at that time intentionally causing.) That belief is involuntary was a claim of Hume. 'Belief consists', he wrote, 'merely in a certain feeling or sentiment; in something that depends not on the will, but must arise from certain determinate causes and principles, of which we are not masters.'[9] But what Hume does not bring out is that this is a logical matter, not a contingent feature of our psychology. For if having a belief in some proposition p was the result of an intentional action, then we would know that it was up to us (i.e. depended on our choice) whether or not we would believe it. But then we would know that we had no reason to believe that our belief that p was in any way sensitive to whether or not p was true; and in that case we couldn't really believe it. This argument reinforces the point made in Chapter 2 that we can only believe that p if we believe that our belief was caused by the event described by p (or some event which would have happened only if p were true). I can only believe that there is a desk in front of me if I believe that that belief was caused by the desk (e.g. via light rays from the desk landing on my eyes) or by some other event which would only have occurred if there was a desk in front of me.

[9] D. Hume, *Treatise Concerning Human Nature*, Appendix.

The second kind of propositional event is thoughts. By a 'thought' I mean a datable occurrent thought of which one is aware, which comes 'into one's mind', that something is so. Thoughts are conscious events. So defined, thoughts will include the conscious beliefs which one expresses to oneself (the ones on which one comments mentally, such as unusual or unexpected events which one perceives), and also expressions to oneself of ideas which one entertains but does not believe. So 'thoughts' will include the acquisitions of unexpected beliefs resulting from perception, 'It's snowing' or 'There's John; I thought that he was abroad'; action-directing thoughts—'It's Tuesday; I must go into town' or 'I'm getting fat; I must take more exercise'; and also the thoughts about what one hopes or fears or wonders about—'I'll win the lottery', 'He'll fall downstairs', or 'Maybe there are a trillion universes'.

When someone has a thought, for example, that the President is dead, often auditory images (sensations) of the words 'President' and 'dead' may flit through their mind. But the occurrence of a thought cannot be analysed in terms of the occurrence of auditory images of words forming a well-formed sentence. To start with, auditory images of words may be images of words of a language the thinker does not understand. I may have liked certain sounds of a foreign language, and they may occur to me again without my having the least idea what they mean, and so without their occurrence constituting the occurrence to me of a thought. Let us suppose the restriction is added that the words be of a language which I understand. There are then three harder difficulties. First, it is not enough for me to know English for the occurrence to me of the words 'the President is dead' to express a thought of mine that some President is dead. They may be the words of a song which pass through my mind without being the vehicle of a thought. A person is usually careful not to say aloud words which they do not mean (for fear of what their hearers might think), but that person may say to him or herself much that they do not mean. Secondly, even given that the words which occur to a subject are words of a sentence which that subject understands as expressing a thought, the words may often not be enough to determine the proposition entertained (the content of that thought). In particular they may be quite inadequate to determine the intended referent. I speak to myself about 'the President', but which President—of the USA, or of China, or of my local history society? The sentence does not fully capture the thought; in having the thought I know of which President I am thinking, but the sentence need not make that clear.

And, finally, even given that we can determine which proposition some thinker's words express, we still do not know the force of that proposition, for example, whether the words express a belief of the thinker (a judgement), or whether that thinker is recalling some past conversation or imagining some future one in which another person says something to them and which they understand in a certain way, but which in no way represents their own current belief. Imagined conversation is different from one's own judgements. 'The President is dead' may be words which I recall someone saying to me in the autumn of 1963 after the assassination of President Kennedy. Or they may even be words which I recall myself uttering on some previous occasion. And yet the thinker knows whether he or she is making a judgement or merely imagining a past conversation, although the pattern of that thinker's sensations does not show this.

So which thought they are having is not determined by the pattern of the thinker's sensations. Something else beside the words is necessary for the thought. Nor are all or even any words necessary. The thought may be expressed in far fewer words than are needed for a grammatical sentence. The word 'old' alone said to myself may serve to express the thought that I am old. And there are grounds for attributing occurrent thoughts to languageless animals. A gorilla seeking to get hold of food out of its reach may suddenly pause, and then use a stick to get it. It is reasonable to attribute to the gorilla as they pause the occurrent thought that the way to get the food is to use a stick. And finally there is the familiar phenomenon of having a thought for which even if we try we cannot find anything like the right words; later the words come, which we recognize as capturing the thought. So a thought is a propositional event not analysable in terms of sensations, though often expressed by means of auditory images of words.

Like sensations, thoughts are as such conscious events. I cannot have a thought of which I was not conscious. And again it should be fairly evident that the occurrence of a thought does not entail the occurrence of any physical event in the thinker; thoughts are the thoughts they are, whatever causes them or whatever the thinker does or does not do about them. And while there may be more to a subject's sensations than they are aware of, there is no more to the subject's thoughts than they are aware of. If someone's thoughts have consequences of which that person is unaware, then those consequences are no part of the thought. Because one's thoughts just are the thoughts of which one is currently aware, one cannot be in error about the content of one's thoughts—one thinks just what one believes that one thinks. And because thoughts are conscious events, and beliefs as such are not, there is no possibility of refusing to investigate whether one has a certain thought; and so no possibility of a psychiatrist knowing better than the subject what thoughts the subject is having. (But when someone doesn't want to admit to others or even to themself the fact that they are having thoughts of certain kinds, others—including psychiatrists—can help that person to do so.) Like most sensations, most thoughts are passive (involuntary) events. Although I can intentionally set myself to think about a certain topic, which relevant or irrelevant thoughts then cross my mind do not depend on my intention. But I can intentionally continue to hold a thought in my mind, or (sometimes) force myself to have a certain thought. And just as a disposition to have the conscious events which are sensations is a continuing mental state, so a disposition to have the conscious events which are thoughts is also a continuing mental state. (Such a disposition will consist only of beliefs if the only conscious thoughts which the subject has a disposition to have are conscious beliefs.)

The next kind of propositional event is intentions (which I assume to be the same as purposes). There is a distinction between an intention in what an agent is currently doing, and an intention someone has to do some action in future. Throughout this book I shall understand by 'intention' an intention of the former kind, except for a brief paragraph or two where I explicitly mention intentions for the future. An intentional action is one which an agent does and means to do, that is, (normally) has the intention of doing. Forming an intention is, however, evidently itself an intentional action, something one does and means to do; but in this case alone one does it without having a further intention to form the first intention. Grammatically 'having an intention' seems to be describing something that happens to one, like having a thought or an after-image. But it is clearly something one does. For to have some intention (in what one is currently doing) just is intentionally to do what (it seems to the agent) will keep one acting in a certain way. Most intentional actions are public actions, achieved by a sequence of bodily movements; but there are also mental actions, achieved by bringing about a mental event or a sequence of mental events (as when I form a mental image or perform 'in my mind' a sequence of calculations). What I write about public actions applies also to mental actions *mutatis mutandis*.

A sequence of bodily movements (under a certain description) constitutes the achievement of an intentional action if (and only if) the subject has some intention in making those movements (under that description). I stress 'under that description'. When I perform the intentional action of walking into town, my bodily movements include movements which I have no intention of making (under that description), such as my foot bending at a certain precise angle at a certain time—I may not even have access to the fact that such movements are occurring. These movements, like the neural events which are their immediate causes, are merely the means by which my body executes my intention. I have the intention of making them only under the description 'walking into town'. We normally suppose that when a person is performing an intentional action, not merely does that person have such an intention in making the movements, but they make the movements because they have the intention; the intention causes the movements. This, however, has been seriously questioned by neuroscientists, and I shall consider this issue of whether intentions cause bodily movements at length in Chapter 4. Meanwhile, in order not to resolve a disputed issue by definition, I shall understand 'having an intention in making them' as 'having an intention which the subject believes causes him or her to make them' rather than— as ordinarily—'having an intention which causes the subject to make them'.[10]

Sometimes the intentions in what we are doing are 'in the forefront of our consciousness'; we are fully aware of them. That is always so when we form a new intention, that is, make a decision, and immediately proceed to execute it. When I decide to order the fish dish rather than the meat dish on the restaurant menu, and then give my order, I am fully aware that I have just formed this intention. And it is

---

[10] There are philosophers and psychologists who claim that they have intentions but do not believe that those intentions cause any movements. It will be a consequence of my arguments in Chapter 5 that if they really believe this, they don't have any intentions. However, for the moment I could allow that they have intentions by amending my definition of 'having an intention in making [the intended movements]' to read 'having an intention of a kind which most people believe causes [the intended movements]'.

normally the case with respect to at least one action which I am doing, that I am fully aware that I have the intention to do that action. When I move my pen to write this sentence, I am fully aware that my intention is to write this sentence. But we may be doing more than one action at a time, and then our main attention is on one of these actions, and we are only half aware of doing the other action (or actions). The latter action is often a longer-term action (one which takes a significant time to fulfil). When ¬ I am driving a car along a well-known route, I may be talking to a passenger or thinking about philosophy at the same time and my attention may be mainly on the latter. But an action is intentional, as I am understanding that notion, if doing the action is something the agent means to be doing; and one can only be doing an action and meaning to do it if one is to some degree aware of doing it.[11] There is a distinction between the driver who is thinking mainly about other things but is nevertheless sensitive enough to the traffic to slow down when they see that they are getting too close to the car ahead, and the driver who is thinking about other things but is so natural a driver that they slow down automatically when getting too close to the car ahead yet without 'realizing' (i.e. coming to acquire a belief) that there is a car ahead to which they are getting too close. I express this distinction by applying the term 'intentional action' only to actions of the former kind. In the latter situation the driver has no 'intention' in my sense, nor is there any other mental event to which they have privileged access directing what they are doing; the driver is simply on 'automatic pilot'.

So, unlike beliefs, intentions are as such conscious events; and, like thoughts, they cannot have elements of which the subject is totally unaware. If I talk about the successes of my children, when your children are 'dropouts', then that hurts you. But if I did not mean to hurt you, hurting you was not an intentional action of mine. (An unintentional action is an intentional action which has an unintended property, normally an unintended effect.) And if I am really meaning to perform a certain action, that is, it is my purpose or goal to perform that action, I cannot fail to believe that this is what I mean to do. It wouldn't be something I was doing as an agent rather than something that was happening to me, if I was ignorant of it. So we cannot be in error about our intentions; but—as with thoughts—we may occasionally refuse to admit them to others or even admit to ourselves that we have those intentions, and others (including psychiatrists) can help us to admit them to ourselves and others.

Intentions to perform actions are often nested. When one does one action in order ¬ to do another action, the former, I shall say, is instrumentally more basic than the latter. Then the agent has an intention to do the first action as part of an intention to do the second action. This may be because, the agent believes, performing the first action is a first stage towards performing the second action, to complete which would require

---

[11] In writing this, I am abandoning the view expressed in some earlier writings such as the paper referred to in the Preface, 'Could anyone justifiably believe in Epiphenomenalism?'

additional subsequent intentional actions, as when I intend to walk along this road because I intend to go to Oriel College, to do which would require me walking along a second road after walking along the first road. Or it may be because the agent believes performing the first action will cause some effect which they intend to cause, and the second action consists in causing that effect. When I open the door by pulling the handle, pulling the handle causes the door to open. Or it may be because, the agent believes, performing the first action in the circumstances in which it is done constitutes performing the second action. Saying 'I will' at a certain point in a marriage service constitutes taking in marriage. One can only do one action as a step towards or as a way to achieve doing another action, if one has a belief that doing the first action is a step towards or a way of doing the second action.

For many actions, having a certain intention (in what one is doing) requires a belief that some other action is a step towards or a way of doing the former action; and how one executes the intention depends on which belief one has. (What I believe about how to go to Oriel College affects which route I take.) The only actions for which this does not hold—which I do without needing a belief about how to do them—are the ones often called 'basic actions'; but ones which, to avoid an ambiguity which I shall discuss in Chapter 4, I shall call 'instrumentally basic actions'. They include almost all actions of moving limbs or tongue, such as waving an arm or saying some particular word. I will call an intention to perform an intentionally basic action a 'basic intention'. I will call an intention which one does not have in order to fulfil another intention an 'ultimate intention'. Such intentions may be long term (to write a book) or short term (to have lunch). I shall discuss basic intentions and ultimate intentions more fully in Chapter 5.

Many philosophers (among those who hold that intentions do cause bodily move-ments) have held that talk about beliefs and intentions is analysable in terms of public actions. But it will be evident from the above that most actions result from combin-ations of beliefs and intentions, and that different combinations of beliefs and intentions may lead to the same public behaviour. I may, for example, tell you that Jupiter is bigger than Saturn, either because I believe this and have the intention of telling the truth, or because I believe the opposite and have the intention of misleading you. Or you have a headache, and ask for an aspirin, I give you a pill; it is a poison pill and you are badly poisoned and nearly die. My action may be the result of a belief that the pill was an aspirin and my intention to cure your headache; or the result of a belief that the pill was poisonous and my intention to kill you. Of course the explanation of my action which claims that my intention is of a kind similar to my past intentions may provide a simpler and so, on the evidence of my public behaviour, more probably true explanation of my action than an explanation which involves me suddenly having developed a quite untypical intention (e.g. to kill you.). But clearly I have a way of learning (by introspec-tion) about which combination of beliefs and intentions is responsible for my public behaviour additional to the ways which others can also use. And since I have privileged access to whether a bodily movement was intended or not, I have privileged access to my basic intentions, as well as non-basic ones. It follows from subjects having privileged access to their beliefs and intentions that these are mental events. And, like sensations and thoughts, so also beliefs and intentions are pure mental events in virtue of the pattern of argument used at the beginning of the chapter, because having some intention or belief by itself entails no physical events involving the believer or agent. So too is a disposition to have intentions, which is a continuing mental state; if the disposition is a felt inclination (explored further), then it will constitute a desire.

All that I have written so far or will write in future (after this paragraph) about 'intentions' (unless otherwise stated) concerns the intentions we have in acting and which—we believe—guide our movements. But we also have intentions for the future. I may intend to go to London tomorrow or to have a holiday in Greece next year without such intentions making any difference (or my believing that they are making any difference) to what I do now. Such intentions are resolutions to do some action at a certain future time, which will—if I recall them—probably influence me later to do that action when I believe that that future time has arrived (e.g. to go to London when I believe that the day I called 'tomorrow' when forming the intention is now today). In that they exist over periods of time during which they are totally absent from my consciousness, they are clearly continuing mental states and not—like intentions in action—conscious events. However, while clearly I may have some intention for the future while I am not conscious of it, I cannot have an intention for the future which I do not believe that I have. An intention which I have forgotten is no longer an intention. It is an important feature of humans that we make plans for the future; but—for reasons of space—my primary concern will be with intentions in action.

The final main kind of propositional events is desires ('wants' in a modern sense of 'want') to do actions of a certain kind or to be in a certain situation. We have desires for short-term and long-term goals—to eat, to play golf, to finish a book, or to be happily married. A desire to do an action of a certain kind is (subject to a qualification) an inclination automatically and naturally intentionally to do that action when it is practically possible; or to do preparatory actions, when it is practically possible to do them, which will make it more probable that one will succeed in doing the former action. A desire to be in a certain situation is (subject to the same qualification) an inclination automatically and naturally intentionally to do actions which will make it more probable that one will be or stay in that situation. A desire to skydive may not be immediately realizable, but one has it if one has an inclination to take any opportunity to skydive, or—if one cannot skydive—to have lessons in skydiving when such an opportunity arises. To desire to be in Rome is to have an inclination intentionally to travel to Rome or to do preparatory actions (e.g. to save money to buy a ticket to travel there), or to stay in Rome if one is already there. Desires, like beliefs, may exist when we are not conscious of them. I have desired to finish writing this book for several years but much of the time I have not been conscious of this. But the desire exists in that if I think about the matter I am aware of an inclination to form the intention, when it is practically possible, to do other actions which will make it more probable that I will finish the book—for example, actions of writing another paragraph or reading an article by someone else which will make it more probable that I shall be able to write a satisfactory paragraph. This account needs the qualification that to constitute a desire an inclination must be one which one does not have solely because of a belief that doing the action or being in the situation would be a step towards achieving some more distant goal. If I am inclined to have a salad at lunch only because I believe that it will benefit my health, then I don't desire (want) to have the salad.

One desires to do what one 'feels' an inclination to do. A desire automatically and naturally leads to the intention, when it is practically possible to fulfil it, in the absence of contrary inclinations. I shall argue in Chapter 7 that value beliefs (in the form of beliefs about what would be objectively good or overall best to do) lead to inclinations to action; but they may not be very strong inclinations or automatically an naturally lead to intentions, and the agent may have to choose whether to do what they most desire to do, or to do what they believe to be best to do. It is often (but not always) the case that when I fulfil my obligations, in natural senses of these words I do not do what I most 'desire' or 'want' to do; I may believe that there is a good reason for doing the action which I believe to be obligatory and in the end do it, but it may not be one to which I feel a strong automatic inclination to yield. So the contrary inclinations which may lead to my not fulfilling my desire when it is practically possible to do so may be either stronger incompatible desires or inclinations produced by value beliefs. I may desire to drink another glass of whisky, but either because I desire not to get drunk (although I do not believe it objectively bad for any reason apart from the fact that I desire this), or because I believe that I ought not to get drunk, I may not yield to the former desire. I shall call the desire of an agent on which he or she would automatically and naturally (form the intention to) act if that agent had no value belief that it would not be the best action to act on that desire their strongest desire; I shall call the desire on which the agent would (form the intention to) act if they didn't have any value belief that it would not be the best action to act on it and didn't have the strongest desire, their second strongest desire, and so on. What happens when we have incompatible desires of equal strength, or a belief that it would not be the best to do what we desire most, will be discussed more fully in Chapter 7.

Desires are not mere felt inclinations to do certain actions, but inclinations to do them intentionally; and so to do them by forming intentions to do the actions. Hence they are inclinations of which we can become aware if we choose to introspect—although, as with beliefs, we occasionally need help from others to get us to introspect and become aware of them, or to admit them to ourselves and others when we are aware of them. If, when buying a lottery ticket, I always choose an even number, but have no knowledge—either readily available or repressed—of this inclination, I do not desire to choose an even number. Hence whatever ways others have of learning about my desires (by studying my brain or behaviour) I can also use, but I have a further way of learning about them—by my introspective awareness of them. Hence desires are mental events. And since talk about intentions cannot be analysed in terms of physical events, neither can the felt inclinations to form intentions which constitute desires. Desires are pure mental events; a desire is the desire it is whether or not it is caused by or causes any brain (or other physical) event.

Like beliefs, desires are involuntary, although I do not think that this is a necessary truth. We humans find ourselves desiring this or that. We can stop ourselves yielding to our desires, but at a given time we cannot help having them. We can, however, take steps which are quite likely to lead over time to changes of desire—for example, a smoker can take medicine which over the course of time is likely to lead to him no longer desiring to smoke. However, at least at present for humans, change of desire is hard to achieve; but perhaps other creatures could change their desires at will, and maybe drugs will be devised which will make this possible for humans.

Beliefs and desires are continuing mental states in that, although much of the time we may not be conscious of them, we have privileged access to them—we become aware of them when we ask ourselves if we have them, or when they become relevant to which intention we should have. Other things being equal, desires together with beliefs about the natures and consequences of alternative actions naturally lead to intentions to do this or that action. But there is an issue about whether the existence of beliefs and desires when we are not conscious of them consists merely in our disposition to become aware of them and act on them when relevant, or whether they still exist as attitudes towards states of affairs, just like conscious beliefs and desires except in the respect that we are not conscious of them. The first view is a dispositional theory—according to such a theory the only categorical mental events (events which do not consist solely of a disposition to produce other events) are conscious events. The propensity to have conscious beliefs and desires and to be guided in our actions in certain ways is what constitutes the continuing mental state of belief. The second view is a categorical theory. According to such a theory beliefs and desires exist as attitudes to states of affairs, which we look into—as it were—when we become conscious of them. I shall return to this issue of dispositional versus categorical theories of beliefs and desires in Chapter 6, when I have considered the nature of the person to whom beliefs and desires belong. But meanwhile, in order to move forward with as few contentious assumptions as possible, I shall assume that the only categorical mental states are conscious ones.[12]

As I wrote earlier, my definitions of (pure) mental events are crafted so as to include all and only those events to which the subject has privileged access. All there is to a

---

[12] My contrast between dispositional and categorical theories of beliefs and desires is different from the normal contrast between 'occurrent beliefs' and 'dispositional beliefs'. This latter is the contrast between the expressions of belief in occurrent thoughts, and the dispositions to have such occurrent thoughts and to manifest beliefs in the way we behave. As 'belief' is ordinarily understood, there is clearly more to it than having an occurrent thought; the account of belief as a disposition must be a correct account of what it is to have a belief. But what I am concerned with is the issue of whether the disposition has a categorical mental basis which causes it (no doubt itself having brain events as a cause), or whether the only cause of the disposition are brain events.

propositional event is a certain kind of way of regarding a proposition; and if a subject does not have access to it as a way of regarding that proposition, he or she does not have access to it at all. Hence, in the way I have analysed these concepts, a subject cannot be in error about what he or she believes, thinks, intends, or desires (although they may refuse to bring into consciousness what they believe or desire, and may need the help of others in order to do so). Sensations, however, are different, because—although they are conscious events—there may be more to a sensation than the subject is aware of; and so their beliefs about them may be in error. And I stress again with respect to the propositional events, that if anyone is moved to act by factors to which he or she has not got privileged access, those factors do not count as 'beliefs', 'intentions', or other mental events in my sense. There are innumerable propositional events of the kind to which we do have privileged access, of which we are aware in ourselves. We are aware that we have attitudes to states of affairs: beliefs that they occur, thoughts that they occur, intentions to bring them about, and desires that they occur. There is an important difference between intentional actions guided by repressed beliefs which need a psychiatrist to help the subject to become aware of them or take them seriously or admit openly to them, and bodily movements which occur solely as a result of physiological processes or intentional actions which exhibit patterns of goal-seeking of which the subject has not the slightest awareness. A similar point applies to intentions, thoughts, and desires. In these respects, I suggest, my classification of the mental 'cuts reality at the joints'.

A subject's privileged access to his or her thoughts, desires, beliefs, etc. would remain, even if we were to discover that all such events as had been previously studied had been caused by brain events in accord with an apparent law-like regularity. For the subject could know about the causal relations so far established just as well as can anyone else, and yet on a new occasion he or she can know better than anyone else whether the law-like regularity continues to operate on this occasion also—in virtue of whether or not he or she is or can become aware of the thought, desire, or whatever, predicted by the law-like regularity.

I have discussed only five kinds of pure mental events—sensations, thoughts, beliefs, intentions, and desires (together with dispositions to have some of these), because—I suggest—all other kinds of pure mental events can be analysed in terms of these five. For example, apparent memory consists of a belief that you did so-and-so, sometimes accompanied by a sensory image. Enjoyment consists in you doing or having happen to you what you desire to be doing or have happen. Different emotional states too consist in different combinations of these five elements. To be afraid is to believe that some event is going to happen which you desire not to happen, to have occurrent thoughts of the details of it happening, normally accompanied by sensory images of it happening and of the sensations you would have when it happened. To be angry is to believe that some harm has been done to you by some person (or animal, or inanimate object) which you desire not to have happened, accompanied by a desire to hurt that person (or whatever), sometimes accompanied by characteristic sensations. And so on. But if there are pure mental events of kinds which cannot be analysed in terms of events of my five kinds, that would not affect my main line of argument in any way.

So—to repeat the main conclusion so far—pure mental events are events, either conscious or accessible to consciousness, additional to physical events. A full history of the world will have to include (or entail the occurrence of) pure mental events as well as physical events: sensations, thoughts, intentions, beliefs, and desires, as well as brain events and behaviour. We have seen that there are different ways of cutting up the history of the world into events; and one could give a full history of the world by listing only events of certain kinds, so long as the list entailed all the events of all kinds which ever have occurred, are occurring, or will occur. We could omit altogether all the impure mental events so long as we included all the pure mental events and the physical events which are entailed by the impure mental events—for example, we could omit from our list the event 'me knowingly seeing a desk' so long as we include the event 'me seeming to see a desk', being caused by the event of a desk being in front of me. Also, on dispositional theories of belief and desire (but not on categorical theories), we could mention only the conscious events which constitute their conscious manifestations—believed thoughts and felt inclinations, as well as the events which caused these actual manifestations (if brain events alone caused these manifestations) and would have caused further manifestations under other conditions; a full account thereof would entail which beliefs and desires a person had. But, explicitly or implicitly, a full history of the world must include all conscious events; and any science or other theory which purports fully to explain the world must explain not merely in general why conscious events occur but why on the different occasions when they occur they are the particular ones they are.

4. Private and public criteria for pure mental events

I have been arguing that there are innumerable events to the content of which the person whose they are has privileged access, and in many cases infallible awareness. But the words I have used and anyone else—psychologist, philosopher, or layperson—uses to describe these mental events are words of a public language. How can a subject use words with a public meaning to describe what is in an important respect private to him or herself? And how can others understand that subject's description of these events?

In *Philosophical Investigations* Wittgenstein argued powerfully that there could not be a 'private language', a language used by only one person for describing their mental life, the meaning of whose words was determined solely by the conventions for their use adopted and practiced by that person. To construct such a language subjects would have to invent predicates describing the properties of their mental events. Wittgenstein imagines a person deciding to call a sensation of a kind which they are currently having 'E'.[13] If 'E' is to function in a language, it must be possible to assert about new sensations either that they are 'E' or that they are not 'E', and such assertions must have a truth-value (be either true or false). But, Wittgenstein claims, the subject can have no criterion for whether they are doing this correctly. The subject cannot look at any privately accessible dictionary which tells him or her what 'E' means, and then check whether the new sensation is correctly so described. And if the language were a purely 'private' language, no public criteria for whether the subject is having that sensation would be relevant. So, Wittgenstein claims, the only criterion for what a subject means by 'E' could be what they believe they mean, and that is no criterion at all. For the very possibility of describing some new sensation correctly depends on the possibility of misdescribing it, and the subject has no criterion for whether they are doing this or not; and that, Wittgenstein claims, means that there is no sense in claiming that a subject has or has not correctly described a sensation: 'whatever is going to seem right to me is right. And that only means that we can't talk about "right"'.

In my opinion Wittgenstein is mistaken in supposing that subjects with a 'private language' of this kind could not misdescribe their sensations. A subject could misdescribe a sensation as 'E', meaning by that that it was qualitatively identical to the previous sensation so described, even if the subject had no way of discovering whether this was so or not. Further, I claimed in Chapter 2, apparent memory is evidence of what happened, and strongly convinced apparent memory is strong evidence of what happened, and one apparent memory can be checked against another apparent memory. An apparent memory that sensations of type E only occur after sensations of type F and an apparent memory of the subject that they had a recent sensation of type F would be evidence that the subject had described their present sensation as 'E' correctly, and an apparent memory of the subject that they had not had any recent sensation of type F would be evidence that the subject had misdescribed his or her present sensation.[14] Despite all that, in the absence of any public test for which mental event some subject is having, the subject (relying only on their apparent memory of their past mental events) must often be uncertain whether they have described it (to him or herself) correctly. And crucially, others could have no knowledge of which mental event the subject is having. That would rule out any possibility of a science of the mental; and whether there could be such a science is a major topic of this book. In fact, however, as Wittgenstein points out, we learn the meanings of words for describing our mental events by the public circumstances which normally cause them and the public behaviour which—we believe—they normally cause. (I assume for the rest of this section that mental events do cause (via brain events) the public behaviour which—it seems to us—they cause. As I have already written, I shall consider whether this assumption is correct in Chapter 4.)

---

[13] L. Wittgenstein, *Philosophical Investigations*, tr. G.E.M. Anscombe, Basil Blackwell, 1953, §§256–8.

[14] This point is developed in A.J. Ayer 'Can there be a Private Language?' republished in his *The Concept of a Person*, Macmillan and Co., 1968.

We saw in Chapter 1 the process by which sentences of a public language come to have the meaning they do; and so how children can be taught that meaning. We come to understand what believing, intending, or desiring (the content of) some sentence to be true consists in by being taught the necessary connection of these propositional events with each other and the public behaviour to which they typically give rise. A belief that there is food only in the cupboard is that belief only if when combined with her intention to get food it leads to a subject forming an intention to go to the cupboard; and a desire to get food is that desire only if, other things being equal, it leads to an intention of the subject to get food. The simplest explanation of many of the bodily movements which we make is often in terms of intentions, themselves caused by beliefs and desires which bring them about; and, as the simplest explanation, such an explanation is therefore most probably the correct one. The movements which can be explained in these ways are only of certain kinds—for example, limb movements and movements of tongue or lip which produce sounds. So children learn to attribute beliefs, intentions, etc. to others on the evidence of their bodily movements. Children also find that when their own behaviour is best explained by a certain set of beliefs, intentions, etc., they are normally aware of having a certain kind of internal attitude towards the state of affairs 'believed' to hold, a different kind of attitude towards the action 'intended', and so on. They then call an internal attitude of the former kind a 'belief' and one of the latter kind an 'intention', and so on. Having got hold of what is meant by 'belief', 'intention', etc., they are then able to describe their mental events in these ways independently of whether on any particular occasion others are able to infer from their behaviour what their beliefs, intentions, etc. are. And since beliefs, intentions, etc. are mental events, those whose events they are have privileged access to them.

That simplicity is evidence of truth is the inductive criterion shared by all humans which gives access to 'other minds', as well as to all our other knowledge of events beyond our immediate experience. The first consequence of the use of the criterion of simplicity is that it is probable—in the absence of contrary evidence (i.e. observed evidence best explained by the contrary supposition)—that people do not suddenly change their character, in the sense of their beliefs and desires and any general pattern of their mental life, for a brief time (e.g. for just two minutes) and then revert to the old character. Hence if I never at any other time hurt anyone physically, and always showed kindness to you, it would be most improbable that I would seek just for two minutes to murder you. So in the example considered earlier in the chapter, we would take as the simplest and so most probably true explanation of my behaviour that I had the intention of curing your headache and believed that the pill which I was giving you was an aspirin. The second consequence of the simplicity criterion is that—in the absence of contrary evidence—it is probable that one human is much like another human in the mental events which the same public circumstances cause in them, and the public behaviour to which those events give rise. It is in virtue of this consequence that we assume that any person who is looking at someone putting food into a cupboard will acquire the belief that there is now food in the cupboard. But other evidence may constitute an overriding or undermining defeater for an assumption that each human is like others in some respect, in the way described in Chapter 2. Then we have to ascribe to that human the simplest overall account of his behaviour; but inevitably sometimes such inferences to the mental lives of others yield false conclusions, and can be shown to yield false conclusions in view of yet further evidence. The inference to one human being much like another in the mental events which public circumstances cause in them and the public behaviour to which those events give rise depends for its strength on the similarity in all humans of the mechanisms—that is, brain events—via which their mental events are caused by public circumstances and cause their behaviour. Any inference to the mental life of a robot constructed in a laboratory out of steel and silicon chips from its public circumstances and behaviour would be far weaker in view of the very different mechanisms which are the immediate causes of its mental events (if it has any) and its public behaviour.

It is, we saw in Chapter 2, a further fundamental criterion (like the criterion that the simplicity of a hypothesis is evidence of its truth) that what others tell us is, in the absence of counter-evidence, probably true. And since many of the beliefs possessed by some other person have no other consequences for how they will behave except consequences about what they will say to us, we often need to rely on the latter if we want to know what that person believes. And the same goes for the thoughts which cross people's minds; the surest and often the only way we can learn about them is from what they tell us. Children learn what a thought is by being told: it's something which you find yourself saying to yourself so quietly that no one else can hear it, or could have put into words but didn't need to. That kind of description enables children to recognize some mental event as a thought. To be a thought, it must be a thought that so-and-so; and so must be able to be expressed by a sentence of some language, although it need not have been so expressed and the thinker may not know the words by which to express it. Hence in principle, though it is sometimes difficult in practice, a thinker should be able to tell others what he or she is thinking, by means of words which have a public meaning.

So all the propositional mental events (beliefs, intentions, desires, and thoughts) have some necessary connection with ways of public expression—if I have a thought and the intention to tell you what the thought is, the thought is what I say that it is; and so on. And often others can learn about someone's propositional events both by inference from their other public behaviour, as well as by what they say about them. With sensations, however, the situation is very different. These have no necessary connection with any public behaviour. Their connections with public behaviour are contingent. People like or dislike (i.e. desire to have or not have) this sensation colour or that taste; and desire, as stated earlier, has a natural public expression. But there is nothing intrinsic to the colour sensation or taste which makes it necessary that most people should like it or dislike it; and their connections with their public causes (outside the body) are similarly contingent. Surfaces which reflect light of a certain wavelength cause a sensation which we call 'red'; and surfaces which reflect light of a certain different wavelength cause a sensation which we call 'green'; but it might easily have been the other way around.

We learn to use the words which describe sensations in virtue of the objects which most people recognize as having the public properties which cause the sensations in us. We learn to describe some food as 'tasting of coffee' because it tastes like the taste which coffee causes in us: and we learn to describe a sensation as red because it has the same colour as the public objects (British post boxes, ripe tomatoes, strawberries, etc.) which people describe as 'red'; and people describe an object as 'red' just because it looks to most people to have the colour these paradigm public objects look to have. Yet why should we suppose that those who make the same distinctions as we do—for example, between red and blue objects, or sweet and sour tastes—make them on the basis of the same sensations as each other?

Some people cannot distinguish between red and green objects; they both look the same to them. So for them either red objects do not look the way they look to most of us and/or green objects do not look the way they look to most of us. So it would not be too unlikely that for one group of people green objects look the way red objects look to another group of people, and conversely. Since many colour sensations can be described in terms of different combinations of colours, the colour-inversion would have to affect the whole spectrum of colours, if it was not to be publicly recognizable. For example, if objects publicly described as 'more red than green' look to one group the way objects which are publicly described as 'more green than red' look to the other group, objects publicly described as 'more green than red' will have to look to the first group the way objects publicly described as 'more red than green' look to the second group. But why should not this sometimes happen?

The situation is even worse with tastes and smells than with colours, since someone could have just one different sensation of taste or smell from that produced in others by the same public cause which could not be recognized even though it was not accompanied by any similar difference in respect of other tastes or smells. This is because—just to consider tastes—there are very many different tastes, only some of which many of us can recognize at all; and we are often unable to describe any taste as a mixture of other tastes. Colours can normally be described in terms of a few primitive colours, and so it is only if someone has different colour sensations affecting several colours, that a difference of colour sensation will not be recognized. It is unclear whether the corresponding inability to describe tastes in terms of other tastes arises from the nature of tastes, or from humans not having made a very serious attempt to develop a fuller vocabulary for describing some tastes as mixtures of other tastes or as tastes of more general kinds (such as 'sweet', 'sour', 'salty', or 'bitter') which can themselves be identified by paradigm examples of those kinds (e.g. the taste of sugar is 'sweet'), than we have at present. In consequence, however, of this inability it is even more likely to happen that the same food may taste differently to different people than that people will have different colour sensations from others, without this ever being recognized. And the same kind of point applies to smells.

In theory neuroscience could help us to discover whether those who make the same discriminations do so on the basis of the same sensations. For the public objects which cause sensations and after which we name the sensations, only cause sensations by causing brain events which cause the sensations. Suppose it were the case that the public events which cause the sensation we call 'red' always did so by causing one group of neurons (nerve cells) to fire; and the public events which cause sensations we call 'green' always did so by causing another group of neurones to fire. And so generally for colour sensations. Then it would be the simplest, and so most probably true, hypothesis that the same group of neurons always causes the same sensation in all subjects (rather than that one group of neurons N_1 cause a sensation S_1 in one group of subjects G_1, but a different sensation S_2 in a different group of subjects G_2). Yet in view of the differences between the brains of different humans (in different persons the parts of the brain which give rise to colour sensations will often have different neurons differently connected), it seems very improbable that the sensation publicly described by the same name always has the same cause. It is much more likely that sometimes two different people give the same name, for example, 'green' to different sensations produced by different groups of neurons. The different reactions which people often have to the same input from the senses supports the hypothesis that the sensations caused thereby are sometimes different in different people. Some people like the taste of curry, others don't. There are two possible hypotheses to explain this; curry tastes the same to everyone but some people like and some people don't like this taste, or curry tastes differently to different people. It would seem highly arbitrary to suppose that the first explanation is correct—let alone suppose that a similar explanation applies to all different reactions to tastes.

I need, however, to make a qualification to all this, that while we may be unable to understand the natures of the individual sensations of others, their sensations may exhibit patterns which are the same as some publicly exemplifiable patterns, and so ones which can be described in a publicly comprehensible way. Thus a mental image of a square has the same shape as a public square. The lines which make up the image may have peculiarities of colour which the subject cannot convey, but they can convey the shape. I shall return to this point in a later chapter.

This serious insurmountable obstacle to our ability to learn fully about the sensory qualities of the sensations of others affects our ability to understand what people say about those propositional events which involve mental attitudes to secondary qualities, such as the colour and sound of public objects. For colours, sounds, etc. are identified as the colours or sounds they are solely by the sensations they cause in us. And if we don't fully understand what someone means when they say that they are having a 'green' sensation, we don't fully understand what that person means when they say that they believe that the colour of their neighbour's house is 'green'. In Chapter 1 I used words designating colour properties of public objects, such as 'red' and 'green' as examples of informative designators on the reasonable assumption that most (though not necessarily all) people who make the same colour discriminations as most sighted people do, make them on the basis of having largely similar colour sensations; and in that case colour words have a public meaning. The assumption was reasonable because although the neural connections underlying sensations are sometimes different in different people, the differences are not often great ones. So we have a public understanding that an object is green iff it looks to someone (more or less) the way it looks to most people who pick out the same objects as each other as 'green'. If, however, my assumption is mistaken, then I would need to replace these examples of informative designators of properties by other examples, in order to illustrate the theses of that chapter. In any case those who don't make the same colour discriminations as we do, and whom for that reason we classify as 'colour blind', do not understand at all fully what is meant by colour words.

Despite these (probably insurmountable) difficulties in discovering fully the nature of the sensory events experienced by others, my earlier conclusion remains that there are public criteria for which humans probably have which propositional events. It is for this reason that we can have informative designators of most of our mental properties. But the public criteria are fallible criteria; and each human is in a better position to know what are his or her own beliefs, intentions, etc. than are others.

5. The errors of physicalism

The subtly different forms of physicalism all hold the doctrine that the only events are physical events, some of which may be also in a sense (although not in my sense) 'mental events'. If we don't use my metacriterion to select a criterion of property identity and so event identity, and use criteria for property and so event identity which have the consequence that we can know all the events which have occurred (under their canonical descriptions) without knowing everything that has occurred, or if we just suppose that we know intuitively when two events picked out in different ways are the same event, the way is open for serious arguments leading to physicalism.

Modern philosophical physicalism claiming that the events which I have claimed to be ⌐ 'mental events' are simply brain events, began in the late 1950s, as I noted in Chapter 1, with the work of U. T. Place; this was subsequently developed by J. J. C. Smart. These philosophers advocated 'type-type identity', the view that 'mental' properties are physical properties: such types of property as having a red sensation, or a desire to eat chocolate just are types of brain-event (e.g. particular patterns of neurons firing). This view was advocated on the grounds that it provided a simple explanation of the occurrence of the kind of events which I have called 'mental'. If we supposed that having a red sensation was a different property from some brain property; and so the events of me having a red sensation and me having some brain property were distinct events, and so generally that mental events were different from physical events, we would have to say that there was a law of the form 'always mental-event of type M_1 occurs when and only when brain event of type B_1 occurs'. There would be innumerable such nomological correlations unconnected with the rest of physical theory, and the success of physics in explaining so much else makes that improbable, type-type identity theorists claimed. But if we say that each type of mental event is a type of brain event, they argued, there would in principle be a simple physical explanation of the mental life, and so—they assumed— one for that reason likely to be true. However, the reasoning of such theorists in essence seems to be this: if current science cannot in principle explain something, then that something doesn't happen—which is of course a highly unscientific attitude. It is obvious that we have sensations, thoughts, etc., and so a good science should recognise both these and brain events as distinct features of the world (distinct for reasons argued earlier in this chapter), and not pretend that they are not what anyone can see that they are. Science starts from these data. We should alter our scientific theories to fit the data, not pretend the data don't occur. We should look for a scientific explanation of the correlations between mental and physical events; but if we cannot find one (as, I shall be arguing in a later chapter, we cannot), that doesn't mean that data are not data; it means only that either the correlations have no scientific explanation or that we are not clever enough to discover the explanation.

Type-type identity theory fairly soon recognized the problem of 'multiple realizability', that the same type of mental event (e.g. pain) may be correlated with different types of brain event in different creatures—for example, the type of brain event underlying pain may be different in humans from what it is in dogs. So, physicalists came to prefer the more moderate theory that mental events supervene on physical events. That is, different types of physical event sometimes give rise (necessarily) to the same type of mental event; but there can be no mental events without the physical events which give rise to them. The natural form of such a theory is 'functionalism' as advocated by Hilary Putnam.[15] Functionalism claims (to use my terminology) that what makes any property a property of a kind which I have called 'pure mental property' is that events with that property have a certain function in a person's life of thought and behaviour, and in particular tend to have certain kinds of causes and effects (in or outside the brain). Thus—to give highly simplified illustrations—functionalists have held that the property of having a pain is the property which events have if they tend to be caused by bodily damage (such as having a needle stuck into one) and tend to cause crying-out or wincing and a desire for the bodily damage to cease. And the property of having a desire to do A is the property which events tend to have if they are caused in certain standard ways and tend to produce an intention to do A. By 'certain standard ways' I mean ways appropriate to the particular desire—for example, the desire to remove bodily damage being caused by bodily damage, and the desire to eat being caused by not having eaten for a long time. These examples of functionalism are highly over-simplified ones, but they should suffice to convey to the reader its central

---

[15]   Hilary Putnam, 'The Nature of Mental States' in his *Mind, Language and Reality, Philosophical Papers*, vol 2, Cambridge University Press, 1975.

idea. What, according to the functionalist, makes a desire or any other mental property the property it is, is the place of events with that property in a whole web of interrelated mental events (thoughts, sensations, intentions, beliefs, desires), of which my simplified examples have mentioned only two or three. Although it is logically possible, the functionalist may admit, for such properties to be instantiated in some creature in virtue of being instantiated in its immaterial soul, the functionalist is almost invariably a substance physicalist in respect of humans (that is, they believe that humans are the same substance as their physical bodies). Functionalists claim that science has shown that the only events in humans caused by input to sense-organs and causing behavioural output are brain events. Hence many brain events are events with functional properties which supervene on brain properties (such as 'having one's C-fibres fire'). A token mental event is then the same token event as some brain event, even though the two types are not always correlated because there are other token mental events of the same type which are identical with brain events of a different type.

I have used the word 'tend' above, because it is used by many writers in their descriptions of functionalism.[16] David Armstrong used a similar word 'apt' in stating his functionalist theory:[17] events are mental events in virtue of being 'apt' to be caused by events of certain types and to cause events of certain other types. What this seems to amount to is that a mental event may be an event of a certain type (i.e. consist in the instantiation of a certain mental property) even if it is not caused in the standard way (people may desire to eat, even when they have just eaten) or does not have the standard effects (we may inhibit our desire to eat), in virtue of its similarity (in its brain properties) to events standardly so caused or causing. In effect, being a mental event of a certain type supervenes on being a physical event of a type which has certain normal causes and effects.

The consequence of an identity theory according to which a brain event is the mental event it is in virtue of the normal causes and effects outside the body of similar brain events is that any brain event would constitute spots in the subject's visual field or that person's intention to hit someone if similar brain events caused or were caused by the normal extra-bodily manifestations of that mental event and not if they didn't. So whether a person had spots in their visual field or intended to hit someone would depend not on what was happening in them but what happens in most other people—

[16] 'Thus for example, a metaphysical functionalist theory of pain might characterize pain in part in terms of its tendency to be caused by tissue damage, by its tendency to cause the desire to be rid of it, and by its tendency to produce action designed to separate the damaged part of the body from what is thought to cause the damage.'—Ned Block, 'What is functionalism?' in his *Consciousness, Function, and Representation, Collected Papers*, vol. I., MIT Press, 2007, p. 28.

[17] D.M. Armstrong, *A Materialist Theory of the Mind*, Routledge and Kegan Paul, 1968. See pp. 82–5 for his account of mental states as ones 'apt' to have certain causes and effects, and Part II for the application analysing 'intention', 'knowledge', 'sensation', etc. in terms of the different causes and effects they are 'apt' to have. For example, (p. 134): 'Suppose I form the intention to strike somebody. My mind is in a certain state, a state that I can only describe by introspection in terms of the effect it is apt for bringing about: my striking that person.'

which is obviously false. The alternative is to leave out the 'normal' requirement and insist that any brain event with certain causes and certain effects outside the body is a mental event of a particular type. Then it looks as if such absurd results would follow as that any event caused by a bodily disorder and causing the subject to wince was a pain, and any brain event which caused the subject to hit someone was an intention to hit them; and so on. Yet we know that people often wince when they think that some medical intervention is going to cause pain, even when it doesn't cause pain; and some people hit others unintentionally. Simple functionalist accounts can of course be made more complicated so as to avoid these difficulties. But the way in which they are made more complicated is by supposing that we already have a prior understanding of what a pain or intention is (as a pure mental event to which the subject has privileged access), then investigating the more complex circumstances under which it occurs, and then giving a definition in terms of the latter. For example, we might discover the many causes of pain and then 'define' pain as an event caused in one of these ways. But the 'definition' will not say what pain is, only what causes it. The investigation already supposes that we know what pain is,

The main and in my view conclusive objection to functionalism is the same as the objection to type—type identity theory. It simply ignores the fact that there are pure mental events, picked out in English by such words as 'pain', 'after-image', 'purpose', and 'thought', to which their possessor has privileged access; and any account of the nature of human beings has got to give these a significant role.

Innumerable subtly different versions of physicalism have been produced over the past 50 years. One more recent version of physicalism claims that the differences between the mental and the physical are just a conceptual difference, two different ways of thinking about the world, not two different features of the world. This is the theme of David Papineau's book *Thinking about Consciousness*. He discusses the issue largely in terms of the relation between physical events and 'conscious events' (rather than all 'mental events'). He begins by asserting as a premiss that 'there is good empirical evidence for the completeness of phyics',[18] that is, 'all physical effects are fully caused by purely physical prior histories',[19] where 'physical effect' is understood as 'inanimate effect', that is, one specifiable 'in any non-biological and non-mental way'.[20] In Chapters 4 and 7 I shall be making the obvious point that quantum theory casts grave doubt on this premiss for reasons having nothing to do with the mind/body problem; the majority interpretation of quantum theory suggests that the physical realm is indeterministic. Papineau merely remarks in a footnote that 'it would seem an odd victory for anti-materialists . . . if the sole locus of sui generis mental action were quantum wave collapses.'[21] I don't see why that would be odd; and in Chapter 7 I give

---

[18] David Papineau, *Thinking about Consciousness*, Clarendon Press, 2002, p. 46.
[19] Ibid., p. 32.   [20] Ibid., p. 42.   [21] Ibid., p. 255, n. 15.

some reason for supposing that it might be true; and in Chapter 4 I argue more strongly that there couldn't be 'good empirical evidence for the completeness of physics'.

Papineau then goes on to reject epiphenomenalism (which he understands as the view that conscious events are caused by but do not cause physical events), on the ground that 'it would require us to deny many apparent obvious truths, such as that my conscious thirst caused me to fetch a beer'.[22] And he further claims that all conscious events have effects, on the ground that there are in nature no examples of 'ontologic-ally independent states with causes but no effects',[23] other than the dubious case of conscious events. It then follows that since all conscious events cause and are caused by physical events, and physical events are caused only by physical events, that all conscious events are physical events. Note that he has reached this conclusion without in any way considering what are the criteria for event identity, what we are claiming when we say that two events are the same. But given that physics being 'complete' entails that it can explain everything physical that happens, we need (for the reasons given in Chapter 1) to understand 'everything' as all the physical events that have occurred on my criterion for two events being the same event. But that criterion will lead us to begin with a premiss far more obvious than that of the completeness of physics, that mental events (including conscious events) are not identical to physical events, to reach the conclusion that physics is not complete.

It is at that point in the argument that Papineau seeks to avoid the obviousness of my premiss by claiming that the same 'property'[24] may be picked out by different concepts; and that the difference between the conscious and the physical is really a difference between concepts, the ways we pick things out, and not between properties and so events in the world. 'Being in pain' and 'having one's C-fibres fire' refer, he claims, to the same ('material', that is, in effect) physical property. But what is it to have two different concepts for picking out the same property? It is, he writes, 'a difference at the level of sense, not reference';[25] a 'sense' or 'mode of presentation' is a way in which we pick something out. Yet a 'mode of presentation' is itself a property—in this case, a property of the one supposedly physical property—by which we pick out the latter property. So if there are two 'senses', there are two predicates designating two 'modes of presentation' by which the properties of the supposedly physical property are picked out. These predicates, 'being in pain' and 'having C-fibres', are normally used in English as informative designators of properties, and since (by the criteria which I expounded and justified in Chapter 1), they are not logically equivalent, they designate different properties. One of these properties ('being in pain') is mental, and the other one ('having one's C-fibres fire') is physical. So the 'two concept' account collapses into another two property account. Even if 'being in pain' was not used as an

---

[22] Ibid., p. 22.
[23] Ibid., p. 23. I shall be rejecting epiphenomenalism in Chapter 4 on very different grounds.
[24] Ibid., p. 48.   [25] Ibid., p. 49.

informative designator of a property, but—as with 'water' in the analogy which Papineau uses—as a rigid designator whose application depends on the physical property underlying the surface property, there are still two different and not logically equivalent ways (by its surface property or by its underlying nature) by which this one supposedly physical property is picked out. Papineau acknowledges this by calling his two different concepts of the underlying property 'phenomenal' (which is in my terminology 'conscious') and 'material' (in my terminology 'physical'). So these two different concepts would pick out this one property by means of different predicates, one of them informatively designating a conscious property possessed by the physical property informatively designated by the other predicate. So, again, there is no escaping the conclusion that if we are to describe the world fully we need to postulate two kinds of property, and so two kinds of (logically disjoint) events.

Someone can only avoid this conclusion by using different criteria for property (and so event) identity from mine. And in that case they would have to admit, instead of an event dualism, that the public world (not merely our description of it) contains some other dualism (an 'aspect'-dualism, for example) which turns out to be just a different way of describing the same feature of the world as does 'event-dualism'. There just are what I describe as 'physical events', and 'pure mental events' (including conscious events) which are different from each other, and philosophers should face up to this.

Physicalism is by no means as popular a philosophical theory as it was twenty years ago. One book strongly influential in leading many philosophers to acknowledge property and so (in my sense) event dualism was David Chalmers's *The Conscious Mind*. There are, he concluded, 'both physical and non-physical features of the world. The falsity of logical supervenience implies that experience is fundamentally different in kind from any physical feature'.[26] For Jaegwon Kim, an influential writer in this field, it is only sensory properties which are in my sense mental properties; we cannot, he claims, 'avoid thinking of intentional/cognitive states, like thought, belief and desire, as supervenient on behaviour and other observable physical facts.'[27] I have argued strongly against this restriction of the mental to the sensory earlier in this chapter. It is vastly implausible to think of occurrent thoughts as supervenient (in the sense analysed in Chapter 1) on behaviour or anything else physical. And although beliefs and desires do have consequences for behaviour (or so, like most of us, Kim assumes), they do not have consequences by themselves but only in combination with each other or other mental states; and different combinations of mental states may have the same consequences for behaviour, while the subject has a privileged view of which

---

[26] David Chalmers, *The Conscious Mind*, Oxford University Press, 1996, p. 124.

[27] Jaegwon Kim, *Physicalism or Something Near Enough*, Princeton University Press, 2005, p. 166. Kim claims Chalmers as an ally in this respect: 'On Chalmers's view, intentional/cognitive properties are physically reducible' (ibid., p. 162). But Chalmers seems to allow the possibility of (what I am calling) 'propositional events' having phenomenal (i.e. in my terms 'sensory') properties, and so not so being fully supervenient on the physical. See *The Conscious Mind*, pp. 19–22.

combination is operative. In affirming the occurrence of propositional events to which we have privileged access, I have not in this chapter (except when otherwise stated) assumed that these have the effect on behaviour which we normally suppose that they do—for example, that when I form the intention to move my arm, that causes my arm to move.[28] I shall argue for that in Chapter 4.

---

[28] The main drive behind 'eliminativism' (as advocated by Paul and Patricia Churchland) seems to be the belief that there is no one-to-one correspondence between types of propositional events such as 'beliefs' and types of brain events (that is, when a propositional event of a certain type occurs, there does not always occur a brain event of one unique type, or conversely). Since in their view there is no privileged access to propositional events, and the only events which cause other brain events and thereby our public behaviour are brain events, we should conclude, the argument goes, that there are no such things as propositional events; and, the argument seems to go, sensations should be treated similarly, since they have no role in any scientific theory. (See Paul M. Churchland, 'Eliminative Materialism and the Propositional Attitudes', *Journal of Philosophy*, 78 (1981), 67–90; and his 'Reduction, Qualia, and the Direct Introspection of Brain States', *Journal of Philosophy*, 82 (1985), 8–28.) I have argued in this chapter for our privileged access to our propositional events, and shall argue in Chapter 4 that beliefs and intentions (via brain events) do cause our behaviour. I do, however, endorse the view that there is no one-to-one correspondence between types of propositional events and types of brain events, and argue from this in Chapter 7 to draw some very different conclusions from those of 'eliminativism'.

4

Interactive Dualism

1. Intentional actions

Fairly obviously most conscious events are caused by brain events which are often themselves caused by physical events in or around the person's body. Our apparent perceptions (if they are really perceptions), for example, such as seeming to see a tree or hear a voice are caused (at least in part) by brain events, themselves caused (via our sense organs) by stimuli from the world beyond our bodies. As I noted in Chapter 3, apparent perceptions normally consist of both sensations (e.g. patterns of colour in my visual field) and beliefs (e.g. that I am now seeing a tree). (I write that these are caused 'at least in part' by brain events, because for brain events caused by light rays to cause my beliefs, it may be necessary for me already to have beliefs about how things of different kinds look; in order for some brain event to cause my apparent perception of a tree, I may need already to have a belief about what trees look like.) And our pains, sensations of touch, beliefs about the positions of our limbs (often misleadingly called kinaesthetic 'sensations') are caused by brain events, themselves normally caused by events elsewhere in the body. And so on, and so on. But it also seems to us that sometimes our conscious events cause our brain events which cause our public behaviour; both our intended bodily movements and unintended events in or around my body—as when my belief that something very unexpected has happened causes a look of surprise on my face. And it also seems that sometimes one conscious event causes another one—as when my intention to add up two numbers in my mind causes a sequence of arithmetical thoughts, leading to a belief about the result of the addition process. By the claim that conscious events cause these effects, I mean only that they are necessary causes—the effects wouldn't have happened but for their causal influence. I do not wish to deny that other events (e.g. many brain events other than ones caused by our conscious events) are also necessary in order for the effects to occur.

Those many thinkers who are convinced that the physical world is closed (that is, no physical events are caused by non-physical events) and also accept the view of Chapter 3 that there are pure mental events and so conscious events, are forced to adopt a view that conscious events never cause brain events, and that all conscious events are caused by physical events (i.e. brain events), which taken together (roughly—a more precise definition will be provided shortly) constitute 'epiphenomenalism'. This chapter will argue that (with a very small qualification) no one could ever be justified in believing the core first principle of epiphenomenalism, that conscious events never cause brain events, and it will conclude that it is very probable indeed that there is a two-way interaction between conscious events and physical events. But before I discuss this issue directly, I need to develop more fully what I wrote in Chapter 3 about the concept of intentional action; and in doing so, for the rest of this section, I shall assume that things are as they seem to be: that when we perform intentional actions, our intentions really do cause our bodily movements.

The most evident way in which our conscious events seem to cause physical events is when—it seems to us—we are intentionally causing those physical events, that is, when we are performing intentional actions. We believe that our intentions (our purposes in acting) guide our bodily movements. I pointed out in Chapter 3 that we often have nested intentions. We often do one action in order to do another action; then doing the former is instrumentally more basic than doing the latter, for which one needs a belief about how doing the former is a means to doing the latter. An action which one does without needing a belief about how to do it is an instrumentally basic action. For most of us moving an arm or saying a sentence are instrumentally basic actions. We do not normally move an arm by intentionally contracting a muscle as a means to making the arm move, or utter a sentence by intentionally twisting the tongue and pursing the lip in a certain way—for most of us do not know which muscle to contract in order to move an arm, or which tongue twisting or lip pursing will cause the relevant sounds to come out of our mouth. We just move the arm or utter the sentence.

We need to distinguish an instrumentally basic action from a causally basic action. An action α is causally more basic than an action β if (and only if) the agent does α intentionally, α causes some effect ϵ (via some process, the operation of which does not depend on the agent causally sustaining it), doing β consists in bring about ϵ, and the agent did α in order to bring about ϵ. Then the agent does β by doing α. If I intentionally throw a brick, the brick causes a window to break, and I threw the brick in order to break the window, then I broke the window by throwing the brick; and throwing the brick was causally more basic than breaking the window. If I intentionally pull the door handle, pulling the door handle causes the door to be open, and I intentionally pulled the handle in order to cause the door to be open, then I opened the door by pulling the handle; and pulling the handle was causally more basic than opening the door. And so on. An action than which no intentional action is instrumentally more basic is an instrumentally basic action, and an action than which no intentional action is causally more basic is a causally basic action *simpliciter*.

Among public intentional actions (and so ones which are mental events but not pure mental events), the instrumentally more basic is normally also the causally more basic and conversely. But not always. There are instrumentally more basic actions which are not causally more basic, as in the example used in the previous chapter: saying 'I will' in certain circumstances is instrumentally more basic than taking in marriage, but—given those circumstances—nothing extra has to happen beyond the former in order for the bridegroom to take the bride in marriage. Or, to take a different example, if

I intentionally insult you by saying 'you are stupid', the latter is instrumentally more basic than the former (it is by saying those words that I succeed in insulting you), but the relation between the two actions is not a causal one. And there are causally more basic actions which are not instrumentally more basic. The way to stretch a muscle is to move your arm in a certain way, but while you may move your arm in order to stretch your muscle, it is stretching the muscle which causes the arm to move.[1]

But in the case of every publicly observable action, and—most of us assume—even in the case of pure mental actions (such as intentionally forming a mental image), various physical events in the brain (and often also elsewhere in the body and in the world beyond the body) need to occur if we are to perform the action. My nerves have to be in working order if I am to pull the trigger, and the safety catch on the gun must be in the 'off' position if I am to kill you by pulling the trigger. And so on. But bringing about such internal bodily events as nerve firings are not normally intentional actions, although we can be trained to bring them about, by learning for which instrumentally basic actions their occurrence is causally necessary.

Since unknown in advance to the agent any of these physical conditions (in or outside the body) necessary for the performance of an intentional action may fail to occur, the agent may try to do the intentional action, and fail. There is, however, an exception in the case of the intentional action of trying to do some other action; inevitably if we try to try, we succeed in trying. Normally one only speaks of someone trying to do an action if it is difficult to do, or if they do not succeed in doing it. We only speak of someone 'trying' to move their hand or give a lecture, if it was difficult for them to move their hand or give the lecture, or if they did not succeed in doing these things. But surely an agent's intentional contribution to a successful action is just the same in kind (even if not in degree) as his contribution to an unsuccessful action, when the lack of success is due to contingencies outside his control. When I open the door without difficulty and when I try to open the door but fail because it is jammed, my intentional contribution—in this case by means of the instrumentally basic action of pulling the handle—is the same. It is just that circumstances outside my control prevented my instrumentally basic action from having its normal effect.

So surely the same applies when I perform a public action than which no other action is an instrumentally or causally more basic action, and when I try to perform such an action but fail, that my intentional contribution is the same (in kind, if not in degree). We can see this from cases where I do not realize beforehand that I would have any difficulty in performing the public action of this kind (such as move an arm), and then suddenly find that I can't do it. I would then have tried but failed; yet all

[1] The two writers who introduced and developed a distinction between basic and non-basic (or mediated) actions are A.C. Danto ('Basic Actions', *American Philosophical Quarterly*, 2 (1965), 141–8) and R.M. Chisholm ('The Descriptive Element in the Concept of Action', *Journal of Philosophy*, 90 (1964), 613–24.) The words 'basic' and 'mediated' are Danto's; Chisholm contrasts making things happen 'directly' and 'indirectly'. Annette Baier ('The Search for Basic Actions', *American Philosophical Quarterly*, 8 (1971), 161–70) pointed out that these authors make slightly different distinctions from each other. She calls Danto's sense of 'basic', 'causally basic', and Chisholm's sense, 'instrumentally basic'; and I am following her terminology.

I contributed intentionally is what I would have contributed normally. Or I may find that while I can do the public action, it needs a little more effort than usual, and so, we may say, I needed to try harder to move my arm before it would move. But there is no difference in kind between a public action which I do easily and one which requires a little effort. So for public actions of this kind, and—I suggest—for all intentional actions whatsoever—trying to do an action is just the same action as having the intention to do the action; although as a matter of linguistic custom we only describe having the intention as 'trying' when the agent does the action with difficulty or proves unable to do it. (For the sake of simplicity of exposition, I shall not always conform to this linguistic custom in future; I shall sometimes describe cases of forming an intention to do A as trying to do A, even when the agent does A without difficulty.) If that is correct and intentional actions (with the exception of the action of having an intention, i.e. trying) are caused by intentions, then the only causally basic actions are having intentions. (These will be instrumentally basic only when the action is difficult to do, and so we need to form the intention first, that is to try as a recognizably distinct act, before we succeed.)[2]

As I noted in Chapter 3, our beliefs are involuntary in the sense that we cannot change them at will; at any given time we are stuck with beliefs we have. So if we have an intention to perform some instrumentally non-basic action, and a belief that a sequence of certain instrumentally basic actions constitutes the best way to perform that action, that belief (together with the intention to perform the non-basic action) causes us to form the intentions to perform the intentionally basic actions; if we believe that each of two such sequences constitutes an equally good way to perform the non-basic action (and that there is no better way), that belief causes us to form intentions to perform one of these sequences of basic actions. The intentions to perform instrumentally basic actions are themselves causally basic actions which cause the movements which (together with the intentions) constitute the instrumentally basic actions; they cause us to move our limbs and utter the words that come out of our mouths, and so make differences to the world beyond our bodies. It is scientifically well established that the movements of our limbs and mouth are fully caused by brain events, and more immediately than by intentions; and so if intentions cause the movements, they do so by causing the brain events. By the principle of credulity (see Chapter 2, section 2), things are probably as they seem to be, in the absence of counter-evidence. It seems to us that we do much of what we do intentionally; and what I have been doing in this section is to bring out what our normal view of this must be thought of as involving. We now need to consider whether there is counter-evidence making it probable that our normal view is mistaken. Various philosophers and scientists have produced arguments, both a priori arguments and arguments based on the detailed results of recent neuroscience or on more general physical theory purporting to show that intentions do not cause brain events.

---

[2] For further argument in support of the thesis that every intentional action involves trying, see Jennifer Hornsby, *Actions*, Routledge and Kegan Paul, 1980, ch.3.

2. An a priori argument for the causal closure of the physical

The claim that intentions do not cause brain events is normally put forward as part of the claim that no conscious events cause physical events; for if conscious events cause any physical events, surely they cause brain events, and if any conscious events cause brain events, surely intentions do. And if no conscious events cause brain events, surely no non-conscious mental events will do so, and so I shall consider this doctrine in the form of the more general doctrine of the causal closure of the physical (CCP), understanding its 'closure', not in the deterministic way understood by Papineau (see Chapter 3, section 5), but simply as the doctrine that all physical events *insofar as* they have causes have only physical causes. Epiphenomenalism, as normally expounded, includes both something like (CCP) and a principle to the effect that all conscious events are caused by physical events (viz. brain events).[3] We could, however, never be justified in holding such a principle in the strong form that all conscious events have physical events as their only immediate causes. For, we saw in Chapter 2 that, to be justified in believing the conclusion of any inference from some propositions as premises perhaps via other intermediate propositions to some proposition as a conclusion, we must believe each conscious belief in an intermediate proposition or in the conclusion is caused immediately by belief in the previous proposition. Fairly obviously this causal condition is satisfied for many inferences which we make, and if it was never satisfied, no argument for epiphenomenalism or any other philosophical or scientific theory would ever be justified. However, it is also surely fairly obvious that most conscious events are caused either directly *or* indirectly by brain events, but the crucial issue is whether all our intentions are so caused. I shall come to consider that issue in Chapter 7. Meanwhile I shall argue that we could never be justified in holding (CCP) which is the core claim of epiphenomenalism.

One often finds in philosophy books an a priori argument for (CCP), that since conscious events and physical events (including brain events) are events of such very different kinds, we would need—in order to be justified in believing that they interact—an explanation of how they interact; and that no one can produce such an explanation. Yet once the two kinds of event are defined in the way I have defined them, it must seem obvious to almost everyone at least that brain events often cause sensations and desires. Sticking a needle into almost anyone does cause some brain

---

[3] The article by W.S. Robinson on 'Epiphenomenalism' in the *Stanford Encyclopaedia of Philosophy* (http://plato.stanford.edu) defines 'epiphenomenalism' as 'the view that mental events are caused by physical events in the brain, but have no effects upon any physical events'. But all discussions bring out that the 'mental events' involved are 'conscious events'. So Robinson in his entry on 'Epiphenomenalism' in *The Oxford Companion to Consciousness* (ed. T. Bayne and others, Oxford University Press, 2009) defines 'epiphenomenalism' as 'the view that conscious events do not themselves have effects', adding that 'some of [our] neural events are . . . causes of our conscious events.' The first clause of this second definition entails that the causation of conscious events by brain events is immediate causation.

event which causes them pain, and this happens whoever sticks the needle in, and whenever they do it. Depriving someone of liquid for many hours causes some brain event which causes almost anyone to have a very strong desire to drink. There are evident simple causal connections of this kind well known to the human race for millennia. If these are not evident causal connections, it is difficult to see what would be an evident causal connection. And to some extent, as I shall comment in Chapter 7, neuroscientists are beginning to discover generalizations about which kinds of brain event cause which kinds of simple sensations and desires. It is true that, as I shall emphasize in that chapter, the most we can hope for is a long list of generalizations which do not fit together into a simple explanatory theory of the kind exemplified by the best theories of physics, such as Newton's theory of gravity set out in Chapter 2. But the fact that no one can provide such a theory does not provide the slightest reason for supposing that sticking a needle into someone does not cause a brain event which causes pain.

Humans have known for centuries how to produce substances of new kinds from ⌐ other substances of very different kinds without having any remotely plausible theory of how this happens; they have known how to produce edible plants from seeds, water, and sunlight, intoxicating wine from grapes, glass from sand, and so on and so on. Only with the development of chemistry in the early nineteenth century did anyone begin to have a plausible theory of how all this happens. But the absence for all previous centuries of a plausible theory of how doing certain things to certain substances produces certain new substances, casts no doubt on the obvious fact that doing those things causes those effects. And even if no-one had ever discovered the underlying chemistry that would never have cast any doubt on that obvious fact. Of course these processes do not always work, but if they work very often whoever does them whenever and wherever, that is a sure sign that the process is a causal process. To deny that some brain event caused by sticking a needle into someone causes pain seems absurd; and it seems equally absurd to deny that (in my sense) brain events are physical events, and pains are not. So the fact that we cannot explain how brain events cause conscious events casts no doubt on the obvious fact that sometimes they do. But if we ⌐\ are justified in believing that brain events sometimes cause conscious events even though these are events of such different kinds, that these are events of different · kinds cannot be a good a priori objection to the claim that conscious events sometimes cause brain events. ⌐⌐

3. Recent neuroscience

So I turn to a posteriori arguments in favour of (CCP) arguments from empirical results of science. These are of two kinds. There are first arguments from recent neuroscience, which depend on evidence about which conscious events (and in particular which intentions) people have how long before or after certain brain events (and so how long before the bodily movements caused by brain events). I will call evidence of this kind α-type evidence. It is claimed that this evidence shows that intentions do not cause the brain events which cause the bodily movements which we suppose they do. And then secondly there are arguments from large-scale physical theory, suggesting that all physical events are caused by and only by other physical events, from which it follows that no conscious events can make any difference to them. The evidence for the physical theory with these purported consequences comes solely from physical events, and I will call such evidence β-type evidence.

Daniel Wegner's *The Illusion of Conscious Will* draws to our attention various kinds of α-type evidence suggesting that 'conscious will might be an illusion, a feeling that comes and goes independent of any actual causal relationship between our thoughts and our actions.' He draws attention to illusions of will, 'cases where people feel they are willing an act that they in fact are not doing' and cases where people 'feel that they are not willing an act that they indeed are doing.'[4] The sense in which Wegner and others use the word 'willing' is the sense in which I am using 'having an intention'; and the sense in which they use 'voluntary action' is the sense in which I am using 'intentional action'.[5] And what Wegner understands by 'cases where people feel they are willing an act that they in fact are not doing' is cases where (in my terminology) people form an intention which they believe causes a bodily movement, but where they are mistaken in this belief—either because no bodily movement occurs, or because the bodily movement which does occur has quite other causes. One of Wegner's examples of the latter is where he got subjects to think that they had stopped a pointer moving, when that effect had in fact been caused by someone else.[6] There are certainly such cases, but they show nothing about whether people's intentions to make a bodily movement normally cause the effect which they believe that they cause. For humans can be subject to illusion in odd circumstances about almost anything; yet that shows nothing about whether we are normally subject to illusion. That some stage magician can lead me to believe (falsely) that I am seeing them saw a woman in half, doesn't show that normally what I think I am seeing is not happening. So if a psychologist can set up a trick situation where they get a subject to believe that he or she has intentionally caused some event when the event had quite other causes, that shows nothing about whether normal judgements about the efficacy of intentions are correct. The subject is not in error about their intentions, only about what they are causing.

If what Wegner has in mind by cases where people 'feel that they are not willing an act that they indeed are doing' are illusions that their intentions are not causing the

---

[4] Daniel Wegner, *The Illusion of Free Will*, MIT Press, 2002, p. x.

[5] In more ordinary usage, a 'voluntary action' is one which one does willingly. Thus an agent handing over money to a gunman who threatens to kill him if he does not hand over the money, would not normally be described as performing a 'voluntary' action. But it is certainly an intentional action; the agent meant to hand over the money. What Wegner and other neuroscientists are concerned with are the actions one believes that one intends to do (that is, one means to do), not the ones one does willingly.

[6] See a description of such an experiment in Wegner pp. 74–8.

intended effect when really they are, a similar comment would apply. But what he seems to have in mind is rather cases where people really are 'willing' an act of a certain kind, but do not feel that they are. Now I claimed in Chapter 3 that people cannot be mistaken about what their intentions are, that is about what they are currently 'willing' in Wegner's sense. And I think that none of the cases of the kind which Wegner describes shows that claim to be false, since there are equally plausible ways of understanding them (which given my argument in Chapter 3 are much more plausible ways). Some of these cases are simply cases where someone's brain events or mental events other than intentions cause movements of their body. Wegner discusses as one example of this the 'Chevreul pendulum'; someone holding a pendulum and in no way aware of willing it to move is in fact causing it to move, although not intentionally. Wegner himself claims that often merely imagining 'a certain pattern of movement (e.g. back and forth toward you, or in a circle)'[7] can cause the imagined movement. Some of these cases are simply cases of people's bodies making movements of a kind characteristic of intentional actions, which they did not intend to make. In automatic writing, hands holding pens write intelligible sentences without any consciousness of what has been written and/or any consciousness of 'willing' it.[8] But it is hardly a new discovery that sometimes our bodies do make intentional-type movements without any intention being involved or our being under an illusion of any kind—for example, when people sleepwalk. The fact that sometimes intentional-type movements occur without our intending this, gives us no reason to suppose that normally our intentional-type movements occur without this. Indeed on the normal view, since our intentions cause our bodily movements by causing the brain events which cause them, it is not surprising that sometimes brain events get out of control and cause the same effects when not caused by intentions to do so.

Some of Wegner's cases are cases where people believe that they had intentions in their past actions which it does not look plausible to suppose that they did have. People 'rationalize' their past behaviour. But I was only claiming in Chapter 3 that people are infallibly aware of their present intentions; they may forget the intentions in their past actions and so seek to provide a reason for having done what they did which makes their behaviour look rational.[9] As Wegner notes, children 'have this odd tendency to

---

[7] Wegner p. 115.

[8] Wegner p. 103.

[9] An example of false memory, but one where no rationalizing is involved, is provided by one recent experiment which shows that people sometimes misjudge the time at which they formed an intention, and so claim to have been guided by an intention at a time at which they were not so guided. H. Lau and others showed that magnetic stimulation (TMS) of a certain brain region (the pre-SMA) just after an action was performed led subjects (after the completion of the action) to ascribe an earlier time to the moment at which they formed the intention to perform the action and a later time to the moment at which they judged the movement to have begun than they would have done without the TMS. Since the stimulation occurred after the action, it could not have affected the actual moment at which the intention was formed or the movement initiated, and hence either subjects' judgements without TMS or their judgements with TMS were illusory. See H.C. Lau, R.D. Rogers, and R.E. Passingham 'Manipulating the experienced onset of intention after action execution', *Journal of Cognitive Neuroscience*, 19 (2007), 81–90. Whether the TMS creates the illusion or

invent false intentions after the fact. It wouldn't be surprising if we [adults] slipped back into this habit from time to time'.[10] Then of course people may be unwilling to admit to inquisitive investigators intentions of which they are aware. The sentence of Wegner's just cited continues with the comment that it would not be surprising if we invented false intentions (that is, knowingly give false accounts of our intentions to others) 'when we knew that no other grown-ups were looking'. And finally of course some of us occasionally refuse to admit to ourselves that we have a certain intention in acting; but we can only refuse to admit to ourselves something of which really we are aware all the time, and so even in that case we do not have intentions of which we are unaware.

Wegner suggests that we can make sense of the 'odd' phenomena of which I have discussed only a few examples, if we suppose that they are not 'odd'; that normally bodily movements are not caused by intentions, and that our beliefs that often they are so caused is what requires explanation.[11] But, I argued in Chapter 2, the principle of credulity tells us to believe that things are as they seem to be and so to believe that our intentions do often cause bodily movements, except in cases where we have positive evidence indicating that we are mistaken. All that Wegner's evidence shows is that just occasionally we do have positive evidence that we are mistaken in believing that someone's intention caused some bodily movement. But that has no tendency to show that normally intentions do not cause bodily movements. And if we ever did seem to have enough evidence, of the kind produced by Wegner, to make it probable that our intentions do not ever cause our bodily movements, it would be open to the objection to all such claims to be presented here that that evidence would need to include evidence about people's conscious events and that we can only have such evidence if their conscious events (conscious beliefs and intentions) cause brain events which cause them to tell us what those conscious events are.

By far the most interesting kind of a-type evidence, which does initially seem relevant to the issue of whether intentions normally cause bodily movements, is that resulting from the research programme initiated by Benjamin Libet. This evidence seems to some investigators to show that brain events of one kind which cause intentional actions consisting of simple bodily movements of a perfectly ordinary kind (not the 'odd' ones or ones done in deceptive circumstances mentioned by Wegner) are not caused by intentions.

---

removes it may be resoluble by further experiments. In Lau's experiment subjects were asked to manifest their judgement of the time of the onset of the intention by an action (moving a cursor to a point on a clock) after the TMS had been applied, but there are ways of getting subjects to manifest their awareness of an intention as soon as it occurs without waiting for its execution which might help to resolve this issue—given that, as I assume, subjects know what their intention is while they have it. On this, see A.R. Mele, *Effective Intentions*, Oxford University Press, 2009, ch. 6

[10] Wegner p.156.   [11] Wegner p.144.

In the original and most influential Libet experiments[12] participants were instructed to move their hand at a moment of their choice within a certain period of time (e.g. 20 sec). While doing this, they watched a very fast clock, and reported subsequently the moment at which they first had the 'intention' (or whatever) to move the hand. They reported the 'intention' to move the hand as (on average) occurring 200 msec before the onset of muscle activity initiating a hand movement. However, electrodes placed on their scalp recorded (on each occasion of hand moving) a build up of 'readiness potential' (RP), which was evidence of a particular kind of brain event (which I'll call B_1) occurring an average 550 msec before the muscle activity. Experiments of other kinds, Libet claimed, showed that subjects report the time of sensations as occurring 50 msec before the time of brain events which caused them.[13] That led Libet to hold that subjects misjudge the time of all conscious events by 50 msec, and so he concluded that (on average) the 'intention' first appeared 150 msec before the muscle activation, and so 400 msec after B_1. So, many have argued, this showed that B_1 caused the hand movement, and that the 'intention' was a mere epiphenomenon.

One problem with Libet's experiments is that Libet and other experimenters describe the conscious event which the subjects report and which I have just described as the onset of an 'intention', sometimes instead as the onset of a 'wish', or of an 'urge' or a 'wanting', or as a 'decision'.[14] There is clearly a big confusion here between on the one hand the passive inclinations with which we find ourselves and which I have called 'desires' and which seem to be the same as what investigators have called 'wishes', 'wantings', or 'urges'; and on the other hand apparent active 'intentions' and formations of intentions which constitute 'decisions'. Since, however, these results were obtained from subjects who were instructed not to pre-plan their movements and to act spontaneously, then (on the reasonable assumption that subjects followed the instructions) any decision (i.e. conscious formation of an intention) and any intention must have been a decision or intention for immediate implementation. And since 'intentions' are the sort of things of which we are conscious (as both I and investigators such as Libet were using the term), and since subjects were asked to look out for their intentions, the first awareness of an intention must have coincided with a decision to act. So any confusion in subjects' reports would be about whether they were reporting the time at which they first became aware of a desire to act, or the time at which they first become aware of an intention to act (i.e. a decision). This is a serious confusion, but since the desire must precede the decision (desires lead to the formation of

---

[12] For Libet's own account of his work, see B. Libet, *Mind Time*, Harvard University Press, 2004, ch.4.

[13] See Libet op. cit. p. 128. See A.R. Mele, *Effective Intentions*, Oxford University Press, 2009, ch. 6 for discussion of some of the literature on the temporal relations between the time of the onset of an intention, the time of the subject's first awareness of this onset, and the time which the subject later believed to be the time of his first awareness of this. Mele allows the possibility that the intention might begin before the subject was aware of it. On my account of intentions, an intention is a conscious intention, and so that is not a possibility.

[14] See A.R. Mele, *Free Will and Luck*, Oxford University Press, 2006, pp. 32–4.

intentions, not vice versa) it does not affect the main result that (if subjects' reports of the times of the events are anywhere near accurate) the decision to act follows B_1. So—to simplify discussion—I will suppose the conscious event dated by the subjects (in these experiments) to be a decision, which is the beginning of an intention. But since this intention needs only to last a very short time to produce its effect, I will use the word 'intention' to describe this event.

So, if the subjects' reports are at all accurate there is a succession of events: a brain event (B_1), then a (conscious) mental event (the intention which I'll call M_2), and then some brain event (which I'll call B_3) which directly causes the muscle activity and so the movement. Many neuroscientists proceed from that to reach this extraordinary conclusion that the intention does not cause the movement. Thus three recent writers conclude that Libet's data 'contradict the naïve view of free will—that conscious intention causes action. Clearly conscious intention cannot cause an action if a neural event that precedes and correlates with the action comes before the conscious intention'.[15] But that is a totally unjustified conclusion, since it is equally compatible with all the data and the most natural explanation of them to suppose that B_1 causes (in the sense of being a necessary causal condition for) the 'conscious intention' (M_2), and that the intention causes the brain event (B_3) which directly causes the movement. Causation is transitive. If I flip the light switch and thereby cause the light bulb to light-up, that doesn't rule out the possibility that my flipping the switch caused an electric current to pass to the bulb and the current caused the bulb to light-up. Despite this obvious point many neuroscientists have come to prefer one of two rival explanations of the data over the natural explanation. One rival explanation is that an earlier brain event (B_1) causes both the intention (M_2) and ('in parallel') a sequence of brain events leading to B_3 which causes the hand movement without the intention causing any brain event. The other rival explanation is that the intention never occurs, and that only after the hand movement does the subject come to acquire a (false) belief that there was such an intention. The scientific evidence, however, now seems to show fairly conclusively that the latter account is not the correct account for most cases of intention formation;[16] and that normally intentions do occur before the brain events which cause the intended bodily movements. That leaves as the only rival to the natural explanation, the 'parallel' explanation.

The last 20 years have seen very considerable progress in understanding the neural basis of intentional actions, made possible by the new techniques of brain imaging, which allow us to identify far more precisely than by measurements of electric potential on the skull which areas of the brain are involved in the formation of intentions how

---

[15] H.L. Roediger, M.K. Goode, and F.M. Zaromb, 'Free Will and the Control of Action', in (ed.) J. Baer, J.C. Kaufman, and R.F. Baumeister, *Are We Free?*, Oxford University Press, 2008. For a collection of similar quotations from neuroscientists see Mele, *Effective Intentions*, pp. 70–2.

[16] See P. Haggard, 'Does Brain Science Change our view of Free Will?' in R. Swinburne, *Free Will and Modern Science*, British Academy, 2011, p. 19.

many milliseconds beforehand. It seems to me that these results give considerable further support to the view that a prior brain event of the kind which gives rise to RP is a necessary condition for the occurrence of an intentional action of a simple bodily movement of the kind studied by Libet. Further, it was a major difficulty of Libet-type experiments that the RP was recorded only when it resulted in such an intentional action, and so B_1-type events might have been happening very frequently without leading to intentional action. If so, much else by way of brain or mental events might have been needed before intentional action resulted. However, subsequent experiments in which subjects had to decide not merely to move a hand, but which hand (left or right) to move, have enabled scientists to detect the occurrence after the RP over the whole brain (or after other evidence of relevant activity in crucial parts of both brain hemispheres) a 'lateralized' RP (or other evidence of greater activity in crucial parts of one brain hemisphere rather than the other), also before the formation of the intention (sometimes several seconds before this). This greater lateralized activity occurred most frequently in that brain hemisphere which was the one more influential in causing the resulting hand movement (that is, the left hemisphere for right hand and right hemisphere for left hand). Since the lateralized RP was measured in these experiments whenever there was an overall RP leading to bodily movement, it made it possible to measure the degree of correlation between prior brain activity of a certain kind (e.g. the lateralized RP) and subsequent intentions. It enabled scientists to predict which hand would be moved with an accuracy of up to 70 per cent.[17] But of course mere 70 per cent accuracy is compatible with the brain activity merely inclining rather than causing the subject to make the relevant bodily movement.[18]

But even if it were shown that some prior brain event B_1 causes a sequence of brain events which are both necessary and sufficient for the bodily movement when that constitutes an intentional action (in virtue of the agent having or believing that he had the intention to make that movement), that still wouldn't show that the intention was not also a necessary part of the cause. B_1 might still cause the bodily movement by

[17] See especially C.S. Soon and others, 'Unconscious Determinants of Free Decisions in the Human Brain', *Nature Neuroscience*, 11 (2008), 543–5.

[18] For accounts and interpretations of the work of the last 20 years on the neural basis of intentional actions, see the surveys by M. Hallett ('Volitional Control of Movement: The Physiology of Free Will', *Clinical Neurophysiology*, 118 (2007), 1179–92), P. Haggard ('Human Volition: Towards a Neuroscience of Will', *Nature Reviews, Neuroscience*, 9 (2008), 934–46.), and W.P. Banks and S. Pockett, 'Benjamin Libet's work on the Neuroscience of Free Will' in (ed.) M. Velmans and S. Schneider, *The Blackwell Companion to Consciousness*, Blackwell Publishing, 2007. Some of this work involves the identification of the brain areas which are the primary locations of the prior brain event which I have labelled 'B_1'. That depends in part on the kind of intention the subject is asked to form; and, as I discuss in the text, if the subject has to choose whether to move his right hand or his left hand, the crucial area turns out to be one on the side of the brain responsible for the chosen movement (e.g. on the right side if the subject eventually moves his left hand). Other of this work affects the issue of whether, as Libet claimed, humans have the power to 'veto' the intentions caused by brain events and so to prevent brain events having their normal effects. The results reported by M. Brass and P. Haggard ('To do or Not to do: The Neural Signature of Self- Control', *Journal of Neuroscience*, 27 (2007), 9141–7) have some tendency to suggest that the 'veto's' also are caused by brain events.

causing the intention to make it. To show that an intention was irrelevant a scientist would need to show that B_1 causes the very same sequence of brain events with or without subjects having the requisite intention (to produce that bodily movement) and so with or without the bodily movement constituting an intentional action. It would only be possible to perform an experiment to show this if scientists could prevent the occurrence of the intention, without thereby automatically preventing the occurrence of the sequence of brain events caused by B_1. That could only be done if either the intention is not caused by any brain event whatsoever, or it is caused by a brain event (i.e. has a brain event as a necessary causal condition) which is not itself part of the sequence from B_1 to B_3. For only if the intention is not caused by an event which belongs to that sequence (although perhaps by a brain event itself caused by an event in the sequence) could the intention be prevented without preventing the occurrence of the sequence of events which caused the bodily movement. If nevertheless scientists proved able to prevent the occurrence of the intention while B_1 still caused exactly the same sequence of events culminating in B_3 and the hand movement, that would show that the intention was not a necessary part of the cause of the hand movement. It would show that the sequence of brain events alone causes the very same movement as would constitute an intentional action if the agent had (or believed that they had) an intention to cause it. As far as I know, no one has attempted to show this. If this were shown, we would have evidence against the natural interpretation of the Libet experiments, that a brain event causes the intention which causes the brain event which causes the bodily movement. But until this is shown, none of this research on the neuroscience of intentional actions has shown or had any tendency to show that, even in the case of the kind of actions with which Libet-type experiments are concerned, our intentions do not cause our bodily movements. The natural interpretation of the evidence obtained so far, I repeat, is that a brain event B_1 is a necessary causal condition of M_2 which is a necessary causal condition of B_3 which causes the movement; this evidence is compatible with B_1 and a sequence of brain events caused by it also being a necessary condition for the occurrence of B_3

4. Physical theory

The other kind of scientific argument in favour of (CCP) comes from general physical theory, based solely on observations of physical events, which I will call β-type evidence. The claim is that our observations of these events makes very probable (in virtue of such criteria as I described in Chapter 2) some very general theory or component of a theory about how the physical world works, from which it follows that physical events are caused by and only by other physical events; and so that our intentions cannot affect our brain events. The normal objection from physics invokes the principle of the conservation of energy; or—more precisely—the following two principles: (1) any causal interaction involves an exchange of energy, and (2) 'the rate of change of total energy in a closed region of space is equal to the total rate of energy flowing through the spatial boundary of the region' or, more loosely, energy only increases or decreases in some region as a result of input from or to a neighbouring region.[19]

The human brain consists of some 10^{12} neurons, each with some thousand or so connections to other neurons. Inputs from muscles, sense organs, etc. cause neurons to 'fire'. When a neuron fires, it transmits electric potential down its axon on to a number of terminals, which in consequence release transmitter chemicals across a 'synaptic cleft', a small gap which separates the neuron from each neighbour. These chemicals attach themselves to receptors on the 'dendrites' of neighbouring neurons, which causes an electric potential to pass up the dendrite to the cell body of the neighbouring neuron. This potential, when added to (or subtracted from) potentials coming through other dendrites may be enough to cause the neuron to fire; and so the process continues, often thereby causing physical events in other parts of the body.

A neuron's mitochondria manufacture energy in the form of ATP molecules used in their reactions, from glucose and oxygen supplied to the neuron by the blood. Also, as energy comes into a neuron from transmitter substances, the energy of the neuron increases. The manufacture and release of chemical transmitters uses energy; and so as the neuron fires, the energy decreases. So, if our two principles govern the brain, any brain event can only be caused by an event with which it exchanges energy; and the only events with which it can do this are contiguous with it. So, the argument goes, there is no scope for conscious events to make any difference to anything which happens in the brain.

There are, however, good reasons to suppose that neither principle (1) nor principle (2) hold in a completely general form. For classical physics was superseded by quantum physics in 1925. It is a consequence of quantum theory that the position and momentum of a particle cannot be measured simultaneously to a joint accuracy of greater than $h/4\pi$, where h is Planck's constant ($\Delta p.\Delta q \geq h/4\pi$). Since the future position and momentum of a particle is a function of its present position and momentum, there is a limit to the accuracy with which the future position and momentum of the particle can be predicted. This result, the Heisenberg indeterminacy principle, follows from the basic structure of quantum theory, and is well confirmed independently—we can show for any instrument which may be proposed for detecting position or momentum, that using it to detect one of these rules out the simultaneous use of that or any other instrument to detect the other. What goes for particle motion goes for various other phenomena covered by quantum theory. Just as you cannot measure position and momentum simultaneously, so you cannot measure simultaneously the energy of a particle and the time at which you measure it, more accurately than within similar

[19] I repeat (in a slightly simplified form) the most general statement of the principle which he calls BPEC (the boundary version of the Principle of Energy Conservation) from Robin Collins, 'Modern Physics and the Energy-Conservation objection to Mind-Body Dualism', *American Philosophical Quarterly*, 45 (2008), 31–42.

limits. If you measure precisely the time at which you are making a measurement of a particle's energy, you will not be able to measure the exact value of that energy, and so to predict its exact subsequent value. All subatomic phenomena are infected by quantum unpredictability. Among the phenomena which in consequence we cannot predict more accurately than within a certain range is the time at which a radioactive atom will decay—all we can say of any given such atom (e.g. an atom of carbon-14) is that it has a certain half-life (e.g. 5,600 years), that is, there is a probability of 1/2 that it will decay during the next 5,600 years.

Most physicists hold that the data explained by quantum theory could not be explained better by any deterministic theory,[20] and so hold that on the small scale nature is not merely not totally predictable, but not totally determined.[21] There is, for example, only a natural probability of 1/2 that an atom of carbon-14 will decay within 5,600 years, or for some particular set-up only a natural probability (e.g. of 1/2 or 2/3) that a photon emitted from a source in the direction of a screen with two slits will pass through one slit rather than the other slit. On the whole these small-scale indeterminacies average out on the larger scale; it is enormously probable that a proportion very close to 1/2 of the atoms in a large collection of carbon-14 atoms will decay within 5,600 years. But there can be systems in which small scale indeterminacies have large scale effects; one could, for example, construct an atomic bomb such that whether it exploded depended on whether some particular atom in a block of atoms decayed within an hour or not.

It follows from all this that all the physical principles of classical physics, such as (2), hold only as statistical generalizations. Small amounts of energy may be gained or lost in the short term. And quantum theory also allows what looks like a causal interaction, without any sort of energy–momentum 'exchange', the EPR correlation, whereby

---

[20] David Bohm produced a rival deterministic theory of the relevant data in 1952, which has been developed by Bohm and some other physicists since then, but this has not obtained any widespread support.

[21] The 'indeterministic' account of the formulae of quantum theory, which I have just given, is, I believe, still that of a majority of physicists. On this account the behaviour of a physical object subsequent to a measurement is indeterministic, either because the measurement itself 'collapses the wave packet' in an indeterministic way (although the wave packet subsequently develops deterministically until next measured), or because the measurement reveals how the wave packet is developing all the time in an indeterministic way. The former version is the 'Copenhagen interpretation' which really amounts to a mere description of what happens, while denying the possibility of any deeper explanation. For the latter version see, for example, the article in The Stanford Encyclopaedia of Philosophy 'Collapse theories', by G. Ghiradi, revised 2007.

An account of the formulae of quantum theory alternative to the indeterministic account holds that the ψ-function is a deterministic function. A measurement splits the world into two or more worlds, and each of the possible outcomes of the measurement occur in some world. There is a very full discussion of this 'Many Worlds' interpretation of quantum theory in (ed.) S. Saunders and others, Many Worlds?, Oxford University Press, 2010. A major problem with this interpretation is that it seems to involve a person being split into two persons—which I claim to be logically impossible (see Chapter 6, section 2). The other major, and to my mind insuperable, problem with this interpretation is that it can give no plausible sense to what quantum theory claims to be a normal result of most measurements that one outcome is more probable than another one—since it claims that every possible outcome will occur in some world or other (and it gives no sense to the 'number' of worlds in which an outcome occurs). So I am presupposing some version of the indeterministic account.

one reading on a detector affects the value of a simultaneous reading of a distant detector (when by the principles of relativity theory simultaneous energy–momentum exchange is not possible).[22] Despite all this, it just may happen that one day quantum theory will be shown to be false and replaced by a rival theory more probably true on the evidence. But at any stage of science we must draw conclusions from the evidence which we have and not that which we guess we might one day obtain. Next century's theory may explain the physical and chemical phenomena which quantum theory purports to explain today in a way entirely different from that of quantum theory. But until such a theory is substantiated by evidence, we must reach our conclusions from the most probable theory which we have.

These possibilities opened by quantum theory have led to various theories about how mental events might influence brain events. Whether the firing of a neuron is transmitted to a neighbouring neuron depends on the exact amount of transmitter chemical released at the synaptic cleft, the exact distance between the neurons (the width of the cleft) and the exact amount of the transmitted chemicals which link to the receptors. The amounts of transmitter chemicals and the distances involved are very small; and so it is often a matter of natural probability of some significant finite value greater than 0 and less than 1 whether the electric potential caused by a neuron firing is transmitted to a neighbouring neuron. Various writers have argued that this is the point at which mental events could affect brain events without violating any physical principles.[23] It remains to be shown, however, whether any such interventions determining whether one neuron fired would affect enough other neurons to determine whether some intentional action was performed. But it may well be that the brain is just the kind of system in which small-scale indeterminacies cause large scale effects.

Here is a recent summary of the state of the evidence about whether the outcome of this process of one neuron causing another neuron to fire is to any significant extent indeterministic:

Current evidence indicates that when an action potential invades the presynaptic terminal, the chance that a single synaptic vesicle will be released can be as low as 20%. Examinations of the precise patterns of vesicular release suggest that the likelihood that a vesicle of neurotransmitter will be released in response to a single action potential can be described as a random Poisson-like process. Vesicular release seems to be an apparently indeterminate process. Careful study of other elements in the synapse seems to yield a set of similar, and highly stochastic, results. Postsynaptic membranes, for example, seem to possess only a tiny number of neurotransmitter receptors,

---

[22] Collins op. cit. p. 39. Since the correlations (e.g. between the directions of spin, of two 'entangled' particles) registered by the detectors, cannot be due to a common cause (given the 'Bell inequality'), there seems no other coherent way to explain them except by simultaneous action at a distance between two particles.

[23] For example, F. Beck and J.C. Eccles, 'Quantum Processes in the Brain: a scientific basis of consciousness' in (ed.) N. Osaka, *Neural Basis of Consciousness*, John Benjamin's, 2003; and J.M. Schwartz, H.P. Stapp, and M. Beauregard, 'Quantum physics in neuroscience and psychology: a neurophysical model of mind-brain interaction', Phil Trans Royal Soc B, online at http://www-physics.lgl.gov/~stapp/stappfiles.html.

and ... during synaptic transmission as few as one or two of a given type of receptor molecules may be activated. Under these conditions, a ... single open ion channel may allow a countable number of calcium or sodium ions to enter the neuron, and there is evidence that the actions of a single receptor and the few ions that it channels into the cell may influence the postsynaptic membrane. Together, all of these data suggest that membrane voltage is the product of interactions at the atomic level, many of which are governed by quantum physics and thus are truly indeterminate events. Under conditions in which the activity of many synapses is correlated and the membrane voltage is driven either way above or way below its threshold for action potential generation, the network of neurons itself would maintain a largely determinate characteristic even though the synapses themselves might appear stochastic [i.e. 'indeterministic']. Alternatively, when the synaptic activity is uncorrelated and the forces of excitation and inhibition are balanced, small uncorrelated fluctuations in synaptic probabilities drive cells above or below threshold. Under these conditions, indeterminacy in the synapses propagates to the membrane voltage and thence to the pattern of action potential generation. Indeterminacy in the pattern of action potential generation, although variable, would reflect a fundamental indeterminacy in the nervous system.[24]

Henry Stapp has developed over a number of years the outline of an account of why we should suppose that intentions, rather than any other conscious events, might make a difference to brain events.[25] Humans bring about a brain event which will eventually cause the bodily movement constituting the action they seek to cause, by concentrating their attention on some neuron when it is in the right state and so freezing it in that state, in virtue of a quantum effect known as the Zeno effect:

If, under appropriate conditions, one repeatedly poses the same probing question at a sufficiently rapid rate, then the sequence of responses will tend to get stuck in place. In the limit of arbitrarily rapid re-posings, the response will become frozen: all the responses will come out to be the same, even though very strong physical forces [from neighbouring neurons and other brain matter] may be working to make them change. Thus a manipulation of the *timings* of the probing actions, which are under the control of the consciousness of agent, can have, even in a warm, wet brain, a very special kind of physical effect. If, by mental effort, an agent can cause a sufficient increase in *probing rate*, then that agent can cause a state of intention and attention to be held in place much longer than would be the case if not such effort were being made.[26]

Stapp thus claims that 'in essence Quantum Theory is already an essentially psychophysical theory' because, following the earlier lead of Wigner, he considers that only conscious beings, not merely physical instruments, can collapse the wave packet.[27]

---

[24] Paul W. Glimcher, 'Indeterminacy in Brain and Behaviour', *Annual Review of Psychology*, 56 (2005), 25–66. See pp. 48–9. I am grateful to Dr Glimcher for permission to reproduce this concise summary of the state of the evidence about indeterminism in synaptic transmission. See also a similar analysis of the extent of brain determinism in H. Atmanspacher and S. Rotter, 'On determinacy or its absence in the brain', in (ed.) R. Swinburne, *Free Will and Modern Science*, British Academy, 2011.

[25] See H. Stapp, 'Quantum Mechanical theories of Consciousness', in (ed.) M. Velmans and S. Schneider, *The Blackwell Companion to Consciousness*, Blackwell Publishing, 2007.

[26] Stapp, 'Quantum Mechanical Theories', p. 306.

[27] op. cit. p. 300.

A very few other physicists have suggested possible extensions to quantum theory which might allow for interaction between conscious events and brain events.[28] While the vast majority of physicists regard Stapp's theory and other developments of quantum physics to account for interaction of conscious events and brain events, as highly speculative and ill developed, it must however be acknowledged that the advent of quantum theory means that it is no longer possible to appeal to a quick argument from deterministic physics to rule out the possibility of conscious events interfering with brain processes. The application of quantum theory to the behaviour of individual neurons, and the development of research on how individual neurons affect larger-scale brain processes, will surely produce interesting results in the coming decades.

5. CCP could never be justified

It is, however, my contention that no experimental results of any science could possibly provide justification for the causal closure of the physical (CCP). I claimed earlier in this chapter that it is 'fairly obvious' that most conscious events are caused by brain events. I shall, however, leave it open until Chapter 7 just which conscious events are caused by brain events, except in one respect. Fairly evidently we are able to recall past experiences only because our experiences cause 'traces' in the brain which we are then able to access subsequently. There is some empirical evidence about one area of the brain in which such traces need to be laid down: short-term true memory of events more than a few minutes earlier (and so of the long-term memory which depends on such short-term memory) depends on the operation of the brain structure called the 'hippocampus'. For example, a patient whose hippocampus was removed proved unable to recall anything subsequent to the removal of the hippocampus, which had happened to him more than a few minutes earlier.[29] So I shall assume that the causal dependence of consciousness is true at least in the respect that true memories of experiences, with the possible exception of ones occurring a very short time earlier, requires those experiences to cause brain events which then cause subsequent memories. Given that assumption, let us consider what evidence would show the causal closure of the physical (CCP) to be true.

(CCP), as a claim about which kinds of event cause other kinds of event, constitutes a scientific theory. I argued in Chapter 2 for what I called the epistemic assumption (EA) that

(1) A justified belief in a scientific theory (which is not itself a consequence of any higher-level theory in which the believer has a justified belief) requires a justified belief that the theory makes true predictions.

---

[28] See the discussion of the Penrose-Hameroff theory in Stapp op. cit. pp. 309–10.

[29] See the description of this patient's condition in R.F. Thompson, *The Brain*, Worth Publishers, third edition, 2000, pp. 392–3.

(2) A justified belief that a theory makes true predictions is (unless this is a consequence of some other theory in which the believer has a justified belief) provided by and only by the evidence of apparent experience, memory, and testimony that the theory predicts certain events and that these events occurred.

(3) Such justification is undermined by evidence that any apparent experience was not caused by the event apparently experienced, any apparent memory was not caused by an apparent experience of the event apparently remembered, or any apparent testimony was not caused by the testifier's intention to report his or her apparent experience or memory.

The fundamental criterion (FC) lying behind (EA) is that justified belief that some event ϵ occurred requires the assumption that ϵ is an event to which the subject has privileged access, or causes some event to which the subject has privileged access—unless ϵ is justifiably believed to occur as a consequence of some higher-level theory which predicts events justifiably believed to occur on grounds independent of that theory. Then a justified belief that a theory makes true predictions requires (unless justified by a higher-level theory) the assumption that both an awareness of the calculations that the theory predicts certain events and the events predicted are accessible or cause effects accessible to the believer. (FC), I claimed in Chapter 2, is a criterion central to our judgements about the credibility of a scientific theory.

So, it might seem, a scientist could be justified in believing (CCP) in virtue of having evidence of when (relative to brain events) various conscious events occur, which I have called α-type evidence. For (CCP) makes predictions about such evidence. As we saw earlier, it predicts that whether or not some type of conscious event occurs during the first part of some sequence of brain events will make no difference to whether or not the sequence is completed (and so cause public behaviour). If this prediction were tested for a large random sample of different types of sequences of brain events (especially those ending with events which are supposed to be caused by intentions) and different types of conscious events (especially intentions), and found to be correct, this—it would seem—would be strong evidence for (CCP). To test such predictions, a scientist would have to learn about the times of occurrence of various conscious events. The way to learn about the conscious events of others is from their behaviour. The obvious kind of behaviour from which to learn about their intentions in the kind of detail needed to construct a scientific theory is from their apparent testimony about them; and scientists doing Libet-type experiments rely on such testimony. We can learn about our own past conscious events by memory, and about our own present ones by experience of them. A scientist testing predictions about the occurrence of conscious events of a particular kind in special circumstances (e.g. the circumstances of Libet-type experiments) could, however, learn about times of occurrence of the relevant conscious events from some wider theory T which had the consequence that certain kinds of brain events always occurred at approximately the same time as certain kinds of conscious event (e.g. intentions); and so the scientist could tell when an intention was occurring from studying the subject's brain and inferring—via T—which conscious events were occurring. But T, being a theory about when conscious events occurred, could itself be justifiably believed only on a range of evidence about when conscious events had occurred in the past, and that would ultimately require relying on apparent testimony (or other behaviour of subjects best explained by postulating such conscious events) and/or apparent memory and experience.

Yet if apparent testimony is to constitute evidence that conscious events occurred, the scientist must—by (EA)—assume that the subjects are caused to say what they do by a belief that the conscious events occurred and an intention to tell the truth about their belief—a causal route which must go through a brain event. Yet if (CCP) were true, no conscious events will cause any brain event to cause the subjects to say what they do. But no theory could be justifiably believed on the basis of evidence about the occurrence of events, about the occurrence of which we could have evidence only if we assume the theory to be false. Hence (CCP) couldn't be justifiably believed on the basis of apparent testimony. The same applies to any inference from other behaviour of subjects to their conscious events which would explain that behaviour; we saw in Chapter 3 that inference from behaviour to mental events presupposes that the mental events cause the behaviour. (It will be seen that my subsequent claims about the assumptions necessary for using apparent testimony as a source of knowledge about the conscious events of others apply also to using any other public behaviour as a source of such knowledge, and so I ask the reader to understand my subsequent references to the assumptions involved in the former to apply also to the latter.)

A scientist might apparently remember his or her own conscious events. (By EA) someone is justified in trusting their apparent memories only on the assumption that they are caused by his or her past experiences. But the scientist will know what I claimed earlier, that virtually all true memories are caused more immediately by brain events; and so the scientist will know that, if those memories are caused by his or her past experiences, those experiences must first cause the brain events—which is ruled out by (CCP). So again (CCP) could not be justifiably believed on the basis of apparent memory, because virtually all apparent memories could only be believed on the assumption that (CCP) was false. Even if people can have justified beliefs about which conscious events they are now having, and can have true memories of very recent conscious events without the need for traces to be laid down in their brains, that would hardly provide any scientist with enough evidence of successful predictions (together with any amount of evidence about brain events) to give even a scientist a justified belief in (CCP). So generally no-one could have a justified belief in (CCP) on the basis of type a evidence for it, because (CCP) rules out the availability of enough evidence of that kind.

Modern neuroscientists doing experimental work of the kind described earlier in this chapter assume that they have access to the conscious lives of many subjects (and so evidence of type α); and that assumption is needed in order to test the prediction discussed earlier, that (in the circumstances of Libet-type experiments) the same sequence of brain events (beginning before the formation of an intention) which causes the bodily movement constituting the intentional action would occur in the absence of the intention. Unless this prediction is observed, the experimental results do not show that the intention does not cause the movement. To test this prediction we need to know when a subject has an intention. The only way to acquire this information is from the behaviour of subjects, and the normal kind of relevant behaviour consists of what subjects tell us. Experimenters assume that subjects' beliefs about their present conscious events (including their memory beliefs about past conscious events) are correlated with their testimony (in the sense that the testimony is a true report of their beliefs). The normal reason for assuming this is provided by (EA)—subjects' intentions to tell the truth about their beliefs plus their beliefs cause the testimony. If we assume that the correlation holds for this reason, then we would already be assuming the falsity of (CCP) in one respect in order to test the crucial prediction necessary to provide justification of the interpretations of the Libet experiments which claim that intentions do not cause the hand movements. So we can only justifiably believe that intentions do not cause the hand movements if we justifiably believe that they do cause the apparent testimony about them.

However, we might have good grounds to believe that in the particular circumstances of Libet-type experiments, apparent testimony is not caused by the intention to produce it, while nevertheless being in general reliable (in correctly reporting the testifiers' beliefs). But these grounds could only be provided by a wider scientific theory about when a testifier's apparent testimony to a belief about their conscious life is or is not correlated with the occurrence of that belief. A justified belief in that wider scientific theory would require a justified belief that that theory made true predictions. The predictions would need to be predictions of when on other occasions subjects' apparent testimony was correlated with their beliefs about their conscious lives. But in order to have a justified belief that these predicted correlations occurred we must rely ultimately on the apparent testimony of subjects to what they believe about their conscious lives (i.e. their beliefs about their present and past conscious events); and so—by (EA)—assume that subjects' apparent testimony is caused by intentions to report true beliefs. And if we are to use subjects' memory beliefs about their past conscious events as evidence about those conscious events, we must also assume a causal relation between the former and the latter which (barring a possible unimportant exception) proceeds via brain events.

I conclude that not merely have Libet-type experiments not so far shown that in their experimental circumstances intentions do not cause bodily movements; but that—even if the crucial predictions necessary to show this proved correct—that would only show that (CCP) held in these special circumstances on the assumption that in general it was false.

It might, however, seem that someone need not rely on evidence about conscious events (a-type evidence) but could rely solely on evidence about physical events

(β-type evidence) to provide a justified belief in (CCP), because of a justified belief in some general theory about the world of which (CCP) was a consequence. The appeals to the principles that energy is always conserved, and that all causation involves energy exchange, discussed earlier in the chapter, are examples of appeal to a general theory about the world which has the consequence that the physical realm is causally closed. But all that is needed is a narrower deterministic theory that every brain event has as an immediate necessary and sufficient causal condition some other brain (or other physical) event. That theory would entail (CCP), for if every brain event has another brain (or other physical) event as its immediate necessary and sufficient causal condition, no brain event can have a conscious event as its necessary causal condition; over-determination would be excluded. It might be thought that we could establish a deterministic physical theory of this kind on evidence solely about which brain events occur when (relative to other brain or other physical events), which would be evidence of the type which I have called type β. If we found that for any random sample of brain events (and especially ones supposed to be caused by conscious events), that it follows from such a theory that each of them has some brain (or other physical) event as its immediate necessary and sufficient cause, that would seem to be powerful evidence in favour of (CCP).

Someone could justifiably believe certain events to be occurring in the brains of others on the evidence of his or her own current observation (a present experience). But to get enough evidence to acquire a justified belief that the deterministic physical theory is true, a scientist would require evidence provided by their apparent memory of past such observations and by the apparent testimony of others to having observed various brain events in the past. But a justified belief in the deliverances of apparent memory of past experiences and apparent testimony to them is—(by CCP)—undermined by evidence that they are not caused by experiences of those events. So—given (EA)—there could not be a justified belief in a physical theory which entailed (CCP).

However, a modified understanding of memory and testimony is possible, which keeps apparent memory and testimony as sources of justified belief, and is still compatible with the fundamental criterion (FC) (lying behind (EA)) that (barring justification by a higher-level justified theory) justified belief in the occurrence of an event is dependent on the assumption that that event is accessible to or causes an effect accessible to the believer. One could understand 'memory' simply as memory of the occurrence of events, and not only of events which are experiences of the occurrence of other events. A subject could be said to 'remember' past physical events in virtue of those events causing traces in their brain, which at a later time cause the apparent memory of those events without any mental-to-physical causation being involved. People sometimes become aware later of details of some event which they observed, details of which they were not aware at the time of the occurrence of the event; and it does not seem too unnatural a use of the word 'remember' to say that they 'remembered' those details. And we could come to understand 'testimony' to amount merely to the public utterance of sentences reporting that a certain event occurred caused by a chain of brain events in the utterer, itself caused by the event reported, a chain which need not include any conscious events. The 'testimony' would not be testimony that the testifier had observed the event, but merely testimony that the event had occurred. This certainly seems to involve giving a stretched meaning to 'testimony', but relying on apparent testimony of this kind to the occurrence of physical events would still be compatible with the fundamental criterion (FC) (though not with (EA)). Given these modified senses of 'memory' and 'testimony', someone could have an apparent memory of or receive apparent testimony to the occurrence of brain events without making any assumption about anyone's conscious events causing brain events. Thus a scientist's eyes could receive light rays from events in a subject's brains, and—because those brain events cause brain events in the scientist—subsequently report them, without that causal chain proceeding through any conscious events. Given this modified understanding of apparent testimony and memory, anyone could have justified beliefs in the occurrence of any set of brain events without presupposing causation of the physical by conscious events; and so could come to believe in the occurrence of the brain events (β-type evidence) predicted by a deterministic physical theory.

This modified understanding of memory and testimony would not, however, make any difference to the unavailability of apparent memory and testimony to provide justified beliefs about the occurrence of conscious events. For even on the modified understanding of these notions any evidence of apparent memory and testimony about conscious events is undermined by the assumption that conscious events do not cause brain events. And so I should add, if this assumption were true, we could not get any evidence about which conscious events are caused by brain events or cause other conscious events; and that would mean that we could not have any evidence in favour of the claim that all conscious events are caused (at least indirectly) by brain events, which is the normal second claim of a fuller epiphenomenalism.

There is, however, a further problem in supposing that even with a modified understanding of 'memory' and 'testimony' we could have a justified belief that some deterministic physical theory gave true predictions about relations between brain (or other physical) events, and so a justified belief that (CCP) is true. This is that we would need not merely a justified belief that certain relations between brain events occurred, but also a justified belief that these relations were predicted by that deterministic theory. But anyone who had not calculated for himself what that theory predicted about the relations between brain events must depend on the evidence provided by the apparent testimony of scientists to have calculated this and 'seen' (i.e. had a conscious belief) that that was what the theory predicted; that is, he must depend on evidence of the conscious events of scientists. But if the deterministic physical theory were true, no scientist would have been caused to give that testimony by any conscious event—neither by their intention to tell the truth or even merely by their conscious belief about what the theory predicted. Hence no-one could justifiably believe what any scientist reported about his calculations, and so believe that the theory made the predictions which he claimed that it did, since believing what the scientist reported would undermine the credibility of their apparent testimony to it. Scientists normally check each other's calculations, but for the same reason—if the deterministic physical theory were true—no scientist could rely on the testimony of another scientist to have made the same calculation as they had. Neither could any scientist rely on their own testimony to him or herself recorded in a diary that the scientist had previously calculated the consequences of the deterministic theory. And since a scientist will believe that their past experiences (with the possible exception of very recent ones) cause their present apparent memories via a causal chain proceeding through brain events, the scientist could not be justified in relying on the evidence of their own apparent memory about their calculations (at least insofar as it concerned calculations more than a few minutes earlier). Only if the scientist could hold in their mind at one time almost all their calculations from which it apparently followed that the deterministic theory predicted certain events could the scientist have a justified belief that that theory made successful predictions, and so a justified belief in (CCP). For most scientific theories and most scientists, this is most unlikely.

I conclude that, given the fundamental criterion (FC) which guides the justifiability of scientific theories, (with the very small exception stated) no one could have a justified belief that any deterministic physical theory of which (CCP) was a consequence made certain predictions, and so no-one could have a justified belief on those grounds in (CCP). This result that (with a very small exception) no-one could have a justified belief in any purely physical deterministic theory applies not merely to theories concerned solely with the functioning of the brain, but to all theories which hold that physical events are caused solely by physical events—such as the principle of the conservation of energy in the form of principles (1) and (2) discussed earlier in this chapter. No one could justifiably believe this because their belief that the theory made successful predictions requires a belief that their own past calculations or those of others have caused the former belief.

6. The frequency of intentions

It follows from the results in section 5 that there cannot be counter-evidence to what seems to us very strongly to be the case, that our intentions often cause our bodily movements. Hence (by the principle of credulity) very probably our intentions do often cause our bodily movements. Given that, we have no reason to deny that other mental events, whether conscious events or continuing mental states, may sometimes cause brain events (and other mental events). So there is no reason to deny that when we seem to remember some past conscious event, probably it happened—unless there is counter-evidence with respect to a particular event; and when someone tells us about their past conscious events, for example, about their assessment of some scientific theory, probably their report about the occurrence of those events is true—again, unless there is counter-evidence with respect to a particular report.

But the fact that our intentions often cause our bodily movements does not entail that we have a separate intention for each intentional action which we perform. When we perform a long sequence of easy bodily movements in order to execute some medium-term intention, the medium-term intention plus the belief that it can be fulfilled by performing a long sequence of movements plausibly causes each of the movements. When someone walks along a street by taking now this step now that step, each of the movements is intentional because he or she has the medium-term intention of walking along the street, and believes about each step that making it is a stage in fulfilling the intention. Given my claim in Chapter 3 that intentions are always to some extent conscious, the action of walking along the street would not be an action which the agent was intending to do unless the agent consciously had such an intention; but the agent's belief about each step need not be conscious. The reason for saying that the intention is causing the movements in such a case is that (normally) it seems to the agent, as they walk along, that they are walking along the street because they intend to walk along the street; and by the principle of credulity the way things seem to the agent to be is the way on that evidence that they probably are, and by the principle of testimony what the agent says about their intentions is on that evidence the way they probably are—in the absence of counter-evidence. Principle (CCP) would provide that counter-evidence, but I have argued that we could not be justified in believing (CCP).

It does, however, seem that sometimes we perform actions of kinds which we could easily have intentionally caused to occur while they were occurring, but which we perform so quickly that we have done them before we have ever had the intention to do them. When a driver turns the car's steering wheel to avoid a pedestrian, or a child withdraws their hand which has touched the cooker's hot plate, no intention has caused the movements; and in retrospect we are often well aware that our actions were as automatic and unintended as reflex actions. Such actions are not intentional actions on my definition of 'intentional action'; and the results of this chapter do not apply to them.[30]

---

[30] The distinctions between kinds of intentions which have been made in Chapter 3 and in this chapter reflect and largely overlap distinctions made in recent years by various philosophers. In 'The Phenomenology of Action: A Conceptual Framework' (*Cognition* 107 (2008), 178–217) Elizabeth Pacherie has tailored her distinctions so as make them useful for analysing the latest psychological results. She follows Alfred Mele (a distinction repeated in his *Effective Intentions*, p. 10) in distinguishing 'distal intentions' ('intentions for the non-immediate future') and 'proximal intentions' ('about what to do now'); but she seems to equate this distinction with the rather different distinction between what I am calling 'ultimate intentions' and 'executive intentions'. (Compare Pacherie p. 182 with p. 188.) The latter distinction is the distinction between what the agent intends to do for no further reason, and what the agent intends to do in order to execute an ultimate intention. But ultimate intentions need not be formed well in advance of their execution; and notoriously distal intentions may get forgotten or may fail to influence an action. Pacherie (pp. 186–7) also makes a distinction between proximal intentions ('P-intentions') and what she calls 'M-intentions', which are the ways (the exact limb or whatever movements) in which the brain causes the body to execute P-intentions. But, given that P-intentions include intentions to perform an instrumentally basic action (such as grasping a cup or uttering a sentence), then the way in which one's body executes such a P-intention is not intended. When I utter a sentence, I do not know, and so do not intend, the exact twists of lip and tongue by which my body executes my intention. So in these cases M-intentions are not 'intentions' at all in the normal sense with which I am concerned.

5

Agent Causation

1. Causation

I argued in Chapter 4 that our intentions often cause our brain events and thereby our bodily movements. But I need now to bring out that that is a slightly misleading way of expressing the conclusion of that chapter. It is, I shall argue in this chapter, we humans, not events which happen in us, who cause our brain events; we cause a brain event by forming the intention to cause some effect of that brain event. And I need to bring out the nature of this intention as causation of a particular kind; forming the intention (that is, trying) to cause a bodily movement is (normally) just causing that movement intentionally (that is, meaning so to do). In order to establish these points, I must begin by defending a particular account of laws of nature, because (since the time when the concept of a law of nature was recognized in the sixteenth century) philosophers have normally recognized an intimate connection between causation and laws of nature. But they have disagreed about whether causation is to be analysed in terms of laws of nature, or laws of nature are to be analysed in terms of causation.

In Chapter 1 I introduced briefly three kinds of account of laws of nature. On the (still very influential) event regularity account of causation deriving from Hume, 'all As are followed by Bs' is a law of nature iff every past, present, or future event of kind A is always followed by an event of kind B. Hence Hume's theory of causation, that a particular event ϵ causes another event γ iff ϵ belongs to some kind (a type) A and γ to some kind B, where 'All As are followed by Bs' is a law of nature.[1] To use one of Hume's own examples:[2] we find that when one moving inelastic billiard ball hits another such ball at rest, the second ball moves away from the first one. From the fact that this always happens it follows, Hume claimed, that an event of the former kind causes an event of the latter kind.[3] Regularity theory needs to be expressed in a more

---

[1] Although Hume seldom used the expression 'law of nature', he regarded what others called 'laws' as sequences of the kind described. See his *Enquiry Concerning Human Understanding* note to §57, where he discusses—but not under that name—Newton's 'first law'. But see too his discussion of miracles where he does use the phrase 'law of nature'—*Enquiry* section 10, and especially §90.

[2] *Enquiry* §59.

[3] In section 10 of the *Enquiry*, as in section 1.3.14 of his *Treatise of Human Nature*, Hume offered two different kinds of account of laws and so of causation—a subjective one in terms of the propensity of humans who think of an event of one kind to think of an event of a certain other kind, and an objective one in terms of regularities of succession of publicly observable events. His objective definition of a 'cause', for example, is

complicated way to deal with the point that not all regularities constitute laws of nature. For example, it may always have been, be now, and be in future the case that on all planets in all universes where there is animal life all dinosaur extinctions are followed by the evolution of mammals 20 million years later, but this is not a law of nature—for there could be a planet on which dinosaurs evolved and became extinct and yet there was no environment suitable for mammals, or all animal life was destroyed by the planet moving too close to its star before mammals could evolve. So we could not infer from the regular succession of dinosaur extinctions followed by mammal evolutions on our planet and maybe other planets too, that the evolution of the dinosaurs on our planet caused the evolution of the mammals on our planet. The succession of dinosaur extinction followed by mammal evolution was a mere 'accidental regularity', not a law of nature.

Regularity theory reached a developed form which tries to take account of this distinction between laws of nature and mere accidental regularities, in the work of David Lewis. For Lewis 'regularities earn their lawhood not by themselves, but by the joint efforts of a system in which they figure either as axioms or theorems.'[4] The best system is the system of regularities which best satisfies the kind of criteria described in Chapter 2 for a probably true explanatory theory, given evidence of all the actual events—whether ever observed by anyone or not—which ever have happened, are happening, or will happen. The true laws are the regularities of the best system. Accidental generalizations are regularities which do not fit into such a system; they float loosely without being derivable from more fundamental regularities. So 'all dinosaur extinctions are followed by the evolution of mammals 20 million years later', even if true, is probably not a law, because it probably does not follow from the best system. This is evidenced by the evident fact that it does not follow from our current best approximation to the best system—a conjunction of quantum theory, relativity theory, and standard particle theory (including the laws of the four forces), from which laws of genetics (determining which organisms are produced) and laws of natural selection (determining which organisms are eliminated) seem to be derived. A particular A causes a particular B—according to Lewis—iff it follows from such a best

that it is 'an object followed by another, and where all the objects similar to the first are followed by objects similar to the second'—*Enquiry* 7(ii), 60. That he understands here by an 'object' an event is shown in the preceding section, where he writes: 'When one particular species of event has always, in all instances, been conjoined with another . . . we then call the one object, *cause;* the other, *effect*'. But if causation is a feature of the world outside ourselves (as almost all of us believe), then human thinking does not make an event a cause, and so it is the objective kind of account which has endured, and is called the 'regularity theory'. In claiming Hume as the source of the regularity theory I am reading him in the traditional way as claiming that the 'necessity' by which a cause is followed by its effect just consists in 'constant conjunction'. Some recent writers claim that Hume has been misunderstood, and that all he was claiming is that we cannot have any more knowledge of the necessity of cause and effect than is provided by constant conjunction. See for example Galen Strawson, *The Secret Connexion: Causation, Realism, and David Hume*, Oxford University Press, 1989.

[4] David Lewis, *Philosophical Papers*, vol. 2, Oxford University Press, 1986, 'A Subjectivist's Guide to Objective Chance', Postscript, p. 122.

system that that A will be followed by that B (and certain other complicated conditions hold).[5] Lewis's account of laws of nature is part of his campaign on behalf of 'Humean supervenience', the view that everything there is supervenes (logically) on a vast mosaic of local matters of particular fact, which he interprets as a spatio-temporal arrangement of intrinsic properties, or qualities.[6] Both laws of nature and causation are, for Lewis, among the things thus supervenient.

Now it seems to me that regularity accounts of laws and causation are perfectly coherent accounts; the sense of 'law' and 'cause' which Hume or Lewis suggest are coherent senses. One could understand 'laws' and 'causes' in the way they suggest. But it also seems fairly evident, even before we consider the phenomenon of intentional causation, that their understanding of laws and causation simply does not fit many paradigm examples of our ordinary talk about 'law' and 'cause'. Their accounts simply do not capture what we are saying when we say that (for example) Newton's law is a 'law of nature' or the position of Saturn caused the recession of Jupiter from the Sun. In particular many of our paradigm examples of 'law' are ones where laws are said to *explain* whether and why one event causes another event. Newton's law of gravity explains why Saturn moving closer to Jupiter causes Jupiter to move further away from the Sun. But for Lewis, since whether some regularity constitutes a law depends not merely on what has happened but on what will happen in the whole future history of the universe, it follows that whether a particular event ϵ causes another particular event γ now depends on that future history. Hence whether ϵ causes γ may depend on what happens in two billion years time; and so if the world ends before then certain events which otherwise would happen (e.g. that some event like ϵ is not followed by an event like γ) will not happen, that may make a difference to whether it is the case now that ϵ causes γ. Yet, on the normal understanding implicit in paradigm examples of one event causing another, what makes it the case that ϵ now causes γ and explains why γ occurs is some state of the world now. What is yet to happen in two billion years' time can make no difference to what is the true explanation of why γ occurs (viz. that ϵ occurred and caused γ)—though, of course, it might make a difference to what we justifiably believe to be the true explanation. (Put another way: that some proposed explanation is the simplest explanation of the data, past and future, is evidence that it is the true explanation; but it does not constitute it being the true explanation.)

Further, it is because of their role in causation, that laws of nature are said to generate counterfactuals (conditional sentences in which it is implied that the antecedent is false). Suppose that it is a law of nature that 'all copper expands when heated', but that I don't heat a certain piece of copper; it is all the same fairly evidently the case that—it would be a paradigm example of a true counterfactual that—'if I had heated that piece of copper, it would have expanded'. But if the statement of a law simply states what does (and did and will) happen, how can it provide any ground for asserting the

[5] op.cit. chapter 21.   [6] op. cit. pp. ix–x.

counterfactual? It would only do that if it affirmed a natural necessity (or natural probability) determining what happens and so what would happen if things were different in some respect from the way they actually are, a necessity deeper than that provided merely by fitting into a system. Fitting into a system could only be evidence
L. of that deeper kind of necessity.[7]

Hume and Lewis would agree that their accounts of law and causation do not fit the way many of us understand these notions. But Hume claimed that the sense of 'natural necessity' (as something other than mere regular succession) implicit in our normal understanding of law and causation is not (in my sense) a coherent sense. This is because, Hume claimed, the only coherent concepts we can have are those derived from experiences of instances of them and we have no experience of physical necessitation.[8] (See my Additional Note D for this theory of 'concept empiricism'.) There could not be, he claims, such things as 'laws' or 'causes' in the normal senses of these words. So Hume is in effect claiming that his accounts of law and causation are the nearest we can get to coherent accounts which have the consequences that many of the paradigm examples of what we naturally regard as laws and causes are laws and causes. I shall be arguing shortly, however, that, contrary to Hume, we are ourselves aware of causing effects, by exerting causal influence which—given the right physical conditions—makes it naturally necessary that they will occur. The innumerable paradigm examples of such intentional causation make the concept of natural necessity intelligible, and so even on Hume's theory of concept empiricism a coherent concept. Lewis finds the RBU account of laws and causation 'unintelligible';[9] but he does not, as far as I know, discuss the SPL account. But even if he allowed that that account was intelligible, he would claim that there is no reason to believe it to be the true account of what happens in the actual world, that is, that substances have powers and liabilities of the kinds it claims.

However, if we assume for the moment the intelligibility of the concept of natural necessity, it is evident from what I have just written that what we are saying when we say, for example, that 'Newton's law of gravity' states a law of nature is that it reports

---

[7] Lewis notoriously claims that what makes a counterfactual true is that there is actually another world in other respects very similar to our world in which both the antecedent and the consequent of the counterfactual are true, and no world equally or more similar to our world in which the antecedent is true and the consequent false. There is a world similar to ours in which I (or –to speak strictly—a counterpart of me) does heat the copper and it expands, and no worlds equally or more similar to our world in which I heat the copper and it does not expand. See his *On the Plurality of Worlds*, Basil Blackwell, 1986. But very few philosophers follow Lewis in holding that, even if there are lots of other worlds very similar to ours, counterfactuals are assertions about such worlds, and that it is what happens in those worlds which makes counterfactuals true.

[8] Our misguided feeling that we do have a coherent concept of natural necessity arises, according to Hume, from the mind having 'a great propensity to spread itself on external objects' and so to suppose, when we find ourselves observing that a kind of event A is regularly followed by a kind of event B and so an 'idea' of the former leads us to have an idea of the latter, that the regular succession of ideas corresponds to some real connection between the events themselves. See his *Treatise* 1.3.14.

[9] 'It's unintelligible how the unHumean constrainer can do its stuff.'- Lewis, *Philosophical Papers*, vol 2, p.xvii.

some natural necessity (or probability) at work in the world. A natural probability (as opposed to an 'epistemic probability' discussed in Chapter 2) is a propensity in the world for some event to occur. (See my Additional Note A.) Probabilistic laws state physical probabilities of kinds of events occurring. (The value of the physical probability of a kind of event occurring is the same as the most probable value of the frequency of an event of that kind in the very long run.) For the sake of simplicity of exposition, when discussing laws, I shall not always mention probabilistic laws. I ask the reader to assume that what I have to say about natural necessity applies also to natural probability.

The two kinds of theory other than the event regularity theory described in Chapter 1 do assume that the concepts of natural necessity and probability are intelligible. They differ in respect of whether they locate that natural necessity (or probability) in something separate from the substances which are governed by it, or whether they locate it in the substances themselves. On the RBU account laws are (logically contingent) relations of physical necessitation or probabilification between 'universals', that is, between properties in my sense. For example, the law that 'all photons have a rectilinear velocity of 299,792 km/sec in empty space' (relative to any inertial frame) is to be analysed as there being a relation of natural necessity connecting the universals of 'photon' and 'having a rectilinear velocity of 299,792 km/sec in empty space'. So when the universal 'photon' is instantiated (i.e. there exists a photon) it brings with it of natural necessity the universal 'having a velocity of 299,792 km/sec in empty space'. The law that 'all atoms of radium-226 have a half-life of 1,620 years' (i.e. a natural probability of 1/2 of decaying within 1,620 years) is to be analysed as there being a relation of natural probability of one half connecting the universals of 'atom of radium-226' and 'decaying within 1,620 years'. On the RBU account, as on the event regularity account, causation is analysed in terms of laws of nature. A particular event ϵ causes another event γ iff ϵ belongs to some kind (a type) A and γ to some kind B, where 'All As are followed by Bs' (and perhaps some other complicated conditions hold) is a law of nature. A particular ignition of gunpowder caused an explosion iff both events occurred and the universal 'ignition of gunpowder' is tied by a relation of natural necessity to the universal 'explosion'.

On the SPL account the fundamental laws are regularities; not regularities of successions of events, but regularities in the causal powers and liabilities of substances—powers to naturally necessitate (or to make naturally probable), that is, to cause effects; and liabilities of natural necessity to exercise those powers under certain circumstances or under all circumstances. Thus 'all photons have a velocity of 299,792 km/sec in empty space' is the regularity that each photon has the same power as each other photon to cause itself to be $299,792n$ km distant after n sec, and the liability inevitably to exercise this power when in empty space. 'All atoms of radium-226 have a half-life of 1,620 years' is the regularity that each atom of radium-226 has the power to decay, and the liability (with a natural probability of 1/2) to exercise this power within 1,620 years. It is natural to think of some of the causal powers of substances and especially of fundamental particles as essential to them, part of what makes a substance that substance. An electron would not be an electron unless it had the power to repel every other electron with a force inversely proportional to the square of the distance between them, and the liability always to exercise that power. By contrast the RBU account has to claim that it is a logically contingent law that electrons repel each other.

Now I suggest that (if we ignore for the moment the relevance of intentional causation) accounts of these two kinds are rival plausible accounts of what is involved in our talk about 'laws of nature', rival plausible extrapolations of the sense of 'law of nature' involved in the paradigm examples of 'laws of nature', and so rival plausible accounts of what we are claiming when we claim that something is a 'law of nature'. They therefore constitute rival explanatory theories which purport to explain the regularities in the behaviour of substances, whereas the regularity theory is not a theory about how the world works and so not an explanatory theory of anything in this sense. Both the RBU and the SPL accounts purport to explain why (for example) the proximity of Saturn to Jupiter causes Jupiter to move further away from the Sun. This happens on the RBU account because there is a law (a component of the world additional to the substances which are governed by it), the law of gravitational attraction, which makes it naturally necessary that, when it is close to Jupiter, Saturn will exert a greater force of attraction on Jupiter than it normally does and so draw it towards itself and away from the Sun. It happens on the SPL account because Saturn itself has the power to exert such a force with that consequence, and a liability to exercise that force when it is closer than normal to Jupiter.

Given that there are laws of nature involving natural necessity, as—I have already argued—all of science supposes, we should adopt a theory of laws of nature of one of the two kinds just outlined. I analysed in Chapter 2 the criteria for judging one explanatory theory to be more probable than another. These two very general theories of how the world works have equal scope and are so general that there is no background evidence with which they can fit. So we must judge that one most probably true which is the simplest and/or makes the evidence more probable. The evidence is the regularities in the successions of physical events, that is, in the behaviour of physical objects, such as the fact that all physical objects behave (at least to a very high degree of approximation) as Newton's theory of gravitation says that they do. These event regularities are rendered equally probable either by there being simple ties between universals (the universals of 'mass', 'distance', and 'force' being tied together by a simple mathematical formula), or by physical objects belonging to kinds which have the same powers and liabilities as each other (all massive bodies having similar simple powers of gravitational attraction to each other). But the SPL account can be expounded in terms of readily accessible concepts. Powers to cause and liabilities to exercise them are familiar things—humans have powers to cause things (and—as described here—it looks as if fundamental particles do too); and dinner plates and glasses have liabilities to break. By contrast, the RBU account needs to be expounded in terms of concepts far from readily accessible; 'universals' tied together in a timeless

heaven. We should not postulate such strange things as relations of natural necessity
between universals unless we need to do so in order to describe or explain phenomena.
For this reason we should prefer the SPL account of laws of nature and so of causation
as more probably the true account of what is happening in the actual world, even
before we come to considerations arising from the nature of intentional causation. (The
event regularity theory does not provide an explanation of event regularities; it merely
states that they occur.) Since powers and liabilities are properties of substances, it
follows (as I claimed in Chapter 1) that we do not need an extra category (beyond
substances, properties, and times) of 'laws of nature' in order to tell the whole history of
the world.[10]

Laws being analysed in terms of the causal powers and liabilities of substances leaves
causation itself as a basic unanalysable relation (that is an unanalysable property), or
rather—it leaves 'exercising causal influence' as a basic relation, unanalysable except in
terms of such a simple synonym as 'making naturally probable'. For, more precisely on
the SPL account, the powers of substances must be regarded on this account as powers
not to cause effects, but as powers to exercise a certain kind and amount of causal
influence. This is because many of the powers which a substance may exercise can be
prevented from causing any effect (or as much effect as they would otherwise cause) by
the exercise of a contrary power by some other substance. A planet may exert force on
another planet, attracting the latter towards it; but have no effect because a third planet
is exercising a force attracting it in the opposite direction. So the SPL account must say
that substances have powers to exercise causal influence of a certain kind and strength
(defined in physics as a 'force') and the liability to do so always or under certain
conditions (e.g. in empty space). The effect produced is a resultant of the amount of
causal influence exerted by different substances. So, on the SPL account exercising
causal influence (that is, making naturally probable) is a basic category. Having made
this point that—strictly speaking—it is 'exercising causal influence' rather than 'causing' which is the basic category on the SPL account, I shall in future sometimes write
loosely about 'causing' rather than 'exercising causal influence' when nothing turns on
the difference, asking the reader always to bear in mind the qualification that substances
cause effects only in the absence of other substances preventing them from doing so.

Contrary to Hume and Lewis (and also contrary to the RBU account), it is then not
an event which causes another event; but a substance or substances which cause an
event. It is not the momentum of the brick but the brick itself which causes the glass
window at which it is thrown to break (in virtue of the brick having the power to break
glass of a certain brittleness and its liability to exercise this power when it has a certain
momentum). Laws of nature are then just generalizations about the powers (of causal
influence) of substances and their liabilities to exercise these powers in different
circumstances. The fundamental physical laws are concerned with the powers and

---

[10] Hence my reason for rejecting also the view of Tim Maudlin (see chapter 1 note 3) that laws of nature
are an unanalysable component of the world.

liabilities of fundamental particles, from which can be derived lower-level laws which describe the powers of substances of different masses and densities composed of these fundamental particles, having, for example (for different velocities), different momenta to exert force on substances of various degrees of strength and rigidity (and so of brittleness). It then follows from the powers and liabilities of the substances involved that the brick having such-and-such a mass has a liability, when it has a certain momentum in contact with a window of a certain brittleness, to exercise its power to break the window, that is, to cause it to break.

The regularity theory of laws confined causation to the operation of laws of nature, holding that for ϵ to cause γ is just for the succession of events to exemplify a regularity. The RBU theory also entails such an analysis: for ϵ to cause γ is for ϵ to belong to some universal kind A and γ to belong to some universal kind B, where there is a relation of natural necessity (or probability) between the kinds A and B. So both Tooley and Armstrong hold that 'states of affairs' (i.e. events) 'cannot be causally related unless they fall under some causal law';[11] although Armstrong emphasizes that this is not logically necessary, and suggests that it is an a posteriori necessity.[12]

On the SPL account causation (or—to speak strictly—exercising causal influence) is a fundamental irreducible relation; and laws are simply contingently true generalizations about its normal operation. The SPL account recognizes that as a matter of contingent fact the physical world consists almost entirely of substances of a few different kinds (e.g. a few kinds of fundamental particles; and larger objects made of these) which belong to a kind in virtue of their properties and especially their causal powers and liabilities to exercise them possessed by all members of the kind. All electrons, to repeat the earlier example, have the power to repel other electrons with a force inversely proportional to the square of the distance between them, and the liability inevitably to exercise that power when there is an electron so placed. A particle wouldn't be an electron unless it had that power and liability.

On the SPL account of cause substances cause effects because they have the powers they do; and if they have a liability necessarily to exercise some power, they will inevitably do so (or if they have a probabilistic liability to do, then—with the degree of probability involved—probably they will do so). But this account allows as metaphysically possible the existence of substances which have powers and liabilities of a kind peculiar to that substance, which would not necessarily be possessed by any substance which had all the same other properties as it; the powers and liabilities of such a substance could be a 'brute fact' about that substance, not deriving from its belonging

---

[11]   Michael Tooley, *Causation*, Oxford University Press, 1987, p. 268. See also D.M. Armstrong, *A World of States of Affairs*, Cambridge University Press, 1997, p. 227: 'The fundamental causal relation is a nomic one, holding between state-of-affairs types, between universals. Singular causation is no more than the instantiation of this type of relation in particular cases.'

[12]   Armstrong writes that 'every singular causal sequence is in fact governed by a law' is 'a likely supposition' (op. cit. p. 227), and suggests that 'the identification of a singular causal sequence with the instantiation of a law' is 'an empirical a posteriori matter' like 'water = H_2O' (op. cit. p. 218).

to some universal kind. Further, since the SPL account treats 'exercising causal influence' as a basic category, not analysable in terms of any other category, it also allows as metaphysically possible the existence of a substance which has a power but no deterministic liability inevitably to exercise that power, or even a probabilistic liability to do so. (By a probabilistic liability to exercise a power I mean a natural probability of some particular value p that the substance will exercise the power.) Such a substance could exercise its power to cause some effect because it intends—that is, tries—to cause that effect, and not because it has a propensity to cause the effect. I now argue that human beings are substances of this kind.

2. Intentional causation

For an agent to have an intention—that is, to try—to perform some intentional action (which will most often consist in intentionally bringing about some physical event ϵ) is for the agent to do whatever they believe will make the performance of that action (e.g. the bringing about of ϵ), more probable than it would have been if the agent had not so intended—more probable in the sense of epistemically more probable given the agent's beliefs. It is for the agent to change the world insofar as they can, in order to ensure that they will successfully perform the intended action (e.g. bring about ϵ) under a greater range of possible conditions of the world than the agent would do otherwise. We saw in Chapter 4 how doing any long-term or complicated action involves doing one or more (instrumentally) basic actions. It involves following a recipe. A recipe for passing some exam might be reading books, taking notes, and going to lectures. What a subject believing this to be such a recipe amounts to is that they believe that, given their beliefs about examiners and the range of questions which they normally set, if they read books, take notes, and go to lectures, the subject will probably be able to answer far more of the questions that will be will set than they would otherwise be able to do. Given the subject's beliefs about examiners they believe that following that recipe would put them in a position where it is epistemically more probable that they will pass the exam than it would otherwise have been. And so, since all the subject can do is to try, trying to pass the exam will consist in trying to read books, trying to take notes, and trying to go to lectures. The former trying then for the subject consists in the latter trying. And there are recipes for performing the latter actions. To try to go to lectures the subject needs to try to get out of bed in the mornings, try to get on the bus, and so on. But in the end there are tryings to do instrumentally basic actions (e.g. to make a simple bodily movement) for which the subject does not need a recipe. For most subjects moving an arm, signing their name, or saying 'Wednesday' are instrumentally basic actions. A subject does not need to follow a recipe in order to do them; all they need to do is to try. Some instrumentally basic actions are ones for which an agent does have a recipe although he or she does not need to follow it—I tie my shoelaces as an instrumentally basic action, but if pressed, I could probably provide a recipe for doing it—first cross this end of the lace over that end, then put it under that end, and so on.

But in the end an instrumentally basic action consists of actions for which an agent has no recipe except to try to do that action.

Trying to do an instrumentally basic action is, we saw in Chapter 4, a causally basic action. Yet many actions which are instrumentally basic for most agents are ones which some other agents find difficult to do, and for doing which they can be given a recipe. For native Russians uttering the hard 'e' is instrumentally basic; native English speakers learning Russian can be taught to pronounce it by being told to say 'er' with the tongue convex in the middle of the mouth and not touching the roof or sides of the mouth. For a good tennis player hitting the ball over the net is instrumentally basic; a beginner player can be taught to do this by being told to hit the ball hard while looking, not at the ball, but at the place on the other side of the net where he or she intends the ball to land. But such teaching takes place by telling the student to do actions which for them are instrumentally basic ('say "er"', 'look at the place on the other side of the net'). For every intentional agent at a given time there is a set of instrumentally basic actions, to do any of which not merely does the agent not need a recipe but the agent has no recipe; all the agent can do is try to do the action, and trying to do that action is itself a causally basic action. Trying to do such an action I will call a basic trying. For me now to try to move an arm or leg or to say 'Wednesday' are basic tryings; and if I suddenly find myself having difficulty in doing them, all I can do about it at this moment is to try harder.

I could not try to do any action, basic or non-basic, unless I believed at the time (it seemed to me then) that my trying was causally influential, although not necessarily in the end effective because other partial causes necessary for the effect are not in the right state—for example, the examiners set untypical questions, or the agent is ill on the day of the exam, so that their trying to pass it does not bring it about that they pass. And the same goes for basic trying, trying to do some instrumentally basic action for which the agent has no recipe. I could not try to lift a weight which I am holding in my hand unless I believed that what I was doing was making some difference to whether or not the weight would be likely to rise into the air—even if I do not in the end succeed, because the weight is heavy, and my muscles are flabby. And, in order to believe of any trying that it is making a difference, I have to believe it of the basic tryings by means of which I try to do other things. And even those neuroscientists who claim not to believe that their intentions (i.e. tryings) have any causal influence on their bodily movements, have to suspend their disbelief for most of their waking lives. For if someone really believes that their basic tryings never have any causal influence, there would be nothing they could do which would constitute trying; and so they would cease to try, and so cease to act.

Given the principle of credulity we should believe things are as they seem to be, that is, as we believe they are, in the absence of counter-evidence. It follows from the fact that when each of us tries to do some action, necessarily he or she believes that they are exercising causal influence which—given the cooperation of other causes—will make it more probable that they will succeed in doing that action (e.g. bring about an intended effect). That is, they must believe (at the time of having an intention) that probably that intention (that trying) is an exercise of causal influence. And, to repeat, to believe otherwise would be to cease to act. I argued in Chapter 4 that there could not be any counter-evidence to the claim that normally intentions cause (via brain events) effects in and outside our body, and thus constitute the performance of actions. That does not rule out there being evidence that our intentions sometimes have no effect, or even sometimes do not in fact (contrary to what we believe at the time) consist in the exercise of causal influence. So we can certainly occasionally justifiably believe that someone else's intentions of a certain kind are not as they seem to the agent and do not constitute the exercise of causal influence; that is, that they do not constitute the exercise of causal influence is probable on the evidence available to others but not to the supposed agent. But even this, given the argument of the previous chapters, is something we can justifiably believe only with respect to a minority of intentions—for otherwise we would not have justified beliefs about matters about which we evidently do have justified beliefs provided by the testimony of others.

Since an agent trying to do an instrumentally basic action for which he or she has no recipe is itself a causally basic action, and does not consist in the agent performing any other intentional action, that is, bringing about some intermediate state of affairs which in turn causes the event they are trying to cause, we must regard such basic trying (normally) as simply the agent intentionally exercising causal influence.[13] To try basically is (normally) to pull the causal levers themselves, not to do something else which in turn pulls the causal levers. When agents try, that does not consist in their being in a state which makes them liable to exercise their causal power; their trying is (normally) their (intentionally) exercising causal power; and so, given the co-operation of other causes, causing the intended effect. And since all other trying is simply a matter of a sequence of basic tryings accompanied by beliefs about their longer-range conse-quences, all tryings by agents (that is, all their intentions) just are (normally) agents exercising causal influence. The exercise of this causal influence may sometimes be a very 'active' matter, as when I try very hard to lift a weight. But the causation may often be largely, although never entirely, 'permissive', as when I walk along a road and my legs move in a semi-automatic way. My action is intentional if I mean to walk along the road, but all my intention may amount to is that I consciously allow my legs to move in this semi-automatic way when I could easily have stopped them.

---

[13] Hume had an argument against the view that we have a direct awareness of exercising causal influence. He claims that the will 'has no more a discoverable connection with its effects, than any material cause has with its proper effect.' Such a connection 'could not be foreseen without the experience of their constant conjunction'. See his *Treatise of Human Nature*, Appendix. I argue above, however, that since an of 'will' (a 'volition' or in my terminology a 'trying') to perform an instrumentally basic action which consists in bringing about ϵ cannot be identified except as that action which the subject believes to be an exercise of causal influence towards the production of ϵ, when the 'volition' is followed by the occurrence of the required event (ϵ) the subject must think of the 'volition' as its cause. I could not even identify a 'volition' of mine as I perform it without thinking of it as causally influential; I do not need to observe any constant conjunctions to reach that understanding.

Now I am not at this stage ruling out the possibility that we caused (e.g. by brain events) to form the intentions we do (that is, to try to do what we do); and such causation may be analysable in terms of the operation of laws of nature. Put in terms of powers and liabilities, it may be that some parts of our brains have liabilities to exercise powers to cause us to form intentions of certain kinds under certain circumstances. I shall discuss this issue of whether our intentions are always caused by brain events in Chapter 7. But what (normally) happens if a brain event causes me to try (for example) to move my hand is that the brain event causes me intentionally to exercise causal influence, and so—given the necessary cooperation of other physical causes—causes me to cause my hand to move. What doesn't happen in any such case is that the brain event directly exercises such causal influence on other brain events, so as—with the necessary cooperation of other physical causes—to cause my hand to move. For, if that happened, I would not be performing an intentional action at all. So it must be the case, if my intentional action is caused, that a brain event causes a mental event and that mental event causes (via other brain events) the bodily movement. But the mental event cannot be a mere involuntary or passive state such as a desire and/or belief with which I find myself. That would not be enough for the occurrence of an intentional action. For a desire, or any other passive mental event, could (via brain events) cause some movement of the agent's body without the agent performing any intentional action; and that could be so even if the mental event is a desire for the movement to occur. A number of examples of how this might happen have been given in the literature. Here is one from Davidson:

A climber might want [i.e. desire] to rid himself of the weight and danger of holding another man on a rope, and he might know that by loosening his hold on the rope he could rid himself of the weight and the danger. This belief and want might so unnerve him as to cause him to loosen his hold, and it might be the case that he never *chose* to loosen his hold, nor did he do it intentionally.[14]

What is required for an intentional action is an active mental event, the agent doing something; and doing is apparently-causing. Given that, as I argued in Chapter 4, very probably our intentions often cause our bodily movements, it follows that my intentions causing consists in me causing, and the content of an intention is what I seek to achieve by causing—which may be a simple bodily movement or some more distant effect thereof. Forming an intention, that is, trying, is the exercise of causal influence, which consists in a substance, the agent, causing (intentionally, that is, meaning to do so); it does not consist in an event, which is a state of the agent, causing

There are surely laws of nature determining when humans have certain powers to perform instrumentally basic actions such as bodily movements, that is, which kinds of brains have the powers to give to humans powers to perform which basic intentional actions. They are laws about which of our intentions to perform instrumentally basic

---

[14]   D. Davidson, 'Freedom to Act' in his *Essays on Actions and Events*, Oxford University Press, 1980, p. 79.

actions will be immediately successful, and which are such that we need to try hard in order to fulfil the intention. Whether our intentions to move our limbs or say words will be fulfilled clearly depends to a considerable degree on whether our neurons have the right connections, and our muscles are in the right condition. But only 'to a considerable degree'; it also depends sometimes on how hard we try (how much causal influence we exert). Whether someone can run 100 m in 10 sec obviously depends on the state of his or her body and brain; and most bodies and brains are not in a condition to allow their owners to do this, however hard they try. For a few athletes, however, success in running 100 m in 10 sec depends, not only on their state of body and brain, but on how hard they try. (I shall urge in Chapter 7 that it is not possible to give a precise numerical measurement to how hard someone tries.)

3. Two species of causation

Now Hume, and following him Kant and most modern philosophers, supposed that most of the paradigm examples from which we derive the concept of causation are successions of inanimate events (e.g. this motion of a billiard ball being followed by that motion of a different billiard ball; these positions and velocities of planets being followed by those positions and velocities of planets). These philosophers then went on to claim that the concept of causation just is the concept of one event being followed by another, when all events similar to the former are followed by events similar to the latter; and that (with qualifications such as those described earlier about which regular successions are causal successions) is the event regularity theory of causation. It should, however, now be evident that the paradigm examples from which we derive our concept of causation include many examples of agents intentionally causing effects. Not merely gunpowder ignitions, but also terrorists cause explosions; not only billiard balls cause billiard balls to move, but billiard players do also. An adequate account of our concept of causation must be such as to exhibit both species of causation (inanimate and intentional) as species of the same genus.

We have seen that the concept of intentional causation is not a concept of one event of some particular kind being followed in a regular way by an event of some other particular kind. To exercise intentional causality is something done by a substance of a particular kind (a person or animal). It does not consist in bringing about some passive mental event (such as a sensation or thought) and then waiting to see what (if any) effects it might have. The concept of exercising causal influence in a certain direction is a concept of something not further analysable (except in some such tautological way as 'making physically more probable'). Exercising causal influence is something which can be done intentionally, and if enough of it is exercised, and the circumstances are right, it will have the intended effect. If inanimate causation is a species of a genus of which intentional causation is another species, the exercise of causal influence must be the same kind of unanalysable thing in both species—with only the necessary minimum difference that in one case the causation is by an agent who intends it, and in the other case by an agent who does not intend it. The only account of inanimate causation which satisfies this requirement is the substances, powers, and liabilities (SPL) account. According to that account, it is substances—planets or billiard balls or gunpowder— which exert causal influence, and they do so in virtue of their powers; if they exert enough causal influence, they often cause effects. Exactly the same holds for intentional causation; substances (in this case, animals or humans) exercise causal influence in virtue of their powers, and if they exert enough of it they often cause effects. The only difference is that in inanimate causation substances have a liability to exercise their powers under various circumstances, whereas in intentional causation substances intentionally exercise their powers. Since this account alone takes seriously the para- digm examples of causation of both kinds, that that is strong reason for believing this account to be the correct account of the sense of 'cause' implicit in the paradigm examples from which we learn to use the word 'cause', and so of the beliefs of most of us about what is happening in the world. Hume claimed that we have 'no internal impression' of necessary connection between cause and effect other than an awareness of regular succession, and so we could have no 'idea' (or as we would now say 'concept') of natural necessity other than an idea of regular succession.[15] But, I have been arguing, it is in part from the experiences of ourselves causing effects that we derive our concept of causation. We do have an impression and so an 'idea' of exercising causal influence and so (in the normal case where our basic tryings are successful) of 'causing'. 'Causing' an event is making its occurrence naturally necessary; and the impression of making the occurrence of an event naturally necessary is generated most evidently when we force the event to occur by exerting a lot of causal influence—for example, by pulling the door hard until it opens, or by smashing the bottle hard until it breaks.

That the two kinds of causation are species of the same genus is not merely the implication of our ordinary concept of causation, but also—I now argue—the correct account of what is actually happening in the world. It is not merely because it is simpler to suppose that the two kinds of causation are species of one genus, but because the occurrence of many events is due to both kinds of causation, acting in unison or opposition to each other—that makes it extremely probable that the same unanalysable force is at work in both kinds of causation. For an agent can cause a succession of a regular kind by doing an instrumentally basic action. I may throw a ball in a certain way (aiming at a window) as an instrumentally basic action; and I can then discover that, when I do so, it hits the window and the window breaks. I can learn to do this so easily, so that breaking a window by throwing a ball becomes an instrumentally basic action. I can thus exercise intentional causation in causing the window to break. But I discover that I cannot do anything after I have thrown the ball to affect what happens subse- quently; and so I can learn that an event of the motion of the ball being followed by the

---

[15] See, for example, Hume's *Treatise of Human Nature*, 1.3.14

breaking of the window is a causal succession of a regular kind which does not depend on me, but—for balls with a certain velocity and windows of a certain normal kind—always happens. When I do throw the ball, this latter succession is a part of the stream of causation which I initiate by throwing the ball. But the regularity of the succession must exhibit causality of the same kind whether I initiate it or not. More generally, I can learn that I can cause effects of certain kinds by causing effects of certain other kinds; I can cause someone to die by submerging them under water, hurt an animal by stabbing it with a sharp stick, break a branch by hitting it with a thicker branch, and so on. And I can also learn that when an event occurs of a kind which I can cause, although on the particular occasion it was not caused by me or any other intentional agent, the same subsequent event occurs. People die by drowning, animals are hurt when impaled on sharp sticks, and branches are broken when the wind smashes thicker branches against them, independently of whether intentional agents cause the earlier events. And so we can learn that some regular successions in nature not initiated by intentional agents are cases of non-intentional causality, but—except in the respect of not being initiated intentionally—a causality of the same kind as that initiated intentionally. There is, however, no obvious intrinsic distinction between regularities of succession of kinds which we have learnt how to bring about intentionally and those of kinds which we have not so far learnt how to bring about intentionally. So surely we are justified in regarding all regular successions of kinds of events of kinds which we are justified in believing to be laws of nature to be causal successions of the same kind.

Another way in which we act intentionally and so learn to apply the concept of causation is by being acted upon. We find ourselves needing to exercise causal power to maintain a status quo, and thus become aware of an opposite causal power in nature which we are resisting. Holding a weight in my hand, I find that I need to exercise causal power to prevent my hand being moved downwards. When I hold the same weight again, I need to exercise what feels like a similar amount of causal power to counteract the causality of the weight in order to keep the hand in place. Since the two causal powers are of equal strength (since they balance each other and stop my hand from moving), they must involve causality of the same kind.

I conclude that the SPL account of causation, and so of laws of nature as contingently true generalizations about the powers and liabilities of substances, is the correct account. This is not merely because the SPL account of all causation is simpler than other accounts, but also because of the fact that the SPL account of inanimate causation represents the two kinds of causation as far more similar to each other than do the other accounts, and so takes account of the fact that so many kinds of events can be caused both intentionally and non-intentionally. I have reached this result by paying careful attention to what we are aware of as happening in many of the paradigm examples by which we are introduced to the concept of causation—just as I suggested in Chapter 2 that we get a certain result about our concept of temporal period if we pay careful attention to what we are aware of in all the paradigm examples by which our temporal concepts are introduced.

Intentional causation, being causation by a substance (an agent) in virtue of its causal powers with some intention (normally an intention to produce some effect) and (except in the case of instrumentally basic actions) in the light of a belief about how that intention can be achieved, is often called 'agent causation'. Almost all writers before the eighteenth century claimed that humans exercise agent causation. Among the few subsequent philosophers who, despite the Humean tradition, have affirmed this are Thomas Reid, Richard Taylor, and Roderick Chisholm.[16] Some writers contrast agent causation with the Humean kind of event causation which, they claim, operates in the inanimate world. I have defended the view that all causation is by substances (and not by events), and the two kinds differ only in respect of whether the substances cause because of an intention to cause an effect, or because of a liability to cause an effect. It is however less clumsy to talk of laws of nature as relating types of events, and of inanimate causation as relating token events, rather than to talk in terms of what I have claimed to be the more accurate account of these concepts; and so in subsequent chapters, when nothing in the argument turns on the nature of laws and causation, I shall sometimes continue to do this.

[16] See the analysis of the views of these writers and the relatively minor differences between them in Timothy O'Connor, *Persons and Causes*, Oxford University Press, 2000, ch. 3.

6

Substance Dualism

1. The synchronic unity of the human person

This history of the world (in the objective sense), I claimed in Chapter 1, is all the events which have occurred; but it can be told by listing any least sub-set of events which entails all the events. Events are the events they are in virtue of the properties, times, and substances involved in them. I argued in Chapter 3 that there are properties and so events of two kinds—physical events and mental events, among the latter pure mental events and among these conscious events—and the history of the world has to include events of both kinds. I turn now to the nature of the substances which are involved in mental events.

I define a mental substance as one for which the possession of some mental property is essential. For a mental substance to exist, when not having a conscious event, it must have some beliefs or desires, or at least a disposition to have sensations or thoughts or form intentions. (Maybe the only conscious events of the most primitive animals are sensations. They continue to exist when not conscious while they still have a disposition to have sensations.)[1] I then define a physical substance as one for which the possession of a mental property is not essential. I define a pure mental substance as one for which only pure mental properties are essential (together with any properties entailed by the possession of pure mental properties). So far I have used the words 'person' and 'human' equivalently and without the need for definition. Now I need to be a little more precise. I shall understand by 'persons' (in what I believe is the normal sense of the word, but nothing turns on that) substances with a capacity (at least after normal growth) for beliefs and actions of the degree of sophistication typical of those present-day earth-inhabitants called 'humans'. I shall understand by 'humans' any persons who have or have had at some time a kind of body and an ancestry similar

---

[1] I have in the past defined a mental substance as one to whose existence that substance necessarily has privileged access, and that definition entails the definition in the text—since having this privileged access is a disposition for having a certain kind of mental event—awareness of one's own existence. But I have some doubt about the converse entailment; it seems odd to say that any animals for whose existence mental properties are essential, have a way of finding out that they exist not available to others, although they certainly have a way of finding out that they are in pain not available to others; they know the latter simply by experiencing the pain. But mental substances, such as adult humans, which have a mental life of any sophistication, have privileged access to their own existence; they have a way of finding out that they exist not available to others—they can be self-aware (not merely conscious, but self-conscious).

to those persons whom we call 'humans' today. With these definitions I can raise the question whether humans are mental substances, and whether they are pure mental substances. (My definitions leave it open at this stage whether there can be persons who are never embodied—that is, never have physical properties—and whether humans can become disembodied.)

I argued in Chapter 1 that there are different ways of cutting up the world into substances, and so we can tell the whole history of the world in many different ways. It might seem that we could tell the whole history of the world if we cut it up in such a way that the only substances are physical substances to which mental properties belong only contingently. Among these would be organisms including humans and other animals, which would belong to some species (defined by certain essential physical properties) and which would continue in existence insofar as they had largely the same physical parts, or their physical parts were replaced only gradually. As mentioned in Chapter 1, there are different ways of cutting up the animal world into species (in a wide sense, that is, not necessarily in accord with any biological definition). It might seem that there are also different limits we could impose on the extent and frequency of replacement of parts which would be consistent with an animal remaining the same animal. For example: we could regard the caterpillar, the chrysalis, and the butterfly as stages of the same animal; or as different animals, such that the death of either of the first two caused the birth of the next one. Many of these animals also have mental properties, in virtue of their causal connection with physical events (such as the animal's brain events). We could regard these, as ordinary language normally does, as properties of the whole animal and not of any part thereof; or as belonging to that part of the animal with which their instantiation is most closely connected causally—that is, their brain, and so to the whole animal in virtue of belonging to its brain.[2] These mental properties could, it might seem, be treated as non-essential properties of the animals. And in all of these different ways, it might seem, we could tell the full history of the world. Then the criteria for the existence and continuing of human beings would be the same as those for the existence and continuing of human bodies, which is what 'animalist' theories of human personal identity advocate.[3] A mental life would then be an inessential feature of humanity.

Contrary to this model, however, it is not possible to have a full description of the world in which all substances are individuated only by physical properties. For it is an evident datum of human experience that conscious mental events of different kinds

----

[2] As proposed, for example, by Jerome Shaffer, 'Could Mental States be Brain Processes?' *Journal of Philosophy*, 58 (1961).

[3] 'There appears to be a thinking animal located where you are. It also appears that you are the thinking thing—the only one—located there. If things are as they appear, then you are that animal. This view has become know as *Animalism* . . . If we are animals, we have the persistence conditions of animals. And as we saw, animals appear to persist by virtue of some sort of brute physical continuity'—article on 'Personal Identity' by Eric Olson in *Stanford Encyclopaedia of Philosophy*, corrected 2010. This view allows that there might be persons other than humans for which different identity criteria are required.

(visual sensations, auditory sensations, etc.) are co-experienced, that is, belong to the same substance, both at one time and over time. Any description of the world which did not include among its components substances which have as their conscious properties all and only coexperienced properties, or did not entail the existence of such components, would not be a full description. I will discuss 'coexperience at one time' in this section, and 'coexperience over time' in section 2.

It is often an evident datum of human experience that it is the same conscious being, one substance, who has simultaneously the conscious experiences of seeing the traffic in the road outside, hearing a knock at the door, smelling the lunch cooking, and so on. So we must include in a full history of the world substances which have all and only conscious properties which are coexperienced at that time. So if this substance has physical properties and so a physical extension, as well as these mental properties, it must include within its borders all the parts of its brain, events in which are immediate causes or effects of conscious events which are experienced simultaneously. And neuroscience seems to indicate that the immediate causes of conscious events of different kinds (e.g. visual sensations, auditory sensations, or olfactory sensations, occurrent thoughts, etc.) include events in different parts of the brain; and also that the immediate causes of different properties (e.g. the colour and the shape) of what we must regard as one conscious event (e.g. perception of a coloured shape) include events in different parts of the brain.[4]

So we would fail to tell the whole history of the world if we traced only the history of each part of the brain, regarded as a separate substance, and the instantiations of mental properties most immediately causing or caused by events in that part; for there would then be truths about properties (such as coexperienced sensory properties) which we would have to attribute—falsely—to different substances. And we would also fail to tell the whole history of the world unless we included among substances with physical properties and so physical parts, substances which are such that events in those parts are the immediate causes or effects of and only of conscious events which are coexperienced with other conscious events belonging to the same substance.[5] So if a coexperiencing substance also has physical properties—as, for example, humans do on our normal way of cutting up the world into substances—then that mental property (of coexperiencing certain properties) will delimit the physical boundaries of the substance, and so help to determine which physical properties it possesses. Hence what constitutes such a substance which has conscious coexperienced properties is— even if it has also some physical properties—determined in part by a mental property,

---

[4] How these different features of a conscious event get bound together constitutes what psychologists call the 'binding problem'. See Tim Bayne, *The Unity of Consciousness*, Oxford University Press, 2010, pp. 229–30 for the distinction between this 'feature binding' and binding of other kinds involved in conscious events.

[5] It could happen—for example, in Siamese twins—that there are parts of a brain, events in which are the immediate causes of two (or more) mental events which belong to different collections of coexperienced events. In this case we must say that these parts are parts of the brains of two (or more) persons, the brains of which overlap.

and so the substance is a mental substance. And of course if the substance does not have any physical properties, it must be anyway a mental substance.

Hence humans are mental substances, since their spatial boundaries are determined by a mental property. So the full history of the world must include mental substances as well as physical substances—though as far as anything I have written so far is concerned, the identity of these mental substances may be determined by physical properties as well as by a mental property. For example, as far as anything I have written so far is concerned, it might be necessary in order for a human being to be a particular human, not merely that he or she coexperiences conscious events, but also that the human has a particular brain.

Almost all the time almost all human-looking bodies move and produce sounds in a unified way so as to lead us naturally and rightly to suppose that each such body is the body of a human being who is doing the moving and speaking, and who has privileged access to all and only the conscious events which are the immediate causes or effects of events in that body's brain at one time. But occasionally in abnormal circumstances some human bodies behave in a disunified way which might seem to suggest that the conscious events connected with the bodies of those persons are not all coexperienced, not events in a single consciousness. In his book *The Unity of Consciousness* Tim Bayne distinguishes three kinds of disunity of consciousness.[6] In describing these, I will describe them as kinds of disunity in the consciousness of one human person—although I shall subsequently claim that one kind of disunity (if it existed) would constitute a disunity, not in one human person but in a human body, since then two different persons would be in control of that body.

The first kind of disunity is 'representational disunity'. A person's 'consciousness' suffers from representational disunity insofar as their conscious events do not give rise to unified or even consistent beliefs about their contents, or about the world which those contents seem to represent. Thus one might experience two colour patches without being aware of which was brighter, or two bodily sensations without being aware of whether they occur in the same limb, or of the sounds 'cob' and 'web' without hearing them as 'cobweb', or experience an object looking square but feeling round. But the existence of such disunity is perfectly compatible with the various conscious events being coexperienced, even if their owner cannot, as it were, get them into focus so as to see them as a whole. The second kind of disunity is 'access disunity', where not all conscious states are 'available to the same range of cognitive and behavioural systems'. Someone may observe things which they cannot report orally (although they have the physical ability to utter the requisite words) but can describe in writing; or a person can commit something to memory which they cannot report to others. In some small degree we are all familiar with this kind of phenomenon in ourselves, and again it is perfectly compatible with all the conscious events involved

---

[6] Bayne defines 'representational unity' and 'phenomenal unity' in op.cit. pp. 10–11, and 'representational disunity' and 'access disunity' on pp. 105–11.

being coexperienced. The third kind of disunity is 'phenomenal disunity' where some of a person's conscious events are not had as parts of one overall conscious event—a person experiences e_1, and at the same time experiences e_2, but does not experience (e_1 and e_2).

In Part II of his book Bayne provides a detailed analysis of various phenomena which might lead us to suppose that the persons involved had a phenomenally divided consciousness. These include anosognosia (where patients seem unable to recognize that they have some impairment of consciousness, such as blindness), schizophrenia, and hypnosis (where someone under hypnosis has been told to perform a certain action at a later stage, they do perform it in their post-hypnotic state, but give some apparently false reason for why they are doing it). Bayne argues that in all these cases all the conscious events involved are coexperienced, and that the strange behaviour is to be explained in other ways—for example, that the person is unable or unwilling to express his or her knowledge of all these events. 'Multiple personalities', where a person seems to have totally different personalities at different times, provide a stronger case for a phenomenally disunified consciousness. At time t_1 a person may have one outlook on life and one set of memories, and at a later time t_2 a quite different outlook and set of memories; and at a still later time t_3 revert to the first outlook and memories; and so on. They may at t_3 refer to the person who had their body at the earlier time t_2 as a different person from themself. This diachronic disunity may spill over into synchronic disunity when the person is aware of two personalities at the same time, and when exhibiting one personality seems to regard the person exhibiting the other personality as a different person inhabiting the same body; and yet, as it were, both personalities strive to express themselves through the same body. For these situations also Bayne gives reason to prefer the view that there is just one person who coexperiences all the conscious events causally connected with that body's brain; that person's strange behaviour is to be explained in terms of their having at different times and sometimes at the same time, two different personalities.

The strongest case for divided phenomenal consciousness is undoubtedly that provided by 'split-brain' cases. The brain consists of two hemispheres, a left hemisphere and a right hemisphere, and a brain stem. Some afferent nerve impulses (including those from the right-side limbs and right sides of the two eyes) go in the first instance to the left hemisphere; and some impulses (including those from the left-side limbs and the left sides of the two eyes) go to the right hemisphere; and the two hemispheres control different parts of the body (the left hemisphere controlling the right-side limbs, and also normally speech; and the right hemisphere controlling the left-side limbs). In the normal brain the signals reaching one hemisphere are immediately transmitted to the other one, and the 'instructions' given by one hemisphere are correlated with events in the other hemisphere. But there have been a few people whose corpus callosum (the main nerve tract between the two hemispheres) has been severed by an operation called 'cerebral commissurotomy'. (Most of such operations were performed some years ago when it was believed that this operation provided a cure for epilepsy. Some few other people do not have a corpus callosum as a result of a genetic abnormality.) In the brains of these 'split-brain' people the two hemispheres act in a much more independent way, which raises the issue of whether all the conscious mental events caused by what seems anatomically to be one brain are coexperienced.

What happens is the following. People without a corpus callosum manifest awareness of stimuli presented to the left visual field only by means of bodily organs controlled by the right hemisphere, for example, by movements of the left hand; and of stimuli presented to the right visual field only by means of bodily organs controlled by the left hemisphere, and so normally by speech. Thus suppose you present to one such person a tray containing miscellaneous items and ask that person to pick out those described on cards presented to them. Among the items on the tray are a key, a ring, and a key ring. You present to him the card reading 'KEY RING', but in such a way that the first word 'KEY' is visible only to his left visual field, and 'RING' is visible only to his right visual field. He then ignores the key ring, but picks out the key with his left hand and the ring with his right hand.[7] Often too in the weeks after surgery behaviour under the control of the two hemispheres is in conflict; a patient's left hand may interfere with what they are trying to do with their right hand. One interpretation of what has happened in such cases is that severing the corpus callosum has the consequence that there is now a phenomenally divided consciousness, which is what most experimenters describe as two separate 'consciousnesses', each dependent on a separate brain hemisphere, one consciousness consisting of one set of conscious events and in control of one range of bodily movements, the other consciousness consisting of a different (but largely qualitatively similar) set of conscious events and in control of a different range of bodily movements. Sperry[8] originally argued for this interpretation. But there are other interpretations of what has happened. One is that the subject has only one consciousness, sustained by the left hemisphere; the severing of the corpus callosum frees many of his or her patterns of response (e.g. those of the left hand in typical split brain experiments) from conscious control.[9] These responses then become as automatic as are many of the movements of my limbs when I am driving a car and talking about philosophy at the same time. Another interpretation, advocated by Mackay,[10]

---

[7] My account of the 'split-brain' syndrome is an account of what might be called the 'classic case'. There are patients who are split for touch and not for vision, patients who can compare stimuli in the two fields but not report them, and others who differ in other ways from the classic case. See Bayne op. cit. ch. 9.

[8] 'Everything we have seen so far indicates that the surgery has left these people with two separate minds, that is two separate spheres of consciousness'—R.W. Sperry, 'Brain Bisection and mechanisms of consciousness' in (ed.) J.C. Eccles, *Brain and Conscious Experience*, Springer, 1996, pp. 298–313; see p. 299. Puccetti took this interpretation further, by claiming that commissurotomy could not create a new 'mind or person'; and that the experiments show that all of us, are 'compounds of two persons' all the time. See R. Puccetti, 'Brain Bisection and Personal Identity', *British Journal for the Philosophy of Science*, 24 (1973), 339–55.

[9] See J.C. Eccles, *Facing Reality: Philosophical Adventures by a Brain Scientist*, 1970, pp. 76–80.

[10] D.M. MacKay, 'Divided Brains—Divided Minds?' in (ed.) C.B. Blackmore and S. Greenfield, *Mindwaves*, Blackwell, 1987.

is that there remains a single consciousness sustained by both hemispheres; and that the disunity of response is (to use Bayne's terminology) only 'access disunity'. Yet another interpretation is Bayne's 'switch model', that consciousness in the split-brain switches between the subject's two hemispheres.[11] Normally perhaps it is the left hemisphere which gives rise to consciousness, but sometimes it is the right hemisphere. When the left hemisphere is conscious, the patient is aware only of the word 'ring'; when the right hemisphere is conscious, the subject is aware only of the word 'key'. The subject is never simultaneously conscious of both 'key' and 'ring'; that the patient seems to be simultaneously conscious of both 'key' and 'ring' separately is 'an illusion generated by the rapidity with which the subject's attention switches between the hemispheres'.

My concern is not with which of these interpretations of the split-brain, multiple personality, and similar phenomena, are correct, but with the more fundamental point that they are all hypotheses postulated to explain data. Investigators must form the best judgement they can by the criteria described in Chapter 2 about which is the true hypothesis on the basis of which gives the simplest explanation of the publicly observed data of stimulus and response (including what subjects say about their experiences) and maybe other publicly observable neuroscientific data as well. Each hypothesis has difficulty in explaining some phenomena. If split-brain patients really have two consciousnesses, it might seem probable that we would find more disunity in their everyday behaviour (outside the special laboratory set-up). But they 'can cook, cycle, swim, and play the piano, and naïve observers are rarely aware that they suffer from cognitive impairments'.[12] Yet it is an objection to the 'switch model' that it is complex, because it is 'anatomically implausible. How could consciousness move between hemispheres, given that the main band of fibres connecting the critical regions has been severed?'[13] The model would require a complicated neural mechanism, which there is no other reason to postulate. So investigators who are not the subjects of these strange phenomena must depend for their justified beliefs about how many consciousnesses are involved on which model provides the best explanation of the data.

Yet there is a truth here which neither entails nor is entailed by those data, and about which the data produce at best fallible evidence—two consciousnesses, one aware of 'key' and the other aware of 'ring', or just one consciousness aware of 'key' and responding to 'ring' by some unconscious mechanism, or some rival hypothesis. Analogously scientists who study photographs of particle tracks in cloud chambers, seek the simplest explanation of just why there are those tracks in terms of there being such and such fundamental particles (muons, pions, positrons, or whatever), and the simplest explanation is that most probably true. But the tracks in the photograph are different from the particles which cause them; and the simplest explanation of the tracks may not be the true one (even though it is most probable that it is), and later

---

[11] op. cit. pp. 209–20. [12] Bayne p. 199. [13] Bayne p. 216.

evidence may show that it isn't. And in the case of the severing of the corpus callosum (or of a person evincing multiple personalities in her behaviour, and such like), however much evidence we obtain about patterns of sensory stimulus and bodily response (including what the subject says), and about the extent of neural connections between parts of the brain, all that evidence would be logically compatible both with all the conscious events being coexperienced, and with there being two groups of coexperienced events, members of each group not being coexperienced with members of the other group, and with some rival hypotheses.

A consciousness is 'phenomenally disunified' (i.e. there are 'two consciousnesses') iff its conscious events (say, e_1 and e_2) are not coexperienced as one overall experience (e_1 and e_2). e_1 and e_2 are coexperienced iff the substance (e.g. the human person) who has the conscious event e_1 also has the conscious event e_2, and so that person will be conscious of having e_2 while he or she has e_1 even if they do not see (e_1 and e_2) as a unified experience (and so suffers from representational disunity), and even if the subject is not able to use all of it to guide their speech and limb movements (and so they suffer from access disunity). Coexperienced events belong to the same substance; events not coexperienced belong to different substances, that is, different persons sharing control of the same body. So the fact that we humans coexperience conscious events entails that we are mental substances; and that the full history of the world must include the history of mental substances—even if such phenomena as split-brains have the consequence that we cannot always determine how many mental substances there are in some situation.

2. The diachronic unity of the human person

What constitutes the unity of a human person over time? What is it for a person P_1 at a time t_1 to be the same person as a person P_2 at a later time t_2? All events take time. Having a pain or having a thought lasts for a period of time, however short—it doesn't just happen at an instant. Any period of time consists of two smaller periods of equal length. (A period of 1 sec consists of two periods, each 0.5 sec). Hence any awareness of a conscious event, for example, a pain, is an awareness of oneself as coexperiencing both the first half of the event and also the second half of the event. So any account of the world which has the consequence that the substance which had the first half of one experience was a different substance from the one which had the second half of the experience would be incompatible with the data of consciousness. But why suppose that mental substances last much longer than the 'specious present', the minimum period of time during which one has a conscious event—that is, the minimum period during which one is aware of things happening? Though the notion of the 'specious present' was not known to Kant, in effect he claimed that we do not have any good reason to hold that any mental substance (a 'self' or 'soul', as he called it) lasts longer than the specious present.[14] And Galen Strawson has recently written at length in defence of a similar view.[15]

However, we normally think of humans as substances which continue to exist for a much longer period of time; and we saw in Chapter 1 that there are answers of two kinds to the question of what constitutes the identity of a substance over time. If substances of some kind do not have thisness and are merely bundles of coinstantiated properties, then (in summary) the identity of a substance S_1 at one time t_1 with some substance S_2 at another time t_2 depends (as well as on both substances having the essential properties of the same kind) on the extent to which the properties of each bundle are similar, and whether the bundles are linked over the intervening time by a (spatio-temporal) chain of very similar bundles, each of which causes the existence of the next member of the chain. If, however, substances of some species have thisness (that is, they are what they are, not merely in virtue of their properties), then the identity of S_1 with S_2 depends on their having (as well as the essential properties of their kind) the same thisness (which in the case of physical substances is being made of the same matter).

Most modern philosophers have given analyses of the first kind for the identity of persons, taking into account (to varying degrees) both physical and what they call 'psychological' properties (in my sense pure mental properties). Both Locke[16] and Hume[17] analysed personal identity in terms of close connections between the

---

[14] Kant suggested that there might be a series of substances, each substance lasting for a short period of time and causing the next substance to have apparent memories (which he calls 'consciousnesses') of its states and to have experiences continuous with its own, so that it would seem to each substance that all the experiences in fact belonging to the distinct earlier substances were really its own experiences: Thus:

An elastic ball which impinges on another similar ball in a straight-line communicates to the latter its whole motion, and therefore its whole state (that is, if we take account only of the positions in space). If, then, in analogy with such bodies, we postulate substances such that the one communicates to the other representations together with the consciousness of them, we can conceive a whole series of substances of which the first transmits its state together with its consciousness to the second, the second its own state with that of the preceding substance to the third, and this in turn the states of all the preceding substances together with its own consciousness and with their consciousness to another. The last substance would then be conscious of all the states of the previously changed substances, as being its own states, because they would have been transferred to it together with the consciousness of them. And yet it would not have been one and the same person in all these states.

(I. Kant, *Critique of Pure Reason*, tr. N. Kemp Smith, MacMillan and Co., 1933, A 363 note.)

[15] See his *Selves*, Oxford University Press, 2009. Part I for discussion of exactly how long selves ('thin-subjects' in his terminology) might last (e.g. perhaps less than a third of a second).

[16] John Locke, *An Essay Concerning Human Understanding*, 2. 27.19, describes personal identity as consisting in 'identity of consciousness' by which he means 'apparent memory': 'If Socrates and the present mayor of Queenborough agree [in identity of consciousness—i.e. the mayor apparently remembers what Socrates experienced], they are the same person; if the same Socrates waking and sleeping do not partake of the same consciousness, Socrates waking and sleeping is not the same person'.

[17] David Hume, *A Treatise of Human Nature* 1.4.6 and Appendix. He claims (in 1.4.6.) that a human is 'nothing but a bundle or collection of different perceptions which succeed each other with an inconceivable rapidity', connected by relations of 'resemblance' and 'causation'. But in the Appendix he expresses doubts about whether this account is correct.

instantiations of conscious properties; and one contemporary philosopher who has followed them very closely in this is Derek Parfit.[18] Parfit analyses the identity of a person P_2 at a time t_2 with a person P_1 at an earlier time t_1 (or—to put his claim more precisely— he analyses the extent to which P_1 'survives' as P_2) as consisting in the extent of their psychological connectedness and continuity, brought about by an underlying cause. For Parfit, connectedness is similarity in crucial respects, while continuity is the 'holding of overlapping chains of *strong* connectedness'. Thus two persons are psychologically connected to the extent to which they have (qualitatively) similar (apparent) memories and character. They are psychologically continuous to the extent to which there are between them overlapping chains of strongly connected persons, that is, chains of persons with very similar apparent memories and character. The 'underlying cause' will normally be that of the (anatomically) same brain. So P_2 at t_2 is psychologically connected with some person P_1 at t_1 insofar as P_2 has some of P_1's apparent memories, and a similar character in the sense of similar moral beliefs and desires (which will give rise to similar intentions and so to a similar kind of public behaviour). P_2 at t_2 is psychologically continuous with P_1 at t_1, insofar as there is a chain of persons connecting P_1 and P_2 over the intermediate period, each of which has almost the same apparent memories and character as its predecessor. Then, according to Parfit, P_1 'survives as' P_2 to the extent to which there is psychological connectedness and continuity between them, caused by the operation of the same brain.

The 'animalist' view described earlier held that only physical continuity is relevant. On the 'bundle view' of physical substances described in Chapter 1, physical continuity consists in a causal relation between bundles of similar properties. If physical substances have 'thisness' (a possibility not normally discussed by those who postulate physical continuity as a criterion of personal identity), then physical continuity would consist in similar properties being instantiated in the same chunk of matter (the same body) or one obtained by gradual replacement of matter from an earlier chunk. Other writers (e.g. Nozick)[19] hold that personal identity is a matter of overall satisfaction of both physical and psychological criteria.

All of these views are versions of what is known as the complex view of personal identity, that personal identity is analysable in terms of degrees of continuity (including in Parfit's sense 'connectedness') of other things, that is, of properties and/or matter. By contrast the simple view holds that personal identity is a separate feature of the world. Although some philosophers may wish to hold that some such continuities (of properties or matter) are necessary but not sufficient for personal identity, I shall defend the simple view in its strongest form that (with one small exception to which I shall come later) no such continuities are either necessary or sufficient for the identity of a person

---

[18] D. Parfit, *Reasons and Persons*, Oxford University Press, 1984, Part III.

[19] R. Nozick *Philosophical Explanations*, Oxford University Press, 1981, Part I.

over time (and so for the mental events of a certain later person to be mental events of a certain earlier person). The simple view, as I shall understand it, is the view that each person has a 'thisness' which makes him or her that person, a 'thisness' other than any thisness possessed by the matter of their brains; and that being that person is compatible with having any particular mental properties or any physical properties (and so body) at all. I begin my defence of this position by arguing that it is logically possible that some person P_2 at t_2 can be the same person as a person P_1 at t_1, even if he or she does not apparently remember anything done or experienced by P_1 at t_1 or earlier and has an entirely different character from P_1, and also has a largely different body (including brain) from P_1. The way to show that this is logically possible is by means of various thought experiments, describing situations which seem logically possible and showing these thought experiments entail this view—in the way described in Chapter 2. There are many such thought experiments discussed in the philosophical literature.

Neuroscientists are beginning to develop techniques which allow them to join individual severed nerves. These techniques have so far been more successful in laboratory animals than in humans, and on peripheral nerves rather than on the spinal cord. But these are early days, and it does not seem in the least unreasonable to predict that in the course of time neuroscientists will be able to repair severed spinal nerves in humans, and then eventually bundles of severed brain neurones. That would enable them to remove some human brain organ and replace it by a similar one from another human. I am very well aware that operations of this delicacy are not at present practically possible; but I cannot see that there are any insuperable theoretical difficulties standing in the way of such operations. We are therefore entitled to ask a further question—how many and which parts of a brain would need to be retained in order for the person whose brain it was to continue to exist? For almost everyone would agree that if you replace P_1's whole brain by a different person's brain the person whose body is controlled by that brain is no longer P_1. For almost any animalist who insists that only physical criteria are relevant for determining identity, the replacement of a whole brain in one operation would constitute too great a discontinuity for the same person to continue to exist. And advocates of any complex theory which insists on the relevance of psychological as well as physical continuity would say the same. For since psychological continuity depends on the continuity of apparent memory and character and these are a matter of beliefs, desires, and inclinations to have occurrent thoughts of certain kinds, and since these mental events are (at least for the most part) caused ultimately by brain events, a total brain replacement would mean there being too little continuity between the earlier P_1 and a later P_2 for these to be the same person. On the other hand all theorists would agree that certainly (or at least very, very probably) the mere replacement of a few neurons would not involve P_1 ceasing to exist. So it would seem to follow that if you replace a certain number of brain parts, P_1 would cease to exist; and at that stage or a bit later as you are replacing P_1's brain parts by more of those of another person, the whole operation would have led to the existence of a different subsequent person P_2 having the rest of the body which was previously P_1's. But how many parts and/or how much psychological continuity is necessary and sufficient for P1's continued existence?

As we have seen, the brain consists of two somewhat similar hemispheres plus a brain-stem. Further, there are to some considerable extent brain events which cause similar mental events by way of apparent memories, beliefs, and desires in both hemispheres of any human being. That is, much of the same 'information' is contained in both hemispheres. So one easy way in which a brain transparent operation raising crucial issues about personal identity could be performed is for half of P_1's brain (one hemisphere plus half their brain stem) to be removed from their skull and to be replaced by a half-brain obtained from an identical twin or clone of P_1, whom we will call 'P_{1a}'. Then the other half-brain could be implanted in the vacant place in P_{1a}'s skull. The implanted half-brains could then be 'connected-up' to the half-brains which remained in their skulls and to the rest of the nervous system of the body into which they were implanted. It might be necessary for each implanted half-brain to be in some way 'tuned' to its new companion half-brain so that their neurons interact in a normal way. In such a case we might reasonably expect that both subsequent persons would be conscious, and that their mental lives (apparent memories and kinds of thoughts) would resemble to some extent those of the previous P_1 and to some extent those of the previous P_{1a}. Hence we would reasonably expect that they would both behave to some extent like P_1 and to some extent like P_{1a}, and claim to remember having done some of the actions which P_1 did and some of the actions which P_{1a} did. So we would have similar evidence in respect of each of them, that they were P_1 and that they were P_{1a}.

But in any such case both resulting persons could not be the original person P_1. For if they were both the same person as the original person they would be the same person as each other (if a is the same as b, and b is the same as c, then a is the same as c) and they are not. They now have different experiences and lead different lives. There remain three other possible results of the experiment: that the person who has P_1's left half-brain is P_1, that the person who has P_1's right half-brain is P_1, or that neither is P_1. (It may be that this traumatic operation destroys P_1, and that although connecting the relevant nerve bundles creates two new persons, neither is P_1.) But we could not be certain which of those three possibilities had occurred.

True, it might turn out that the result of this experiment (as shown by the subject's memory claims and behaviour) was that one resulting person had a mental life very similar to that of the earlier P_1—it might be the person who had the same body (other than brain) as P_1, while the other person had a mental life very different from that of P_1. In that case there would be no room for serious doubt about which resulting person was P_1. But then a different experiment of transplanting brain parts would be likely to yield two equal moderately good candidates for being P_1. We could remove both of P_1's half-brains, and put each in a skull of a different clone from which a half-brain had been removed. Or we could exchange only certain brain parts from both halves of the brains. So there are various possible partial brain transplants in which we could very probably create two more or less equally plausible candidates for being the original person.

It just might, however, turn out that all such experiments designed to create two persons, each containing parts of the brain of two previous persons, never had the outcome that both new persons were equally good candidates for being the original person P_1. Perhaps there would always be one resulting person who had a mental life much more like that of P_1, than did the other candidate; or—alternatively—it might always happen that neither candidate was much like P_1. That, however, still wouldn't settle the issue of what had happened to P_1, since as with the similar issue at stake in section 1, the traumatic operation might—it seems logically possible—have had the consequence that P_1 lost much of their memory and came to have quite a different kind of mental life, while the other resulting person who was not P_1 came to resemble P_1 much more in their apparent memories and mental life. Even if this is improbable, it seems strongly to remain a logical possibility, and so very probably is logically possible.

It is tempting to say that it would be a matter of arbitrary definition which of the three possibilities (this resulting person was P_1, that resulting person was P_1, neither resulting person was P_1) was the actual one. But there seems to be a crucial factual issue here—which can be shown if we imagine that before any split-brain operation was done, P_1 was captured by a mad surgeon who tells them that such an operation is going to be performed on them; and the surgeon tells them just which parts of P_1's brain will be transplanted into which skulls. The surgeon tells P_1 (and—let us suppose—P_1 has good reason to believe the surgeon) that one of the two subsequent persons will receive a million dollars and have a subsequently enjoyable life, and that the other subsequent person will be subjected to a life of torture. The surgeon asks P_1 to choose whether the person who will receive such-and-such parts will be rewarded and the other person tortured, or the person who will receive the other parts will be rewarded and the first person tortured; and the surgeon promises to carry out P_1's wishes (and again let us suppose that P_1 has good reason to believe the surgeon). Being selfish, P_1 wishes to be rewarded and not tortured. So how is P_1 to choose? Whether someone's future life will be happy or painful, or whether they will continue to exist at all after the operation (which is how I am understanding a later person being the 'same person' as the earlier person) do seem very clearly to be factual questions. Yet, as P_1 awaits the transplant and knows exactly what will happen to his or her brain, they are in no position to know what will happen to them, and so in no position to know how to choose which subsequent person will be rewarded. Any choice would be a 'risk', as Bernard Williams, who first introduced a similar example into the philosophical literature, put the point.[20] When we know everything about which planks in the ship of Theseus (see Chapter 5, section 5) have been replaced or reassembled when, then we know all there is to know

---

[20] See his 'The Self and the Future', *Philosophical Review*, 77 (1968).

about what is the same and what is different about the subsequent ships; although there are different ways in which we can describe what has happened, they are logically equivalent to each other. But when we know everything about the extent to which later persons have the same brains and the same apparent memories and other mental life as the earlier persons in the half-brain transplant experiment, it does look very strongly that there is still something all-important to know—as the mad surgeon addition to the story brings out: it is the all-important fact about who survives the operation and what happens to them. The difference arises because persons have conscious lives, and are not simply inanimate objects. This thought experiment does suggest very strongly to almost anyone that the continued existence or non-existence of a person are both logically compatible with a person having only some of that person's brain matter and some mental continuity with him or her.

Parfit claims that what matters in such cases is not identity (that is, which—if any—later person is me), but what he calls 'survival', which is for Parfit a matter of degree. I 'survive' on Parfit's definition, given more precisely above, to the extent to which the mental life of some later person involves 'apparent memories of' and is caused by my mental life. So what matters, according to Parfit is whether some later person 'apparently remembers' my past experiences and is caused to do so by those experiences. But, whether or not that matters, another thing that many people think matters (as Parfit would—I think—acknowledge), is that they themselves survive (in the normal sense of 'continue to exist'). The mere existence of a later person whose mental events are in large part caused by and include apparent memories of my past life is not what I hope for, when I hope to survive an operation (in the normal sense of 'survive'). I want a subsequent person to be me, whether or not that person can remember much of my previous life. But, whatever I or Parfit or anyone else hope for, my point is that there is an evident crucial difference between these two suppositions. There could be a hundred different future persons whose mental events are in large part caused by mine and include apparent memories of my past life; what would make at most one of them me cannot be such mere similarity and causal connection. And conversely I could—it is logically possible—continue to exist even if I had forgotten my past life, and my character (my personality) had changed.

The complex theories discussed so far all assume that in any situation there is one correct answer to the question of which (if any) later person is P_1. An alternative form of complex theory holds that personal identity is a matter of degree. P_2 is the same person as P_1 to the extent to which P_2 has P_1's brain, apparent memories, and character. And so, this form of theory would hold, really none of us are the same person as the person whom we are normally thought to have been 20 years ago—since our brains consist to some extent of different neurons and we have different apparent memories. It would then follow that the result of half-brain transplant operations would be a division—a 'fission'—of P_1 into two persons; each of the later persons would be partly the original person. This theory would certainly avoid the problem of the arbitrariness of any normal form of complex theory—it seems arbitrary to claim that P_2 is the same person as P_1 iff he has just so many of P_1's brain parts and apparent memories, but not if he has very slightly fewer of these. I cannot, however, make much sense of this theory. For—to consider again the mad surgeon story—if the mad surgeon carries out his plans on P_1, one subsequent person will be rewarded and one subsequent person will be tortured. If both persons were partly P_1, it would follow that P_1 has a subsequent life partly of enjoyment and partly of torture. Yet neither of the future persons will have such a mixed life. For this kind of reason, fission of a person seems logically impossible. But even if fission were a possible result of the operation, it cannot be a necessary truth that the operation will have this result, because the history of all the physical bits and all the mental properties associated with them seems logically compatible with neither subsequent person being only partly the original person. It seems to be still a possibility that, just as it does seem very strongly at least logically possible that the resulting person is fully me if my heart is replaced, so one of the subsequent persons will be fully P_1 even if some of P_1's brain is replaced and they have a new body. If, however, we include both subsequent persons being partly P_1 as only a logically possible result (and not a necessary result) of the operation, we would now be ignorant about which out of four (rather than three) possible results of the operation had in fact occurred. Since the possibility of partial survival does not affect the fact that we would still be ignorant of the result of the experiment, I shall ignore this possibility in future.

So what follows from this thought experiment is that at least for many possible replacements of brain parts it is logically possible that the replacements take place and the person remains the same, and it is also logically possible that the replacements take place and the person does not remain the same. The preservation of certain brain parts is neither logically necessary not logically sufficient for personal identity.

In the thought experiments described so far each subsequent person has some of the brain of the original person. But here is a thought experiment where this isn't the case. Suppose that P_1 undergoes an operation in which a small diseased part of his or her brain (a tenth of the whole brain) is replaced by a similar part from another brain (perhaps that of a clone of P_1). People sometimes do have parts of the brain of that size removed, and it is normally supposed that the person after the operation is the same as the person before the operation. It is plausible to suppose that adding a replacement part after removing the diseased part wouldn't change the identity of the person whose brain it was. So it seems at least logically possible—and plausibly true—that this operation keeps the original person alive, that the new brain is still that person's brain. But now suppose that each year a different tenth of P_1's brain is removed and replaced by a similar part from another brain (perhaps that of a different clone of P_1 on each occasion). At the end of ten years there is a person whose brain is made of entirely different matter. It seems at least logically possible that—because the process has been gradual and each new part has become integrated into the brain before a new operation is done—the resulting person is still P_1. It seems of course also logically possible that the resulting person is not P_1. Once again, there seems to be a truth about whether P_1 has survived the series of operations (in the normal sense of 'continued to exist' through the series of operations), which is not entailed by and does not entail any truth about the amount of brain matter and the similarity of mental life shared between the original and finally resulting persons.

I now add a further detail to the above thought experiment to make it even more plausible that it is logically possible that P_1 would survive such a series of operations. I noted earlier that every conscious event lasts for the short period of the 'specious present' and so consists of two co-experienced events which each last for half that period. A pain which lasts for 1 sec consists, for example, of two pains which each last for 0.5 sec, co-experienced by the same person. So every experience whatsoever involves an owner of that experience. Conscious events which occur in periods of 'specious present' may overlap. The second half of the experience of a pain during a specious present may overlap with the first half of an experience of some noise; this noise may continue for a short time (during several overlapping periods of specious present), and overlap with a certain tactual experience, and so on. (I distinguish an overlap of experiences from the different case where one experience begins at the instant at which another experience ends.) When two conscious events overlap, they are events of the same substance; the overlap entails this.[21] Given the overlap, the events are events of the same mental substance, whether or not any physical criteria for sameness are satisfied.[22] And it is an evident datum of human experience that sometimes conscious events do overlap, and so that we are mental substances who last longer than the specious present. To deny that it is evident that we sometimes experience such overlaps would be to deny that we are sometimes aware of tunes or long sentences, which last longer than the specious present in which we hear a single note or word.

Now suppose that during each of the ten operations in which brain parts are replaced, the patient remains conscious and has a series of overlapping conscious experiences lasting for the whole of the operation. That seems logically possible. (It is normal for patients to be kept conscious during brain operations, since the brain has no pain sensors.) If P_1 did have such series of overlapping experiences on all ten occasions, clearly P_1 would have survived all the operations. So if it is logically possible that there be such series of overlapping experiences, it is logically possible that P_1 survives the series of operations (in the normal sense of 'survive'). So anyone who denies the logical possibility of someone surviving this ordeal is committed to denying the logical possibility of someone remaining conscious with overlapping experiences during

---

[21] Galen Strawson allows that two experiences may overlap, but claims that even if they do there is no reason to suppose that the subject of the first experience is the same substance as the subject of the second experience which it overlaps: 'There could very well be a temporally continuous period of experience that isn't an experientially unitary period of experience' (op. cit. p. 395). I find this remark perplexing, since the claim that experiences overlap just is the claim that they are experienced by the same substance (the same 'thin-subject' in Strawson's terminology).

[22] I owe this argument from the overlaps of experiences to John Foster. See his 'In Self-Defence' in (ed.) G.F. MacDonald, *Perception and Identity, Essays presented to A.J. Ayer*, Macmillan, 1979—'it is in the identity of a stream that we primarily discern the identity of a subject' (op.cit. p. 176). See also his *The Immaterial Self*, Routledge, 1991, pp. 246–50.

each of the ten operations. I doubt if many philosophers would really want to deny that. So I suggest that it is very plausible indeed to suppose that it is logically possible that a person should continue to exist with a totally new brain produced by gradual replacement of parts.

I have found that when such stories are told in sufficient detail, it does begin to seem to most people (even to those who still deny that the different outcomes are all metaphysically possible) that each of the different outcomes (e.g. me surviving and me not surviving) is logically possible. I argued in Chapter 2 that what seems logically possible probably is logically possible. And, given that some person surviving in the cases just discussed is logically possible, there seems no reason to insist that any continuities of body or physical and mental properties whatsoever are either logically necessary or (with one small exception) logically sufficient for the continued existence of a particular person. The exception is that to which I have drawn attention in the previous paragraph: the occurrence of overlapping conscious events is a sufficient condition for their being events of the same person. That (with this exception) no such continuities are logically sufficient is suggested by the thought experiment considered by Kant and by Galen Strawson, to which I referred earlier. It does seem logically possible that (given that the two sets of conscious events do not overlap) one person might have the conscious events caused by a given brain up to a certain instant, and a different person have the conscious events caused by the same brain after that instant, while the latter person has qualitatively the same desires and beliefs (including apparent memories), and so the same character, as the earlier person. That no such continuities are logically necessary is suggested by fictional stories in which some person acquires a new body (without the new body resulting from any gradual replacement of parts of their old body) with a new character, having forgotten all their past life. While an advocate of the simple theory acknowledges that the more brain parts you replace in one operation, the more probable it is that the resulting person is not P_1, the complex theorist is committed to the view that being P_1 is constituted by having a brain to some degree continuous with that of the earlier P_1. But the disagreements between different complex theorists about what degree of continuity is needed for a person to continue to exist, and the implausibility (indicated by the already mentioned thought experiments) of insisting on any particular degree of continuity, do indicate very strongly that our concept of personal identity is not a concept of the complex kind.

Given that it is logically possible that a person continue to exist without there being any continuity of physical or mental properties, the next question is whether it is metaphysically possible that each of us, each human being—not merely some logically possible person in some logically possible universe—should continue to exist without the existence of such continuities. Is it metaphysically possible that I should acquire a new body and/or lose my apparent memories, and find myself with a new character? Or that the person in interaction with my brain until they fell asleep last night was not me, but a different person with qualitatively identical beliefs and desires to me when

I woke up this morning? I suggest that all the thought experiments described here seem equally logically possible for each of us when 'I' is substituted for 'P₁'. Yet if we were ignorant of what 'I' referred to, then what is logically possible might not be metaphysically possible. I argued in Chapter 1 that a logically possible sentence is metaphysically possible iff the substances designated in it are picked out by informative designators. A rigid designator 'ϕ' is an 'informative designator' iff anyone (when favourably positioned, faculties in working order, and not subject to illusion) can recognize when something is (now) ϕ and when it is not, merely in virtue of knowing what the word 'ϕ' means (that is, having the linguistic knowledge of how to use it), and can make simple inferences involving ϕ. So what sort of designator is 'I' or our own name as used by each of us? What sort of designators are 'I' or 'Richard Swinburne' as used by me? These seem to be informative designators. If I know how to use these words, then—when favourably positioned, with faculties in working order, and not subject to illusion—I can't be mistaken about when to apply them; and when I am considering applying these words to a person in virtue of that person being the subject of a present experience, no mistake at all is possible. I am in Shoemaker's phrase 'immune to error though misidentification'.[23] I cannot know how to use the word 'I', recognize that someone is having some conscious event (e.g. some pain), and still wonder whether it is I or someone else who is having that event, in the way that an early explorer can know how to use the word 'Everest', and yet wonder whether the mountain at which they are looking is Everest. My knowledge of how to use 'I', like my knowledge of how to use 'green' and 'square', means that I know the nature of what I am talking about when I use the word. Hence if 'I will exist tomorrow with a new brain' or 'I will exist tomorrow without any memory of my previous existence' or 'I will continue to exist when my brain, memory, and character are replaced all at once' or 'I began to exist only a minute ago inheriting all the beliefs and desires of another person who previously interacted with my brain' are logically possible, they are also metaphysically possible. And since I can know this merely in virtue of knowing to what my use of the word 'I' refers, other people can know the same about themselves. Each of us, we may properly conclude, can continue to exist without any continuity of brain, memory, or character. It follows that the simple theory of personal identity is true.

Of course I can still misremember what I did in the past, and indeed misremember how I used the word 'I' in the past. But this kind of problem arises with every claim whatsoever about the past. 'Green' is an informative designator of a property, but I may still misremember which things were green and even what I meant by 'green' in the past. The difference between informative and uninformative designators is that (when my faculties are in working order, I am favourably positioned and not subject to

---

[23] Sydney Shoemaker, 'Introspection and the Self' in (ed.) Q. Cassam, *Self-Knowledge*, Oxford University Press, 1994, p. 82. I can of course misidentify myself if I pick out myself by means of a body—for example, believing falsely that the person seen in the mirror is me—but that will be a case of illusion.

illusion) I can recognize which objects are correctly picked out at the present time by informative designators, but not necessarily when they are picked out by uninformative designators (in the absence of further information). And so I always know what a claim about the past or future amounts to when it is made by informative designators, but not when it is made by uninformative designators, whether or not I have any reason for supposing it to be true. For to claim that some informatively designated object a will exist or have an informatively designated property ϕ tomorrow is to just claim that a existing or being ϕ today, something I can understand, will hold tomorrow. It follows that I can understand what it is for me to exist in a new body tomorrow or to have had a different body yesterday, or to have such-and-such experiences yesterday or tomorrow. My situation contrasts with the examples of 'Everest' and 'water' discussed in Chapter 1. I would not know what would constitute a past or future substance being water or Everest if I was merely in the position of the 'water' user in the eighteenth century, or the early explorers who named the mountain seen from Tibet 'Everest'.

What led to the complex theory of personal identity, either as an account of the identity conditions of logically possible persons or—more strongly—as an account of the identity conditions of actual humans, was an attempt to analyse a concept derivable from only some properties of the paradigm examples on which our actual concept is based. We certainly can construct concepts having some connection with the actual concept which are versions of the complex view, according to which 'personal identity' is a matter of the degree of continuity of brain or behaviour (including speech), or of the kind of mental events which we ascribe to others on the basis of their behaviour, such as memory or character. Concepts of this kind are natural concepts to derive from paradigm examples of one earlier person being the same person as some later person, when neither of these persons is oneself, together with paradigm examples of what each of us remembers in respect of the content of what the remembered person did and experienced at various past times. But our actual concept of personal identity is in fact derived not only from the content of paradigm examples of our memories in respect of what the remembered person did and experienced, but also from their content in respect of who did and experienced these things, and also from certain paradigm examples of present experiences. For it is part of the content of apparent memories that the rememberer was the person who did and experienced these things, and our present experiences include experiences of conscious events lasting some time longer than that of the specious present.

These latter experiences are experiences of events consisting of two or more successive overlapping events being had by the same substance (oneself). Thereby we derive an understanding of what personal identity over time consists in; that is, in being a particular subject of experiences (that is, of conscious events), and so a mental substance who exists over that time. This understanding of what we are experiencing over time in no way derives from beliefs about physical continuities or continuities in respect of memory or other mental events.

This concept of being a particular mental substance, whose continuity is not to be understood in terms of continuities of other kinds, is reinforced by our personal memories of what we did or experienced a short time ago. A personal memory is an apparent memory 'from the inside' of what one did or experienced oneself which one has straight-off, not by inference from a diary or from what someone else told one that one had done or experienced; it is not merely apparent memory of what someone else would have seen one doing or experiencing. The content of such apparent memory will often, though not always, include faint images of the perceptions and intentions involved in doing the actions or having the experiences. But for an apparent memory of mine to qualify as my apparent personal memory, something else (additional to it being an apparent experience 'from the inside') is necessary—the belief, not resulting from inference from anything else, that it was I who did or experienced those things 'from the inside'. After all my brain might have been tampered with in such a way that it caused a belief that someone had done and experienced certain things accompanied by images (of how things felt from the inside) qualitatively identical to those which someone who did and experienced these things would have had; but if I had no belief about who did and experienced the things of which I was aware 'from the inside', I wouldn't count as having an apparent personal memory of these things. A belief about someone having done or experienced certain things doesn't count as a personal memory belief if it requires an inference to establish that those things happened to the believer. Who did the action or had the experience is part of the content of the apparent memory. As Reid put it, 'my memory testifies not only that [a certain past action] was done, but that it was done by me who now remembers it.'[24] Sydney Shoemaker devised the term 'Q-memory'[25] to describe an apparent memory 'from the inside' in which it is not part of the content of the Q-memory that the memorizer was the same person as the person who did and experienced the things Q-remembered. There are no doubt such Q-memories. But most of us do not have them very often, if ever; and the content of apparent personal memories, of which virtually all of us have innumerably many, concern what one did or experienced oneself.

Not merely do we derive our concept of personal identity in these ways, but—given the principle of credulity that we should believe that things are as they seem to be in the absence of counter-evidence—it is such a strong deliverance of experience for all of us that we are aware of ourselves as continuing mental substances for very short periods of time during which we seem to recall overlapping experiences that it is hard to see that

---

[24] Thomas Reid, *Essays on the Intellectual Powers of Man*, III.4.

[25] Sydney Shoemaker, 'Persons and their Pasts', *American Philosophical Quarterly*, 7 (1970), 269–85. Contrary to what Shoemaker seems to suggest, it is not—I suggest—part of the content of the claim that 'I' did so-and-so, that the person who did so-and-so was spatio-temporally continuous with myself. However, as I acknowledge in the text, the existence of such spatio-temporal continuity is evidence in favour of a claim that some apparent personal memory is indeed a real memory; and evidence that 'I' do not have spatio-temporal continuity with the person who did so-and-so is evidence against the apparent memory claim being a real memory. But none of this is conclusive evidence, given the account in this chapter of the meaning of such claims.

there could be any counter-evidence to rebut this result, that we really are such subjects.[26]

But while such overlaps entail that the same person is having the experiences, overlap is not necessary for sameness of persons.[27] For the understanding of ourselves as mental substances derived from innumerable paradigm examples of overlapping experiences, reinforces the understanding provided by our apparent personal memories of conscious events which do not overlap with our memories of them as memories of the mental substances which we are, and again the principle of credulity makes us justified in taking these apparent memories as true memories in the absence of counter-evidence. It is the past of the mental substance which we are that we recall in personal memory. Having understood what our past existence amounts to, we can then see what our future existence would amount to, and it is with the future of this substance that our self-centred hopes and fears are concerned. It is because we derive our concept of personal identity in the ways which I have just described that we naturally regard the thought experiments already discussed as descriptions of logically possible events.

It then seems to follow that since continuity of body (and in particular of brain) and of physical and mental properties with some past person are not what constitute me having been that past person, and since they obviously provide grounds for claims about who I was, their role must be evidential—that is, they make it to different degrees probable that I was that person. When my brain is at time t2 much the same as ⌐

---

[26] Hume claimed that we have no idea (i.e. no coherent concept) of the self, because we do not find an impression of the self which remains 'invariably the same, thro' the whole course of our lives, from which we could device that idea'. For 'when I enter most intimately into what I call *myself*, I always stumble on some particular perception or other, of heat or cold, light or shade, love or hatred, pain or pleasure. I never catch *myself* at any time without a perception.' (*A Treatise of Human Nature*, 1.4.6.) Hume is surely correct to claim that he never catches himself without a 'perception' (i.e. a conscious event); but his bare datum is not 'perceptions', but simultaneous coinstantiations of 'perceptions', or successions of overlapping 'perceptions' experienced by a common subject himself.

[27] Foster (*The Immaterial Self*, pp. 251–61) argues that identity after an interval of unconsciousness is entailed by what he calls 'potential serial consciousness'. Suppose a series of experiences A to be followed by a period of unconsciousness followed by a series of experiences B. He claims that A and B are experiences of the same person iff, had A continued until the time of the beginning of B and then B occurred, A would have merged into B. If the owner of A had not fallen asleep but stayed awake until the time of B, he would have owned B. This seems correct, but of no use as a criterion for determining whether the owner of A is also the owner of B, since whether 'A would have merged into B' depends on who owns B. In order not to beg the question in advance that the two series of experiences are experiences (conscious events) belonging to the same person, we must individuate them as series of types of conscious events (e.g. series of notes of a certain pitch) caused in a certain way (e.g. by the same brain). But then the mere fact that if A had continued, it would have changed into *a* B (in the sense of *a* series of notes of exactly the same pitch) does not guarantee that the actual B which occurred after the interval was an experience of the same person as experienced A. For in the interval in the actual world some other person could—it is logically (and I suggest—for the kind of reason given in the text—metaphysically) possible—have taken over that brain and experienced *a* B, a change of ownership which—we may suppose—would have been prevented by the continuance of A. In order to rule out that possibility, we have to individuate B, not merely by the types of conscious events which it contains and the brain events which caused them, but by who experiences B, and then we beg the question. Of course if B is experienced by P who is the person who experienced A, then if A had continued and B had occurred, A would have merged into B.

the brain of a person between t1 and t2, I at t1 and the person with my brain all the time between t1 and t2 have strongly continuous apparent personal memories of what the person at t1 did and experienced which—on other evidence—coincides with what that person did and experienced, and a character at t1 strongly continuous with the character of the person with my brain from t1 to t2, it is enormously probable that I was the person who had my brain at t1 and thereafter. The reason it is enormously probable that under those normal conditions I was that person is that (1) (apparent) memory beliefs are probably true (in the absence of counter-evidence) and my apparent memories of myself concern the actions and experiences of the person who had a brain strongly continuous with my present brain, and (2) our mental life affects our public behaviour, and the simplest supposition about the strong continuity of the public memory claims and character caused by the operation of a brain strongly continuous from t1 to t2, itself caused (as I argued in Chapter 4) by the mental events of the person whose brain it is, is that the latter are mental events inhering in the same person. It would be less simple and so less probably true to suppose that the strongly continuous public memory claims and character caused by the same brain are caused more ultimately by mental events of different persons. But insofar as a person does not have memory beliefs about the actions and experiences of the person who had a brain strongly continuous with his or her present brain (and perhaps ones concerning the acts of a person or persons with different brains) and does not have a character strongly continuous with the character of the person who had his or her brain previously, it is less and less probable that the brain, memory, and character are those of the same person.

It would be a mistake to deny that our evidence of our own personal identity can be very strong, on the grounds that it depends crucially on our apparent memory. For, as I noted in Chapter 2, all our knowledge about the past depends ultimately on apparent memory. We depend for that knowledge on our apparent memories of what we did, of what other people testify that they did, and on what the words of their (oral or written) testimony mean. And insofar as our knowledge of the past depends on inference from physical remains, we depend on the probable truth of some scientific theory to provide justification for that inference, and that too—we noted in Chapter 2—depends crucially on apparent memory. The coincidence of apparent personal memories with each other, and with the simplest explanation of certain phenomena, does render it very probable that they are true. But our justification for our belief that they do coincide in this way depends on our own apparent personal memory that they do; and so we must have very considerable justification for believing our own apparent memory if we are to have any well justified belief about the past at all.

I conclude that there are truths about which later person is the same person as an earlier person, some of which we are justified in believing and some of which are quite undiscoverable. Hence a full history of the world must include or entail the history of mental substances, which (with the small exception that I have noted) are the sub-stances they are quite independently of any continuities of matter or properties. If we were to divide up the world solely into physical substances, and allow them to have conscious events only contingently, something all-important would have been omitted. As it is with the past of the mental substance which we are that our regrets and self-satisfactions are concerned, and on the future of that substance that our self-centred hopes and fears are focused, our concern is with personal identity as analysed by the simple theory. So in future I shall assume that persons are mental substances of the kind analysed by the simple theory. The continued existence of a person over time consists in the continued existence of a mental substance; and it is metaphysically possible that that substance acquire a totally new body, totally new apparent memories and character. I and each of my readers, being persons, are mental substances in this sense; and having at some time a kind of body and an ancestry similar to those persons called 'human' today, we are human persons.

3. Humans are pure mental substances

Is it logically possible that a person could continue to exist without a body at all? I suggest that it is. A body is a physical substance, which is the body of some animate being. For a physical substance to be my body, something like the following is required. I must be able to move it and some of its parts as (instrumentally) basic actions, its changing states caused by changes elsewhere in the physical world (e.g. via light rays impinging on my eyes or sound waves impinging on my ears) must be the means by which I learn about the rest of the physical world, and I must be (at least to some extent) tied down to acting and acquiring knowledge through it. Now suppose I find myself able at will gradually to bring it about that the region of the world containing physical substances which I can move by basic actions and through which I learn about the physical world gradually changes, and that it is then physical substances within that new region which I can move as basic actions and which provide the means by which I learn about the rest of the physical world. I might for example gradually find myself able to bring it about that I become able to move the chair in the corner instead of my present body as a basic action, and at the same time to learn about the world from the light rays and so on impinging on that chair instead of the light rays landing on my present body. If I had such powers, I would no longer be tied down to acting through one physical substance. So in the postulated situation, it would seem, not that I had a new body (the chair), but rather that I had no body at all. Some readers might want to say that in the postulated situation I would still have a body, but a different body as I move around the world. Yet now suppose I lost all causal contact with the physical world, and yet continued to have thoughts and sensations. I argued in chapter 3 that it is logically possible that there be pure mental events which do not supervene on physical events. I argued earlier in this chapter that any mental event lasts for a period of time, and that what makes it one event is that its two half-events are coexperienced by the same person. So a person can have successive pure mental events. I have now argued that the identity of a person is quite independent of any physical continuities. Hence it is logically possible that I lose all contact with the physical world and yet continue to have thoughts and feelings. Given the logical possibility of these two situations, or at least the logical possibility of the second situation, entails that it is logically possible that I could exist without any body. And so, as before, since 'I' is an informative designator, it is not merely logically possible but also metaphysically possible that I could exist without my body; and what goes for me goes for any other human person.

But if a person can exist without a body, and so without any physical properties, only pure mental properties are essential for his or her existence, and so a person is a pure mental substance. So no pure mental substance supervenes on any physical substance. On the understanding of a human person as one who has or had at some time a body and a mental life similar to that of persons currently called 'human', it follows that we humans are pure mental substances.

For me to exist, I need only to have some pure mental property (for example, some belief). I do not need to have any particular mental properties. But I would pick out the same substance if I used to pick out myself fewer or more of the mental properties of which I am currently aware as co-instantiated. Thus suppose I pick out myself as the subject of two separate sensations (say, a visual sensation and a tactual sensation). But if at the same time I also had two other sensations (say, an auditory sensation and a gustatory sensation) which I did not have, I could have picked out the same myself by means of those latter sensations. And if I had done so, the fact that I had the former (visual and tactual) sensations would have made no difference to who was picked out. But then the same person would have been picked out if I had not had those (visual and tactual) sensations at all, the only ones I did have. So I would have been the same person if I had had quite other sensations instead. And so for mental properties generally. And yet I might only exist long enough to have these particular sensations or thoughts. The examples therefore suggest that for a pure mental substance who exists for a longer period of time, there can be no principled argument for claiming that there are any limits at all to the kind and length of mental life which can be had by that substance. And, as we have seen, which (if any) body and physical properties a pure mental substance possesses makes no difference to who they are. It follows that each pure mental substance (and so each person) has a thisness which makes that person who they are, which is independent of any thisness possessed by physical matter.

This point is brought out by the apparent logical possibility of there being a different world instead of our actual world W_1, a world W_2 in which for each substance in W_1 there is a substance which has the same properties as it and conversely (and any physical matter underlying the properties is the same in both worlds), but where a person S who exists in W_1 does not exist in W_2. The person who lives in W_2 the life (physical and mental) which S lives in W_1 is not S. And surely our world could be different solely in the respect that the person who lived my life was not me. For it is not entailed by the full description of the world in its physical aspects and in respect of which bundles of mental properties are coinstantiated (at a time and over time) that I, picked out as the actual subject of certain mental properties, should have the body and the particular physical or mental properties which I have; or that the person who has that body and those properties should be me. We can see this if we imagine that before this world exists we are shown a film of what is going to happen in it; and that the film in some way shows us what will be the mental lives of the people in the world. Each of us would still not know—am I going to live one of the lives in this world? And if so, which one? So because W_2 can be seen, I suggest, when we reflect on it, to be logically possible; and because—as before—persons can be picked out by themselves by the informative designator 'I' or a name which is their own name for themselves, W_2 is a metaphysically possible world. So again it follows that each person has a 'thisness', a uniqueness, which makes them the person they are quite apart from the particular mental properties they have and any physical properties (and any thisness) possessed by their body. (Although I can know what the difference between a world in which I exist and a qualitatively identical world in which I do not exist consists in, because 'I' and 'Richard Swinburne' as used by me are informative designators, other people cannot know this in a full way—because they must refer to me via some uninformative designator which picks me out in virtue of non-essential publicly observable properties. As used by others 'Richard Swinburne' is an uninformative designator. Others can know that there would be a difference between the two worlds in respect of who exists in them, but they cannot know who it is that exists in one world and not in the other in the sense that they cannot know the essence of that person.[28])

We normally suppose that a person's body is part of the person and that the physical properties which belong to that body (e.g. shape and mass) belong to the person. But in that case, given my arguments, the body is only a contingent part of the person, and the body's properties are only contingent properties of the person. I suggest that a way of describing the world which treated a person's 'body', not as a part of the person, but as a separate constituent of the world with which the person was in close causal interaction would enable us to give just as full a description of the world, as does our more normal way of describing the world.[29]

Although my arguments, I claim, show that the existence of consciousness requires a pure mental substance whose consciousness it is, why should we suppose that that substance continues to exist when it is not conscious[30] (i.e. does not have conscious

---

[28] Thus using the expression 'semantically stable referring to' in the same sense as my 'having an informative designator for' (see Chapter 1, section 2), John Hawthorne writes: 'We do not have any semantically stable way of referring to any given person, such as Saul Kripke. I can't take a cognitive photograph of his haecceity....Whatever the means I have of referring to him, it seems clear that there will be a counterpart community that uses the same reference-fixing devices to refer to a different individual.' (Hawthorne, 'Causal Structuralism' in his *Metaphysical Essays*, p. 218.)

[29] Descartes is often supposed to think about the world in this other way, understanding his body as a substance distinct from the substance which is himself (his self or soul). But in fact Descartes seems to oscillate between these two ways of thinking. For examples and commentary, see pp. 63–6 of Brian Smart, 'How can Persons be ascribed M-Predicates', *Mind*, 86 (1977), 49–66.

[30] Descartes holds that 'thinking', by which he seems to mean 'having conscious experiences', is essential for a person's existence:

I saw that while I could conceive that I had no body . . . I could not conceive that I was not. On the other hand, if I had only ceased from thinking . . . I should have no reason for thinking that I had existed. From this I knew that I was a substance the whole nature or essence of which is to think and that for its existence there is

events. I am still conscious in my sense if I am dreaming)? While we recall some periods of dreaming when we wake up, we have no reason to suppose that we are having conscious experiences all the time we are asleep. For some of the time we are asleep, we exhibit 'rapid eye movements' (REMs), and our brain rhythms are much more similar to those of awake persons than are the rhythms during non-REM sleep. If a person is woken up during a period of REM-sleep, they typically report that they were in the middle of a dream, the details of which they can report; whereas if a person is woken up during a period of non-REM sleep, they typically report only having 'thoughts' while being woken. Since we can seldom recall much about our dreams unless we write them down or tell someone about them immediately on waking, it may well be that we are conscious all the time we are asleep—perhaps vague images and incoherent thoughts cross our minds every moment of our waking and sleeping lives. But this does not seem very probable. So, on the assumption that we have periods of dreamless sleep when we do not have conscious events, and so in such periods there is no conscious person having the brain of the human person who was previously conscious, why suppose that a person with that brain exists at all? Why suppose that human mental substances continue to exist while asleep? My answer is that wherever the person having the brain of a previously conscious person is woken up, he or she will claim to have apparent memories of the conscious events of that previous person. It is clearly far simpler to suppose that the same person continues to exist rather than they are recreated each time they awake, and for that reason it is probably true that that person continues to exist during dreamless sleep. While asleep a person will still have the beliefs and desires which they had before ceasing to be conscious. But when a person's brain ceases to function in the kind of way which can be stirred into causing conscious experiences, then it is most improbable that the brain is any longer the brain of a living person. Yet since any pure mental substance (and so any person) needs only some pure mental property (not necessarily a conscious property) in order to exist, a person may still exist (even in a non-conscious state) with or without a body. We would however need further evidence in order to have a justified belief that when their brain ceases to function, the person does still exist. This might be evidence that some subsequent person has the apparent memories and character of the original person, when there is no more probable explanation of why this happened; or evidence making it probable that the teaching of some religious tradition has been authorized

---

no need of any place, nor does it depend on any material thing. (R. Descartes, *Discourse on the Method*, (trans. E.S. Haldane and G.R.T. Ross), *Collected works of Descartes*, vol. I., Cambridge University Press, 1972, p. 101.)

I argue above that a person can continue to exist without having conscious experiences. But if we read Descartes's 'thinking' as 'having pure mental events', then I am happy to endorse his conclusion. For I argued earlier that our continued existence depends on our continuing to have mental events, but they may be continuing mental events (e.g. beliefs and desires), not necessarily conscious events. The usual objection to the possibility of Descartes' supposition is that maybe 'I' designates merely my body; but, given that 'I' is an informative designator, that objection fails.

by God, where that teaching includes teaching that persons continue to exist after their death on earth.

I set out in Chapter 3 two alternative theories of what it is for a person who is not currently conscious of having a certain belief or desire to have that belief or desire: the dispositional theory, that the person has a disposition to become aware of the desire or belief and act on it when relevant, and the categorical theory that the desire or belief exists as an attitude toward an apparently conceivable event, just like a conscious belief or desire except in the respect that the person is not conscious of it. In his picture of the unconscious in his *New Introductory Lectures on Psychoanalysis*, Freud seems to take literally the notion of a realm of beliefs and desires, which are just like conscious beliefs and desires except that they are unconscious, to be distinguished from the 'somatic processes' which cause the unconscious beliefs and desires.[31] Although Freud's formal position was a thoroughly physicalist one, he gave us good reason to understand the human mental life as consisting of a structure of interacting beliefs and desires, some of them conscious and some repressed from consciousness. And if we accept the need to postulate repressed beliefs and desires as categorical mental states, there is no reason to deny that status to all the beliefs and desires of which we are not currently conscious, even if we have not repressed them.

It is noteworthy that despite a recent boom in psychological research into which unconscious beliefs and desires we have,[32] there is virtually no consideration by psychologists and very little by recent philosophers of mind of what having such beliefs and desires consists in. The most thorough discussion of this is in three chapters of C.D. Broad's book *The Mind and its Place in Nature*, first published in 1925. Broad's conclusion (if we ignore his views about the relevance of parapsychology) is in effect that—despite the Freudian-type argument of the need to postulate such categorical unconscious states in order to explain the data of psychoanalysis—while either theory might be true of humans, it is simpler not to postulate categorical states when all the conscious phenomena and behaviour can be explained by brain events which cause

---

[31] Thus: 'The oldest and best meaning of the word "unconscious" is the descriptive one; we call "unconscious" any mental process the existence of which we are obliged to assume—because, for instance, we infer it in some way from its effects—but of which we are not directly aware. We have the same relation to that mental process as we have to a mental process in another person, except that it belongs to ourselves. If we want to be more accurate, we should modify the statement by saying that we call a process "unconscious" when we have to assume that it was active *at a certain time*, although *at that time* we knew nothing about it. This restriction reminds us that most conscious processes are conscious only for a short period; quite soon they become *latent*, though they can easily become conscious again. We could also say that they had become unconscious, if we were certain that they were still something mental when they were in the latent condition.' (S. Freud, *New Introductory Lectures on Psychoanalysis,* trans. W.J.H. Sprott, Hogarth Press, 1937, p. 93.) Freud writes of the id, the largest part of the unconscious, that 'it is somewhere in direct contact with somatic processes, and takes over from them instinctual needs and gives them mental expression' (op. cit. p. 98).

[32] See the large volume (ed.) R.R. Hassin and others, *The New Unconscious,* Oxford University Press, 2005.

dispositional states.[33] In that case the only categorical mental properties possessed by humans would be conscious properties. Our character, our whole attitude to life, is, however, a matter of our continuing mental states, our beliefs about what the world is like and our desires to behave in this or that way. So if (as I have argued) we are essentially pure mental substances, it would then follow that our characters are not intrinsic to us but depend on the brains with which we are in causal interaction—although of course our brains (and so the conscious desires and beliefs to which they later give rise) are formed partly by our previous conscious choices of how to act. Nevertheless it follows on the dispositional theory that if we became disembodied, we would have no character.

The dispositional theory does however seem to have a major problem, that it is forced to postulate the operation of quite different processes when we reach theoretical conclusions or form intentions, dependent on whether we are influenced by conscious or non-conscious beliefs. I argued in Chapter 4 that we must hold that when we consciously form a belief from some other consciously held belief in accord with some rational process, we must suppose that the latter belief causes us to form the former belief. Analogously, given the falsity of epiphenomenalism, it seems fairly obvious that when we form some ultimate intention (e.g. to walk home) and have some conscious belief about how to fulfil the intention (e.g. the belief that the Woodstock Road leads home), and so form the basic intention to begin to walk along the Woodstock Road, that the ultimate intention together with the belief cause the basic intention. So it is natural to suppose that something similar happens when the relevant belief is not conscious. (In this example my belief that the Woodstock Road leads home would not normally enter my consciousness—it is so obvious to me that if I intend to walk home, I must intend to begin to walk along the Woodstock Road.) But on the dispositional theory a quite different process must be involved if I am not conscious of my belief from the process when I am conscious of my belief. For, according to the dispositional theory, all that my unconscious belief amounts to is its disposition to cause effects, and the manifestation of this disposition on this occasion consists in brain events causing the ultimate intention to be followed by the basic intention. Whereas on the categorical theory a categorical mental state of an attitude to a proposition is at work in both cases—the only difference is that in the second case the belief is below the level of consciousness.

---

[33] C.D. Broad, *The Mind and its Place in Nature*, Kegan Paul, Trench, Trubner and Co , 1924, chs 8–10. Broad calls his preferred theory, which I have called a 'dispositional' theory, 'epiphenomenalist'; but it is not 'epiphenomenalist' in the sense which I defined in Chapter 4 and which is, I think, the normal sense. Broad is not claiming that our unconscious beliefs do not cause effects, but rather that their sole nature is to cause effects. Broad emphasizes that the categorical theory is compatible with the view that persons are essentially embodied (i.e. have essential physical properties), although he suggests that it fits more naturally with what he calls the 'pure ego' view, that is the view that the person is a pure mental substance. He qualifies the view of chs 8–10 by claiming that insofar as there is evidence of life after death (and so of our existence without our present bodies) that would tip the balance in favour of the categorical theory (which he later calls the 'compound theory'); and he suggests in a later chapter that there is some such evidence provided by parapsychology.

What holds for this simple example applies generally. Most of the beliefs involved in our inferences to other beliefs, and most of the beliefs which lead us to do this action rather than that action, are taken for granted rather than expressed to ourselves in conscious thoughts; and yet we are influenced by them in virtue of their propositional content in just the same way as we would have been if they had been conscious. Consider a longer example of a detective expressing to himself his reasoning leading to the conclusion 'Jones did the murder'. Each new step in his reasoning constitutes the expression in judgement of a newly acquired belief. What leads the detective to acquire that belief is what has gone before. Yet in such a case, and especially when the reasoning is not deductive, often each step would not have been taken but for other beliefs which the detective takes for granted but does not express to himself. Thus he may move from 'Smith said he was in Edinburgh on Wednesday morning and two people claimed to see him there' to 'he was not in London on Wednesday morning'. In the background are a number of beliefs which alone made this a reasonable step to take, for example, 'Edinburgh is 400 miles from London', 'trains take more than four hours to travel 400 miles', 'Smith would not be at all likely to travel by air', etc. The previous beliefs, both expressed and unexpressed, lead to the new belief. Now the detective looking back on the process will affirm that he came to acquire his new belief under the pressure of reasons, through seeing what was involved in the old beliefs, guided by beliefs which he did not need to express to himself; he was, it seemed to him, drawing out the consequences of the beliefs which he did so express. It seems clear to the detective that he would not have reached the new belief but for his old beliefs (both those which he expressed to himself and those which he did not express to himself). So it would seem a simpler and so more probably true theory to suppose that the same kind of process is at work when non-conscious beliefs influence us, as when conscious ones do; and that is what the categorical theory claims: that non-conscious beliefs are categorical states (attitudes to propositions) exactly like conscious beliefs except that we are not conscious of them. And what applies to beliefs applies for similar reasons to desires.

The categorical theory pictures humans as having a vast number of largely unconscious categorical mental states, beliefs, and desires connected with each other in rational ways. (We cannot consciously hold beliefs known to be incompatible; and we tend to hold beliefs which follow from and are compatible with a general worldview.) Our system of value beliefs and desires constitute our character. When we reason consciously we 'look in' on these beliefs and desires; and they then give rise to conscious intentions and thoughts. It seems evident, however, that brain events must also be at work in holding in place such a system of unconscious beliefs and desires; and that brain events interact all the time with our beliefs and desires to sustain our processes of rational influence or to lead us on occasion to reason and behave irrationally. I shall discuss this interaction more fully in Chapter 7. I am, however, sensitive to the difficulty that the categorical theory involves postulating a very large number of unobserved events to provide the best explanation of observable ones; and my subsequent argument in Chapter 7 is in no way dependent on the categorical theory.

4. The human soul

I have been arguing that it is compatible with any full description of the respects in which some subsequent person is (or is not) continuous with an earlier me in having such-and-such parts of the brain of the earlier me, and such-and-such continuity of physical and mental properties (other than overlapping conscious properties) with the earlier me, that that person is me and also compatible with that person not being me. Yet, I argued in Chapter 1, although the principle of the identity of indiscernibles is not a necessary truth, what is a necessary truth is a stronger principle which I called 'the principle of the identity of composites', that 'there cannot (logically) be two things which have all the same parts having all the same properties, arranged in the same way.' A substance made of the same parts with the same properties arranged in the same way must be the same substance; and so if a substance is a different substance from some earlier substance, there must be some parts or properties which are different. Hence, given that an earlier person who had all the same physical parts as me, and all the same physical and mental properties as me, could, it is metaphysically possible, not be me, and could, it is metaphysically possible, be me, it follows that the difference must consist in the presence or absence of some non-physical part. I must now have a non-physical part (i.e. a part which is a pure mental substance) which makes me me, which the earlier person (even if they were in all other respects the same) would not have had if they were not me. We may call this non-physical part of me my 'soul'. In using the word 'soul' like this I am using it in the way that Plato uses '$\psi\upsilon\chi\acute{\eta}$' to denote the essential part of a human.[34] Further, given that it is metaphysically possible that I become disembodied, it follows that—whether embodied or not—I need only a pure mental part, my soul, in order to exist. My soul therefore carries my 'thisness'. However—given the normal understanding of a human being on earth as constituted (in part) by a body—it follows that humans, unlike other possible pure mental substances such as ghosts or poltergeists, each have their body as a contingent part. So I now consist of two parts—my soul (the essential part) and my body (a non-essential part), each of them separate substances. My physical properties are mine in virtue of belonging to my body; and since—given the metaphysical possibility of disembodiment in which I continue to possess pure mental properties—mental properties are mine in virtue of belonging to my soul. But that does not have the consequence that there are two events of thinking going on when I am thinking—my soul thinking and me thinking; for since the two canonical descriptions of the event mutually entail each other, the events are the same (see Chapter 1, section 4).[35]

---

[34] Plato *Phaedo* 105c. In answer to the question 'What causes the body . . . to be alive?' Socrates gives the answer, 'the soul'. He goes on (106e) to affirm that when a human dies, the immortal part, the soul, goes to Hades.

[35] For discussion of the claim of Eric T. Olson that there are serious difficulties in compound dualism (the view that the person who I am has on earth two parts, body and soul) which do not arise for 'simple dualism' (the view that I always have only one part, my soul, and my body is not part of me) see Additional Note G.

It follows from all this that, whether or not physical substances are mere bundles of co-instantiated properties, pure mental substances are not. If physical substances have thisness, then the hylemorphic account applies to them. They are forms (essential properties) instantiated in matter (which is what provides the 'thisness' which individuates them). The plausibility of this account of physical substances if they have thisness, gives rise to a temptation to give a similar account of pure mental substances (which—I have argued—definitely do have thisness) and to analyse them as forms (essential properties) instantiated in some mental stuff, soul-stuff. St. Bonaventure held that the human soul consists of 'spiritual' stuff (*materia*) informed by a form (properties);[36] and in the first edition of my book *The Evolution of the Soul*[37] I adopted this view myself. But it now seems to me that we understand by 'stuff' something capable of being divided into smaller chunks of the same stuff; and given my earlier argument that humans (and so their souls) cannot be divided, the soul cannot be made of any stuff.

Aristotle held that the soul was the 'form' of the body, but he understood 'soul' in a very different sense from Plato. The soul, for Aristotle, is a collection of certain properties which someone needs to have in order to be human (a certain bodily shape, certain ways of behaving and thinking). The human soul is thus the same in all humans. When a chunk of matter is endowed with these properties (i.e. is informed by the human soul), it becomes a human being (which is the same as a functioning human body). What makes one human a different human from another human is the different matter of which each human (i.e. each human body) is made.[38] This is a straightforward physicalist (or perhaps property dualist) theory of the identity of human persons.

Aquinas tried to produce a version of Aristotle's theory that the soul is the form (in Aristotle's sense) of the body compatible with the normal Christian view that the souls of the dead exist immediately after death in Heaven or elsewhere where they have some sort of conscious life, but are only reunited with a body later at the General Resurrection. Unlike the souls of inanimate things and of animals, the human soul is, he holds, a 'subsistent thing', which is capable of existing (after death, for a period) without being united with a body.[39] He calls it, in his earlier work *Summa Contra Gentiles*, an 'intellectual substance',[40] but stresses in *Summa Theologiae* that, as Eleanore Stump puts, it is not a 'complete substance in its own right'.[41] This is because it is not in its 'natural' condition unless it is united to the body. The soul on its own is not fully a human. But, as Aquinas seems to allow even in *Summa Theologiae*, the soul is a substance;[42] and he is surely right to

[36] See Bonaventure, *II Sentences*, 17.1.2. Responsio.

[37] op. cit. pp. 153–4. This passage in the first edition (1986) is repeated in the main text of the revised edition (1997), but corrected in the New Appendix C to that edition (pp. 327–32).

[38] 'When we have the whole, such and such a form in this flesh and these bones, this is Callias or Socrates; and they are different in virtue of their matter (for that is different), but the same in form (for that is indivisible)'—Aristotle *Metaphysics* 1034ª, 5–7.

[39] For Aquinas's view on this, see his *Summa Theologiae*, Ia.75 and 76 and *Summa Contra Gentiles*, 2.46–end.

[40] See, for example, *Summa Contra Gentiles*, 90.1.

[41] Eleanore Stump, *Aquinas*, Routledge, 2003, p. 210.

[42] See *Summa Theologiae*, Ia.75.4. obj. 2, and how Aquinas responds to this objection in ad. 2.

concede this, since in his terminology as well of course as in the terminology of this book, whether something is a substance is independent of whether it is in its 'natural' condition. It is after all, Aquinas holds, by its nature 'immortal'.[43] Stump claims that one reason why Aquinas would not wish to call a soul a substance is that it is not an *integral* part of a human being';[44] it is rather what makes the matter of what becomes a human body into that body. It is the principle of its operation. For that reason, Stump claims, Aquinas holds that the soul 'could not interact causally with the matter which it informs';[45] the principle of operation of a thing is not a part of that thing. But, since the soul can exist independently of the body, it clearly is a part of the whole living human being; and its presence, Aquinas must hold, is a necessary and sufficient causal condition of the body behaving in the way characteristic of the human body. So Aquinas clearly is telling us that this form (the soul of a human being) is a substance.

And so, Aquinas has to hold, it is a very unusual form in that, unlike the forms of inanimate things and of animals, it can exist and have a life without being instantiated in matter. Further, he holds that the soul of each human differs from the soul of each other human. He claims that a soul is individuated by the body which it is 'fitted' to occupy—souls differ from each other because they have the relation of 'fitting' to different bodies; unlike normal forms, a human soul can fit only one body.[46] But, as Duns Scotus objected,[47] that could only hold if there was something intrinsic to a soul which made it fit only one body; and then that intrinsic feature would already be enough to individuate the soul. If a key differs from another key in virtue of being able to fit a different lock, then that entails that it has a different shape. So in order to hold that the soul is the form (in Aristotle's sense) of the body, Aquinas has to hold also that the form of each human body is not a universal (a collection of properties), but an individual substance which can exist independently of being instantiated in matter. But with these changes to the understanding of 'form', the only remaining content to the claim that the soul is the 'form' of the body is that the soul is naturally equipped to operate through a body. It is the kind of thing which can acquire beliefs and execute intentions through a body, and its typical desires (both sensory—to eat and drink—and non-sensory—to interact with other persons) are desires which are naturally expressed through a body. Humans have a natural inclination to act through bodies. Maybe Plato did not stress this point, but Descartes may be making just this point when he writes that 'it is not sufficient that [the rational soul] be lodged in the human body like a pilot in his ship.'[48] But while noting that Plato and Descartes may not stress this point enough, and that Aquinas expresses his view in a very misleading terminology and seems not to acknowledge that the differences between souls must be intrinsic to them, I can detect no real difference in their accounts of the relation of soul and body

[43] *Summa Theologiae*, Ia. 75.6.   [44] Stump, op. cit. p. 209.   [45] op. cit. p. 210.
[46] *Summa Contra Gentiles*, 81.8.   [47] *Ordinatio*, II d3. p1.q7 nn. 230–1.
[48] Descartes, op. cit. p. 118.

between Aquinas's view and the Plato–Descartes view with which many writers contrast it.

So, I conclude that the human soul cannot be analysed as composed of form and matter; it is non-physical and indivisible, and possesses only pure mental properties. This is the view of Plato and Descartes, and—if he is read in a certain way—also the view of Duns Scotus (to whom philosophers owe the concept of 'thisness', *haecceitas*).[49] Each of us on earth is a compound of a soul (a simple) and a body (an organism). Under normal circumstances a soul can only function (have a conscious life) if the brain with which it interacts functions in the normal way, and it can only operate on the world via operating on that brain. A non-physical substance does not 'occupy' space in the sense of filling it and excluding other things; and so if we wish to say that it has a location, we need to define the sense in which it has a location. If it interacts with the physical world, it is natural to define it as being located in the place where it interacts with that world. On this definition a person's soul is located where their brain is. Yet we are not (normally) aware of interacting with our brains. We are aware of what is happening in the world by its effects on our bodies (e.g. on our sense organs) and have non-inferential awareness of what is happening in various parts of our bodies (but not of the brain events which cause that awareness), and we perform movements of parts of the body other than our brains as instrumentally basic acts (without being aware of the brain events through which we cause these movements). It therefore seems natural to think of ourselves, and so our souls, the essential part of ourselves, as located in that part of the physical world of which we are most directly aware and which we can influence most directly. The soul of a human living on earth is located (in one sense) in that human's brain and (in another sense) in the whole of that human's body. But under abnormal circumstances (e.g. at death), my argument shows that it is (metaphysically) possible that the soul could become connected to (i.e. interact with) a new body, or exist (and even have a conscious life) without a body. And if in the latter case there was then no particular region of the world on which it could act (even temporarily), we could not then say that it had a location at all.

The conclusion of this long chapter is that a full history of the world will have to include (or to allow us to deduce) the histories of both human bodies and human souls; and that—it is metaphysically possible—there can be bodies without souls and souls without bodies, although under the normal circumstances of earthly life there is no reason to suppose that souls and bodies come apart.

---

[49] For a more detailed account of Duns Scotus's treatment of this topic and two different ways of understanding it, see my *The Christian God*, Oxford University Press, 1994, pp. 47–50.

7

Free Will

1. Moral beliefs and the scope for decision

I argued in Chapter 4 that brain events often cause mental events including conscious events, and that conscious events often cause brain events and also other conscious events. Among the conscious events which cause brain events are intentions, and the brain events which they cause in turn cause public behaviour. I argued in Chapter 5 that intentions are simply the intentional exercises of causal influence, normally via a brain event in order to produce some bodily movement and thereby affect the world in a certain way. I argued in Chapter 6 that humans are pure mental substances. So humans are pure mental substances who intentionally cause their bodies to move in certain ways. I turn in this chapter to examine the extent to which humans are caused by other events to form their intentions, that is, to exercise causal influence. In this section I consider the influence of mental events of other kinds on the formation of our intentions.

Humans are in part rational beings, and—in the respect that we form the intentions which we do because we have reasons for forming those intentions—fully rational. Most of our intentions are intentions about how to fulfil some other intention, and so in the end about how to fulfil what I called our 'ultimate' intentions. These intentions about how to fulfil ultimate intentions I will call 'executive intentions', our reason for having which is to fulfil an ultimate intention. Our ultimate intentions determine our executive intentions. If an agent has only one ultimate intention, and a strong belief about what is the quickest way to fulfil that intention, they inevitably form an intention to take that way. If—when staying at a hotel—I form an ultimate intention to go to bed, and believe strongly that my hotel bedroom is number 324 on the third floor, I will form an executive intention to go to the third floor and look for number 324. If I believe strongly that the lift is situated at the end of the corridor, and that the lift will provide the quickest way to get to the third floor, I will form the intention to go to the end of the corridor. And so on. The dynamics of the interaction of beliefs and ultimate intentions in forming executive intentions is more complicated when an agent's ultimate intention is more complicated, for example, if the agent has an ultimate intention to achieve two separate goals, the intention to achieve one being stronger than the intention to achieve the other. I may, for example, intend to go to bed, and also intend to stop at a hotel shop on the way so long as the extra time involved is not longer than five minutes. My belief about what is the quickest way of fulfilling the combined intention will be different from my belief about what is the quickest way of fulfilling the single intention. The dynamics become more complicated still if I have competing beliefs of different strengths, for example, if my belief that the probability that the lift is at the end of the corridor is only somewhat stronger than my belief that it is in the other direction where there are also stairs by which I can reach the shop, albeit less quickly than by the lift. We do not of course normally go through an explicit reasoning procedure in working out how to execute our intentions (and we could not normally ascribe numerical values to the relative strengths of the ultimate intentions and the probabilities of different ways of fulfilling them). I am claiming only that we respond in the way that we believe is probably the quickest way to execute our intentions, given their relative strengths. When we believe that there are two· or more different equally quick ways to execute some ultimate intention (and no quicker way), we need to choose between these ways by an arbitrary decision, and any such decision will constitute a rational way of executing our ultimate intention in the light of our beliefs about how we can do so.[1]

Our reasons for forming some particular ultimate intention will be either that we desire to do so and/or that we believe that it is in some way a good thing to do so for a reason other than that we desire to do so. The reader will recall from Chapter 3 that I understand by an agent having a desire to do some action, the agent having an inclination to do that action not solely because of a belief that doing so would be a step towards achieving some other goal. A desire which leads to an ultimate intention may be a very short-term one; someone may swear simply because they desire to swear. But of course most of us have desires to achieve longer-term goals. Normally we regard fulfilling any desire as such to be a good thing. But we also often believe that an action is intrinsically good to do for a reason independent of whether we desire to do it; and we sometimes believe that the intrinsic goodness of doing an action makes it on balance good to do even if we have a strong desire not to do it.

Value beliefs (in the sense in which I shall understand this notion) are beliefs about the objective intrinsic goodness or badness of doing actions of different kinds, and about their overall goodness or badness (that is whether they are good or bad on balance when all their different properties are weighed together). I mean by the beliefs concerning the 'objective' goodness or badness of actions that the beliefs are beliefs that their goodness or badness is a fact about certain actions which does not depend on the believer believing it to be such or desiring to do it. Value beliefs as such, unlike other beliefs, motivate us. All other beliefs need to be combined with some desire in order to incline us to act—a belief that there is food in the cupboard will only lead to any action when combined with some desire, for example,

---

[1] For a fuller account of how complicated beliefs and intentions interact see my *Epistemic Justification*, ch. 2, especially pp. 40–6. (What I call 'intentions' here, I called 'purposes' there.)

to eat some food. A belief that an action is good in this sense, however, by itself gives the believer a reason for doing it and thereby at least a minimum inclination to do it, and a belief that it is bad gives that person a reason for not doing it and thereby at least a minimum inclination not to do it. And the stronger the value belief, the stronger the inclination to conform to it (although this inclination may still be weak). An agent has most reason to do the action which is—the agent believes—best overall among incompatible alternative actions. But the agent may also have a stronger desire to do some different alternative action; and they will then have to choose whether to do what they most desire or what they believe would be best to do. (The reader will recall from Chapter 3 that I define the strongest desire as the one on which the agent would act automatically and naturally if they had no value belief that it would not be the best action to do so; the second strongest desire is the one on which the agent would act if they had no value belief that it would not be the best action to do so and did not have the strongest desire. And so on.)

A person's values may be of a very peculiar kind. A person may believe, for example, that the only actions worth doing by them or anyone else are actions of walking on alternate paving stones. But such beliefs will still be value beliefs if the agent sees them as providing a reason for doing the action, which may conflict with the agent's desires. The agent who believes that some action would be overall best because it would be an action of walking on alternate paving stones, may still feel tired and fed up with doing such actions and have a strongest desire not to bother doing them in future. In that case the agent will have to choose between forcing him or herself once again to do the overall best action (as they believe it to be), and yielding to a desire not to do it. A desire to do an action other than the best is naturally called a temptation.

It would of course be very peculiar for someone to have as their only value belief, that the only actions worth doing by them or anyone else are actions of walking on alternate paving stones. When our value beliefs overlap substantially with the beliefs of most other humans about the overall goodness or badness of actions of different kinds, we recognize that our value beliefs and theirs are beliefs about a special kind of overriding goodness, and that the value beliefs of other such humans which we do not share as well as the ones which we do are beliefs of this kind. I shall call all such beliefs 'moral beliefs'. Although much of what I shall have to say about conflicts between desires and moral beliefs applies, I believe, to all conflicts between desires and value beliefs of any kind, for reasons of space I will concern myself only with conflicts of the former kind, because that is the form which the desire/value belief conflict takes in almost all of us. Because our moral beliefs are of crucial importance in the formation of our intentions, and also because—I shall be arguing in Chapter 8—we need them in order to have a certain kind of free will. I need to say a lot more about what I understand by a 'moral belief', the relevance of some of which will not be apparent until Chapter 8.

Although there is in the world a wide diversity of beliefs about which actions are good or bad, overall good or overall bad, almost all of us have some beliefs in common with most of those who disagree with us about some of the properties which make actions overall good or bad—different beliefs in common with different groups; and many of us share many such beliefs with many others. The community of all humans, I suggest, is a community with overlapping beliefs of this kind. Among such beliefs about which actions are good are beliefs about which actions are obligatory to do (of overriding importance to do); and among such beliefs about which actions are bad are beliefs about what is obligatory not to do (overriding importance not to do), that is, wrong to do. (I shall understand by a 'right' action one which is not wrong.) Obligations are debts to others. Hence, we suppose, it is normally more important to fulfil one's obligations than to do good actions which are not obligatory; and it is more important not to do what is wrong than not to do bad actions which are not wrong. Almost all people agree that—except perhaps under certain circumstances—causing pleasure and saving life are good actions; keeping promises, feeding and educating their children, caring for their aged parents, are obligatory actions; telling lies, killing or wounding others who have done no harm are wrong actions. But then different groups put different qualifications on these very general claims—killing is good if it is a punishment for serious wrongdoing, pleasure is good only if it is pleasure at what causes others no pain; and so on. Hence the considerable extent of disagreement about what is overall good or bad or of overriding importance to do or not to do. But the extent of this disagreement must not obscure the fact that the disagreement takes place within a network of considerations about which there is very considerable agreement. We thus derive from similar examples of beliefs about which actions are 'overall' good or bad, or of 'overriding' importance to do or not to do, the reasons for doing which have some connection with the beliefs of others of us about these matters, the concept of a 'moral' belief.

I stress the wide sense in which I am using the expression 'moral belief'. I am not using it in any of the many different narrower ways in which it is sometimes used—for example, merely to denote a belief about obligations, or a belief about obligations to other humans, or a belief about obligations in respect of personal relations. A belief that it is better for me to give a certain amount of money to feed the hungry than to use that money for a foreign holiday which I need in order to refresh myself is in my sense a moral belief. But so too, on this definition, would be a belief that it would be better for me to use the money for a foreign holiday than to give it to feed the hungry—so long as my belief fits in with beliefs about the overall goodness or badness of actions which many other people have. It may fit in with such beliefs, for example, if I believe it because I believe that I am weary and that it is good that everyone (not only I) should refresh themselves when weary. (In such cases people sometimes say 'I owe it to myself' to do the action.)

My definition of 'morally good' actions includes actions of benefiting others in ways in which we have no obligation to benefit them; these are 'supererogatory' good actions. No one is obliged to sacrifice their own life to save the life of some stranger, but it is a supererogatory good action if they do (so long as they do not thereby fail to fulfil an obligation to some third person), an action even better than merely fulfilling an obligation. My definition of 'morally' good actions also includes actions which are worthwhile even if they benefit no one except oneself—for example, keeping physically fit, or learning a foreign language, or sculpting a beautiful ice-statue which will be seen by no one else and which will melt the next day. Such actions are clearly not obligatory. Nevertheless, most of us are inclined to think, it is good if someone does not waste their 'talents', but develops and applies them creatively. Plausibly also there are bad actions which are not wrong—for example, slouching in front of the TV all day watching pornographic films, even if this wrongs no one. I call such actions 'infravetatory' actions.

Moral beliefs as such, I suggest, like all value beliefs and unlike other beliefs, motivate us. I could not believe that some action was really morally good to do (as opposed to being what other people call 'morally good') and yet not see myself as having a reason for doing it. And I could not see myself as having a reason for doing it unless I had some inclination to do it. And the better I believe some good action to be, the greater as such is my inclination to do it. But such a moral inclination may be weak, and agents may show 'weakness of will' in yielding to some incompatible inclination (including merely the inclination not to do the relevant action) instead.

To call some mental event a moral 'belief' implies that it is a belief in a proposition about how things are; one which in the believer's view corresponds to how things are. I claim that almost all of us have moral beliefs in this sense. Some philosophers have seemed to deny this, claiming that 'moral beliefs' are really not beliefs at all, but merely attitudes towards, in my terminology desires about, the propositions said to be 'believed'. On such a 'non-cognitivist' view, to 'believe', for example, that it is always wrong for a state to allow capital punishment (i.e. allow the imposition of the death penalty for a crime) is merely to have a desire that capital punishment be not practiced, or that the agent and others campaign against it.[2] Now certainly some people may not have moral beliefs (in my sense) but merely desires about the occurrence of actions about which the rest of us have moral beliefs, but I suggest that almost all of us have moral beliefs. We believe that the propositions we are said to 'believe' would be true independently of whether we believed them. It may however be the case, as other philosophers have maintained, that we are under an 'error' or 'illusion' in believing that propositions about the objective goodness or badness of actions are or even could (logically) be true; and that therefore we ought to regard our attitudes to those propositions as mere desires. I will call those who hold that some moral beliefs are true moral objectivists, in contrast to moral subjectivists who deny that any moral beliefs are true.[3] My concern in this chapter being with the effects of the beliefs which

---

[2] The best known forms of moral non-cognitivism are the 'emotivism' of C.L. Stevenson, which holds that moral utterances are expressions of emotion which the utterer desires others to share; and the 'prescriptivism' of R.L. Hare, which holds that moral utterances are expressions of commitment which the utterer desires others to follow.

[3] The best known defender of 'error theory' is J.L. Mackie. See his *Ethics, Inventing Right and Wrong*, Penguin, 1977, ch. 1.

most of us have, not with whether those beliefs are or could be true, I need to take no view at this stage about whether moral objectivism is correct. I assume merely that almost all of us are in fact objectivists about morality,[4] and I shall now spell out what moral objectivism involves. We believe that certain particular actions are good and other particular actions are bad, and we believe that if anyone disagrees with us they are mistaken. For example, most people believe that Hitler did a morally wrong action in commanding the extermination of the Jews. We do, however, of course differ from each other considerably in our beliefs about which actions are morally good, or bad; and some people believe that most actions are morally indifferent (neither good nor bad).

Like our non-moral beliefs, our moral beliefs are held partly because of other beliefs which we hold and change as those other beliefs change. Moral beliefs have logical connections of two kinds with other beliefs, which influence how they change as the other beliefs change. The first connection arises from the logically necessary truth that moral properties (being good or bad, obligatory or wrong) supervene on non-moral properties, often called 'natural properties'.[5] In Chapter 1 I illustrated the concept of supervenience by the example of the moral theory of utilitarianism, according to which moral properties supervene on hedonic properties; different moral theories have different views from utilitarianism about which are the non-moral properties on which moral properties supervene. What this supervenience amounts to is that particular actions are morally good or bad, right or wrong, because of some non-moral properties which they have. Thus, plausibly what Hitler did on such and such occasions in 1942 and 1943 was morally wrong because it was an act of genocide; what mother Teresa did in Calcutta was good because it was an act of feeding the starving; and so on. No action can be just morally good or bad; it is good or bad because it has certain other non-moral properties—those of the kinds which I have illustrated. And any other action which had just those non-moral properties would have the same moral properties. The conjunction of non-moral properties which gives rise to the moral property

---

[4] In thus tying believing an action to be morally good to having some inclination to do it, while maintaining that the content of a moral 'belief' (the proposition believed) is in the believer's view true, I take an internalist realist view of the content of moral beliefs. One alternative view to this is moral externalism, the view that believing an action to be morally good, is just like believing an action to have any other property such as causing pain or giving pleasure, and has to be combined with some inclination to do morally good action before it leads to an inclination to do the action. The other alternative view is moral non-cognitivism, which can be described more precisely as 'moral internalist anti-realism': the view described above that 'believing' an action to be good is simply being inclined to approve it, or act or react in some other way with respect to it, without the content of the belief being true or false. Internalist realism about morality seeks to combine the positive insights of the two alternative approaches to moral philosophy just described. It accepts the positive insight of non-cognitivist theories that having a moral belief gives the believer some inclination to act on it when it is relevant to the believer's decisions; but it also accepts the positive insight of externalist theories that 'beliefs' about what is morally good or bad really are beliefs which are in the believer's view true. For three recent discussions of views about the nature of moral belief, all largely favouring both internalist realism and moral objectivism, see Michael Smith, *The Moral Problem* (Blackwell, 1994), Russ Shafer-Landau, *Moral Realism* (Oxford University Press, 2003), and Derek Parfit *On What Matters* (Oxford University Press, 2011), Parts I and VI.

[5] 'Everyone agrees that it is an a priori truth that the moral supervenes on the natural' (Smith op.cit. p. 22.)

may be a long one or a short one. It may be that all acts of telling lies are bad, or it may be that all acts of telling lies in such and such circumstances (the description of which is a long one) are bad. But it must be that if there is a (logically and so metaphysically possible) world W in which a certain action *a* having various non-moral properties (e.g. being an act of killing someone to whom the killer had a certain kind of relation) was bad, there could not be another world W★ which was exactly the same as W in all non-moral respects, but in which *a* was not bad. A difference in moral properties has to arise from a difference in non-moral properties. If a certain sort of killing is not bad in one world, but bad in another world, there must be some (logically contingent non-moral) difference between the two worlds (e.g. in social organization or the prevalence of crime) which makes for the moral difference.

The supervenience of moral properties on non-moral properties must be supervenience of the kind analysed in Chapter 1. Our concept of the moral is such that it makes no *sense* to suppose both that there is a world W in which *a* is wrong and a world W★ exactly the same as W except that in W★ *a* is (overall) good. It follows that there are metaphysically necessary truths of the form 'If an action has non-moral properties A, B, and C, it is morally good', 'If an action has non-moral properties C and D, it is morally wrong', and so on. If there are moral truths, there are necessary fundamental moral truths—ones which hold in all words. I re-emphasize that, for all I have said so far, these may often be very complicated principles—for example, 'All actions of promise breaking in circumstances C, D, E, F, and G are wrong', rather than just 'All actions of promise breaking are wrong'. All moral truths are either necessary (of the above kind) or contingent. Contingent (particular) moral truths (e.g. that what you did yesterday was good) derive their truth from some contingent non-moral truth (e.g. that what you did yesterday was to feed the starving) and some necessary moral truth (e.g. that all acts of feeding the starving are good). The fundamental moral truths are necessary truths. The only way to deny this latter claim is to deny that there are true moral propositions.

Given this logical supervenience of the moral on the non-moral, it follows that our particular moral beliefs are causally sustained by a conjunction of particular non-moral beliefs, and fundamental moral beliefs, that is, beliefs in some necessary moral principles. Someone's belief that executing some particular person Jones, found guilty of murder, is right might, for example, be causally sustained by some non-moral belief that the prospect of capital punishment for murder deters would-be murderers, and the fundamental moral belief that it is good to deter would-be murderers. In practice most people will have several relevant fundamental moral beliefs which need to be weighed against each other in order to determine whether a particular action about which they have several relevant non-moral beliefs is overall good or bad, right or wrong. Thus someone may have, as well as the previous belief, the fundamental moral belief that it is bad to execute someone unless a jury has found them guilty by a unanimous vote, and that Jones was not found guilty by a unanimous vote. They may hold a further explicit moral principle about how to weigh fundamental principles against each other, or

merely believe that with respect to any action which has the same non-moral properties as some particular action that the balance of principles favours one moral belief over
another, for example the belief that executing the condemned man is wrong over the
rival belief. But the general point remains that particular moral beliefs are sustained in
part by non-moral beliefs, and so will change as the non-moral beliefs change. Or
rather this will happen unless the change of non-moral belief simultaneously causes a
change of fundamental moral belief. A change of the latter kind would be an irrational
process, for while non-moral propositions together with fundamental moral propositions make particular moral propositions probable, non-moral propositions do not by
themselves make fundamental moral propositions probable.

I analysed in Chapter 2 some of the criteria for when some (non-moral) propositions
make other (non-moral) propositions probable, and these are the criteria determining
when a rational believer will change his non-moral beliefs in the light of other beliefs.
I derived these criteria by considering what most of us would say after reflection are the
actual criteria which we would be right to use in forming probable beliefs on the basis
of other beliefs, and so—to the extent to which my account of this is correct—humans
must often form their particular moral beliefs in the light of new non-moral beliefs
using these criteria. Humans are not always rational in their processes of belief formation, but they are quite often.

Particular moral beliefs are also causally sustained in part by fundamental moral
beliefs, and change (or rationally should change) as they change. It is, I suggest, a highly
plausible contingent truth that people do often change their beliefs about fundamental
moral principles by using the method of reflective equilibrium (as described in Chapter
2). Thus we might be told by our parents and teachers that it is morally obligatory to
feed your family or your close neighbours if they are starving, yet it is not merely not
obligatory but wrong to feed foreigners if they are starving. But we may come to doubt
the latter claim by reflecting that the obvious simple principle which makes the former
obligations obligatory is that it is good to feed any starving human. Human need is the
same in the cases of all who are starving, and what is good for our family and
neighbours must be good for foreigners also; and so even if, given limited resources,
we have greater obligations to those close to us, it cannot be bad, let alone wrong to
feed foreigners. Or we may be told that it is morally right (i.e. not wrong) for the state
to execute those found guilty of murder and for anyone to kill in order to save their
own or others' lives, and also that killing in a duel to defend one's honour is morally
obligatory. But we may then come to derive through reflection on the former
situations and other possible situations where we are told that it is not permissible to
kill, a general principle that someone's life is a very valuable thing, so valuable that it
should only be taken from them to save a life or in reparation for a life which they have
taken away; that is, that no one should ever try to kill anyone except to prevent them
killing someone or as a punishment for killing someone. So we conclude that although
it is not wrong to kill in a war to save the lives of fellow soldiers or to execute a

convicted murderer, it is wrong to kill in a duel to defend one's honour. This kind of reflection can lead each of us and (over the centuries) the whole human race to improve our grasp of what are—on the objectivist view—the necessary truths of morality. This process is often facilitated by personal experience of some events of the kinds at issue: those who think that torture is sometimes not wrong might well change their mind when they actually see someone being tortured and so understand more fully what torture involves.

We have seen that on a moral objectivist view particular moral propositions rely for their justification in part on fundamental necessary moral propositions. What kind of necessity do these latter propositions have? My own belief is that the fundamental moral principles are logically necessary truths; the sentences which express them are true in virtue of the senses of such phrases as 'overall good' and 'overriding importance'. I analysed in Chapter 2 the methods by which we can resolve disagreements about whether some sentence (and so the proposition which it expresses) is a logically necessary truth. While the paradigm way to show some sentence to be logically necessary is to deduce a contradiction from its negation, any attempted deduction of a contradiction from the negation of a purported necessary moral principle is likely to be controversial. Yet, as we have just seen, the less direct method of reflective equilibrium does offer hope for progress towards agreement. And given my claim that almost all humans have quite a lot of paradigm beliefs about the 'overall goodness' or 'overriding importance' of various kinds of cases of actions in common, and given that humans have similar cognitive mechanisms for extrapolating from particular examples to the implicit general principles, it follows that reflection on those paradigm examples is bound to yield to some extent a common view of the principles involved in them. So the view that the true fundamental moral propositions are logically necessary explains the utility of the method of reflective equilibrium in beginning to secure agreement about what they are.

Other philosophers have held that the fundamental moral propositions are metaphysically but not logically necessary, that is are a posteriori necessary.[6] On that view 'overall goodness' (or whatever) pick out properties by (in my terminology) uninformative designators, but what makes some action 'overall good' (or whatever) are properties which underlie these. If the fundamental moral principles are in this way metaphysically but not logically necessary (and so necessary a posteriori), it needs to be explained how humans can acquire many justified beliefs about morality and why the

---

[6] This is the view expounded, for example, by Robert Adams in his *Finite and Infinite Goods*, Oxford University Press, 1999, ch. 1. He holds that the underlying property of actions picked out as 'good' by the superficial properties of (for example) manifesting 'kindness' and 'creativity' is 'resembling God'. So, on his view, it is necessary a posteriori that goodness consists in resembling God. This does have the consequence that many actions which seem to us obvious paradigm cases of good actions might turn out to be bad when we learn what God is like, unless we make it a matter of definition that God has a certain character such as being kind and creative. But the latter move would make the necessity of 'it is good to be kind' a priori. Adams seeks to deal with such objections at the end of his chapter.

method of reflective equilibrium would enable them to acquire many more. It seems to me, however, that a moral subjectivist could explain the utility of reflective equilibrium. For while a moral subjectivist cannot regard it as a method for discovering some necessary moral truth, they can regard it as showing the similarity between (for example) one's family who are starving and foreigners who are starving as giving someone an inclination to take the same attitude towards both groups, and so perhaps no longer to regard feeding starving foreigners with disapproval.

Those who begin to align the moral judgements about the overall worth or overriding nature of different kinds of actions by the method of reflective equilibrium must already have to some extent a shared understanding of what it is to believe that some action is 'overall good' or 'of overriding importance'. So although different people derive their concept of the morally good from different kinds of examples, there must be enough overlap between the examples to give rise to a sufficiently similar concept of moral goodness for them to begin to sort out which actions are morally good, that is, on which non-moral properties moral goodness supervenes. By contrast, there seem to me no grounds for saying that someone who does not share with many of us quite a few beliefs about which actions are overall good and bad, of overriding importance to do or to avoid doing, has 'moral beliefs' in anything like my sense. If someone believes that no action is 'overall good' except walking on alternate paving stones, or of 'overriding importance' except killing anyone who lives close to them, I suggest that they do not have any belief at all about what is morally good or obligatory. This is because that person does not understand 'overall' goodness and 'overriding' importance—the terms by which I am elucidating our concepts of 'moral' goodness and obligation—in nearly the same kind of way as the rest of us. Even if that person is angry with him or herself if they do not act on their weird beliefs, that person is not angry with him or herself for the same kind of reason as other humans are when they tell a lie when they believe that it was 'wrong' to do so. This person's 'conscience' would not have the same flavour as ours. Such a person is a psychopath beyond moral assessment.

So much for the way in which particular moral beliefs are causally sustained by non-moral beliefs and fundamental moral beliefs, and the way in which fundamental moral beliefs in their turn are sustained by particular moral beliefs, which in turn sustain new particular moral beliefs.

Beliefs, I claimed in Chapter 3, are, at a given time, involuntary states; we cannot change them at will; and normally too, I claimed, the desires of humans are also involuntary. It follows that if I have equally strong desires (felt inclinations) to do any of two or more available actions (e.g. to give money to this charity or to that charity) and no stronger rival desire, but believe that one of these actions is the overall best action to do (i.e. the one which, I now understand as the 'morally best action), I will inevitably form the intention to do the latter action. For my reason provides the extra inclination, which I have no desire to oppose, beyond the 'felt' inclination, of my desires, which leads to action. If I believe that it would be equally good to do any of two or more incompatible actions (e.g. to lunch at this restaurant rather than that one), and that there is no better rival action, but I desire to do one of these actions more than the others, I will inevitably do that one for I have no reason not to do so. In either of these circumstances the formation of my intention does not require a decision between alternatives. I form the intention I form inevitably.

But when I have equally strong desires to do any of two incompatible actions (and no stronger desire to do a different incompatible action) and believe each of the actions to be equal best actions, neither reason nor desire can determine what I will do. I will have to make an arbitrary decision. In these circumstances the formation of whatever intention I form will be fully rational, for whatever I do, I have a reason to do it, and no better reason for not doing it. The same applies when I have to form an executive intention about which of two equally quick ways to take in order to fulfil an ultimate intention.

Finally there is the situation where the action which I most desire to do (or each of the actions which I most desire equally to do) is incompatible with what I believe to be the morally best action to do. Here too neither reason nor desire can determine which intention I will form; it cannot be determined solely by the strengths of my desires relative to each other or by my belief about which action would be best to do. For as I am understanding these terms, beliefs and desires are measured on incommensurable scales; a belief is strong insofar as the agent believes it to be very probably true, whereas a desire to do an action is strong insofar as the agent is spontaneously and naturally inclined to do it. A moral belief may be strong, while the inclination to act on it may be weak.

Here I have to decide whether to yield to desire and do the less good action, or to force myself—contrary to my strongest desire—to do the best action. This is a familiar situation vividly described by Plato in *Phaedrus*,[7] and by St Paul in his letter to the *Romans*,[8] when yielding to desire manifests 'weakness of will'. This situation I will call the situation of *difficult moral decision*. Both in the situation of having equally strong desires and moral beliefs, and in the situation of conflict between strongest desire and moral belief, if the agent's intention is fully caused, the route of causation must involve brain events—since the (accessible) mental events cannot determine which action the agent will do. I should add that since moral beliefs as such motivate—that is, incline us to act—some desire may be the strongest partly (or for some occasional saintly agents, wholly) because the agent desires to do the best action. In that case the agent will inevitably do the best action. We may suppose that when Luther took the path which led to the Reformation with the words 'I can do no other', that was his situation. But, too often for many of us, our strongest desires conflict with our moral beliefs and so we

---

[7] 'In each of us there are two ruling and leading principles, which we follow wherever they lead; one is the innate desire for pleasures, the other is an acquired belief which strives for the best. Sometimes these two within us agree, and sometimes they are at war with each other; and then sometimes the one and sometimes the other prevails.' (*Phaedrus*, 238e.)

[8] 'So I find it to be a law that when I want to do what is good, evil lies close at hand. For I delight in the law of God in my inmost self. But I see in my members another law at war with the law of my mind, making me captive to the law of sin that dwells in my members.' (*Letter to the Romans* 7: 21–3.)

have to decide whether to yield to felt inclination and follow our strongest desire, or to resist it and do (what seems to us to be) the best action.

When the issue is important, we often deliberate about what to do before reaching a decision—as a result of a prior decision to deliberate, itself motivated by a desire to reach, or a belief that it would be morally good to reach, a well justified belief about which action would be the best to do or would best satisfy our considered desires. Such deliberation consists of intentionally bringing about thoughts relevant to whether or not to do so-and-so, and drawing out their consequences—which is itself a mental intentional action. The process is completed when we form an intention, that is, decide. Sometimes a decision for immediate execution is simply the conscious first stage of having the intention which immediately influences our movements. At other times, and especially when it is a decision to do some important action which would take some time to execute, there will be a recognizable short gap between the decision and the first stage of its execution. But if the decision is one for execution in the more distant future, then, if we do not forget it, it remains ready to guide our movements at the relevant time, though as a continuing mental state, not as an event of which we are all the time conscious.

As well as being in part creatures of reason, we humans are also largely creatures of habit. Even most of our ultimate intentions are habitual ones. We go to lunch at the same restaurants, watch the same television programmes, and attend the same football matches—out of habit. It is the same desire or the same belief about what would be best to do, which inclines us to form the same intentions when similar circumstances recur. Most of our executive intentions are also habitual—we have particular routes along which we walk to the restaurant, certain routines we follow in shaving or dressing. This is because we have over periods of time the same beliefs about the quickest ways to fulfil our ultimate intentions. And when the action is a fairly short-term one and easy to do, and especially when it results from a desire rather than a moral belief, the causal role of the resulting intention is 'permissive' rather than 'active'. I let my body carry on the way it is tending to do.

I have argued that beliefs and desires are caused, and I shall assume (since nothing in my argument turns on this) that all other mental events with the possible exception of intentions are also caused. I shall assume that all such causation (with the possible exception of causation of intentions) is deterministic and of a law-like kind—that is, for any such brain or mental event which causes another one, any event of the same type as the cause is a sufficient causal condition of an event of the same type as the effect. Clearly some desires and sensations are caused directly by brain events without any other mental events having much influence on the causal process; desires to drink or sleep, and sensations of pain or noise are normally[9] surely in this category. But almost all our propositional events—most of our desires and, I suggest, all of our beliefs and

---

[9] The strength of pain felt (and even sometimes whether it is felt at all) is, however, affected by mood and by whether one is engaged in an attention-absorbing activity. For a general survey of the current research on pain, its causes, and cures, see a popular article 'Pain be gone' by Claire Wilson, *New Scientist*, 22 January 2011.

occurrent thoughts—couldn't be had without belonging to mutually sustaining packages of other beliefs and desires; or be conscious without being sustained by other conscious beliefs and desires. I could not have a desire to be Prime Minister without it being sustained by many beliefs about what prime ministers do, as well no doubt as by some brain events causing me to desire to be famous or powerful. And I couldn't even come consciously to believe (through perceiving it) that there is a lectern in front of me without having many other (at least to some degree) conscious beliefs, such as a belief that lecterns are used for giving lectures and so a belief about what lectures are.

I shall understand by a total conscious state at a time all a person's conscious events happening at that time, and by a total brain state at a time all that person's brain events happening at that time. Many total conscious states are large ones, containing many beliefs and sensations (consider merely the sensory content of our visual field and the beliefs which we acquire about the objects we see, as we enter a room), and often also occurrent thoughts and intentions (we often have some ultimate intention and some executive intention we are trying to fulfil). The part of the brain state which sustains even the conscious part of any mental state will also be a large state; recent neuroscience suggests that it consists in a 'temporal synchrony between the firing of neurons located even in widely separated regions of the brain', between which there are 'reciprocal long-distance connections', a synchrony which attains a 'sufficient degree and duration of self-sustained activity'.[10] Different conscious events are sustained by different variants of this pattern of activity. So if we are to make predictions of future conscious events and brain events, we would need a theory of which aspects of a total brain state (which types of brain events) cause or are caused by which aspects of a total mental (including conscious) state (which types of mental events). Then we could predict that any new total brain state which contained a certain type of brain event would cause a certain type of conscious event, including perhaps a certain type of intention.

2. Obstacles to assembling data for a mind–brain theory

To have evidence in favour of such a theory we would need to acquire a lot of data in the form of a very long list of particular ('token') total conscious states occurring approximately simultaneously with token total brain states. To get information about which conscious events are occurring, we must depend ultimately—for reasons given in Chapters 3 and 4—on the reports of subjects about their own conscious events. There are, however, two major obstacles which make it difficult or impossible to get full information from subjects.

---

[10] See Jeffrey Gray, *Consciousness*, Oxford University Press, 2004, pp. 173 and 175. The 'global work-space' model has been confirmed by recent work of Raphael Gaillard and others; see R. Robinson (2009), 'Exploring the "global Workspace" of Consciousness', PloS Biol 7 (3) doi 10.1371/journal.pbio.1000066.

The first obstacle concerns the 'propositional' mental events, thoughts, desires, beliefs, and intentions. The problem is that while the content of most of these events can be described in a public language, as I commented in Chapter 1, its words are often understood in slightly different senses by different speakers. One person's thought which they describe as the occurrent thought that scientists are 'narrow-minded', or the belief which that person describes as the belief that there is a 'table' in the next room, or the desire which they describe as the desire for a 'jolly' holiday in Greece has a slightly different content from another person's thought, belief, or desire described in the same way. What one person thinks of as 'narrow-minded' another person does not, some of us count any surfaces with legs as 'tables' whereas others discriminate between desks, sideboards, and real tables, and different people have different views about what would constitute a holiday being 'jolly'.[11] This obstacle can be overcome by questioning subjects about exactly what they mean by certain words. But it has the consequence that, since beliefs and so on are the beliefs they are in virtue of the way their owners think of them, relatively few people have exactly the same types of beliefs, desires, etc. as anyone else—which makes the kind of experimental repetition which scientists require to establish their theories very difficult to obtain.

There is, however, a much larger obstacle to understanding what people tell us about their sensations, which I discussed in Chapter 3. This is, that we can understand what they say only on the assumption that the sensations of anyone else are the same as we would ourselves have in the same circumstances—and that is often a highly dubious assumption. This obstacle applies to all experiences of colour, sound, taste, and smell (the 'secondary qualities'). We can recognize when someone makes the same discriminations as we do in respect of the public properties of colour and so on, but we cannot check whether they make the discriminations on the basis of the same sensations as we do. And, I argued in Chapter 3, there are good reasons to suppose that different people do not always make the same discriminations on the basis of the same sensations. Maybe green things look a little redder to some people than to others, or coloured things look fainter to some people than to others, or curry tastes differently to different people, when none of these differences affect their abilities to make the same discriminations. The ways things look and feel, however, inevitably affect the way people react to them. Our inability to discover fully how things look and feel to others has, as I pointed out in Chapter 3, the consequence that we cannot fully understand what they mean by some sentence which uses words whose meaning derives from the way things look or feel. For example, our understanding of colour terms derives from the way objects of a certain group look; and if we don't know exactly how green objects look

---

[11] Though it hardly needs such support, this point is born out by recent experiments showing that presenting some image to a group of subjects produced in all subjects similar patterns of activity in different regions, but slightly different patterns for each subject. See S.V. Shinkareva and others (2008), 'Using fMRI Brain activation to identify cognitive states associated with perception of tools and dwellings', PloS ONE 3(1):e1394.doi10.1371/journal.pone.0001394.

to someone else, we don't fully understand what they mean when they describe a house as 'green'. I did, however, make a qualification to all this in Chapter 3, that while we may be unable to understand the natures of the individual sensations of others, their sensations may exhibit patterns which are the same as some publicly exemplifiable patterns; and so we can know what someone means when they describe a mental image as 'square'.

3. The high improbability that human behaviour will be predictable

So, bearing in mind these limits to the kinds of data about the conscious events of different subjects we can have, what are the prospects for forming a theory supported by evidence which will not merely explain and so predict how brain events ultimately cause conscious (and other mental) events of other kinds but how these (together with brain events) cause our subsequent intentions? On the account of the criteria for the probable truth of a scientific explanatory theory given in Chapter 2, to be fairly probable a scientific theory must be fairly simple—that is, postulate mathematically simple relations between only fairly few properties of entities of similar kinds—and make many correct predictions therefrom. Mathematical relations can hold only between properties which have degrees, greater or less, which can be measured on some scale.

What makes a scientific theory such as a theory of mechanics able to explain a diverse set of mechanical phenomena is that the laws of mechanics all deal with the same sort of thing—physical objects, and concern only a few of their properties—their mass, shape, size, and position, which differ from each other in measurable ways. (One may have twice as much mass as another, or be three times as long as another.) Because the values of these measurable properties are affected only by the values of a few other such properties, we can have a few general laws which relate two or more such measured properties in all physical objects by a mathematical formula. We do not merely have to say that, for example, when an inelastic object of 100 g mass and 10 m/sec velocity collides with an inelastic object of 200 g mass and 5 m/sec velocity, such and such results; and have a quite unrelated formula for what happens when an inelastic object of 50 g mass and 20 m/sec collides with an inelastic object of 150 g mass and 5 m/sec velocity, and other unrelated formulae for each different mass and velocity of colliding inelastic objects. We can have a general formula, a law saying that for every pair of inelastic physical objects in collision the quantity of the sum of the mass of the first multiplied by its velocity plus the mass of the second multiplied by its velocity is always conserved. As I illustrated in Chapter 2, what made Newton's theory very probably true is that it contained only four simple laws relating the masses and velocities of all bodies, and made successful predictions about innumerable bodies, small and large. But there can only be such laws because mass and velocity can be measured on scales—for example, of grams and metres per second. And we can extend mechanics to a general physics including a few more measurable quantities (charge, spin, colour charge, etc.) which interact with mechanical quantities, to construct a theory with laws making testable predictions.

A mind-brain theory, however, would need to deal with things of very different kinds. Brain events differ from each other in the chemical elements involved in them (which in turn differ from each other in measurable ways) and in the velocity and direction of the transmission of measurable electric charge. But mental events do not have any of these properties. The propositional events (beliefs, desires, etc.) are what they are, and have the influence they do in virtue of their propositional content (and strength—to which I'll come shortly), often expressible in language but a language which—I noted earlier—has a content and rules differing slightly for each person. (And note that while the meaning of a public sentence is a matter of how the words of the language are used, the (narrow) content of a propositional event such as a thought is intrinsic to it; it has the content it does, independently of how the subject or others use words on other occasions.) Propositional events have relations of deductive logic to each other; and some of those deductive relations (the relations of mini-entailment) determine the identity of the propositional event. My belief that all men are mortal wouldn't be that belief if I also believed that Socrates was an immortal man; and my thought that $2 = 1 + 1$, and $3 = 2 + 1$, and $4 = 3 + 1$ wouldn't be the thought normally expressed by those equations if I denied that it followed from them that $2 + 2 = 4$. And so generally. Much of the content of the mental life cannot be described except in terms of the content of propositional events; and that cannot be done except by some language (slightly different for each person) with semantic and syntactic features somewhat analogous to those of a public language. The rules of a language which relate the concepts of that language to each other cannot be captured by a few 'laws of language' because the deductive relations between sentences and so the propositions which they express are so complicated that it needs all the rules contained in a dictionary and grammar of the language to express them. These rules are independent rules and do not follow from a few more general rules. Consider how few of the words which occur in a dictionary can be defined adequately by other words in the diction-ary, and so the same must hold for the concepts which they express; and consider in how many different ways described by the grammar of the language words can be put together so as to form sentences with different kinds of meaning, and so the same must hold for the propositions which they express.

So any mind–brain theory which sought to explain how prior brain events cause the beliefs, desires, etc. which they do would consist of laws relating brain events with numerically measurable values of transmission of electric charge in various circuits, to conscious (and non-conscious) beliefs, desires, intentions, etc. formulated in propos-itional terms, and also sensations (of different strengths). The contents of the mental events do not differ from each other in any measurable way, nor do they have any intrinsic order (so that one can be thought of as greater than another). Those concepts which are not designated by words fully defined by other words designating other concepts—and that is most of the concepts we have—are not functions of each other. And they can be combined in innumerable different ways which are not functions of each other, to form the propositions which are the contents of thoughts, intentions, and so on. So it looks as if the best we could hope for is an enormously long list of separate laws relating brain events (of certain strengths) and mental events (of certain strengths) without these laws being derivable from a few more general laws.[12]

But could we not have at least an 'atomic' theory which would state the causal relations of particular types of brain events involving only a few neurons to particular aspects of a total conscious state—particular types of beliefs, occurrent thoughts, etc., the content of which was describable by a single sentence (of a given subject's language), in such a way that we could at least predict that a belief with exactly the same content would be formed when the same few neurons fired again in the same sequence at the same rate (if ever that happened)?

The 'language of thought' hypothesis[13] (LOT) is a particular version of such an atomic theory. It claims that there are rules relating brain events and beliefs of these kinds, albeit a very large and complicated set of them. It holds that different concepts and different logical relations which they can have to each other are correlated with different features in the brain. For example, it holds that there are features of the brain which are correlated with the concepts of 'all', 'man', 'mortal', and 'Socrates', and that there is a relation R which these features can sometimes have to each other. When someone believes that Socrates is mortal, this relation R holds in their brain between the 'Socrates' feature, and the 'mortal' feature; when someone believes that Socrates is a man, R holds between the 'Socrates' feature, and the 'man' feature; and when someone believes that all men are mortal, R holds between the 'man' feature and the 'mortal' feature. (The holding of this relation might perhaps consist in the features being connected by some regular pattern of signals between them.) The main argument given for LOT is that unless our brain worked like this, the operation of the brain couldn't explain how we reason from 'all men are mortal' and 'Socrates is a man' to 'Socrates is mortal', since our reasoning depends on our ability to recognize the relevant concepts as separate concepts connected in a certain particular way. Beliefs, thoughts, etc. then, the theory claims, correspond to 'sentences in the head'.

I argued earlier, however, that no belief can be held without being sustained by certain other beliefs—for logical reasons; which other beliefs a given belief is believed

---

[12] Donald Davidson is well known for arguing that 'there are no strict psychophysical laws' (see p. 222 of his 'Mental Events', republished in his *Essays on Actions and Events*, Oxford University Press, 1980). This thesis (if we understand 'strict' as 'general' is the same as mine, and his reasons for it are similar to mine. However, he uses this thesis in defence of his theory of 'anomalous monism', that all events are physical while some of them are also 'mental', and so physical-mental causal interaction is law-like causal interaction of two physical events. But, contrary to Davidson, I am assuming (for all the reasons given in chapter 3) that there are events of two distinct types, physical and 'mental' (in my sense); and so I reject Davidson's resulting theory.

[13] This theory was originally put forward by J.A. Fodor in his *The Language of Thought*, Harvard University Press, 1975.

to mini-entail determines in part which belief the former belief is. Now consider two beliefs, the belief that a particular object is square and the belief that that object has four sides; someone couldn't hold the first belief without holding the second. So these two beliefs cannot always be correlated with different brain events, since in that case a neuroscientist could eliminate the brain event corresponding to the latter belief without eliminating the brain event corresponding to the former belief. On the other hand these two beliefs cannot always be correlated with the same brain event since someone can have the belief that the particular object has four sides without having the belief that that object is square. We can generalize this result as follows. In every believer a belief q 'this object has four sides' must be sustained by every brain event x which (if it occurred) would sustain any belief r which is such that the believer believes that r mini-entails q—for example, the belief r 'this object is a rectangle', the belief 'this object is a rhombus', and so on. And every belief which the believer believes to be mini-entailed by q but not to mini-entail q must be sustained also by some brain event other than x. And what goes for the beliefs just discussed clearly applies generally. All the distinct beliefs which any believer has must be sustainable in them by very many different brain events which sustain other beliefs also. That leads naturally to the view that it is the type of the total mental state to which propositional events belong which is correlated with and so causally related to the type of a total brain state without there being correlations between small parts of the mental and brain states. This view is that of connectionism,[14] the rival theory to LOT, which holds that mind–brain relations are holistic. Only if connectionists hold, as they often do, that mental events are identical with (or supervene on) brain events, is it an objection to connectionism that, according to it brain events do not have to each other the kind of relations between sentences and so between propositions characteristic of rational thought. But given my arguments in Chapter 3 to the effect that mental events are events distinct from brain events (and do not supervene on them), mental events can have a sentential structure without the brain events which sustain them having such a structure. So, given connectionism, a mind–brain theory could at best predict the occurrence of some mental event only in the context of a large mental state (a large part of an overall mental state, consisting of many beliefs, desires, etc.) and of a large brain state (events involving large numbers of neurons).

We must suppose that mental events often cause other mental events in a rational way. To deny this would involve holding that the only justified beliefs are those caused by experience, memory, and testimony. We saw in Chapter 4 that no argument could show that beliefs never cause other beliefs—since one is only justified in believing the conclusion of an argument on the basis of its premises if one believes that believing the premises causes one to believe the conclusion. It would be equally self-defeating to believe the conclusion of an argument purporting to show that no-one believes the

---

[14] For a selection of papers on both sides of the language-of-thought/connectionism debate see Parts II and III of (ed.) W.G. Lycan and J.J. Prinz *Mind and Cognition: An Anthology*, 3rd edition, Blackwell Publishing, 2009.

conclusion of an argument because the premises make it rational to believe the conclusion. So (by the principle of credulity) we should believe that things are as they seem to be, that many of us come to believe that some historical, scientific, or philosophical belief is true because we have reached it by a process of rational thought. And the criteria for premises supporting conclusions used by scientists and other investigators are merely sharpened up versions of those used in less sophisticated activities, such as working out the way to go home or the cost of a holiday. As I have already illustrated, the laws of rational thought include the criteria of valid deductive inference, and these can be codified only by lists as long as those of the dictionary and grammar of a human language. They also include the criteria of cogent inductive inference—that is, the criteria of epistemic probability, of which propositions make which other propositions probable, some of which were analysed in Chapter 2. They also include the criteria for forming moral beliefs, analysed earlier in this chapter. But at a given time each person has slightly different criteria from other persons, in part because of the slightly different concepts with different deductive relations, with which their inductive and moral criteria are concerned. And of course humans are not always rational even by their own criteria of rationality, and so we would need laws stating when and how brain events disturb rational processes; these laws would vary with the overall mental and brain states of the subject, and the mental states which disturb rationality would often need to be described in terms of the concepts with which that subject operates (e.g. some particular fixation preventing someone reasoning rationally about a particular subject matter).

As I noted earlier, moral beliefs and desires vary in strength. And so do all other mental events, apart from occurrent thoughts. One person's sensation of the taste of curry may be stronger than another person's. One person's belief that humans are causing global warming and that it is good to prevent this may be stronger than another person's (i.e. the first person believes this proposition to be epistemically more probable on their evidence than does the second person on their evidence). And one person may have a stronger intention (i.e. may try harder) than another person to bring about some effect.

These differences of strength affect the influence of mental events on each other in a rational way. Someone who dislikes the taste of curry (i.e. desires not to taste that taste) will be more likely to stop eating curry, the stronger is that taste of curry. Someone will be more likely to choose to travel by bus rather than by car, if they have a moral belief of a certain strength that it is good to prevent global warming, the stronger is their belief that petrol-driven cars cause global warming. The stronger is someone's intention (i.e. the harder they try) to lift a weight, the more likely it is that the brain event which will cause that person's arm to raise the weight will occur. So although there cannot be a mathematical law relating changes in types of brain event to changes in types of mental event except in the context of a whole brain state and a whole mental state, perhaps in the context of such a state there could be a law determining how some change of brain event could increase or decrease the strength of a particular mental event. Then maybe we could calculate from the strength of the belief or sensation the strength of the intention which they could cause. But in order to determine that influence on intentions in a new situation where there are many conflicting influences, we need a measure of the absolute strength of sensations and so on (not merely of their strength relative to that of a similar event in a different past situation) which can play its role in an equation connecting these; and subjects cannot provide that from introspection. While subjects can sometimes put sensations in order of strength in virtue of their subjective experience, what they cannot do is to ascribe to them numerical degrees of strength in any objective way. People do not have any criteria which would enable them to answer the doctor's question 'Is this pain more than twice as severe as that pain?' There is no clear meaning in someone saying that one pain is or is not twice as severe as another one.[15]

The same applies to beliefs and other propositional events. There is a long philosophical tradition of trying to measure the strength of a subject's belief in some proposition by which actions that person is prepared to do (in effect, which intentions they would form) in different circumstances.[16] But even if we take the subject's word for how they would act in some different circumstances, we cannot use this information to measure the strength of the subject's beliefs unless we could measure the strength of their desires (and moral beliefs) in those different circumstances on some scale. For, as we have seen, what someone does depends not only on what that person believes will result from their actions, but how much they desire (or believe it good to achieve) that result. We can measure the strength of a subject's desires relative to other desires by what a subject tells us; and if we make the implausible supposition that the subject's brain state and the rest of their mental state remain exactly the same, we may be able to make some predictions about which intention the subject will form without knowing the absolute value of their desire. It would, for example, follow that if the subject got food from a cupboard

---

[15] This, despite the fact that 'psychophysics' has been trying to measure the strength of sensations for the past 150 years. See the article by D.R.J. Laming, 'Psychophysics', in (ed.) Richard L. Gregory, *The Oxford Companion to the Mind*, second edition, Oxford University Press, 2004. He writes: 'Most people have no idea what "half as loud" means...In conclusion, there is no way to measure sensation that is distinct from measurement of the physical stimulus'.

[16] This tradition originates from the work of F.P. Ramsey ('Truth and Probability' in his *The Foundations of Mathematics and other Logical Essays*, Routledge and Kegan Paul, 1931.) It typically measures someone's degree of belief in a proposition (the 'subjective probability' which they ascribe to it) by the lowest odds at which they believe that they would be prepared to bet that it was true. If someone is, they believe, prepared to bet £N that q is true at odds of 3 to 1 (so that they would win £3N if q turned out true, but lose their £N if q turned out false) but not at any lower odds (e.g. 2–1), that—it was claimed—showed that they ascribe to q a probability of ¼ (because then in their view what they would win multiplied by the probability of their winning would equal what they would lose multiplied by the probability of their losing). But that method of assessing subjective probability will give different answers varying with the amount to be bet—someone might be willing to bet £10 at 3–1 but £100 only at odds of 4–1; which shows that people's desire for a sum of money does not increase in proportion to the sum. And surely too how it increases with the sum varies with the person betting, and people have desires and moral beliefs which affect whether or not they bet, which have nothing to do with the sum of money which they might win. Again, none of this information obtained from subject's beliefs about how they would act in different situations will yield precise numerical values of beliefs, desires etc. to enable us to calculate how they would act in a still different new situation.

yesterday and today had a desire to eat stronger than yesterday's desire, and a belief that there was food in the cupboard no weaker than yesterday's belief (and everything else in the subject's mind and brain were the same) that they would form the intention to get the food. But in order to make a prediction about what the subject will do in any new circumstances (where their other desires and brain states are slightly different) we need to know the absolute value of the strength of the subject's beliefs and desires in that situation on an objective scale—just as we need to know the exact masses and velocities of two billiard balls in order to predict accurately what their velocities will be after a certain collision. And all of this is complicated by the fact that people do not always act on their moral beliefs in a way which reflects the 'strength' (in the sense in which beliefs are strange) of those beliefs. All of this suggests that we could not derive from data about what a subject believed that they would do under different circumstances any absolute situation-independent numerical values of the strengths of their beliefs or desires.

So could neuroscience provide those exact values which subjects cannot provide from introspection? On a common scale which reflects the influence of the different mental events neuroscience might discover that greater activity of certain kinds of brain event causes (for example) the beliefs caused by those brain events to be stronger. But for prediction of their effects we would need to know how much stronger were the resultant beliefs. So we would need a theory by means of which to calculate this, which gave results compatible with subjects' subjective reports about the relative strengths of their beliefs. But although almost all adults have brains containing the same interconnected parts—thalamus, hippo-campus, amygdala, and so on, they vary in size and have different connections with each other in different people, and the brain circuits, rates of firing etc., which sustain beliefs in different people, are so different from each other that it is difficult to see how there could be a general formula connecting some feature of brain events with the absolute strength of the mental events which they sustain.[17] Again, we could only have a long list of the kinds of brain activity which increase or decrease the strength of which kinds of mental events.

So the part of a mind–brain theory which predicts human intentions and so human actions would consist of an enormous number of particular laws, relating brain events to subsequent mental events (some of them conscious), and these (together with other brain events) to subsequent intentions, having the following shape: Brain events $(B_1, B_2 \ldots B_j)$ + sensations $(M_1 \ldots M_j)$ + Beliefs (including moral beliefs) $(M_j \ldots M_k)$ + Desires $(M_k \ldots M_1)$ → Intention (M_n) + Beliefs (about how to execute the intention) $(M_p \ldots M_q)$ + Brain events → bodily movements. The B's designate events in individual neurons, and each law would involve large numbers of these; the M's designate mental events with a content

---

[17] For a summary of some of these differences between people see Michael Gazzaniga, *Who's in Charge?*, HarperCollins, 2011, pp. 195–8. For one example see the paper of Michael B. Miller and others, 'Extensive individual differences in brain activations associated with episodic retrieval over time', *Journal of Cognitive Neuroscience*, 14:8 (2002), 1200–14. These authors showed that when subjects were asked to recall words which they had previously been shown, although in most subjects this process involved activations in the right anterior prefrontal cortex, it also involved activations in different parts of that cortex and in different other places in each different subject. When subjects were retested several months later each subject had activations in similar brain areas on each occasion. These variations between individuals were connected with differences of memory ability and character.

describable by a short sentence and with a certain strength, and again each law would involve large numbers of these. The strength of an intention measures how hard the agent will try to do the intended action. The arrow designates 'causes'.

There would be an enormous number of different laws for each person relating total brain states to total mental states, including total conscious states, and relating these and subsequent brain states to subsequent intentions. So we could not work out what a person will do on one occasion when they had one set of brain events, beliefs, and desires, on the basis of what that person (or someone else) did on a previous occasion when they had a different set differing only in respect of one belief. For there could be no general rule about the effect of just that one change of belief on different belief and desire sets; the effect of the change would be different according to what was the earlier set, and what were the brain events correlated with it. But no human being ever has the same overall brain state and mental state at any two times, or as any other human does at any time; and—I suggest—no human being considering a difficult moral decision ever has the same conscious state, let alone the same brain state in the respects which give rise to consciousness and determine its transitions, as at another time or as any other human ever. For making a difficult moral decision involves taking into account many different conflicting beliefs and desires. The believed circumstances of each such decision will be different, and (consciously or unconsciously) an agent will be much influenced by her previous moral reflections and decisions.

Consider someone deciding how to vote at a national election. That person will have beliefs about the moral worth of the different policies of each party, and the probability of each party executing its policies; they will desire to vote for this candidate and against that candidate (liking or disliking them) for various different reasons; they will desire to vote in the same way as (or in a different way from) their parents, and so on. This person will have slightly different beliefs and desires of these kinds, different from those of almost any other voter. Further, that part of the voter's total brain state which determines the strength of their different mental events, and how rationally they will react to them, will almost certainly be different from those of any other voter. So because exactly the same overall conscious state would never have occurred previously together with its brain correlates, there could not be any evidence supporting a component law of the mind–brain theory to predict what would happen this time. It might just happen that a very similar conscious state had occurred on one previous occasion (in the same or a different voter) correlated with a not too dissimilar brain state, which would support a detailed law about the effects of that similar conscious state. But that suggested law would (because of the slight difference in the conscious events and brain events) only make it quite probable what would happen this time, and the law itself would only be very weakly supported by one piece of evidence about what happened on the one previous occasion.

What applies to the example of the voter applies even more evidently to the difficult moral decisions over which people agonize from time to time: whether to begin a sexual relationship, get married, have children, leave one's husband or wife, accept a new job, move house, give up a job to look after aged parents, join a religious community, etc. In each case so many different mental events will be involved. The conscious state of someone agonizing over what to do will differ from the conscious state of someone else agonizing over a decision of the same kind. Our images of and beliefs about the others involved will be different, and the moral beliefs and desires and their strengths which we bring to the decision process will be different; and so too will be the brain events which sustain them.

Add to all this the points made in section 2 about the difficulty involved in getting some of the evidence required to support any mind–brain theory, and I conclude that a prediction about which difficult moral decision someone would make, and so which resulting action they would do, could never be supported by enough evidence to make it probably true. Human brains and human mental life are just too complex for humans to understand completely. That conclusion is of course compatible with human behaviour being predetermined (but its laws too complex to be inferred from a finite collection of data about prior brain and mental events), or not being fully predetermined, by prior brain events. But it does have a crucial consequence that those brain events which most immediately cause the movements which constitute human actions of deepest moral significance will never be totally predictable.

4. Brain indeterminism and physics

I pointed out in Chapter 4 that the normal indeterministic interpretation of quantum theory has the consequence that no physical system is totally deterministic, and that there can be systems in which small-scale non-determined events cause large-scale effects. It is possible that the brain is just such a system, and, we saw in Chapter 4, there are theories developed from quantum theory which purport to explain how intentions can affect brain events.

Nevertheless if sequences of brain events must conform to the laws of quantum theory, it will surely be fairly rare for a very small change in the brain (of a value within the limits of unpredictability stated in the Heisenberg indeterminacy principle), to make a difference to which bodily movements an agent makes. It will still normally be the case that which brain events cause which bodily movements will be unaffected by variations within those limits. This is because only some variations within those limits will make any difference to whether potential is transmitted to an adjoining neuron, the potential transmitted at one synapse will relatively seldom (in view of all the other changes of potential arising from that neuron's other synapses) make any crucial difference to whether or not the neuron fires, and the firing of one neuron will relatively seldom (in view of the behaviour of other neurons) make any crucial difference to whether a bodily movement occurs. As I wrote in Chapter 4, we simply do not know just how many is 'some' and how 'seldom' is relatively seldom.

I argued earlier, however, that most of our executive intentions follow inevitably from our ultimate intentions and our beliefs. I argued also that in the case of ultimate intentions, if we have no conflicting moral belief, we inevitably form the intention to do what we most desire; and, if we have no conflicting desire, we inevitably form an intention to do what we believe best. Given, as I assumed earlier, that all our beliefs and desires at a given time are caused ultimately by prior brain events, any intention we form will in these cases also be so formed. Hence in these cases any sequence of brain events which leads to an intentional action will be caused by an intention which is caused by the brain events which cause our beliefs and desires; and so the role of the intention will be merely 'permissive'. We allow our brain events to cause those movements which they are already 'on track' to cause us to perform, and thereby we constitute those movements as intentional actions; it would be contrary to our intention to interfere in this process. Almost all our intentional actions are like this.

If, however, in the absence of any relevant moral belief we have two (or more) conflicting desires of equal strength to do alternative actions, or we believe that it would be equally morally good to do any of two (or more) alternative actions and our desires do not favour one over others, we have to make a decision; but we believe that it doesn't matter how we choose. Either way our conduct is rational; and so we have no reason to interfere with whatever would otherwise be determined by brain or mental events.

It is only when our strongest moral beliefs conflict with our strongest desires that we have to make a decision that matters about which action to do. In this case there are clearly brain processes inclining us to do two different incompatible actions, in the form of brain events drawing our attention to our moral beliefs and other brain events causing contrary desires. Our strongest desires are our strongest inclinations and will inevitably determine what we will do unless we force ourselves to do the best action. So the brain processes causing the agent's strongest desires will inevitably determine what he will do, unless he interferes in the process. And alone in this situation of having to make a difficult moral decision, unlike in the other situations, the agent has good reason to interfere in the brain processes. My guess is that on average humans are faced with such choices maybe once a day; but clearly there are conscientious people who are faced with such choices much more often than that, and other people less sensitive to moral dilemmas who face difficult moral decisions only perhaps once a month.[18] But for everyone surely the occasions on which they face a difficult moral decision are very rare in comparison to all the other occasions on which they form intentions. Hence the proportion of occasions on which variations in the brain within the Heisenberg limits

---

[18] There has been a recent study of the frequency of 'experienced desire' and of attempts to resist it by 'willpower' among Germans living near Wurzburg. The study concluded that 'the average adult spends approximately eight hours per day feeling desires, three hours resisting them, and half an hour yielding to previously resisted desires'! W. Hoffmann and others, 'What people desire, feel conflicted about, and try to resist in ordinary life', *Psychological Science*, 23 (2012), 582–88. However, the detailed tables of which desires were resisted for what reasons suggest that what the authors call 'moral integrity' was a very infrequent reason for resisting a desire. The normal case of resisting a desire would therefore seem to be merely the case where one has a stronger desire. In such a case, as I argue in the text, the relative strengths of the desires inevitably determine the outcome. Moral conflicts only arise when someone believes that it would be overall good to resist a desire for a reason other than that they desire to do something incompatible with fulfilling it.

would make any difference to our movements may well coincide with the proportion of occasions on which we are faced with having to make difficult moral decisions. On this model the greater the natural probability that some sequence of brain events will eventually lead to the occurrence (or non-occurrence) of certain bodily movements, the stronger the desire which its earlier stages will cause in the agent to allow it to continue. But in this situation of a conflict with their moral beliefs the agent has a reason to interfere; yet the greater that natural probability (relative to the natural probability of the sequence of brain events causing the action believed best), the harder it will be for the agent to do so, and so the less probable it will be that they will do so. Nevertheless on this model the agent can force themself to do a less desired action which they believe would be the best one to do (despite having only a weaker inclination to do it), and it would be compatible with quantum theory that the agent should do the less desired action by their intention to do so causing the sequence of brain events to bring about a naturally less probable outcome. (This model yields a way of measuring the strength of a desire (relative to that of a rival desire including one to do an action believed best) by the degree of this natural probability, the possibility of which I doubted earlier.) Hence it may well be that humans can make difficult moral decisions which they are not fully caused to make, in a way compatible with the full conformity of the operation of the brain to the laws of quantum theory.

Yet even if it should turn out that quantum theory has the consequence that it is immensely improbable that a change in the brain within the Heisenberg limits could affect the pattern of our bodily movements as frequently as the occasions on which humans make difficult moral decisions, or even if it should turn out that quantum theory is replaced by a (very probably true) deterministic theory which makes the behaviour of physical systems other than the brain totally predictable, it follows inevitably from the argument of Chapter 4 that it will not be possible fully to predict brain behaviour by means of a theory of physics alone. For if it was the case that every brain event was caused by another brain event in a totally deterministic way in accord with physical laws, then our intentions would not cause brain events—and I argued in Chapter 4 that no evidence could make that conclusion probable. Either quantum theory or some rival theory must find a place for intentions to influence the brain, if that theory is to provide a fully adequate account of the brain. As I have already argued in this book, it should not be too surprising that the brains (of humans and perhaps higher animals also) are different from other physical systems, since the brain is unlike any other physical system in that—quite apart from whether intentions cause brain events—brain events cause innumerable conscious events. And if intentions cause brain events in the light of beliefs and desires, then, I have already argued, how these will interact to yield an intention in the case of difficult moral decisions is too complicated to be predicted by any mind–brain theory which could be well justified by evidence.[19]

---

[19] I give a brief assessment of J.R. Lucas's argument from Godel's theorem for the indeterminism of human conscious life in Additional Note H.

5. What neuroscience can discover

The limits to the ability of neuroscience to predict mental events arise, I have claimed, from the enormously large number of detailed laws which would have to govern any interaction of many different kinds of mental (including conscious) events and brain events. But neuroscience may be able to discover, and has begun to discover mind– brain laws which do not involve such complicated interactions. Thus it has begun to discover which particular brain events are necessary and sufficient for the occurrence of those non-propositional events which do not involve the inaccessible aspects of sensations, but only the patterns of sensations. A mental image has the same sort of properties of shape and size as the properties of public objects such as brain events. So neuroscience is on the way to discovering a law-like formula by which it can predict from a subject's brain events both the images caused by the public objects at which they are looking and the images which the subject is intentionally causing.[20] But that formula will not tell us what the subject regards their image as an image of—for example, as an image of a television set or of a shiny box. Which beliefs subjects acquire about what they are seeing is clearly going to vary with their prior beliefs about the way objects of different kinds look, for example, that something of such-and-such a shape is a television set. But if the neuroscientist discovers these prior beliefs in some other way than from observation of brain events (e.g. from what subjects tell them, or by analogy with the neuroscientist's own beliefs), then theyt should be able to predict from a subject's brain events not merely the shape of the image which the subject is seeing, but the subject's belief about what they believe that they are seeing.

Similar considerations apply to the other senses. Which words a subject hears depends on the pattern of sensed sounds rather than their intrinsic qualities; and patterns of sensed sounds have the same describable shape as patterns of public noises, that is, air vibrations. So it should be possible to construct a formula describing how the brain events caused by certain patterns of public noises cause patterns of sensed sounds. Given people's linguistic beliefs (their beliefs about what words mean) discoverable in some other way, it should then be possible to predict from their brain events what they understand to be the content of what is being said to them. So scientists should be able to arrange for sentences to be 'heard' by the deaf whose auditory nerves no longer function, by means of electrodes in their brain causing the appropriate brain events.

Desires to do basic actions can occur in the absence of a large set of beliefs. Hence neuroscience could discover the brain events which are the immediate causes of desires to form intentions to do instrumentally basic actions, these being intentions which can be had independently of any beliefs, such as to drink or scratch. It could also discover the brain events which are the immediate effects of intentions to perform basic actions

---

[20] K.N. Kay and others (2008) devised a decoding method which made it possible to identify, 'from a large net of completely novel natural images, which specific image was seen by an observer.' See their 'Identifying natural images from human brain activity', *Nature 452* (20 March 2008), 352–5.

of a kind which are normally done in order thereby to do a less basic action, such as to move a hand, or utter a certain sound. That will enable it to detect what 'locked in' people are trying to do, and so to set up some apparatus which will enable them to succeed.[21] But in order to predict which non-basic action a subject has the intention of performing, a neuroscientist would need to know the subject's beliefs about which basic actions would bring about the performance of the non-basic action. Hence we need to know subjects' linguistic beliefs in order to know which proposition as opposed to which sounds subjects are trying to utter.

Neuroscience may be able to make various kinds of statistical predictions, to the effect that a change in the pattern of certain kinds of brain events will probably lead to an increase or decrease in the strength of certain kinds of desire or belief and so make more probable the formation of certain intentions. Thus it may be able to discover how certain brain events affect the relative strengths of very general kinds of desire (e.g. for fame or power). Desires influence but, when the subject also has competing desires and moral beliefs, do not determine a subject's intentions and so behaviour. And which intention a general desire will tend to cause will depend on the subject's beliefs (e.g. about how fame can be obtained). So again in the absence of a formula for calculating beliefs of any complexity from brain events, and in the absence of a formula for calculating intentions from competing beliefs and desires and brain events, all we can hope for is statistical predictions to the effect that the more or less of some physical quantity that brain events have, the greater or less the desire to do so-and-so, and so— probably—the greater the proportion of subjects who will do so-and-so. Hence drugs or mirror neurons may indeed promote or diminish altruistic desires,[22] or strengthen or weaken a desire to commit suicide. But such increases or decreases of desires only yield probable statistics; they don't tell you who will do what, since we all have different rival desires of different strengths and different value beliefs of different strengths.

However, it follows, finally, that neuroscience should be able to predict what individual humans will do in order to execute certain general instructions which have as a consequence that their behaviour will depend on only one simple desire of a kind caused directly by a brain event. For example, in the Libet experiments discussed in Chapter 4 subjects were told to move their hand at any time within a short period when they decided to do so; and since they would not have had any moral beliefs about when to do so, they must have decided to do so when they 'felt like' it, that is, desired to do it. Such a desire is like an itch and so presumably has a direct cause in a brain event. If subjects disobeyed the instructions, and didn't move their hand within the period—either because they didn't feel the requisite desire or because they had rival

---

[21] See the work described in S. Kellis and others, 'Decoding Spoken Words using local field potentials recorded from the cortical surface', *Journal of Neural Engineering*, 7 (2010), 1–10.

[22] Paul J. Zak and others found that increasing testosterone in men makes them less generous in the game situations created by psychologists. See their 2009 paper 'Testosterone Administration Decreases Generosity in the Ultimatum Game' PloS ONE, 4(12):e8330.doi:10.1371/journal.pone.0008330.

desires (e.g. to be a nuisance) or rival moral beliefs (e.g. that it was immoral to take part in the experiment)—their actions would not count in assessing the experiment. So under these experimental conditions neuroscience may be able to correlate prior brain events with the movements which they cause, via the desire which causes the agent to form the intention to cause them. Hence in this case 100 per cent success in predicting hand movements is by no means impossible. But once again that tells us nothing about how people will behave in situations of conflicting desires and moral beliefs.

But despite the possibility (and in some cases the actuality) of all these advances in neuroscience, the main conclusion of this chapter remains that for the prediction of individual behaviour in circumstances where there are many different variables, both brain events and mental events of different and competing kinds and strengths affecting the outcome, neuroscience would need a general formula well supported by evidence to enable it to relate the strengths of these kinds of events to each other; and that very probably cannot be had.

6. The probability that human behaviour is not fully determined

The argument so far leads to the conclusion that (at least sometimes) humans (as pure mental substances) cause brain events which cause bodily movements which they intend to cause, and that when they make difficult moral decisions we will never have enough evidence to predict in advance what they will decide. Yet, even if it is unpredictable which intention we will form and how strong it will prove, what reason do we have for supposing that that intention (with its particular strength) is not caused (in a way too complicated to predict) by brain events? After all, I have acknowledged, our intentions often are caused—when they are caused by a strongest desire and we have no contrary moral belief, by a strongest moral belief when we have no contrary desire, and when they simply execute (in the way which we believe to be the quickest way) some ultimate intention.

My answer to the question posed is that it is in those circumstances where desires and moral beliefs are in opposition to each other or we have equally strong competing desires and moral beliefs, and only in those circumstances, that we are conscious of deciding between competing alternatives. We then believe that it is up to us what to do, and we make a decision. Otherwise we allow ourselves to do as our desires and moral beliefs dictate—which is so often just to conform to habit. The principle of credulity (Chapter 2, section 2) says that things are probably the way they seem to be in the absence of counter-evidence. So we should believe that in these circumstances where we believe that we are making a choice without being caused to choose as we do, that we are indeed doing just this. In other cases it does not seem to us that we are choosing without being caused to choose as we do, and so we should not believe that we are then making an uncaused choice. The phenomenology of deciding between rival possible actions, ones which are not determined by our mental states (our existing desires and beliefs with their relative strengths), is so different from the phenomenology of doing the everyday things we do intentionally, that we should expect the underlying brain processes to be similarly different. And the apparent indeterminism of the physical world suggested by quantum theory (see Chapter 4, especially note 21) gives us a further reason for expecting that the mental world will not be fully deterministic.

There may be people who do not have much opportunity to exercise any significant choices for a long time; slaves may not have much opportunity even to choose between equally strong desires (for example, to spend a rest day doing either this or that), and no moral beliefs that it would be good to rebel against their servitude. Some mentally retarded persons may simply both desire and have moral beliefs to do what they are told to do. A few others perhaps simply have no moral beliefs; their choices are confined to arbitrary choices between equally desired alternatives. And then there are others who do have a choice (as well as between equally desired or equal moral best alternatives) between their strongest desires and their moral beliefs, but their strongest desires are so strong and their moral beliefs so weak, that it feels to them too difficult to try to rebel against their desires, and indeed it is almost inevitable what they will do. Drug addicts or children under the powerful influence of domineering adults are often in this situation. But when slaves suddenly become aware of simple alternatives (for example, they are allowed a rest day on which they can do either this or that) or are stirred to an awareness that it would be good to rebel against their servitude, they become conscious of having a choice. And when the drug addiction is weakened by some medicine or therapy, or the children leave home and meet others with different life styles and moral beliefs, then they become conscious of a significant freedom: 'it's really up to me what I am to do'. And most of us are very conscious of it being up to us whether we yield to temptation or fulfil what we believe to be our obligation—sometimes giving into temptation knowingly ('Why should I always be moral?', 'It won't matter if I am not moral this time'), or trying to persuade ourselves that we don't really have an obligation in this case. So, in the absence of counter-evidence (in the form of a deterministic theory of our behaviour in such circumstances, rendered probably true by much evidence), in those circumstances we probably are choosing without our choice being caused. Our situation is like that where we are being pulled by ropes tied to our body exerting different degrees of force upon it; it is easier to yield to the strongest force and move in its direction, but we have the power to resist it.

Having avoided using this expression up to now, I shall in future write of an agent having 'free will' insofar as the agent acts intentionally without their intentions being fully determined by prior causes. 'Free will' is a term which can be used in different senses, and needs to be defined before anyone argues about whether humans have free will. I think that the definition which I have just given captures the normal understanding of claims made by those who are not professional philosophers; that humans do or do not have 'free will'. Many philosophers, however, understand 'free will' in such a sense that someone has free will to the extent to which that person is morally responsible for their actions. I shall investigate the issue of when people are 'morally responsible' for their actions in Chapter 8, but meanwhile I suggest that it is desirable to be able to discuss whether humans have free will without investigating at the same time whether they are 'morally responsible' for their actions.

It is natural to suppose that there follows from someone having free will in my sense a principle called 'the principle of alternative possibilities' (PAP) that:

A does x freely only if he could have not done x (i.e. could have refrained from doing x).

By 'A could have refrained' is meant 'it is naturally possible', not merely 'metaphysically' possible, that A refrains. Harry Frankfurt produced a thought experiment designed to show PAP to be false, which has provoked a large philosophical literature. Frankfurt supposes that a scientist, Black, has acquired the power to intervene in Jones's brain processes so that Jones acts in one way rather than another.[23] It is evident to Black, Frankfurt supposes, by some instrument which gives information about Jones's brain state, when Jones is about to do a certain action. So if Jones was about to choose to do some action which Black did not wish him to do, Black has the power to intervene and make Jones choose not to do the action. Now suppose that Black wants Jones to do A, and would have intervened if Jones had been about not to do A. But in fact, Frankfurt supposes, it turned out, there was no need for an intervention—Black saw that Jones was about to choose to do A anyway. So Black did not intervene, and Jones in fact did A. In this situation, argues Frankfurt, one way or the other Jones could not have not done A. But that fact by itself cannot have made his actual action unfree—since the actual action could have been done as a result of forming an intention which he was not caused to form by any prior cause. Although Jones could not have not done A, his actual action could still have been free. Hence, argued Frankfurt, PAP is false.

In response to Frankfurt, David Widerker[24] argued that even if Frankfurt's argument works for what Widerker calls 'complex actions', ones involving an intention and something further (e.g. its effect), in my terminology actions which are not causally basic, it would not work for intentions themselves. An interferer can prevent the occurrence of a complex action by preventing the second part (the effect of the intention), when he observes the occurrence of the intention. If Black observes that Jones has freely formed an intention to do A, he can prevent the intention having any effect. But the same argument will not work for intentions themselves. For in the postulated actual situation either Jones is predetermined by prior causes to form the intention to do x, or he is not. In the former case Jones does not form the intention freely. In the latter case, before having formed any intention, Jones could still not form

[23] Harry G. Frankfurt, 'Alternate Possibilities and Moral Responsibility', *Journal of Philosophy* 66 (1969), 829–39; reprinted in (ed.) G. Watson, *Free Will*, second edition, Oxford University Press, 2003 (see p. 173).
[24] My argument in the next two paragraphs is in essence that of David Widerker, see his 'Libertarianism and Frankfurt's attack on the Principle of Alternative Possibilities', *Philosophical Review*, 104 (1995), 247–61, republished in (ed.) Watson.

the intention to do x. Only if some person or mechanism, such as Black, could know in advance whether Jones is going to form the intention to do x if they do not intervene can they ensure that Jones does not form the intention. But Black (or any other person or mechanism) can only know that for certain if there is an infallible sign indicating which intention Jones is going to form; and there can only be such an infallible sign if that sign is a sufficient cause of the intention, or has a sufficient cause of the intention as a necessary causal condition. There cannot be an infallible sign if the intention does not have a sufficient cause. A Frankfurt scenario gives no reason to suppose that PAP does not apply to intentions.

Given that, it then follows that Frankfurt's argument does not show the falsity of 'A does x freely at time t only if A could have refrained from doing x at t'. For A could only have done x at t if they had the intention to do x at t; and Frankfurt's argument does not show that some agent could have infallibly ensured that they would form that intention unless (by the agent's act or some other means), A was caused (fully, that is, by a sufficient cause) to form the intention to do x at t. But of course Black has the power to make Jones do A at an immediately subsequent time, if Black fails to do it at t. So Frankfurt's argument does show that it is false that 'A does x freely at t only if (if A had not done x at t) he could also have not done x at an immediately following time (t + 1)'. But this is not the significant result which Frankfurt's argument seemed to reach. In a more precise form (PAP★), 'A does x freely at t only if he could have done not-x at t instead' is surely true.

My claim that human intentions and so actions are not fully determined by prior events, depending on my claim that they will never be fully predictable, is one for which I have produced what I regard as strong probabilistic arguments, the kind of arguments from evidence which can be produced for the existence of electrons or the theory of evolution by natural selection. But of course scientific theories which are probable on the evidence available at a time can be overthrown by new evidence. In the case of theories which really are very probable, this is most unlikely to happen. I do not regard what I have written in this chapter as immune from any possible future scientific discoveries, whereas I do regard what I have written in all the previous chapters as immune from any possible future scientific discoveries. No science could possibly show that mental events (in my sense) are identical to physical events, or that no intentions cause brain events or that humans are not pure mental substances. But my argument in this chapter depends on the claim that no scientist will ever be able to find enough subjects having at a given time sufficiently similar brain events over a large brain area and a large enough number of sufficiently similar mental events, so as to be able to check whether those events are always followed by the same intentions (of the same strength). If this could be done, my claim that they will not always be followed by the same intentions could itself be checked, and—it is logically possible—be confirmed or refuted.

7. The arguments of Pereboom and van Inwagen

Derk Pereboom and Peter van Inwagen have both given arguments claiming that it is inevitable that, if our intentional actions are not fully determined, the overall pattern of those movements will be such as it would be if the movements were determined by 'chance'; and that that is good reason to suppose that they are determined by chance. Hence, they claim, there is no good reason to suppose that they are determined by the free will of an agent.

Pereboom's argument is directed against theories of the kind I described above which hold that while quantum theory determines what happens in the brain and so there is sometimes a certain natural probability significantly greater than zero and less than one of some bodily movement occurring, the agent can then intervene so as to bring it about that the movement will occur or that it will not occur without violating physical laws. He objects that if what happens in the brain is subject to quantum theory (or the statistical laws of any similar indeterministic theory), then if an event of a certain kind has a natural probability of occurring of p (e.g. 1/10), then in the long run, he concludes, 'it is overwhelmingly likely'[25] that events of that kind will occur approximately a proportion p (e.g. 1/10) of the time. But, he argues, 'the agent-causal libertarian's proposal that the frequencies of agent-caused free choices dovetail with determinate physical probabilities involves coincidences so wild as to make it incredible'.

I argued in previous sections that the agent can only make a difference to which bodily movements he or she makes in two kinds of circumstance—where there are equal strongest desires and moral beliefs or where there is a conflict between desire and moral belief. In the former case the outcome will indeed be determined by 'chance', that is, the natural probability of different sequences of brain events—the greater the natural probability of a sequence, the more such sequences will occur in the long run. But this will happen because the agent will rationally allow it to happen—since the agent has no inclination or reason to do one intentional action rather than a different one. In the latter case, I have just argued, the more probable is it that a sequence of brain events will lead to certain bodily movements the greater the agent's inclination (in the form of the strength of the agent's strongest desire relative to the strength of the inclination produced by their moral belief) to allow that sequence to occur; and so it is more probable that the agent will allow it. So it is true that if the whole brain were in exactly the same state in relevant respects at various times, then it is 'overwhelmingly likely' that there would be no difference in the long run, between the actual frequencies of choices and the frequencies that would occur if the choices of agents were not free at all. But the view that the agent sometimes intervenes in the brain can explain why that happens. It is because the stronger is an inclination to do some action, the more effort it requires to resist it; and the agent only has a reason to resist it where that agent has a contrary moral belief. Although, as such, this does not entail that the strength of an inclination can be given a

---

[25] Derk Pereboom, *Living without Free Will*, Cambridge University Press, 2001, pp. 84–5.

precise numerical value, it is to be expected that 'in the long run' agents will do what requires less effort. No 'wild' coincidences are involved. But, I argued earlier, human brains are very seldom, if ever during a human life, in exactly the same state in relevant respects; and, as Keynes famously remarked 'in the long run we are all dead'. And even if we lived for far longer than we do today, what is 'overwhelmingly likely' may still not happen. There is no reason to suppose that in the course of a short life, a human's brain will always behave in the most probable way; and, if my conclusions so far are correct, that human can ensure that it doesn't. I conclude that the fact that given quantum theory, 'it is overwhelmingly likely' that there would be no difference in the long run, between the actual frequencies of choices, whether or not agents have free will, is not a good objection to the claim that they have free will.

Peter van Inwagen's argument is more general, and doesn't presuppose that what can happen in the brain is limited by quantum theory or any other physical theory. It is designed to show that, whatever agents do, if it is not determined how they will act, we can only conclude that agents' choices are 'a matter of chance'.[26] In effect—though this is not how van Inwagen would describe his argument—it is an argument developed to show that indeterminism forces us to suppose that some law-like principle having the same indeterministic character as quantum theory is operative, and from that he reaches a similar conclusion to that of Pereboom. Here is van Inwagen's argument. Suppose that at time t_1 Alice has a choice of lying or telling the truth; and tells the truth, and that her choice was not predetermined. Then,

suppose that God a thousand times caused the universe to revert to exactly the state it was at t_1 ... what would have happened? ... We observers shall—almost certainly—observe the ratio of the outcome 'truth' to the outcome 'lie' settling down to, converging on, some value ... Let us imagine the simplest case: we observe that Alice tells the truth in about half the replays and lies in about half the replays. If, after one hundred replays, Alice has told the truth fifty-three times and has lied forty-eight times ... is it not true that we shall become convinced that what will happen in the next replay is a matter of chance?

For the reasons given above in cases where an agent has a strongest desire and no contrary moral beliefs, or incompatible desires of equal strength and a strongest moral belief, the issue will be determined. But, when an agent has equal strongest desires and moral beliefs of equal strength, van Inwagen is right to claim that it is immensely probable that the result of many repetitions will be the same if the agent caused them intentionally as if they are caused by 'chance'. I have acknowledged that free will does not operate in the first two situations, and that chance operates in the third situation—but only because any agent rationally allows it to do so. But in the situation where the agent has a conflict between what he desires and a belief about what is best to do, why

[26] Peter van Inwagen, 'Free Will Remains a Mystery', *Philosophical Perspectives 14: Action and Freedom*, 2000, pp. 1–19.

should we suppose that the outcome of the series of choices will converge on some value, unless some physical law such as a law of quantum theory determines this?

To claim that a series of heads or tails resulting from a coin toss converges on a value p of the proportion of heads, for example, 1/3, is to claim that if you record the proportion of heads to total throws as you toss the coin more and more times, there is for any small value δ a finite number of tosses after which always the proportion of heads will vary between $p + \delta$ and $p-\delta$. If the series yields heads and tails as follows HTTHHHHTHTH, the proportions of heads after each throw will be 1/1, 1/2, 1/3, 2/4, 3/5, 4/6, 5/7, 5/8, 6/9, 6/10, 7/11, and so on. Now if we do not know what is the mechanism producing the series, we can only come to a justified belief about whether the series will converge on the evidence of what happens in a finite part of the series. We would need to examine whether the proportion of successes is very similar in each of several disjointed segments of the series of equal length—for example, whether the proportion of heads is similar in the second, third, and fourth hundred throws from what it is in the first hundred. That would increase the (epistemic) probability that this will hold for (almost all) indefinitely many future segments; and if so, it is evidence that the series is convergent. But if the proportions in different segments get on average larger or smaller as the series gets longer, that would increase the (epistemic) probability that the series is divergent. And if the proportions vary considerably, not in accord with any simple formula, that leaves it as probable as it was initially that the series is either convergent or divergent. But in ignorance of the mechanism producing the series we would need to examine a large number of segments before we could reach a conclusion which was more probable than not. Evidence that the series was convergent would in its turn make it (epistemically) probable that the mechanism producing the series has an inbuilt bias of a measurable kind; that on each occasion there is a certain natural probability of a certain outcome. But if the evidence did not point to the series being convergent, we would have no reason to believe that the mechanism had any inbuilt bias of a measurable kind.

Now van Inwagen has given us no reason to suppose that if Alice had the same choice in exactly the same circumstances 100 further times, as well as the 100 times in which she told the truth 53 times, the proportion of times she told the truth would be roughly the same; let alone that this would be the case also for many more segments of 100 opportunities to tell the truth. If we don't have evidence one way or the other on this matter, we may still know enough about the mechanism to know what will probably happen. For some mechanisms we know that, although they operate in a virtually deterministic way, the outcome depends on very slight variations of initial conditions, which typically vary in such a way as to produce a roughly similar pattern of outcomes when repeated frequently. Coin-tossing is such a mechanism. The pattern is determined by a certain measurable bias in the weighting of the coin. And we also know what to expect for any process where physical theory indicates that there is a fixed probability of outcome from exactly the same initial conditions. The spread of points on a screen marking the arrival of a photon sent towards it through a small slit is due, we justifiably suppose, to an inbuilt bias (a natural probability) in the photon-plus-slit apparatus. We know this from the principles of quantum theory without doing the measurements each time. But in the case of a person making choices all we know is that the person is responding to the influence of reason against stronger desires, and (unless we suppose that some theory such as quantum theory governs the brain) we don't know that that process is characterized by a measurable bias; and so in the absence of evidence of convergence of the kind described above, we have no reason to suppose that on each occasion of choice Alice has any fixed bias in favour of one outcome. But if there is no fixed bias, no natural probability on any particular occasion that Alice will tell the truth, the claim that there is a certain 'chance' with a precise value that she will has no meaning. I have given a sense to one desire being stronger than another in terms of which action the agent would do if they had no moral contrary beliefs. But I have given no sense to this strength having any precise numerical value except in the case where a physical theory such as quantum theory provides a way of measuring this, in the way described above.

But suppose that the result of the repetition of the experiment many times was that Alice told the truth approximately the same number of times in each of many segments of 100 opportunities, what should we conclude? If Alice were simply a machine which did not make conscious decisions, we should indeed conclude that there was a fixed bias towards truth-telling on each occasion, making the result a matter of measurable 'chance'. But as the outcome results from Alice's conscious choice, we should surely regard a 'fixed bias' of p (e.g. 1/3) as measuring how easy it is for her to resist the temptation to lie. In that case she would be in the same situation as that of a brain governed by quantum theory in which the agent can intervene only to the extent allowed by that theory. The stronger the temptation is, the harder it will be to resist, and so the less likely she is to succeed.

I have urged that the natural probability of a sequence of brain events leading to some movement may correspond to the relative strength of a desire to bring about that sequence. It is hardly news that it is harder for humans to do some free acts than to do other free acts; but that doesn't mean that we don't have free will. It means only that our free will is a limited one. An agent can still do what he or she is on balance inclined not to do. So I argue against van Inwagen, as against Pereboom, that in any finite human life it may often be that the most probable outcome does not occur because the agent may do what they are on balance inclined not to do. And it is what the agent does, not what they are inclined to do which matters.

I have been arguing that we have not the slightest reason to suppose that if van Inwagen's experiment was done, the outcome would have the kind of result van Inwagen expects. However, van Inwagen's experiment is most unlikely to be done—it is most improbable that God will cause the universe to revert to an earlier state a thousand times. And the actual choices of normal human beings are crucially unlike the outcome of a normal coin toss with a fixed physical bias in a further respect beyond the one discussed here. In normal coin-tossing the outcome of a second toss is unaffected by the outcome of the first toss. If the coin lands heads first time, it is no more likely than it would be otherwise to land heads or to land tails next time. Humans, however, are so made that if we make a certain kind of choice once, then that makes us more inclined to make a choice of that kind next time. As Aristotle wrote, 'we become just by doing just acts, prudent by doing prudent acts, brave by doing brave acts.'[27] Every time we overcome a bad inclination, it is easier to resist it the next time we are subject to it. In this way over time humans can change the strengths of their desires. As we come to recognize an action of some kind as good, and force ourselves to do it when we have a stronger contrary desire, we can in the course of time make ourselves such that it becomes natural, that is, it becomes our strongest desire, to do an action of that kind when the occasion arises. Conversely we can lose our moral beliefs through neglect. If we always yield to the desire to do the (believed) bad action, the time may come when it never even crosses our mind to do the good action—we don't even have a moral belief that it would be bad to do the bad action.[28] And one of the opportunities which we have at times is to choose to reflect on our moral beliefs and—through experience of the world and talking to others—improve them; or we may neglect to do this. In these ways over time we can either make ourselves naturally virtuous beings or allow ourselves to become amoral beings.

---

[27] Aristotle, *Nichomachaean Ethics*, 1103b.

[28] Recent psychological studies have shown that not merely does forcing yourself to do some action which is difficult to do make it easier to do an action of the same kind next time, but forcing yourself to do difficult actions of one kind makes it easier to do difficult actions of another kind. See R.F. Baumeister and J. Tierney, *Willpower*, Penguin Press, 2011, ch. 6. These studies were not, however, concerned only or mainly with actions done because the agent believed that they were morally good, and so with their effects on moral character. Willpower can be exercised to weaken the influence of one purely selfish desire (e.g. to stay in bed) and so make it easier to fulfil another selfish desire (e.g. to get rich).

8

Moral Responsibility

1. The concept of moral responsibility

Many people like to think that they have free will (in the sense defined in Chapter 7), and so given that by their will they control their bodily movements (as I argued in Chapters 4 and 5) they have (within limits) some control over their lives independent of nature or nurture. I argued in Chapter 7 that (probably) they often do have this free will and so this control which they like to think that they have. And it is indeed in my view a great intrinsic good for us that we do have this free will. Many people also think that it is because we have free will that we are morally responsible for our intentional actions, that is, morally culpable for certain such actions and morally praiseworthy for other such actions. This chapter will investigate what are the criteria for someone being morally responsible for their actions, and in particular whether having free will is enough to make us morally responsible. In this first section I seek to analyse the kinds of actions for which, if an agent is morally responsible, he or she can be held morally culpable or praiseworthy. I shall phrase my arguments on the assumption that there are objective moral truths, and so necessarily true propositions about which particular moral propositions supervene on which non-moral propositions. But anyone who does not hold an objectivist view of morality may instead regard the argument of this chapter as commending certain attitudes to certain non-moral propositions.

People have blamed each other for their morally bad actions, and praised each other for their morally good actions for millennia. But since the praise or blame is being ascribed not to an action, but to an agent who did that action, people gradually became sensitive to the point that it was not right to praise or blame someone for their unintentional actions. If I slam the car door in such a way as to crush your fingers (when I did not intend to crush them and had good reason to suppose that your fingers were not in the way of the door), I do not deserve blame (I am not culpable) for that action. On the other hand if I slam the door on your fingers intentionally, then it begins to be plausible that I do deserve blame and am culpable. This point was recognized very early in the Judaeo-Christian tradition. The Hebrew Bible book of Numbers[1] distinguished between sins done 'unintentionally' for which some small

---

[1] Numbers, 25: 22–31.

sacrifice would atone; and sins done 'highhandedly', the agent of which should be 'cut off' from among the people, that is, killed.

But then it follows by a similar argument that no-one is culpable or praiseworthy for not acting on a moral belief, unless they have that moral belief; and people began to realize that often others do not have the same moral beliefs as themselves. So in recent centuries there evolved among many people in many different societies the view that people only deserve praise or blame, at least in any deep important respect, for acting or not acting on their own moral beliefs. Some people believe that stealing from the rich is not wrong; and so if I have this belief and also the belief that you are rich, I would not be culpable for stealing from you. For a person to deserve blame in this sense is (subject to qualifications below) to deserve blame because they are morally guilty (of rebelling against their understanding of morality) if they do what they believe to be morally bad; and to deserve praise in this sense is to deserve praise because they are morally meritorious (for conforming to their understanding of morality) if they do what they believe to be morally good. Aquinas held that a person's *conscientia* could err over some pretty fundamental matters, but that nevertheless the good person is the one who follows their own conscience:

To believe in Christ is good in itself and necessary for salvation; all the same this does not win the will unless it be recommended by reason. If the reason presents it as bad, then the will reaches to it in that light, not that it really is bad in itself. . . Every act of will against reason, whether in the right or in the wrong, is always bad.[2]

But, since—as we saw in earlier chapters—all an agent can do is to try, that is, to form an intention, and whether the intention has its intended effect is up to nature, it follows that—strictly speaking—an agent must deserve praise or blame not for what he or she succeeds in doing but only for what they try to do. Someone is just as culpable for trying to blow up a civilian aircraft although prevented from doing so by the police discovering the bomb, as they are for succeeding in blowing up the aircraft. The criminal law has various good reasons for punishing someone less severely for an

---

[2] St Thomas Aquinas, *Summa Theologiae* Ia. 2ae. 19.5. Translation from the Blackfriars edition, 1964. In medieval terminology an agent's *conscientia* informed him or her of which actions were instances of conformity to or failure of conformity to very general moral principles (e.g. that taking this grape is stealing, and purporting to marry that woman is bigamy, and so that both actions are wrong). But the quoted passage shows that Aquinas held that *conscientia* can err over some pretty fundamental matters. The medievals, including Aquinas, held that we have a different faculty, *synderesis*, which informed us about what are the most general moral principles, and that according to Aquinas could not err. But the examples which Aquinas gives of these moral principles about which we cannot be in error are so general as to look like simple tautologies—e.g. 'evil ought not to be done' and 'God is to be loved' (when by definition God is perfectly good.) What Aquinas might have been getting at by his claim that *synderesis* cannot err, while *conscientia* can, is that there are logical limits to the possibility of erroneous moral belief, because—as I suggested in Chapter 7—beliefs which have no connection with paradigm moral beliefs are not moral beliefs at all. For Aquinas' views on the fallibility of *conscientia* and the infallibility of *synderesis*, see the extract from his *Quaestiones Disputatae: De Veritate*, as well as extracts from discussions of the issue in other medieval writers and a most valuable introduction to them, in T.C. Potts, *Conscience in Medieval Philosophy*, Cambridge University Press, 1980.

attempted murder (or other crime) than for a successful murder (or other crime). For example, it is harder to prove what someone was attempting to do than what they actually did, and so there are grounds for giving a punishment which reflects that greater possibility that the verdict may be mistaken. Also, if the punishment for attempted murder was normally the same as the punishment for successful murder, someone whose attempt had failed would have no incentive not to try again—because they would already be liable for the same punishment as that for a successful murder. But these grounds for the law punishing failed attempts at wrongdoing less than successful attempts do not invalidate the point that some factor outside the agent's control which prevented his action being successful does not diminish his culpability.

I now suggest that a person is morally meritorious and so deserves praise only for their intentions in doing actions which they believe to be morally good (and normally only for those which they believe not to be obligatory), and morally guilty and so culpable (blameworthy) only for their intentions in doing actions which they believe morally wrong. What seems to be meant when philosophers and others discuss whether people are 'morally responsible' for their actions is that they have moral beliefs and deserve praise or blame for reasons of these kinds; and I shall understand being 'morally responsible' in this sense.

I distinguished in Chapter 7 among good actions those which are obligatory from those which are supererogatory and creative, and among bad actions those which are wrong from those which are infravetatory. I am suggesting that normally a person can be praiseworthy, not for doing any action which he or she believes to be morally good, but only one which they believe not to be morally obligatory. A person can be praiseworthy for doing a (believed) supererogatory good act; greatly praiseworthy for doing a greatly supererogatory act, such as sacrificing their own life to save someone else's life; and mildly praiseworthy even for doing a (believed) creative act, such as not wasting their life, but applying or developing their talents. Normally, however, people do not deserve praise merely for fulfilling their (believed) obligations. If I keep a promise to repay some money, or if I provide meals for my own children, I do not deserve praise for this; it is what is expected of a normal human being. Similarly we are not culpable for any act at all which we believe to be bad, but can be culpable only for failing to do what we believe to be obligatory, or doing what we believe to be wrong (i.e. obligatory not to do). Given these points, I shall henceforward for the sake of simplicity of exposition normally write about culpability or praiseworthiness for doing a good, bad, or whatever action, and omit the clause 'what the agent believes to be' which belongs in front of the 'good', 'bad', or whatever. I ask the reader to take that clause for granted, and assume that culpability or praiseworthiness really belong to actions in virtue of the agent's beliefs about their moral quality, not in virtue of their actual moral quality.

A belief that an agent is morally responsible is a belief that a certain moral proposition is true—yet not a proposition about the morality of an action, but a proposition about the morality of an agent of an action. Hence we must assess it in the light of all the considerations about the nature of moral propositions and how they can be rendered probable by evidence adduced in Chapter 7. A proposition that a particular individual is morally responsible will be true or false in virtue of some contingent non-moral proposition about that person, and of some fundamental moral principle which states under which circumstances people are morally responsible. The latter principle must be a necessary truth (in my view a logically necessary truth), and most likely to be reached by the method of reflective equilibrium. While a moral subjectivist cannot acknowledge that any arguments can establish a true answer about whether some moral proposition is correct, he or she may still regard the method of reflective equilibrium as giving them an inclination (though hardly a reason) to adopt an approving attitude to those who do good beyond obligation, and a disapproving attitude to those who do wrong.

Now I suggest that there is fairly general agreement about two further principles—which on the objectivist account are necessary truths—connecting non-moral features of actions with moral responsibility for them. The first of these is that a person is not culpable for not doing some action which they had an obligation to do if it was not within their physical power to do it. I am not culpable for not fulfilling my promise to have lunch with you, if I have been kidnapped. But if the reason why it is impossible for someone to fulfil an obligation at a particular time is that they have done or failed to do some action at an earlier time which they believed made it improbable that they would be able to fulfil the obligation, then they may be culpable—not for the failure to fulfil the obligation at the later time, but for allowing themself to get into a situation where they believed that it would be improbable that they would be able to fulfil the obligation. If, at a given time, it is impossible for you to fulfil some promise and you realized when making it that that was likely to happen, then you may be culpable for making the promise. It may happen that a person has at a given time two or more obligations of which they can only fulfil one at that time. If I have one sick brother who lives a hundred miles west of me and needs my help, and another sick brother who lives a hundred miles east of me and also needs my help, I am not culpable for not fulfilling both obligations. I could only be culpable for failing to fulfil what I believe to be the strongest of two competing obligations, or failing to fulfil either of what I believe to be two equally strong obligations.

Secondly I suggest that there is fairly general agreement that the degree to which someone is praiseworthy or culpable for doing or not doing some action is affected crucially by how easy or difficult it was for them to do it or not to do it. While in general people do not deserve praise for fulfilling (what they believe to be) their obligations, they do so if it is very difficult for them to do this—because it would require great effort of will to do so (to overcome contrary desires). A person deserves praise for fulfilling their obligations to repay money if the foreseen consequence was that they would have no money to buy food for the next two days—given their strong desire to eat in the coming days. The witness who tells the truth in court, although it involves testifying against a family member whom they like and when that person's upbringing has emphasized that their family will punish them for disloyalty to it, is indeed praiseworthy; whereas someone who knew that their family would always think well of them for telling the truth and has no special liking for the person against whom they are testifying, is hardly praiseworthy for telling the truth. Conversely people do not deserve blame (or nearly as much blame) for not fulfilling their (believed) obligations if it is very difficult for them to do so. If I am threatened with a gun or tortured, I am hardly blameworthy if I hand over the key to the firm's safe. If a young man steals when all his peers are stealing and would insult and despise him if he did not steal, we judge him less culpable. Conversely those who do what they believe to be wrong when they have little temptation to do so are more culpable than they would be otherwise.

2. General criteria for being morally responsible

Yet with the exception of these principles, there is significant disagreement among philosophers about what are the necessary and sufficient conditions of moral responsibility—that is, the conditions under which an agent is culpable for trying to do what he or she believes wrong and praiseworthy for trying to do what he or she believes to be good but not obligatory. There are two kinds of philosophical theory, 'compatibilist' and 'incompatibilist', about what makes someone morally responsible (in the sense delineated in section 1) for their actions. They are (on an objectivist moral theory) theories about what are the non-moral conditions on which moral responsibility supervenes. An incompatibilist theory is one which holds that moral responsibility requires free will (as defined in Chapter 7, that is, that an agent has free will iff he or she is not fully caused to form the intentions they form) and has moral beliefs. Moral responsibility, as defined in section 1, only applies to someone who has moral beliefs; and an additional necessary condition for someone being morally responsible is their having free will to act or not act on those moral beliefs. Or rather in the case of an action believed wrong, it is having free will to do an action morally better than the one an individual actually does; and in the case of an action believed good but not obligatory, it is having free will to do an action morally worse than the one a person actually does. The point of this qualification is that, for example, someone is not culpable for doing some wrong action if the only other action which they had the free will to do is—they believe—equally bad or even worse. I ask the reader to take for granted this qualification in the subsequent discussion, when I write about 'free will' to act or not act on moral beliefs. It will be evident that rival theories will need a similar qualification. I shall argue shortly that these conditions together must be regarded by such a theory as a sufficient condition; on an incompatibilist theory anyone who has free will (in the sense just specified) and moral beliefs is morally responsible.

By contrast a compatibilist theory holds that having free will is not necessary for moral responsibility. Modern compatibilist theories hold that moral responsibility supervenes on agents having their intentional actions caused (totally or partially) by certain kinds of reason-related causes. The moral issue between incompatibilist theories and compatibilist theories is, I shall be urging, to be resolved by the method of reflective equilibrium, by finding the simplest and so (on an objectivist moral theory) most probably true moral principles which explain most of our intuitive judgements about different kinds of example.

The philosophical discussions of the different theories can prove confusing, because most philosophers who discuss them use 'free will', not in my sense, but in the sense that an agent has free will iff that agent is morally responsible. On that definition of 'free will' 'compatibilism' is the view that 'free will' is compatible with determinism (the view that all events including intentions are fully caused); and 'incompatibilism' is the view that these are not compatible. But it should be apparent that the incompatibility and compatibility between the absence of free will (in my sense) and moral responsibility amounts to the same as the incompatibility and compatibility between 'free will' (in the other sense) and determinism. I shall continue to phrase the issues in terms of my definition of 'free will' because I believe this to be the more common one outside philosophy.

I shall express these contrasting theories more often in the form of their consequences for actions rather than for omissions to act, simply in order to avoid long cumbersome clauses. But whatever view is taken about responsibility for doing some action will also apply to responsibility for failure to do an action. And, I repeat, the responsibility with which we are concerned is really the responsibility for one's intentions, doing one's best to perform some action; and so I shall discuss these issues on the assumption that agents have the requisite physical ability to do the action and are not impeded by unexpected obstacles. I shall also conduct the discussion mainly in terms of what makes an agent culpable for doing what he or she believes to be wrong rather than what makes an agent praiseworthy for doing what he or she believes to be good but not obligatory. Contemporary discussions typically give far less attention to the latter; but I shall assume that whatever factors make someone not culpable if they do what they believe to be wrong also make someone not praiseworthy if they do what they believe to be good but not obligatory.

As I noted, it is generally agreed that physical inability to do some action excuses failure to do it. Some early modern philosophers seem to hold a very simple form of compatibilism, claiming that is the only reason which makes someone not morally responsible for his or her intentional actions. This would naturally lead them to hold that only if physical forces literally force the agent to do something (e.g. someone forces their finger against a trigger so that it makes the gun fire) and so the action is no longer an intentional action, is the agent not morally responsible for the action. Hobbes wrote that a person's 'freedom' consists in that person finding that they have 'no stop in doing what he has the will, desire, or inclination to do'.[3] And Hume wrote that 'when applied to voluntary actions', 'by liberty . . . we can only mean a power of acting or not acting according to the determinations of the will; that is, if we choose to remain at rest, we may; if we choose to move, we also may'.[4] Both writers mean by 'freedom' or

---

[3] Thomas Hobbes, *Leviathan*, 2.21.
[4] David Hume, *An Enquiry Concerning Human Understanding*, section 8, Part I.

'liberty' the kind of control which makes an agent morally responsible. So, on this view, agents are responsible for all their intentional actions.

Modern compatibilists have added to this simple form of compatibilism the requirement that to be morally responsible someone must not be influenced exclusively by some irrational desire but must exhibit some kind of rationality in the formation of their intentions. A psychopath or someone acting solely under the influence of an overwhelming craving for heroin or agoraphobia without having any moral beliefs about the matter is not, they hold, morally responsible.

Thus Harry Frankfurt[5] distinguished first-order desires (to eat, drink, smoke, etc.) from second-order desires, which are desires to act or not act on some first-order desire rather than another. (He includes among other second-order desires what I have called 'moral beliefs'.) Thus I might have a second-order desire that I do not act on my first-order desire to smoke or to inject heroin. We have, in Frankfurt's view, 'free will' (which he equates with moral responsibility) to the extent to which we exercise the capacity to conform out 'volitions' (i.e. intentions) to our second-order desires (or higher-order desires if we have them). Without second-order desires, we are mere 'wantons'; and if we have second-order desires but they do not influence us, we are in the same situation as wantons, since we are subject to addictions and phobias which make us not morally responsible for our actions.

Gary Watson[6] pointed out that Frankfurt gives no reason why anyone should prefer their second-order desires as such to their first-order desires. Why, he asks, should someone who has both a first-order desire to take heroin and a second-order desire to be moved by the first-order desire be deemed 'free', whereas someone who has only the first-order desire but not the second-order desire be deemed 'unfree'? Watson suggests that the second-order desires which matter are those which reflect the agent's conception of what he or she has reason to do or be, that is, the agent's moral beliefs. So, Watson suggests, having 'freedom of will' (which, like Frankfurt, he uses in the sense of 'being morally responsible') consists in conforming one's will to one's moral beliefs. The problem with that suggestion, as with many similar ones which equate free will with rationality, is that it seems to make us free if we overcome temptation but not free if we don't. So how can anyone be culpable for yielding to temptation and exhibiting 'weakness of will', as we normally suppose that sometimes they can be?

Over many years J. M. Fischer (sometimes in collaboration with Mark Ravizza)[7] has developed a much more sophisticated compatibilist account of the rationality requirement for moral responsibility for their actions, which deals with this problem. His account explicates people's moral responsibility in terms of their sensitivity to different kinds of

---

[5] Harry G. Frankfurt, 'Freedom of the Will and the Concept of a Person', *Journal of Philosophy*, 68 (1971), 5–20, republished in (ed.) Watson.

[6] Gary Watson, 'Free Agency', *Journal of Philosophy*, 2 (1975), 205–20, reprinted in (ed.) Watson.

[7] See in particular J.M. Fischer and M. Ravizza, *Responsibility and Control*, Cambridge University Press, 1998.

desires (in his terminology, of their motivation by different kinds of reasons) in different kinds of circumstances. Fischer distinguishes different grades of reason-responsiveness. An agent who does A is strongly reasons-responsive if that agent would recognize sufficient reasons for not doing A if they were presented to him or her, and would act on those reasons. But of course few of us are totally strongly reasons-responsive. We sometimes refuse to recognize sufficient reasons for not doing some action, when they are presented to us; or if we do recognize them, we do not act on them and so exhibit 'weakness of will', for which sometimes—as I have already claimed, we normally suppose—we should be held morally culpable. So it seems too strong a requirement for an agent being morally responsible for doing A, that he or she recognizes and acts on sufficient reasons for doing A. Fischer distinguishes strong reasons-responsiveness from weak reasons-responsiveness. An agent is weakly reasons-responsible for doing A if he or she would recognize some possible reason, however crazy, as a sufficient reason for not doing A, and under some possible circumstances would act on it. But this, Fischer argues, is too weak a requirement. He considers an example of a madman who is utterly insensitive to any reason for not killing any fellow passenger on a ferry, except one crazy reason; the madman recognizes the reason that the passenger is smoking a Gambier pipe as a reason for not killing him. It seems unreasonable to hold such a madman responsible for his action of killing a passenger who was not smoking a Gambier pipe. So Fischer prefers what he calls moderate reasons—responsiveness as the necessary condition of moral responsibility. The agent must exhibit an 'understandable pattern of reasons-recognition': they must be able to recognize some reasons for not doing A of a kind which connect with each other in ways which we can understand, and it must be possible that in some circumstances such reasons would lead the agent not to do A. If there is some reason which the drug addict will recognize as a reason for not taking drugs (e.g. that they would need to kill someone in order to get the drugs), and in some circumstances would act upon the reason—for example, they would not kill several women in order to get drugs—then according to Fischer, the agent satisfies the reason-responsiveness necessary condition of moral responsibility. Fischer also proposes a further necessary condition of moral responsibility for an action, which I'll call the condition of agent-recognition: that the agent recognizes the action as his or her own; does not think of it merely as a series of movements produced by some other agent.

I suggest that two of the reasons-related requirements which Fischer adduces are already taken account of by the simple requirement analysed in the previous section that a person is responsible only for his or her intentional actions of conforming or not conforming to their moral beliefs; and that the other one is unnecessary. Thus Fischer's first condition that the agent must exhibit an understandable pattern of reasons-recognition is just another way of stating the requirement that the agent must have relevant moral beliefs, which I construed in terms of having beliefs overlapping with the beliefs of most other people about the overall reasons for doing actions. Someone who believes that the only reason for not killing a particular man is that he is smoking a Gambier pipe does not have a relevant moral belief. And Fischer's third condition that 'the agent recognise the action as his own' is just the condition that moral responsibility applies only to intentional actions—given my earlier understanding of an action as intentional only if the agent means to do it. But Fischer's second condition, 'that in some circumstances such reasons' would lead to a difference of intentional action, seems, however, unnecessary. So long as an agent has the relevant moral beliefs, whether he or she would act on them in other circumstances does not seem relevant to assessing that agent's responsibility for acting or not acting on them in the actual circumstances—unless the fact that the agent would not act on those beliefs in any circumstances is regarded as evidence that the agent is psychologically compelled not to act on them. But in that case Fischer is adopting an incompatibilist criterion.

Fischer's compatibilist theory is only one of several sophisticated modern versions of compatibilism. I shall not discuss other versions, since they all have different versions of a rationality requirement together with the insistence that while physical inability to do some action or physical force exacted by another agent making one do the action, has the consequence that the agent is not responsible for not doing it or doing it, the mere fact that the agent was predetermined by some cause to do the action intentionally does not as such make that agent no longer responsible. Some sort of rationality requirement is indeed necessary if we are not to hold psychopaths or addicts lacking 'second-order desires' morally responsible, but I suggest again that it is satisfied by the requirement that moral responsibility belongs only to those who have moral beliefs. This is because having moral beliefs is having beliefs of the requisite kind about reasons for action.

I suggest, however, that by far the simplest principle which explains the two fairly generally agreed principles about moral responsibility set out at the end of section 1 is the incompatibilist view that moral responsibility requires free will and moral beliefs. The reason why public physical force deprives an agent of moral responsibility is that the agent cannot do the action. So, surely if any other cause makes that peson unable to do the action, he or she should also be deemed not morally responsible for not doing it. And if that applies to omissions to act, it is simpler to suppose that it applies to actions as well. If someone is predetermined to steal, they are unable not to steal and so surely not morally responsible for stealing. Hence whether it is an irresistible desire or a moral belief caused by a brain event which fully causes an agent to do some action (i.e. is a sufficient cause of this), then surely he or she is not morally responsible for doing it. The compatibilist, however, claims that there is the crucial difference between the case where an agent is prevented by external force from doing an action and the case where he or she is fully caused not to do it by some desire or brain state, that in the latter case the agent intends not to do the action whereas in the former case he or she does not intend not to do the action. But, replies the incompatibilist, if the agent cannot help his or her intentions why should that difference matter?

The second generally agreed principle, however, is that the degree to which someone is culpable or praiseworthy for doing some action is crucially affected by how easy or difficult it was for them psychologically—that is, given their desires arising from nature or nurture—to do it. As I pointed out, if a bank employee is threatened with a gun or subjected to torture, we do not judge that employee greatly culpable if he or she hands over the key to the firm's safe despite holding the view that it would be wrong to do so—in view of his or her very strong desire to go on living or to cease to be tortured; or if a young man steals when all his peers are stealing and would insult and despise him if he did not steal, we judge him less culpable than he would be otherwise. It is a simple extrapolation from the fact that the stronger someone's contrary desires, the less they deserve blame for not doing what they believe wrong, that if those desires (or other causes) are totally irresistible, they do not deserve any blame at all. The simplest form of this incompatibilist principle is that having moral beliefs and free will (in my sense) is not merely necessary but sufficient for moral responsibility. I shall understand incompatibilism in this form of future; moral responsibility supervenes on free will and moral beliefs.

A different powerful argument showing the ad hoc and so complex and so improbable nature of any compatibilist account of the criteria for the ascription of moral responsibility to an agent has been given by Derk Pereboom. He describes a series of cases of an agent being caused inevitably to do an action by causes outside him or herself, beginning from one where almost everyone would admit that the agent is not morally responsible for the action to one where many compatibilists would claim that the agent is responsible.[8] He urges—to my mind correctly—that 'no relevant difference can be found among these cases that would justify denying responsibility in the first case while affirming it in the last case.' In all the cases the common action is that Professor Plum murders Ms White. In the first case Plum was created by neuroscientists who manipulate his every action at the time of the action by radio-like technology. They manipulate his desires and reasoning processes at the relevant time so that he commits the murder as a result of his higher-order desires and reasons—responsive beliefs. In this case almost everyone would agree that Plum is not morally responsible for the murder. In the second case also Plum was created by neuroscientists; but, having created him, they are no longer able to control him subsequently. However, they have created him with such brain and mental processes that it is inevitable that he will murder Ms White. But, Pereboom reasonably urges, surely the mere difference of time when Plum was manipulated cannot make Plum morally responsible. In the third case Plum is an ordinary human, but predetermined by special training processes at an early age to have just the desires and reason-responsive beliefs which would cause him to commit the murder. Yet surely the difference in the causes of the desires and belief-processes being inculcated cannot make Plum morally responsible for what happens. What happens subsequently is no more under his control than it was in the second case. In the final case Plum is generated and raised under normal circumstances, which makes him the sort of person who will inevitably commit the murder—although his upbringing was not designed by anyone to have that effect. But how can the inevitable fact that another agent is responsible for what happens make all the difference to Plum's

---

[8] Derk Pereboom, *Living Without Free Will*, Cambridge University Press, 2001, pp. 112–17.

responsibility for it? It would not make Plum responsible in the first and second cases if a machine rather than neuroscientists had created him. So surely if an agent is caused inevitably to do an action by any process over which he or she has no control, that deprives the agent of moral responsibility for the action.

The simple incompatibilist has a simple principle about the non-moral conditions on which moral responsibility supervenes (having moral belief and actions not having a sufficient cause) fits all the agreed intuitions concerning these particular cases (both those concerning the degree of culpability or praiseworthiness, and those concerning the first two cases in Pereboom's thought experiment). By contrast a compatibilist has to offer a more complicated principle to the effect that certain kinds of sufficient cause do and other kinds do not make someone morally responsible. This makes us justified in adopting the incompatibilist account of the disputed cases (e.g. those concerning Pereboom's last two cases). The method of reflective equilibrium leading to the general principle discussed in Chapter 7, that it is wrong to kill someone except to prevent them killing someone else or in reparation for a killing, led to a simpler principle which fits our agreed moral intuitions better than does the same principle with a qualification added permitting killing in a duel. That provided reason to recognize the former principle. The same kind of consideration should lead us to accept the incompatibilist view of moral responsibility.

There is, however, one consequence of the incompatibilist theory which may initially seem implausible to some readers, but which—I suggest—should on reflection seem plausible. This is that the theory entails that the hero who is caused inevitably (e.g. by his strongest desire) to do a supererogatory action—for example, to agree to be executed for a crime he did not commit in place of the actual criminal because the latter has a wife and family who would be deprived of his love if he was executed—is not praiseworthy. This is because the action comes so naturally to him—he has such a natural love for others that he really wants to do that action. Such a hero to whom the heroic action comes so naturally does not have to make a difficult moral decision in order to do it. But we do not judge the rich man who has no interest in what riches can buy morally praiseworthy for giving much of his wealth to feed the poor; and that is because he has no desire to keep the money. And if the hero is in just the same situation of having no desire to do anything else, it would follow that we should make a similar judgement about him. Of course the hero has a superb character for which he deserves enormous admiration. But what is so good about him is his nature, not his action; and so he deserves a different kind of admiration—just as what is so bad about the totally wicked man who has no conscience is his nature, not what he does with it; that is not within his control. It may, however, also be the case that the hero's heroic character is the result of his own actions of doing good actions when it did require a difficult moral decision to do them, in the way described at the end of Chapter 7. In that case he would be greatly morally praiseworthy for those earlier actions which produced his subsequent heroic character.

Not merely does the compatibilist have to give a more complicated account of what makes an agent morally responsible than does the incompatibilist. It is also the case that the compatibilist finds it difficult to say what is so good about being morally responsible on his theory. Why is it so good if your intentional actions are caused by your brain events rather than by irrational desires? Fischer's answer is that 'the value of acting so as to be morally responsible is the value of a certain sort of artistic self-expression'; 'we transform our lives in such a way that the chronicles of our lives become genuine stories or narratives'.[9] What he seems to have in mind here is that if we show moderate reasons-responsiveness, then whether or not our actions are fully caused, they will have to some extent a consistent pattern over time. But since someone's actions could easily exhibit a consistent pattern arising from conformity to totally immoral beliefs, it cannot be the consistency of the pattern alone which makes it a good thing, but also the fact that the individual actions which make it up are reason-responsive. And the natural explanation of why that is good is that it is good that any action at all is reasons-responsive (whether part of a pattern or not); and so of course it is good if the agent seeks to make his or her actions reason-responsive, and therefore—I now suggest—it is even better if the agent is the ultimate source of his or her attempt to make their actions reason-responsive.

An incompatibilist has this very simple answer about what is so good about an agent's action satisfying incompatibilist criteria for moral responsibility: this is, that such an action derives ultimately from the agent's own choices. Freely pursuing the (believed) good despite difficulty makes the agent meritorious; freely allowing oneself to do (believed) wrong makes an agent 'morally guilty', guilty for breaking the moral law—it stains the agent. It is because his or her actions result ultimately from the agent's own choice that the agent of a praiseworthy action which benefits someone deserves gratitude, and the agent of a culpable action needs to apologize to anyone wronged by it.[10] Such reactions to the agent of a particular action are appropriate, whether or not the action constitutes a contribution to a narrative. Since compatibilists normally hold that it is good that we are morally responsible for our actions, that is reason for them— in the absence of a better account—to adapt the incompatibilist account of what makes moral responsibility a good thing to have.

Such considerations and the thought experiments which I adduced earlier are designed to show that we are justified in believing that the concept implicit in the paradigm examples by which we learn what it is to be 'morally responsible' is the incompatibilist one. Hence on an objective theory of morality, the necessary moral truth is 'A person is morally responsible iff he or she has moral beliefs and free will'. More precisely, a person is morally responsible in respect of those actions in respect of which he or she has free will; for a person may be subject to irresistible desires in respect of actions of certain kinds but not in respect of actions of other kinds, and—as I commented in Chapter 7—not all humans may always have much free will. Moral

---

[9] J. M. Fischer, 'Semi-compatibilism and its rivals', *Journal of Ethics*, 16 No. 2 (2012), 117–43.

[10] For fuller discussion of the appropriateness of talk of 'merit' and 'guilt', and of the appropriate reactions to good and wrong actions by way of gratitude by a beneficiary and apology by a wrongdoer, see my *Responsibility and Atonement*, chs. 4 and 5.

responsibility is incompatible with determinism. A moral subjectivist will not regard the discussion of this chapter as showing some necessary moral truth. But a subjectivist can regard it as showing the similarity between (for example) those who are caused to do some wrong action by an irresistible desire caused by a brain event caused by a neuroscientist and those who are caused to do some wrong action by a moral upbringing which made it inevitable that they would do that action. Awareness of this similarity might well give the moral subjectivist an inclination to take the same attitude towards both kinds of agents, and so perhaps no longer to regard the latter agents with moral disapproval.

My treatment of compatibilist–incompatibilist controversy may seem rather brief in view of the very considerable amount of recent philosophical writing devoted to it. But I do not think that there are deeply new arguments relevant to this issue, or any unobvious features of the paradigm examples of moral responsibility which require more careful analysis, in the way that, for example—I argued—there are such features of the paradigm examples of causation, which some philosophers have not noticed. So having put forward the arguments for incompatibilism and believing it to be the concept of moral responsibility to which most people implicitly ascribe, I shall have—for reasons of space—to leave the argument at this point.

3. The coherence of libertarianism

Determinism, I have argued, rules out moral responsibility. Other philosophers have argued that indeterminism would rule out moral responsibility, claiming that if our actions are not caused, then we cannot be held responsible for them. Some of these philosophers are compatibilists, such as some of those discussed in section 2, who hold that we are morally responsible for our actions so long as they are caused in certain ways but not if they are caused in other ways. Hume was one such philosopher. At a later point in the section from which I quoted earlier, he made the additional claim that we are responsible only for actions which are in character and which are determined by our character. It follows that if we had free will in my sense, no action would be fully caused by the agent's previous character, and so no agent would be responsible for his or her actions. He writes:

Actions are by their very nature temporary and perishing; and where they proceed not from some cause in the character and disposition of the person, who performed them, they infix not themselves upon him, and can neither redound to his honour, if good, nor infamy, if evil. The actions themselves may be blameable; they may be contrary to all the rules of morality and religion: But the person is not answerable for them; and as they proceeded from nothing in him that is durable or constant, and leave nothing of that nature behind them, it is impossible he can, upon its account, become the object of punishment or vengeance.[11]

---

[11] Hume, op.cit. section 8, Part II.

I argued in sections 1 and 2 that our understanding of moral responsibility assumes exactly the opposite. If someone well brought up, who is normally benevolent and truth-telling, commits perjury in a law court, we blame them more than we would blame a habitual liar for doing the same. And we praise more the person brought up in an atmosphere where people habitually tell lies, if they give honest testimony in a law court despite being threatened with violence if they do so.

Other philosophers who claim that indeterminism would rule out moral responsibility are what I shall call 'incoherentists'. They hold that both determinism and indeterminism rule out moral responsibility, because the concept of moral responsibility is not a coherent concept—no-one could be morally responsible for any action in the sense discussed in sections 1 and 2. The argument for incoherentism is as follows. If an action is uncaused, then, whether it happens or not is a matter of 'chance'. We can properly be blamed or praised no more for uncaused actions, than can a photon be blamed for passing through one slit rather than another (see Chapter 4, section 4), or an atom of radium be blamed for decaying at this moment rather than at some other moment, when the laws of quantum theory have the consequence that which event happens in these cases is a matter of natural probability (i.e. chance). Over many years Galen Strawson has defended the view that to the extent to which actions are uncaused their occurrence is a matter of chance, and to the extent to which they are caused by previous events their occurrence is a matter of natural necessity, and so neither way is the agent 'ultimately responsible' for any action.[12] He argues that our interest in free action is an interest in actions done for a reason; and that when one acts for a reason, what one does is a function of how one is, 'mentally speaking'. So if one is to be truly responsible for how one acts, one must be truly responsible for how one is, 'mentally speaking'. But this means that one must have chosen to be the way one is in light of principles which one has chosen. But then if one is to be responsible for those principles, one must have chosen them in virtue of earlier principles; 'and so on. Here we are getting out on a regress that we cannot stop'.

But actions may be done for a reason, even if one chooses which of alternative actions to do, for each of which there is a reason to do it; and the fact that there are no 'principles' of choice determining how one will choose (as opposed to how it would be good to choose) in these circumstances—as, I have argued, there are no principles when one has to choose whether to fulfil a moral obligation or to yield to a strong desire to do what is in one's narrow self-interest—does not seem to me to entail that one cannot be held responsible for one's choice.

I think that it would entail this if all that is going on is that some brain event or other mental event caused another mental event (the decision about what to do) in virtue of some law of nature that there is a physical probability p (less than one and greater than zero) that an event of the first kind will be followed by an event of the second kind—in

[12] See, for example, Galen Strawson, 'The Impossibility of Moral Responsibility', *Philosophical Studies*, 75 (1994), 5–24, reprinted in (ed.) Watson.

the way in which a 'law of nature' is analysed by a regularity or RBU theory of causation. For in such a case the fact that the first event is causally influential is not inbuilt into that event, but is due to the pattern of other events (on the regularity theory) or to a law which exists independently of the events governed by it (on the RBU theory). So if our brain were so arranged that the decay of an atom caused a decision to do A_1 and its failure to decay caused a decision not to do A_1, we would not—on either of these theories of causation—hold the atom (or any larger entity to which it belonged) responsible for the action. And if the causal process was of this same kind (constituted by the pattern of other events or brought about by a law independent of events) when consideration of reasons causes a decision, it would seem equally unreasonable to hold the agent responsible. I suggest that it is this picture of how reasons affect decisions which gives rise to the incoherentist view. However, as I have already argued, intentional actions are caused not by events (physical or mental passive states of agents) but by agents themselves; and, I have also argued, whatever the analysis of the causation of physical events by other physical events, agent-causation cannot be analysed in either of these ways. If I decide to tell a lie, this is to be analysed as a person (me) intentionally causing the utterance of words which I believe form a false sentence; it does not consist of any event in me (other than me causing) bringing about the latter. It is I who cause the words to come out of my mouth, whether or not there is a cause of me causing the words to come out of my mouth; and if there is no fully determining cause of me causing the words to come out of my mouth, the ultimate responsibility for this clearly belongs to me. Hence when I choose consciously in the light of reasons for acting, whether to go along with these reasons or to ignore them, I am morally responsible for what I do.[13]

It is not a good objection to this to say that {I cause the words to come out of my mouth} entails that {I cause the action of me causing the words to come out of my mouth}; and that the phrase within the second set of brackets itself describes an action which I cause {the action of causing the action of me causing the words to come out of my mouth}; and so ad infinitum. There is indeed an infinite regress of propositions here, but since each of these propositions entails each of the others, all these propositions describe one and the same event.

In the absence of any further significant objections known to me, I suggest that we should hold the view that someone who has moral beliefs and does an intentional action is morally responsible for that action, unless he or she is fully caused to do it (i.e. unless there is a full sufficient prior cause of their doing it). Hence—in the absence of such a cause—someone is morally blameworthy for doing the action if they believe it wrong, and morally praiseworthy for doing it if they believe it good but non-obligatory. And, as I argued earlier, the degree of blameworthiness or praiseworthiness depends on the

---

[13] While Pereboom argues that humans are never morally responsible for their actions, he acknowledges that if humans were agent-causes and there were not sufficient causes of their actions, they would be morally responsible. See op.cit. p. 129.

strength of the causal influences on the agent to do or not to do the action. I argued earlier that there is no sufficient cause for our doing an intentional action, when our choosing to do it results from a choice between two incompatible actions regarded as equally morally good (and better to do than any incompatible action) and each of which we desire equally to do (and desire to do more than any incompatible action); and also when it involves a choice between one action which we regard as the morally best to do and an incompatible action which we desire to do more than any other one. Hence we are morally responsible for doing any such action at the time when we exercise our choice to do or not do that action. This view is commonly called 'libertarianism'.

4. Responsibility for past actions

But does the passage of time diminish or abolish moral responsibility? Am I culpable for a murder which I committed 20 years ago? The answer, I suggest, depends on what humans are.

If human persons were merely physical organisms, then, as I discussed in Chapter 6, our identity over time would depends on the extent of our physical continuity. An organism P_2 at a later time t_2 is the same organism as an organism P_1 at t_1 insofar as P_2 is made of matter resulting from gradual replacement of the matter of P_1 by new matter having the same function, and there is continuity of physical properties between them. As humans get older, cells are replaced, organs decay and may be replaced by transplanted organs; and over time too we may develop different patterns of behaviour. Although normally the gradual nature of the replacement and change of behaviour patterns makes it natural to say that there is a single organism continuing through change, we would not misdescribe the world if we supposed that at some arbitrary moment (e.g. at puberty or menopause or when someone suddenly adopts a new attitude to life) the organism ceases to exist and is replaced by another one made of almost the same matter. As we have seen throughout this book, there are different ways of cutting up the world into substances, and the history of the world can be told in different ways. But since, on an objectivist view of morality, it is not an arbitrary matter, dependent on the way we choose to describe the world, whether someone is morally responsible for actions done long ago, application of the principle of reflective equilibrium would, I suggest, lead us to the conclusion that responsibility for the actions of an earlier human belongs to whatever organism is continuous with that earlier human. And since continuity is a matter of degree—bodily matter and patterns of behaviour may change more or less gradually—the degree of responsibility for past actions depends on the extent to which the organism's bodily matter and patterns of behaviour are the same, or have changed only very gradually. To the extent to which a human being is made of different matter and behaves in different ways, especially if that results from a sharp change, that human is much less responsible for actions done by the human with which he or she is continuous many years ago. It seems in no way obvious that a human would bear as much, or indeed any, responsibility for the actions of a previous human 20 years ago simply in virtue of some minimal continuity of organiza-tion lying behind almost total replacement of its constituent matter.

A similar conclusion, I suggest, follows if we suppose that the identity of the person over time depends on the extent of mental as well as physical continuity, or of mental continuity alone. While the rate of change in physical constitution and organization is very similar in most humans—for example, our cells are replaced at similar rates—the rate of change in memory and character is very different in different people. Some have a very similar character to their character 20 years ago; others not so. Some can remember quite a lot of what they could remember 20 years ago, others can remember virtually nothing of this. Some of such changes may be very sudden. Someone may experience a sudden loss of memory through a brain injury, or undergo a sudden religious conversion which leads to a significant change of character. In so far as we become rather different in these respects from the human who had largely the same body, it would seem to follow—by an argument similar to that just given—that our responsibility for the past actions of that earlier human should be much diminished. John Locke thought that being 'the same person' depends on continuity of 'consciousness', by which he meant continuity of 'apparent memory'; and so he drew the natural conclusion that we should not be punished for past actions which we could not remember.[14]

But a different conclusion follows from the account of personal identity which I advocated in Chapter 6. On that account humans are essentially pure mental sub-stances. A pure mental substance has only one essential part, its soul. I claimed in Chapter 6 that it is very probable that the same soul is connected to the same body while that body is the body of a living human. A pure mental substance may be connected to a body which changes over time, and it may gain or lose various contingent properties (including those of memory and character). But the mental substance whose properties they are (in virtue of their being properties of his soul) has exactly the same essential properties (being a person) and the same thisness (which makes him or her the same person) throughout life. So that human, in his or her essence exactly the same, who did some action 20 years ago for which they were then morally responsible, would be no less responsible for that action as a result of any change of character, memory, or bodily constitution.

If, as I believe, the stain of moral guilt involved in moral responsibility for a wrong action can be removed it is by the agent's repentant apology and reparation, and by his or her being forgiven by whoever he or she has wronged, or alternatively by the agent being punished.[15] And then the agent is no longer culpable—he or she deserves no more

---

[14] Locke writes (op. cit. 2.27.22) that while human laws punish a 'man' 'for the act he commits when drunk, though he be never afterwards conscious of it', that is only because human courts of law cannot determine whether the man does or does not remember his actions when drunk. 'But in the great day when the secrets of all hearts shall be laid open, it may be reasonable to think, no one shall be made to answer for what he knows nothing of.'

[15] For my account of how guilt may be removed by repentant apology and reparation and being forgiven, see my *Responsibility and Atonement*, ch. 5.

blame—and so is no longer morally responsible for the action. But if humans are essentially as I have analysed them, the mere passage of time cannot remove moral responsibility for a wrong action. For similar reasons the mere passage of time cannot remove the merit involved in moral responsibility for a good-but-not-obligatory action. When the action is a supererogatory action benefitting someone else, then there may be a debt of gratitude to be paid by others. But my intuition is that nothing can remove the merit acquired by the agent of such an action; he or she always deserves praise but there is a limit to any obligation on others to give it to her.

5. The limits to free will

Humans, I have claimed, have a freedom to choose between alternative actions independently of the causes which influence them, and they bear moral responsibility for their decisions. But clearly it is a limited free will. First, there are limits to our powers, that is, to the effects we can bring about, however hard we try. There are for each of us limits to the instrumentally basic actions we can perform at a given time—I cannot play a tune on the piano, ride a horse, or speak Mandarin. Secondly, there are also for each of us limits to our knowledge which in turn limits the non-basic actions we can do. I could no doubt make my computer work if I knew how to do so, or translate this book into Italian if I had a much larger Italian vocabulary than I have. Among the limits to our knowledge which limit our choices are our inadequate moral beliefs about which actions are the best. I can only successfully pursue the good if I know what it is. If I don't believe that it is wrong to hit a man just because he has insulted me, I shall not have the choice between yielding to the desire to hit him and doing the right thing by restraining myself. Our ability to make good choices is limited by our moral views. And thirdly, within the class of actions which we have the power and knowledge to do, our choices are limited, I argued earlier, to choosing between equal best actions which are equally desired, equally desired actions where we do not believe that it would be better to do one rather than another, and—all-importantly—between actions we desire most to do and actions we believe best to do. But for some such choices our desires to do an action less than the best are enormously strong. There are heroic moral actions which we have the power and knowledge to do and which we believe would be the best actions to do, but which it would need an enormous effort of will to choose to do. For some agents sometimes it would be very hard indeed to force themselves to sacrifice their life to save a comrade, to give all their money to a worthy cause, or to withhold information when tortured and threatened with much more painful torture. But, within these limits of possibility and difficulty, if the argument of Chapter 7 is correct, each of us has a limited range of choices, between which it is up to us how we choose.

We can, however, alter the range of actions open to us. We can by practice improve our powers so as to be able to do instrumentally basic actions previously beyond those powers, and improve our knowledge of how to produce effects by means of our actions. Among other kinds of knowledge we can improve is our knowledge of which actions are good and which are bad, and more generally which kind of life is worth living; and so we can put ourselves in a better position to do what really is good. We may seek to improve our knowledge of fundamental moral principles by applying the method of reflective equilibrium by spending time reflecting on moral issues and discussing them with others; and improve our knowledge of particular moral principles by taking trouble to discover what effects our different actions have on those affected by them. Further, we can move the range of actions which are 'live options', in the sense of actions which it does not need an enormous effort of will for us to decide to do. By resisting desires to do actions of a certain kind to which we could easily have yielded we may strengthen our (second-order) desires not to yield to temptations of this kind in future, so that eventually we don't even desire to do actions of that kind. By doing quite good actions of a certain kind, we may make it easier for us to do more heroic actions of that kind. Or if we yield too often to temptations (in the sense of desires to do an action which we believe to be wrong or otherwise bad) of a certain kind when we could have resisted them, it may become very difficult to resist them in future; and by doing wrong actions of moderate seriousness of a certain kind, we may find ourselves desiring to do very wicked actions of that kind which previously we did not even desire to do. If I force myself to tell the truth today when it would damage my reputation among a small group of not very close colleagues, I may find it a little easier tomorrow to tell the truth even if it would damage my whole career. But if I yield to the temptation to lie today in the former circumstances, I may find myself open to the temptation to lie in a court of law in return for a bribe—which wouldn't previously even have crossed my mind as a possibility. A person's character is a matter of how he or she behaves and thinks. This in turn depends on what that person has the power to do, what he or she believes about how to attain goals, what he or she desires to do and have (and so what kind of behaviour comes naturally), and what that person believes about what is morally good and bad. While there may be limits (different for each of us) to what we can achieve in these ways, nevertheless (helped or hindered by others) we can to a significant extent form our own characters—if we choose to do so. We can make ourselves naturally loving and cheerful, or allow ourselves to become bitter and gloomy. Within many limits, we can over time change ourselves.

Conclusion

I have argued that it is an unavoidable datum of experience that we are pure mental substances; and that when we perform intentional actions it seems to us strongly that we are exercising causal influence. It is a fundamental epistemic principle, which I called the principle of credulity, that things are probably the way they seem to be—in the absence of counter-evidence. I have argued that there could not be any counter-evidence to the claim that humans often do cause the bodily movements which they make intentionally, and so cause the brain events which are the more immediate causes of those movements. When we have to make a difficult moral decision about what to do it seems to us that it is up to us, independently of the causes influencing us, how we are to decide. It is very improbable that there could be counter-evidence to that belief. This is because, in view of the enormous complexity of the causal interactions between our brain events and our conscious life, it is very improbable that there could ever be a scientific theory able to predict precisely which intentional actions we will decide to perform when faced with such a decision. So such decisions are very probably up to us. The principle of credulity, backed up by the evidence of brain continuity and continuity of memory and character in the way analysed in Chapter 6, also leads us to acknowledge that the pure mental substances which we are probably continue to exist as long as the period of time between the birth and death of our bodies; our continued existence does not consist in any continuity of mental or physical properties, but simply in the continued existence of our one essential immaterial part, our soul. Because we are agent-causes who act intentionally without being fully caused by anything else to do what we do, we are morally responsible for our actions. And because we are in essence exactly the same person as the person who had the same body during all that body's life, the mere passage of time cannot remove our moral responsibility for actions which we did earlier in our lives.

Additional Notes

A. *Three kinds of probability* (see Chapter 1 note 4 and Chapter 2 note 3)

It is important to distinguish three basic kinds of probability—natural, statistical, and inductive. I used the concept of natural probability in Chapter 1. Natural probability is a measure of the extent to which nature has a deterministic propensity towards bringing forth events. If there is a natural probability of 1 at a time t that an event of a certain kind will occur, then the state of the world at t naturally necessitates its occurrence; it cannot but occur; if there is a natural probability of 0 at t that such an event will occur, then the state of the world at t necessitates its non-occurrence. A natural probability between 1 and 0 measures the strength of the propensity in the world inclining such an event to occur. (Like other writers, in my book *Epistemic Justification* and elsewhere, because discussion of the operation of this kind of probability usually concerns only its operation in the physical world, I called natural probability 'physical probability'. But since this book is also concerned with the possibility of its operation in the mental realm, I am using the more general term 'natural probability'.) Statistical probability is a measure of the proportion of events of one type in some class of events of another type. The class may be a class in the actual world—for example, the proportion of Russians in 2012 who favour capital punishment; or a class in some possible world—for example, the proportion of heads in a trillion tosses of a certain coin under such-and-such conditions. And finally there is inductive probability, which is the probability of one proposition (which may be some hypothesis) on another (which may be the evidence for and against that hypothesis). A proposition p has an inductive probability of 1 on a proposition q iff q makes p certainly true; and an inductive probability of 0 on q iff q makes p certainly false. Intermediate values measure the degree of inductive support which q gives to p. There are two kinds of inductive probability, which I shall call 'epistemic probability' and 'subjective probability'. I shall understand by epistemic probability the probability of one proposition on another by correct criteria of inductive probability; and by subjective probability the probability of one proposition on another by the criteria of inductive probability used by a certain person or group. (In my book *Epistemic Justification*, pp. 62–71, I made a distinction between what I called there 'epistemic probability' and what I called there 'logical probability'. I ignore that distinction here as irrelevant for the purposes of this book.) All scientific inquiry presupposes that there are correct criteria of inductive inference, and in Chapter 2 I present some of these criteria. My main concern in this book is with correct criteria and so with epistemic probability, not with the actual criteria used by some person or group of people. Among the hypotheses rendered epistemically probable by evidence may be a hypothesis that a substance has a natural probability of doing something (e.g. decaying within the next 1,620 years). And the evidence which gives some epistemic probability to some proposition may include some proposition of statistical probability; for example, the proportion of times some coin has landed heads so far (e.g. 604 times in 1,000 tosses) which gives a particular epistemic probability (e.g. 0.604) to a hypothesis that the coin will land heads next time.

B. *Alternative conceptual systems* (see chapter 1 note 7)

Some philosophers have proposed alternative systems of categories which do not include the familiar categories of substance, property, and time in the senses I have been analysing, as reflecting more perspicuously the structure of the world. But all the alternative systems known to me seem to be reinterpretations in ways which their advocates regard as more fundamental, of the history of the world described in familiar terms—that is, as a list of events (in my sense). They do not involve postulating kinds of entities additional to the familiar ones. For each entity in the alternative system there is a corresponding entity in the familiar system, which the advocates of the alternative system regard as the illusory or derivative phenomenon undergirded by the reality which they describe. So if—as I argue in this book—some accounts of human nature described in familiar terms omit important aspects of it, the same will apply to those accounts described in unfamiliar terms. Hence it does not affect the argument of this book if some alternative system of categories is to be preferred to the familiar system of substances, properties, and times in providing a full history of the world.

I illustrate this point with respect to the two best known alternative systems, the system of tropes and the system of perdurance. Trope theory dispenses both with the category of a substance and with the category of a property in the sense of a universal, and replaces them with the category of a particular property otherwise known as a 'trope'. On this theory every so called substance is really just a bundle of particular properties instantiated together—this redness, that squareness, that 2 m distance from another bundle, and so on, each of which particular properties is a 'trope'. The history of the world is then on this theory just the history of tropes—how long different tropes existed, to which bundles they belonged at each time, and which tropes are similar to other tropes in which respect. But even if everything we normally express in terms of substances and properties corresponds to something expressible in terms of tropes (which I doubt), there is no reason to doubt that anything which can be expressed in terms of tropes corresponds to something which can be expressed in terms of substances and properties. Talk about bundles of tropes corresponds to talk about substances (consisting of bundles of instantiated universal properties); talk about the similarities of tropes to each other corresponds to talk about substances having the same universal property. Of course the trope theorist wants to say that his theory provides a more fundamental account of what exists, than the familiar account. But he provides no reason for supposing that the familiar account leaves out any particular kind of happening from the history of the world, even if it does not describe it in the most perspicuous way. For the history of trope theory—its merits and demerits—see Cynthia MacDonald, 'Tropes and other things' in (ed.) S. Laurence and C. MacDonald, *Contemporary Readings in the Foundations of Metaphysics*, Blackwell, 1998.

Perdurance theory (alias temporal-part theory, or four-dimensionalism) holds that objects do not 'endure' through time, but 'perdure'. Given that what we ordinarily regard as physical substances have three spatial dimensions, perdurantists hold that the real constituents of the physical world are not such physical substances but four-dimensional substances (each having three spatial dimensions and one temporal dimension); and so, for example, they include not my desk but my-desk-throughout-its life. The desk as it is today is a 'temporal slice' of the four-dimensional object. On the normal account of substances (analysed in Chapter 1), substances exist totally at each moment of time when they exist; a substance continuing in existence is then described as it 'enduring' through time. On the perdurantist account only a 'temporal slice' of a substance exists at a time; the substance then 'perdures' through the period of time during which a corresponding substance in the normal sense would be said to exist. (If they acknowledged non-physical substances, perdurantists would have to say that they too do not exist all-at-once, even if they do not have four dimensions.) But anything which can be described by a perdurantist account of the world corresponds to something which can be described by a normal account. For example, if you knew the different properties possessed by each time slice of the temporally extended desk, then you could deduce from that all that the familiar account would claim had happened to my desk at each period of its history. Even if the four-dimensional account gives a more fundamental account of what happens, it doesn't have the consequence that the familiar account leaves out any particular kind of happening in the history of the world. For a defence of perdurantism see, for example, Mark Heller, *The Ontology of Physical Objects*, Cambridge University Press, 1990, ch. 1.

I conclude that if some account of the history of the world expressed in terms of our familiar system of categories—substances, properties, and times—leaves out some particular kind of happening, the best known rival systems of categories, trope and perdurantist accounts, will also leave it out.

C. *Logical Impossibility* (see Chapter 1 note 14)

I claimed that there is no reason to suppose that there can be any logically impossible sentences (that is, sentences which are as strongly impossible as those which entail a contradiction) which do not themselves entail a contradiction. My argument for this is as follows.

A sentence can only be logically impossible if the impossibility is detectable merely by understanding the sentence. To be logically impossible a sentence must have the form of a declarative sentence, in which the component words already have a sense in the language (determined in the way outlined in Chapter 1, section 3). It will be a subject-predicate sentence, an existential generalization, or some other one of many recognized forms of declarative sentences. It will—to put the point loosely—assert something about some substance or property or event or whatever that it has or does not have some property or relation to some other substance, property, etc.; or that there are or are not certain substances, properties, or whatever. Words designating a substance or property (or whatever) have a sense in so far as it is clear what are the criteria for something to be that substance or property (or whatever)—they therefore delimit a boundary to the sort of object or property it can be or the sort of properties it can have. Hence it will be inconsistent to affirm that an object picked out by some expression is of a kind ruled out by the very criteria for being that object. And the form of a sentence will exclude some alternative; and so it will be inconsistent to affirm the sentence together with that alternative. It follows therefore that sentences which used to be called 'category mistakes', for example, 'Caesar is a prime number' or 'this memory is violet' are—in my sense—logically impossible sentences. (I take these examples from the article on 'Category mistake' by Jack Meiland in (ed.) R. Audi, *The Cambridge Dictionary of Philosophy*, second edition, 1999.) Words and sentences mean what users of the language mean by them. If a sentence cannot be recognized as entailing a contradiction in these ways, it cannot be recognized as impossible merely by understanding the sentence. In that case we could have no a priori reason to suppose that that sentence is metaphysically impossible, and so no reason to suppose that it is logically impossible.

Philosophers have often tried to adduce examples of sentences which we can 'see' to be logically impossible (or whatever) but whose impossibility doesn't depend on entailing a contradiction. But I believe that all such examples turn out either to entail a contradiction or not to be in the least obviously logically impossible. Robert Adams has one example of what, he writes, 'seems to be a necessary truth': 'Everything green has some spatial property'. He claims that this sentence cannot be shown to be 'analytic'. (See Robert Adams, 'Divine Necessity' republished in his *The Virtue of Faith*, Oxford University Press, 1987, pp. 213–4.) 'Analytic' may be understood in different ways, but one way which Adams mentions is being true 'solely in virtue of the meanings of its terms'; and he claims that this account is 'so vague as to be useless'. But when it is spelled out in terms of the negation of the sentence entailing a contradiction, the notion is clear. I suggest that being 'green' can be understood in two possible ways, and that the cited sentence with 'green' understood in either of these ways can be shown to be such that its negation entails a contradiction. Being green is a property of a thing. One can understand the word 'green' in such a way that a thing being 'green' entails that thing being a publicly observable thing. A publicly observable thing must have a spatial extension—for what one observes one observes as occupying a region of space. In that case the negation of the cited sentence clearly entails a contradiction. But one can understand 'green' in a sense in which (not merely a public observable thing, but also) a private thing experienced by only one person, the content of a mental event such as a sense-datum (or, less controversially, an after-image), could be 'green'. Clearly what it would be for that private thing to be green is to have the same visual appearance in respect of colour as a green public object. It must look like a surface or a volume which is green; and so must have the visual appearance of a spatial thing. For a private object to have a visual appearance of a spatial thing entails it looking as if it occupies a region of public space, and it can only do that if it occupies a spatial region of one's visual field. So again, even if one allows the existence of private objects which are green, the negation of 'everything green has some spatial property' entails a contradiction. Adams's example does not disconfirm my claim that the logically necessary is simply that the negation of which entails a contradiction, and that similar equivalences hold for logical possibility and impossibility.

D. *Concept empiricism and logical positivism* (see Chapter 2 note 13)

Two modern philosophical movements—Hume's 'concept empiricism' and logical positivism— have tried to enunciate quick general principles by which we can distinguish the logically possible (often called the 'conceivable' or the 'coherent', or even the 'meaningful') from the logically impossible, or the logically contingent from other sentences have proved totally inadequate for the purpose. Hume's 'concept-empiricism', holds that the only coherent concepts (Hume called them 'ideas') are ones formed of simple concepts ultimately derived from sensations (in Hume's terminology from 'impressions'). (See David Hume, *An Enquiry Concerning Human Understanding*, (ed.) L.A. Selby-Bigge, second edition, Clarendon Press, 1902, section 2.17.) The account, which I gave in Chapter 1, of how words get senses (and so we acquire the concepts which they designate), is an account of concept-empiricism. We derive a concept of a duck from being told that of certain objects which cause sensations in us that we are seeing 'a duck'. But I point out in Chapter 2 that observing the same paradigm examples of their application and so having the same sensations when teachers utter simple identifying sentences may lead to different speakers ascribing different senses to the same words and so acquiring different concepts, some of which may not be coherent. And even given common concepts derived from sensory experience, we might still put the words which designate them together into sentences in such a way as to make obvious nonsense. To take the examples cited in

Additional Note C, we can derive the concepts of 'memory', 'violet', 'Caesar', and 'prime number' from sensory experience (including experience of sentences of mathematics); and yet it is nonsense to claim (in any literal sense) that 'This memory is violet' or 'Caesar is a prime number'. So we need paradigm examples of how words derived from sensory experience are to be used—that is, examples of situations in which they are used correctly in sentences of different forms. And yet different speakers may still derive different concepts from the same paradigm examples of simple sentences in which a word is used, and so make different judgements about whether some new sentence is or is not logically possible.

The other movement is logical positivism, developed by the Vienna Circle in the 1930s and made widely known by A.J. Ayer's *Language, Truth, and Logic* (Victor Gollancz, 1936). This movement enunciated the verification principle that 'to be factually meaningful', that is, to be logically contingent, 'a sentence must be verifiable'. But if 'verifiable' is to mean 'conclusively verifiable', virtually no sentence we ordinarily think to be logically contingent would be factually meaningful. And if 'verifiable' is to mean 'is such that it is logically possible that someone at some time could make an observation which would increase or decrease the probability of the sentence being true', the account still needs a definition of 'logically possible'; and anyway there is in my view no good reason to suppose that there is this close tie between logical contingence and probability. Such general philosophical principles prove inadequate to settle issues of what is logically possible or contingent; these issues can be settled only by detailed conceptual inquiry on a case-by-case basis in the way described in the text.

E. *Williamson on disagreement about the logical status of sentences* (see **Chapter 2 note 14**)

In his *The Philosophy of Philosophy* (Blackwell Publishing, 2007) Timothy Williamson emphasizes that disagreements about logical status of sentences occur among philosophers who are linguistically and conceptually 'competent'. But, I suggest, all that being thus competent can amount to is that the philosophers agree with speakers of the same language in their use of relevant terms *almost* all the time. In the example discussed by me in the main text (Chapter 2, section 3), advocates of the view that the world could have begun a year later than it did agree with their opponents almost all the time as much as their opponents agree with each other, about the dates of mundane events. Williamson seems to see any disagreement as arising from a lack of 'logical' understanding (his p. 91) or 'deductive competence' (p. 112), a difficult skill. But I am claiming that it results sometimes, not from such logical incompetence, but from a failure to see the coherence of more than one concept which can be derived from the same linguistic training, the applications of which normally but not always coincide with each other. There is a sense in which, to cite a position which Williamson (p. 122) ascribes to both Noam Chomsky and Donald Davidson, 'there is no such thing as a shared language'. The sense is that the same word may come to be used in two slightly different senses, in order to express slightly different concepts, the differences between which have hitherto escaped our notice. And that, to my mind, is the correct analysis of the examples which Williamson discusses in his chapter 4. There are speakers whose use of 'all' differs in a few circumstances from that of others—for example, in holding that 'all As are B' entails 'there are As'. This does not, in my view, happen because they violate the rules of English, which does not seem to me to have a recognized rule of mini-entailment that 'all As are B' entails 'there are As', nor a rule that 'all As are B' is compatible with 'there are no As.' Rather, two different but very similar concepts can be derived from the same paradigm examples by which the use of 'all' has been introduced to many of us.

F. *Kripke on the non-identity of mental and physical events* (see Chapter 3 note 2)

It may be useful to compare my argument for pure mental events not being identical to physical events with Kripke's somewhat similar argument for the falsity of 'my pain is my being in such-and-such a brain state'. I analyse the version in Kripke's paper 'Identity and Necessity' in (ed.) M.K. Munitz, *Identity and Individuation*, New York University Press, 1971. Kripke claims, first, that 'my pain' (which I shall understand as 'me being in pain') and 'my being in such-and-such a brain state' (which I shall understand as 'me being in such-and-such a brain state') are 'both rigid designators' (p. 162). Kripke and I are entitled to use these expressions in this way, and that is surely their normal use. But a conclusion will only follow about whether or not they rigidly designate the same event, given an understanding of what it is for some event to be the event it is. In this case, Kripke claims, we pick out the events 'by essential properties'. That is, being a pain is essential to the first event and not the second event; and being a brain state is essential to the second event and not the first event. On my view (for which I have given reasons) an event is the event it is in virtue of the substances (or events), properties, and times involved in it. Since the substances and (I assume) times are the same in the events in question, the issue terms on whether the properties designated are the same. The conclusion that the two events are not the same will follow only if 'being in pain' and 'being in such-and-such a brain state' are being used not merely as rigid designators of properties, but as informative designators of the properties of being in pain and being in such-and-such a brain state, and so do not designate some underlying property by means of its superficial properties of being in pain or being in such-and-such a brain state. I am explicitly using these expressions as informative designators; I would claim it to be the most natural understanding of them, and I am clearly entitled to use the words in this way. Kripke is equally entitled to think of the properties designated by informative designators, involved in the events as ones essential to the events—but only given my view that we are entitled by definition to say which properties are essential to an event. Kripke's argument seems to be relying on an intuition that the properties stated are essential to the event; but there is no need for him to do that. He can make it a matter of definition. The conclusion of the non-identity of the pain and the brain state does, however, need a further argument. It will only follow—given my criterion (or some similar criterion) for property identity—that to be identical two properties have to have logically equivalent informative designators, that is, logically equivalent sets of necessary and sufficient conditions for their application (and I have given reasons for using that criterion). From that it will follow that the properties involved in the two events are not the same, and so the events are not the same. Without this an opponent of Kripke might say that the property of being in pain just is the property of being in such-and-such a brain state. I think that Kripke would be sympathetic to this final move of mine, but he does not actually make it.

G. *Olson on simple and compound dualism* (see Chapter 6 note 35)

In 'A Compound of Two Substances' (in ed. K.Corcoran, *Soul, Body, and Survival*, Cornell University Press, 2001) Eric T. Olson argued that there are serious difficulties for compound dualism (the view that the person who I am has on earth two parts: body and soul) which do not arise for 'simple dualism' (the view that I always have only one part, my soul, and my body is never part of me). The first supposed difficulty is that mentioned in the text—that if we (embodied on earth) are not mere souls although our souls think, then there are two thinking things—I and my soul. In the text I argue that this is unparadoxical, since there is only one act of thinking going on—I think, in virtue of my soul thinking. Olson admits (his p. 76) that 'there are some properties we have in a derivative sense. We are tattooed insofar as our skin is tattooed', but he seems to think this unimportant. However, innumerable similar examples can be adduced (I give the example of a table and its top in Chapter 1). The reason these examples do not have paradoxical consequences is because the different descriptions ('I being tattooed' and 'my skin being tattooed') are descriptions of the same event, since the descriptions mutually entail each other. I have argued in several places in this book that there are many different ways of describing the world, but some of them do not describe anything 'over and above' others of them.

The other difficulty which Olson finds in compound dualism is (his p. 81) that it has the 'absurd consequence that one could come to be identical with something that was previously only a part of one'. Suppose I am embodied on Monday, but my body is then destroyed and I continue to exist in a disembodied state on Tuesday. Then, Olson claims, according to compound dualism, (1) I on Monday am the same as I on Tuesday, (2) I on Tuesday am the same as my soul on Tuesday, and (3) my soul on Tuesday is the same as my soul on Monday. But it follows from these premises, (4) I on Monday am the same as my soul on Monday, which is a conclusion incompatible with compound dualism. But this argument contains a premise, (2), which the compound dualist will regard as false. I on Tuesday have one and only one part on Tuesday, my soul. But I on Tuesday am not the same as my soul on Tuesday. (That one thing should be identical with one substance at one time, and not identical with that substance at another time would constitute 'occasional identity'; for arguments showing this to be an incoherent notion see Gallois, *Occasions of Identity*, pp. 113–17.) Clearly substances (of many genera) may gain or lose parts while remaining the same substance: and there is no good reason to deny that a substance might come to have only one part. The 'absurd consequence' does not follow.

H. *Gödel's theorem and human indeterminism* (see Chapter 7 note 19)

In 1931 the Austrian mathematician Kurt Gödel proved that for any consistent formal system in a language L and axioms and rules of inference S containing a certain part of arithmetic, a sentence G (a 'Gödel sentence') can be constructed which can be shown to be true but which is such that it is not provable in S. A formal system, a calculus, is a collection of axioms with rules of deductive inference. To derive a theorem from such a system is to derive it by a computable process, or to use what is called a sound algorithm. Since—if we assume that he knows his formal system to be consistent—any human mathematician of modest ability can construct such a sentence which he can know to have this character, it follows that 'human mathematicians are not using a knowably sound algorithm in order to ascertain [every] mathematical truth' (Roger Penrose, *Shadows of the Mind*, Oxford University Press, 1994, p. 76.). Human mathematicians must have cognitive processes which enable them to recognize truths of a system apart from consciously deducing them from explicit axioms.

J.R. Lucas has argued over many years that our ability to formulate Gödel sentences shows physical determinism to be false (see for example his *The Freedom of the Will*, Oxford University

Press, 1970, pp. 124–72). He understands by 'physical determinism' the theory that all events are fully caused by (i.e. have sufficient causes in) physical events in accord with physical laws. Lucas's argument, if cogent, would show any law-governed determinism of conscious events by other events (conscious or physical) to be false, and I shall treat it as an argument against any such law-governed determinism. Such a determinist, Lucas points out, must claim that the process whereby a human reaches a conscious conclusion can be represented by a formal system S, consisting of axioms describing the brain events and conscious events which cause him to reach that conclusion, and rules of inference which describe the laws governing this causal process. (Inevitably since the descriptions of the events and the laws of their operation are by hypothesis true, S will be consistent.) Lucas claims that for any S of this kind, there are some mathematicians—or at least one—'who can follow Gödel's argument, and if told that any particular logistic calculus S represents his intellectual output, produce as true the Gödelian formula of S', that is, the formula not provable in S which he can see to be true (op.cit. p. 140. I have replaced Lucas's 'L' by 'S'). Hence, Lucas argues, whatever calculus the determinist claims governs our processes of occurrent thought production, a human mathematician can show that those processes are not fully deterministic by having an occurrent thought that a certain Gödel sentence is true, his production of which that calculus could not have represented.

Now I have emphasized in the book that there are in a human brain at any time a vast number of brain events which play a role (together with conscious events) in influencing the occurrence of other conscious events. So if a conscious belief is fully caused by brain events and other conscious events, it is caused by a large number of them. It would take any mathematician at least a short period of time to discover what were his or her brain events and conscious events at a given instant, represent them in a calculus together with the rules representing his or her causal processes, and calculate the Gödel sentence of the resulting system. The mathematician can surely do this calculation, but while they are doing it, new brain and conscious events are occurring in the mathematician, which—in the view of the determinist—are causing him or her to do that calculation. So a new calculus with new axiomes would be needed to represent the process by which the mathematician reached the previous Gödel sentence. The mathematician could calculate the Gödel sentence of the new calculus, but the process by which they did it would need yet another different calculus to represent it. And so on. To generalize, no mathematician could produce the Gödel sentence of the calculus which represents the process by which he or she produced it, merely one which represents a different process in him or herself or someone else. But that is perfectly compatible with every Gödel sentence of one calculus which he calculates being a theorem of some other calculus which represents a deterministic process in his brain and consciousness. I conclude that Lucas's argument does not show that humans are not deterministic systems.[1]

---

[1] Thanks to Dan Isaacson and John Lucas for help with understanding Gödel's theorem and Lucas's resultant argument.

Index